THE **COMMITTEE** TO **DESTROY** THE **WORLD**

THE **COMMITTEE** TO **DESTROY** THE **WORLD**

INSIDE THE PLOT
TO UNLEASH A SUPER CRASH
ON THE GLOBAL ECONOMY

MICHAEL LEWITT

WILEY

Published by John Wiley & Sons, Inc., Hoboken, New Jersey.
The first edition was published by Wiley in 2010.
Published simultaneously in Canada.

For general information on our other products and services or for technical support, please contact our Customer Care Department within the United States at (800) 762-2974, outside the United States at (317) 572-3993 or fax (317) 572-4002.

Wiley publishes in a variety of print and electronic formats and by print-on-demand. Some material included with standard print versions of this book may not be included in e-books or in print-on-demand. If this book refers to media such as a CD or DVD that is not included in the version you purchased, you may download this material at http://booksupport.wiley.com. For more information about Wiley products, visit www.wiley.com.

Library of Congress Cataloging-in-Publication Data:

ISBN 978-1-119-18354-9 (Hardcover)
ISBN 978-1-119-18369-3 (ePDF)
ISBN 978-1-119-18370-9 (ePub)

Printed in the United States of America

10 9 8 7 6 5 4 3 2 1

For Marcie, Alessia, Alexander, and Preston

And in memory of Laurence G. Lewitt, 1930–2015

This disposition to admire, and almost to worship, the rich and the powerful, and to despise, or, at least, to neglect, persons of poor and mean condition, though necessary both to establish and to maintain the distinction of ranks and the order of society, is, at the same time, the great and most universal cause of the corruption of our moral sentiments.

—Adam Smith

For historians each event is unique. Economics, however, maintains that forces in society and nature behave in repetitive ways. History is particular; economics is general.

—Charles Kindleberger

CONTENTS

ACKNOWLEDGMENTS

As someone who has spent the last 25 years in the world of credit, I am unduly aware of the importance of acknowledging the debts we owe to other people. Despite the arguments found in the following pages, not all debts are onerous. In particular, the debts we owe other people are gifts, and it is my privilege to be able to acknowledge them publicly.

Many people like to say that life is short, but that is not true. Life is long. It is long in possibilities, long in the people we affect, and long in what lives on after we are gone. Life is also long in the people who affect us. This is my opportunity to thank the people who have enriched my life in ways that I am pleased to acknowledge here.

First and foremost, I want to thank my family. My wife Marcie is an unending source of strength and wisdom and love without whom my life would be unthinkable. I am blessed with a true life partner in every sense of the world, a wonderful friend and a wise and beautiful woman who has helped me accomplish much more than I could have on my own; I owe her everything. My children Alessia, Alexander, and Preston are the greatest gifts in our lives and have grown into warm, caring, and accomplished young adults largely due to the remarkable guidance of my wife. I could not be prouder of each of them.

My parents, Laurence and Roberta Lewitt, gave me the gifts of education, self-respect, and respect for others. They helped make me who I am and I love them very much. My father passed away shortly before publication of this book after a long and active life. He taught me to speak out and I hope that this book and the rest of my work lives up to his example. My brother David is a gifted musician and teacher who makes me proud every day.

My in-laws Lester and Peggy Engel welcomed me into their family 30 years ago and made me feel like one of their own from the first day I met them. Peggy passed away shortly before my father and she lives on in her three wonderful children and nine grandchildren. My brother-in-law Dr. Marc Engel and my sister-in-law Lesli Sugerman have always made me feel like we grew up in the same house.

When I started writing *The Credit Strategist* in January 2001, I had no idea whether anybody would be interested in what I had to say. Since then, the publication has taken on a life of its own. It has also introduced me to people around the country from all walks of life who have broadened my understanding of the world. I owe a great debt to my readers to whom I am enormously appreciative.

One of the greatest things to have come out of *The Credit Strategist* is the community of brilliant people to whom it has introduced me and who continue to educate me about the markets on a daily basis while in many cases also becoming friends. It is my great pleasure to thank them here: Peter Boockvar, Paul Brodsky, Gil Caffray, Albert Edwards, Marc Faber, Martin Fridson, Joshua Friedlander, Dennis Gartman, James Grant, Dan Greenhaus, Fred Hickey, Lacy Hunt and Van Hoisington, Ed Hyman and his team at Evercore/ISI, Doug Kass, Bill King, Andrew Lapthorne, Richard Lehmann, John Mauldin, Rafael and David Mayer, James F. Meisner, Russell Napier, Raoul Pal, Lee Partridge, Pedro J. Ramirez, David Rosenberg, Edward Scott, Kirby Shanks, Michael Shaoul, David Stockman, David Rocker, Cole Walton, Peter Warburton, Kate Welling, Christopher Whalen, Grant Williams, Christopher Wood, and Mark Yusko. Needless to say, I alone am responsible for the contents of the book.

I also continue to benefit from the enduring friendship, wisdom, and support of two of the wisest and most accomplished investors of our generation, Leon Cooperman and Steven Einhorn.

I am grateful for the support and friendship of my colleagues at The Third Friday Total Return Fund, L.P. – Michael Shatsky, Steven Artzi, Daniel Goldburg, as well as Perry Lerner, Chris Calise, Mitch Ackles, and Daniel Strachman.

My friends and colleagues Philippe Blumenthal and Greger Hamilton have helped me learn about the world outside the United States and are a constant source of wisdom and support.

I am very fortunate to enjoy the personal friendship of Dr. Paul Belsky, Gerald Brodsky, Fred and Sara Chikovsky, Mark Dern, Thomas Donatelli, Michael Felsher, Warren Greenspoon, Richard Hehman, Michael Kirsh, Donald Kittredge, Thomas Loucas, Jedd and Anna Novatt, Eric Oberg, Michael O'Rourke, Jeffrey Queen, Thomas Romero, Keith Rosenbloom, Dr. Amer Rustom, Azzam ("Skip") Rustom, Jeffrey Schreiber, Randall Shaw, Dennis J. Stanek, Jr., Charles Swanson, John Schiller, Laurence Silverman, Laura Stein, Burt Sugarman and Mary Hart, William Vanech, William Villafranco, Greg Walker, and Barry Wish. I am sure I left some people out inadvertently—please forgive me.

Chris Andersen and Frederick McCarthy have been great friends and mentors to me for many years since I met them at Drexel Burnham in the late 1980s.

My friends at Money Map Press and *Sure Money* have been wonderful supporters of my work. Mike Ward is the greatest editor in the business. Valerie Dowdle is the force behind *Sure Money* and was invaluable in bringing this book to press. Elizabeth Latanishen is a constant source of energy and ideas at *Sure Money*. Greg Madison helps make sure that my weekly market reports get out on time and make sense. If all of Baltimore were run by Mike and his team, the city's problems would be solved.

My teachers have been among my most important lifelong influences. Arnold Weinstein, Edna and Richard Salomon Distinguished Professor of Comparative Literature at Brown University, has been a lifelong friend and intellectual and moral influence along with his incredible wife Ann. Mark Taylor, Chairman of the Religious Studies Department at Columbia University, has taught me Hegel, Kierkegaard, and a thousand other things and is a wonderful friend.

I also had the privilege to study with the equivalent of the 1927 Yankees in literary studies as a graduate student at Yale University in the early 1980s: Harold Bloom, Paul de Man, Geoffrey Hartman, Thomas

Greene, J. Hillis Miller, Peter Brooks, Frederic Jameson, R. W. B. Lewis and Peter Gay. Jacques Derrida and Umberto Eco would stop by to lecture and meet with us from time-to-time as well. I sometimes pinch myself to remember how lucky I was to interact with these great minds.

And while I haven't seen them since leaving Vanderbilt Hall, my first-year teachers at New York University School of Law had a much greater influence on me than I realized at the time: John Sexton (civil procedure), who went on to become the dean of the law school and later president of the university; the late Daniel Collins (contracts); Sylvia Law (torts); James Jacobs (criminal law); and Lawrence Sager, now Dean of the University of Texas Law School (constitutional law). Former Dean of the law school Ricky Revesz brought me back to NYU after many years and for that I am very grateful as well.

Going further back, Professor John Halperin first inspired me to want to read and write when I met him at Camp Lenox, and my high school teachers at Paul D. Schreiber High School in Port Washington, New York, William Mock and Blaine Bocarde, taught me how to read and write.

Last but certainly not least, 25 years ago I had the good fortune to work at Drexel Burnham Lambert, Inc. for a brief period of time. That experience was a crash course in finance followed by a second crash course in human nature and markets when my two-man firm was chosen to manage the Drexel Burnham Employee Partnerships in the 1990s. My childhood friend Jonathan Sokoloff, who has brilliantly guided the pre-eminent private equity firm Leonard Green & Partners for many years, generously helped bring me to Drexel and while I have thanked him privately many times I am pleased to do so publicly here.

I am also grateful to have had the privilege to work with Michael Milken, Lowell Milken, Richard Sandler, and Peter Ackerman managing the Drexel Burnham Employee Partnerships and on other projects. I am confident that history will show not only that Michael, Lowell, and Drexel Burnham were ill-treated by the U.S. government, but that Drexel democratized capital in ways that will be felt for generations. Michael changed the world and paid a huge price for doing so, but like many artists and revolutionaries was not sufficiently appreciated while he was accomplishing his greatest feats. History will be kinder to him than his contemporaries.

INTRODUCTION

The Committee to Destroy the World

> In a theater, it happened that a fire started offstage. The clown came out to tell the audience. They thought it was a joke and applauded. He told them again, and they became still more hilarious. This is the way, I suppose, that the world will be destroyed – amid the universal hilarity of wits and wags who think it is all a joke.
>
> —Soren Kierkegaard

The 2008 financial crisis didn't materialize out of thin air—and neither will the next one. The worst financial crisis since the Great Depression was caused by policy errors that encouraged economic actors to borrow too much and spend or invest the money unproductively—and the next one will follow the same script. Surveying the debris of their work after the crisis, politicians, central bankers and regulators swore they would never allow such a crisis to happen again. Predictably, their promises were broken virtually the moment they were uttered.

By the time the first edition of this book was published in early 2010 under the title *The Death of Capital*, financial markets had stabilized but economies were still struggling to recover. Almost six years later, they are still struggling—except the world is much more leveraged, the geopolitical landscape is much more fractured, American politics are more divided, and policymakers have run out of answers.

1

Post-crisis economic reforms followed two paths: heavy regulation and activist monetary policy. Both of them missed the mark because neither addressed the rising tide of debt that is steadily suffocating the global economy. In fact, all of the responses to the financial crisis involved the creation of more debt. On the surface, it appeared that conditions were improving but under the surface the imbalances that caused the crisis were intensifying.

The post-crisis recovery was based on a mirage: an epic accumulation of debt created by central banks lowering interest rates to zero and engaging in trillions of dollars of quantitative easing. In their wisdom, policymakers decided to solve a debt crisis by creating more debt out of thin air, guaranteeing an even more severe crisis in the future. And it wasn't just the United States that saw its debt grow significantly. Debt also increased in Europe and Japan after the crisis. But in China, the country most responsible for driving the post-crisis global recovery, it exploded beyond reason. China's growth was built on the biggest debt bubble in history.

China's debt explosion was either ignored or cheered on by the financial press and Wall Street. These observers adopted the unfounded belief that China was exempt from normal economic forces. Some of us dissented from this view and warned that China's debt-fueled growth was unsustainable, but our voices were drowned out by the bubbled masses. But when China's economy began to slow sharply in 2014, it became apparent that China was playing a role in the post-crisis global economy analogous to that played by the U.S. housing market before the crisis. In the mid-2000s, the U.S. housing market created huge amounts of debt that not only inflated housing prices at home but ended up inflating asset prices around the world. In a similar fashion, China's so-called "economic miracle" inflated the prices of commodities, real estate, and other financial assets around the world. In 2007, the world experienced a debt crisis that originated in the U.S. housing industry and radiated out into the global economy. In 2016, the world faces a debt crisis that originated in China and commodities and is spreading out into the global economy. The common ingredient is excess global liquidity created by central banks.

According to the McKinsey Global Institute, China's total debt increased from $7 trillion in 2007 to $28 trillion by mid-2014.[1] To place these figures in context, household debt in the United States increased by $7 trillion in the period leading up to the financial crisis in 2008.

And America's federal deficit increased by roughly $7.5 trillion between January 2009 and mid-2015.[2] So China, an economy only 50 to 60 percent as large as the United States, saw its debt increase by three times as much as America's household debt grew during the housing bubble or, alternatively, three times as much as America's federal deficit grew during the first six-and-a-half years of Barack Obama's presidency (a period that included four consecutive years of $1 trillion deficits). Moreover, much of China's debt was directed into wasteful and unproductive real estate and commodity investments that will never produce a reasonable return or generate enough income to service or repay the capital that funded them. So much for China's "economic miracle."

In a globalized world, the effects of China's epic debt explosion were not confined to that country's borders; China's unconstrained borrowing created unsustainable demand for commodities and massive overproduction in mining, mineral, chemical, and related industries throughout the world. It left in its wake massive overcapacity in commodity-related industries across the globe. Once this debt-fueled expansion began to run out of gas in mid-2014, China's growth began crumbling, commodity prices began collapsing, credit markets began collapsing, and global growth began slowing from already depressed post-crisis levels.

Then central banks did what central banks do—they compounded their earlier policy errors by repeating their old ones. They doubled down on the failed policies they were employing to stimulate economic growth in an over-indebted post-crisis world. On October 31, 2014, Bank of Japan Governor Haruhiko Kuroda announced unprecedented new stimulus measures in another desperate attempt to break Japan's decades-long economic spiral. In January 2015, European Central Bank (ECB) President Mario Draghi followed suit with Europe's first-ever quantitative easing initiative. Only Janet Yellen's Federal Reserve was moving in the opposite direction by ending its own quantitative easing program, but this was primarily through sins of omission that strengthened the dollar and exerted additional downward pressure on commodity prices, U.S. corporate profits, and the global economy.

By mid-2015, serious cracks began to appear in global markets. Greece defaulted and had to be bailed out again by the European Union while solidifying its status as a failed state and global security threat as an entry point for refugees from a shattered Middle East. Emerging markets were melting down with particular weakness in Brazil and Russia. China's stock market was crashing and the country shocked global markets by beginning a concerted effort to devalue the yuan. Puerto Rico declared itself insolvent (something anyone with a functioning cerebellum already knew was the case). Leveraged oil and gas companies in the U.S. were filing for bankruptcy left and right. And then the U.S. stock market, which had struggled to rise all year, suffered sharp losses and extreme volatility in August and September, shaking the confidence of investors. The post-crisis debt party had run long past midnight—and nothing good ever happens after midnight.

With interest rates around the world stuck at zero, there was little prospect that the $200 trillion of debt suffocating the global economy could ever be repaid by conventional means. The world is incapable of generating enough income to pay the interest and principal on that much debt. Instead, it was obvious that this debt could only be repaid through a combination of currency debasement, inflation, and defaults. Stated plainly, this means that the value of fiat money is going to be obliterated. Of course, politicians, central bankers, and policymakers have been destroying the value of money for years. But now they are going to have to accelerate their efforts. Out-of-control debt is metastasizing, crippling global growth and sucking the lifeblood out of the global economy. Central bankers badly miscalculated when they decided to try to solve a debt crisis by printing trillions of dollars of additional debt.

A Regulatory Theocracy

The 2008 financial crisis and, before that, the 9-11 attacks drastically reshaped the world. Each of these seminal tragedies unleashed massive policy responses that radically altered American life for the worse. As a result of the 9-11 attacks, the United States invaded Iraq and Afghanistan and launched anti-terror operations in Pakistan, Yemen, and Somalia; passed the Patriot Act that expanded surveillance of its citizens; and established a massive new bureaucracy in the Department of Homeland Security to protect the nation. As a result of the expansion of the radical Islamic terrorism around the globe that triggered the 9-11 attacks, Americans can no longer travel freely or feel secure in public places due to the growing threat of random violence. American police forces are militarized and the freedoms enjoyed by our parents and grandparents are limited by our own fears and our government's failure to effectively fight our enemies at home and abroad.

Financial regulation was supposed to improve after the financial crisis, but instead it deteriorated into an orgy of mindless rulemaking. In a perverse interpretation of his campaign promise of "Hope and Change," Barack Obama left post-crisis financial regulation in the hands of the same cast of inept economic policymakers that led America into crisis in the first place.

He named Lawrence Summers as his chief economic adviser, a man whose inflated opinion of himself dwarfs his meager accomplishments such as rejecting CFTC Chair Brooksley Born's pleas to regulate derivatives in the late 1990s despite himself knowing virtually nothing about derivatives. He named Timothy Geithner, who ran the Federal Reserve Bank of New York before the crisis while Wall Street leveraged itself into insolvency right under his nose, as his Treasury Secretary.

And, in perhaps his most disappointing move, the president brought in Mary Schapiro, an undistinguished career regulator who had mastered the art of failing upward, to run the already ineffective Securities and Exchange Commission (SEC). Among Ms. Schapiro's notable failures was allowing Bernard Madoff to run the largest Ponzi scheme in history right under her nose as she served as a senior regulator and ultimately the Chair and CEO of the National Association of Securities Dealers in the mid-to-late 1990s, the height of Mr. Madoff's fraud.

Rather than new blood and new thinking, Mr. Obama relied on the same people responsible for the policy errors that contributed to the crisis to fix those errors. Those who had warned of the problems before they happened were nowhere to be found.

In the aftermath of the financial crisis, Congress passed The Dodd-Frank Wall Street Reform and Consumer Protection Act (Dodd-Frank). Naturally, this bill turned into a regulatory and lobbying orgy that ended up sapping liquidity and vitality from the financial system while leaving derivatives inadequately regulated and the individuals who committed crimes that contributed to the financial crisis unpunished. Dodd-Frank was 14,000 pages in length and included 398 rule-making requirements, rendering it almost impossible to administer by the SEC and other agencies charged with administering it. Like the badly flawed Affordable Care Act, which House Majority Leader Nancy Pelosi famously (and disgracefully) said had to be passed into law in order for the members of Congress to know what it actually said, Dodd–Frank was another piece of absurdly complex legislation that was voted on by people who didn't read it or understand its contents or its unintended consequences.

The gargantuan Dodd–Frank bill was the government's main regulatory response to the financial crisis. The law required banks to reduce leverage and risk-taking activities using taxpayer money (reforms that I proposed in the first edition of this book). While some of these goals were accomplished, the forms in which they were implemented rendered the financial system less liquid, more rigid, and more susceptible to another financial crisis.

Legislators and regulators failed to recognize that inflexibly bolstering bank capital would severely reduce market liquidity, yet that is precisely what occurred. By 2014, liquidity in fixed income markets had dried up as banks restructured their businesses to meet the demands of the new law. Corporate bond inventories held by dealers dropped by 70 percent while Treasury market liquidity evaporated. This happened as debt markets increased dramatically in size; by 2015, the U.S. corporate debt market had doubled in size to $4.5 trillion since before the crisis, yet it had become much more difficult to trade bonds than a decade earlier. The evaporation of market liquidity will inevitably make the next crisis more severe than the last.

The government's role in the economy and its intrusions into the daily lives of its citizens are immeasurably greater today than on September 10, 2001. The costs in terms of lost privacy and freedom are incalculable. We live in a world run by regulators who are operating in the dark while exercising increasingly untrammeled power. We are lorded over by a growing regulatory state to whom courts—particularly the Roberts Supreme Court—have granted enormous and undue deference. The Tyranny of the Alphabet—the FBI, IRS, SEC, FINRA, NLRB, EPA, OSHA—governs our lives. The rise of the regulatory state coupled with the epic increase in debt are smothering the economic vitality of the United States and dooming this country and the rest of the world to generations of sluggish growth.

The expansion of the regulatory state is appalling in breadth. Over the last decade, 768,920 pages of federal regulations have been added to

Figure I.1 Apocalypse Then
SOURCE: *Time*, February 1999.

the *Federal Register*, an average of almost 77,000 pages a year.[3] A nearly incomprehensible 36,877 new regulations were added during that period.[4] It is a miracle that the American economy can function at all under the weight of all of these rules, many of which can give rise to substantial criminal and civil penalties in the hands of overzealous and corrupt prosecutors (of which there are no shortage).

We have come a long way from February 1999 when *Time Magazine* celebrated "The Committee to Save the World"—Alan Greenspan, Robert Rubin, and Lawrence Summers (see Figure I.1). *Time*'s misguided anointment of these three men coincided with the birth of the European Union, which enslaved vast swathes of southern Europe in an economic straitjacket. Shortly before the three men were celebrated by *Time*, they had successfully thwarted efforts by U.S. Commodity Futures Trading Commission chair Brooksley Born to regulate over-the-counter derivatives, a decision that contributed less than a decade later to the worst economic crisis since the Great Depression. As we came to learn, with men like these in charge of saving the world, the world was going to find itself in deep trouble.

A decade later, Mr. Greenspan admitted to Congress that his basic assumptions about economics and human behavior were wrong. Mr. Rubin was trying to justify his $100 million sinecure at Citigroup, Inc. while refusing to acknowledge any responsibility for the actions of his underlings that pushed that bank into insolvency and a federal bailout on his watch. And Mr. Summers kept failing upward, retaining his sneer of intellectual superiority while consistently demonstrating why academic economists like him are the last ones anyone should ask for economic policy advice.

Unfortunately, economic governance would get much worse and "The Committee to Save the World" was succeeded by "The Committee to Destroy the World" (see Figure I.2) after the 2008 financial crisis (although the mainstream press never identified them as such, leaving that to me in *The Credit Strategist*[5]). In 2015, the troika leading the world's largest central banks was still pursuing crisis-era policies long after the crisis had passed. By that time, new strains were appearing in

Figure I.2   The Committee to Destroy the World
Source: Haruhiko Kuroda photo by Michael Wuertenberg, https://commons.wikimedia.org/wiki/File:Accelerating_Infrastructure_Development_Haruhiko_Kuroda_(8410957075).jpg#filelinks; Mario Draghi photo by Remy Steinegger, https://commons.wikimedia.org/wiki/File:Mario_Draghi_World_Economic_Forum_2013.jpg; Janet Yellen photo by Day Donaldson, https://www.flickr.com/photos/thespeakernews/16165619661.

the global economy due to the failure of fiscal policymakers to adopt meaningful pro-growth policies and the perpetuation of crisis-era monetary policies long past their sell-by date.

Governed by intellectual fallacies and cowed by markets, The Committee to Destroy the World adopted policies that were guaranteed to lead the world straight into the jaws of another financial crisis. Global interest rates were kept at, near, or below zero for years while central banks purchased trillions of dollars/yen/euros of government bonds based on the delusion that these policies would stimulate economic growth. Naturally, they did precisely the opposite.

Einstein supposedly said that the working definition of insanity is repeating the same mistake and expecting a different result. That remark should be applied to the working definition of stupidity and central bankers. By 2014 (if not earlier), there was abundant and irrefutable evidence that quantitative easing was failing to stimulate growth in the United States. In fact, it was sapping economic vitality and market liquidity and contributing to the most disappointing economic recovery in memory. In the 2011–2014 period, GDP growth in the United States averaged a measly 2.0 percent according to the Bureau of Economic Statistics. And during Barack Obama's presidency, the high point for annual GDP growth was a tepid 2.5 percent in 2010.

Nonetheless, faced with mounting evidence that their policies were not working, central bankers, demonstrating that there is a difference between being educated and being smart, refused to change course; instead, they persisted with their failed policies. Their subsequent expectations for economic growth never came close to materializing. Table I.1 shows the "central tendency" projections of GDP growth by

Table I.1 "Central Tendency" Projections of GDP Growth Compared to Actual GDP in the 2011–2015 Period

Year	Fed Projections	Actual
2011	3.0–3.6%	1.60%
2012	2.5–2.9	2.2
2013	2.3–3.0	1.5
2014	2.8–3.2	2.4
2015	2.6–3.0	1.5 (first half)

SOURCE: Federal Reserve Board.

Federal Reserve governors and bank presidents compared to actual GDP in the 2011–2015 period.

Looking at this record, one could reasonably conclude that it would be more useful to ask a group of English professors to forecast the economy.[6] In the wake of their failures, the Fed left behind a grossly over-leveraged economy whose fragility was disguised by artificially inflated stock prices, artificially low interest rates, and artificially suppressed volatility. You have to hand it to Ben Bernanke and his progeny—they couldn't have designed a more disastrous set of policies had they consulted Dr. Victor Frankenstein.[7]

Things didn't have to be this way. A sounder and more creative intellectual approach and bolder political initiatives would have produced far better results. But there are no Paul Volckers running central banks today and no Winston Churchills leading the world. Mr. Volcker was willing to battle inflation while being demonized in the press and Churchill fought the Nazis from an underground London bunker while being bombarded by the Luftwaffe every night.

Today, we are left in the hands of people like Janet Yellen and Barack Obama. Mrs. Yellen was terrified to raise interest rates by a mere 25 basis points for years for fear of upsetting markets while Mr. Obama, who tellingly removed Churchill's bust from the Oval Office, loaded the American economy with job-killing regulations and multi-trillion dollar entitlements while appeasing tyrants, betraying our allies, and apologizing for American power and principles. They say that societies get the leaders they deserve. I say we deserve better.

A Crisis Wasted

Shortly after President Obama took office in 2009, I received a telephone call from one of the Obama administration's top economic advisers. I was asked whether I was willing to speak to the small group advising the president how to regulate derivatives after the financial crisis. The individual who called me said he was uncertain whether he could get me a hearing but felt it was important for them to hear my views (which were published, among other places, in the first edition of this book) since the president and Lawrence Summers, the president's top economic adviser, believed it would be appropriate to leave regulation of derivatives in the hands of regulators. My view, which the caller had shared with the group, was that regulators do not understand derivatives and are not qualified to regulate them. After some back and forth, I was not invited to share my views with the group; there was little appetite to hear them, and derivatives regulation was left in the hands of people who do not understand them.

On the first page of his magnum opus, *Stabilizing an Unstable Economy*, the great economist Hyman Minsky wrote: "Economic theory is the product of creative imagination; its concepts and constructs are the result of human thought."[8] There is nothing foreordained about economics; it is merely a series of intellectual constructs about how the world works. It is a soft science. Accordingly, its forecasts are more often wrong than right. As a human intellectual construct, it is subject to the deficiencies of human thought—in the shorthand of the markets, greed and fear. These flaws lead economists to make less than optimal policy choices, and that is nowhere more apparent than in the responses to the 2008 financial crisis.

After the crisis, the government consistently sought advice, not from those who correctly predicted the housing bubble and resulting market collapse, but instead from those economists and strategists who missed the obvious warning signs and those investors who lost enormous sums of money. If your fund was down 80 percent, you were at the top of the list of the people the government called for advice. Of course, many of these people purchased their seats at the table with large campaign contributions; that is what happens in a system of crony capitalism. Nonetheless, it was a shame that we were calling on the same individuals who led us to the brink disaster to lead us out of it. We can see the results of that approach six years later: an over-leveraged and over-regulated financial system that is failing to fuel sufficient economic growth to pay our current and future obligations.

In the midst of the crisis, presidential aide Rahm Emanuel (who was not the individual who called me) famously said that it would be a shame to let a crisis go to waste. But that is exactly what happened. Despite heroic efforts to prevent a complete collapse of the financial system after the failure of Lehman Brothers and the near demise of insurance giant AIG, policymakers failed to address many of the underlying regulatory, fiscal, and monetary policy failures that led to the financial crisis while also creating new ones.

That is not to say that they did nothing: they took some important steps to reform the U.S. banking system and make it better capitalized. But they failed to address the two biggest elephants in the room: (1) the incessant growth of debt in the U.S. and around the world; and (2) the $650 trillion derivatives infrastructure that hangs over the entire edifice of global finance like a dark cloud waiting to burst. Excess debt and all that comes with it pose the greatest risk to global financial stability since the Great Depression and absolutely nothing has been done to tame this beast.

The Death of Fiscal Policy

Mr. Obama inherited an extremely difficult situation upon taking office, but he made it worse through a series of deliberate policy choices that further weakened the American economy. His proclivity for government rather than market solutions imposed enormous regulatory burdens on the economy that impeded private sector growth while loading the government with trillions of dollars of future obligations that it can't afford to pay.

The first large piece of economic legislation that Mr. Obama promoted was the $800 billion American Recovery and Reinvestment Act. The president touted this so-called stimulus bill as a massive boost for the American economy when it was passed by a Democrat-controlled Congress in February 2009, but it proved to be a bust. Very little of the money was spent to increase the productive capacity of the American economy as proven by the economy's sub-par growth in the years that followed. We may not have been building bridges to nowhere like Japan and China, but we weren't building bridges to the future either.[9]

Then Mr. Obama decided to impose a new multi-trillion-dollar entitlement on one-sixth of a struggling American economy—The Patient Protection and Affordable Care Act (familiarly known as ObamaCare). Unable to get the highly unpopular law passed in Congress by conventional means, he worked with Senate Majority Leader Harry Reid and House Speaker Nancy Pelosi to force the bill through via the federal budget reconciliation process that only requires 51 votes rather than the normal three-fifths majority. This legislative device was inserted in the Congressional Budget and Impoundment Control Act of 1974 to end filibuster, close debate, and pass controversial budget bills. Of course, ObamaCare was much more than a mere budget bill, but this was only the first of many instances where the Obama administration trampled on the rule of law to pursue its ideologically driven policy goals. The Democratic leadership dressed up the healthcare bill as a phony civil rights measure, even parading former civil rights leader and House member Elijah Cummings up the steps of the Capital on the day of passage, to push the law through Congress over the opposition of the Republicans and much of the American public.

In order to gain business support, the administration bought off the health insurance, hospital, and healthcare industries that stood to gain millions of new patients whose bills would be paid by the government. The merger boom in these industries in the years following passage of the law (with no meaningful antitrust review) coupled with escalating drug costs (with no complaint from the administration) spoke to the devil's bargain that paved the way to so-called "healthcare reform."

While most people agree that all American citizens should have access to healthcare, the harried, procedurally irregular and politically dishonest way in which the law was passed imposed a deeply flawed and prohibitively expensive bill on American taxpayers. ObamaCare is another multi-trillion-dollar entitlement whose true costs were deliberately delayed until after Mr. Obama leaves office. By late 2015, the law was already struggling due to its high costs and flawed incentives. More than half of the regional coops set up under the law had failed, year-end 2016 enrollment was projected to come in at half the 20 million originally projected by the Congressional Budget Office, and the country's largest healthcare insurer, United Healthcare, announced in November 2015 that it was considering withdrawing from ObamaCare exchanges due to massive losses. We are also learning that the true costs of the law's expansion of Medicaid to the states is going to be in the tens of billions of dollars as federal subsidies roll off, placing enormous burdens on state budgets after Mr. Obama leaves office. The law asks nothing of its beneficiaries and provides no means to pay for itself. Its dubious economics are only rivaled by it questionable legality. The law survived two near-death challenges in the Supreme Court only because Chief Justice John Roberts flouted long-established standards of statutory interpretation to rewrite the statute, severely damaging his institution's integrity and reputation in the process.[10] In truth, Mr. Obama's dream of universal healthcare is an economic and political nightmare.

Monetary Policy Follies

The Failures of the Fed

Since the financial crisis, the Federal Reserve and its foreign counterparts have engaged in policies that failed to stimulate sustainable economic growth and, once they saw them fail, refused to change course and instead intensified the same policies.[11] While former Federal Reserve Chairman Ben Bernanke was rightfully praised for the steps he took during the financial crisis to prevent a total collapse of the financial system, his successor, Janet Yellen, kept emergency policies in place far too long after the crisis ended. The result was seven years of zero interest rates and trillions of dollars of quantitative easing that boosted financial markets but left the economy struggling to grow.

These policies also created inflation in the prices of many of the products and services used by consumers despite these higher prices not being reflected in official government inflation statistics. They also contributed to a dramatic increase in wealth inequality in the United States, which exacerbated social instability and political divisiveness during an administration that purported to be benefitting those most damaged by the policies designed to help them.

Monetary policy led to massive inflation in the prices of financial assets such as stocks and bonds as well as art and other collectibles, high-end real estate, and anything else denominated in increasingly debauched paper money. These assets experienced what the economist Irving Fisher termed a "money illusion" in which the inherent value of the assets themselves was not increasing; instead, the value of the fiat currencies used to purchase them was deteriorating.[12]

At the same time that consumers were being told by the government that the prices of the everyday goods they need in order to live were barely increasing, these prices were actually rising sharply. In a word, the government was lying to them. Figure I.3 shows the rise in inflation as measured by the government.

These numbers are, of course, utter nonsense despite the fact that Wall Street and other establishment economists accept them at face value. For the real story, look at Table I.2, which shows the actual increase in

U.S. core PCE price inflation

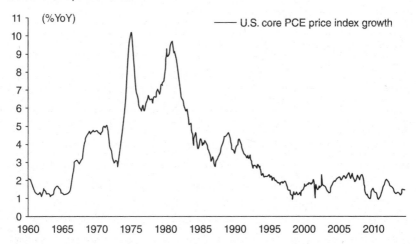

Figure I.3   Rise in Inflation as Measured by the Government
SOURCE: CLSA, U.S. Bureau of Economic Analysis.

Table I.2   Increase in Prices over the Last 15 Years

	2000	2014	Change (%)
Money Supply (millions) (1, 5)	$612.00	$3,989.00	564%
CPI Index (1)	$174.60	$235.10	35%
4-year avg. college tuition (2)	$14,000.00	$23,700.00	69%
Avg. annual healthcare cost per individual	$4,672.00	$9,400.00	101%
LA median house price (4)	$200,000.00	$560,000.00	180%
Six pack of beer pre-tax	$3.00	$6.30	108%
Oil (1)	$33.00	$98.00	197%
Spot gold (1)	$272.00	$1,282.00	371%
Copper (1)	$84.00	$322.90	284%
Corn per bushel (1)	$1.90	$3.90	105%
Beef per pound (4)	$2.60	$5.50	112%
Ave price of cable television	$20.00	$65.00	225%
Total government expenditures (bns) (3)	$3,087.00	$5,800.00	88%

SOURCE: (1) Bloomberg, (2) National Center for Education Services, (3) St. Louis Fed, (4), Trulia, (5) St. Louis Fed.

the prices over the last 10 years of many of the products and services actually used by consumers.

Only a professional economist would really believe that the prices of goods and services are not increasing at a rate that threatens the ability of ordinary Americans to maintain a reasonable standard of living. "Official" government inflation statistics, which guide monetary policy, bear little relationship to what is happening in the real world. The fact that monetary policy is based on these numbers is not only an intellectual insult, it is a profound moral betrayal that violates the government's social compact with its citizens. Monetary policy is guided by a deliberate falsehood perpetrated by a government robbing its citizens of their money and their freedom.

The Fed's post-crisis policy was driven by a deliberate attempt to ignite inflation despite the fact that prices are rising just fine on their own in the real world. This policy confiscated the savings of ordinary Americans while triggering serious geopolitical consequences such as the Arab Spring, which was unleashed by higher food prices in the Mideast, and a race by China and Russia for valuable energy resources around the world. There was an enormous disconnect between an activist monetary policy that sought to inflate already inflating prices and a fiscal policy that was shut down during the first six years of the Obama presidency by Senate Majority Leader Harry Reid.

To some extent, the incredible vitality and innovation of the U.S. technology sector helped counteract some of the effects of these disastrous policies. But despite the revival of Apple, Inc. and the Apple ecosystem of products as well as the advent of new companies such as Facebook, Inc. and Tesla Motors, Inc. and the growth of Amazon.com, Inc. and Google, Inc. and new products pouring out of the biotechnology industry, the United States still saw a disappointing recovery coupled with the largest debt increase in history while the world around it grew dangerously indebted and unstable. In the end, iPhones, "friending," and producing 50,000 or 100,000 electric cars a year are not going to save us.

The European Monetary Experiment

As problematic as U.S. monetary policy was since the crisis, it was even more misguided in Europe. While low rates effectively deprived American savers of enormous amounts of income over the past six years, Europeans experienced a much more dangerous phenomenon beginning in early 2015 when more than €2 trillion of European debt started trading at negative yields in response to a long-awaited and ill-fated quantitative easing program announced by ECB President Mario Draghi in January 2015.

Like the U.S., European governments failed to implement the types of fiscal policies necessary to grow their economies. This left Mario Draghi with little choice (in his own mind at least) but to mimic the failed policies of other central banks. By February 5, 2015, as Table I.3 illustrates, 10-year bond yields in Europe had dropped to historically low levels.[13]

These yields deprived individual savers as well as institutions such as insurance companies and pension funds of the ability to earn any meaningful return on their capital. A few months later in April 2015, German 10-year bund yields sank to a mere 5 basis points before markets came to their senses and sold off viciously, moving the yield back up to the high double digits (still absurdly low but better than near-zero). By way of comparison, U.S. 10-year Treasury yields were 1.81 percent

Table I.3   10-Year Yields at February 5, 2015

	Yield
Switzerland	−0.12
Denmark	0.21
Germany	0.37
Netherlands	0.42
Austria	0.45
Finland	0.48
France	0.59
Belgium	0.7
Iceland	0.99
Norway	1.26
Spain	1.51
Italy	1.55
UK	1.55
Portugal	2.44
Greece	9.53

DATA SOURCE: *Financial Times.*

on February 5, 2015. When the bond yields of functionally insolvent countries like Spain and Italy are lower than those of the United States, markets are seriously distorted. Even Greece's 9.53 percent yields were delusionally low; by June they would be 20 percent higher as the country teetered (once again) on the brink of financial collapse.

The ECB's QE program was not only doomed to fail for the reasons that all QE programs unaccompanied by meaningful fiscal reforms are doomed to fail but also because European bond markets were ill-suited to such a regime. European bond markets were already illiquid prior to the launch of QE and quickly became dangerously more so afterwards; front-running of the ECB's bond purchases by hedge funds and other investors depressed yields to absurdly low levels. Many of these investors suffered losses when the market reversed in May 2015 (as I warned in *The Credit Strategist*) because there were a limited number of buyers for bonds that were little more than certificates of confiscation. The ECB was limited in the bonds it could buy under the terms of its QE program, and private sector buyers started coming to their senses, putting an end to another momentum trade. In broader policy terms, however, QE is what happens when fiscal policymakers lack the courage and wherewithal to enact pro-growth economic reforms and leave it to monetary policymakers to fill the gap.

The ECB was forced into QE because European politicians were unwilling to stop spending other peoples' money to prop up over-indebted welfare states like Greece, Spain, Italy, and Portugal. Greece is the most blatant example of a failing state dependent on borrowing money from its neighbors that it can never hope to pay back. But it is not the only example: Spain, Italy, and Portugal (and likely France) are not far behind. Mario Draghi is prepared to tax all Europeans with future inflation (both directly and through currency debasement) to keep these countries afloat and the flawed European Union intact, but that is a promise bound to be broken in the future because it sunders the social contract between governments and their citizens. Sooner or later these countries will not be able to finance their deficits and will move towards default.

Under the current form of the Maastricht Treaty, the ECB is legally barred from directly financing member states by printing money, but QE is the first step down that road. Markets rely on the ECB to support European sovereign debt, which is why European bond yields dropped to such low levels during the first half of 2015 (and returned to those levels again late in the year). At some point, however, the ECB's existing tools will prove insufficient and either the Maastricht Treaty will have to be amended (a tall order) or abrogated or European sovereign debt will no longer enjoy the confidence of markets (the latter being the more likely outcome for investors).

Even more disturbing than the sight of negative yields was the market's complacency in the face of a phenomenon that violated the very tenets of capitalist economics. If this was the nineteenth century, there literally would be blood in the streets, but modern man has been fooled into worshipping central bankers. The problem with this brand of religion is that investors may think they are worshipping God but are really worshipping the Devil because central banks have made it very clear that they intend to confiscate their citizens' money through inflation and currency devaluation.

The Bank of Japan has been doing that for years only to be followed by its Western counterparts. When members of The Committee to Destroy the World complain that inflation is too low in a world in which goods and services grow more expensive every day, they are admitting that they intend to destroy the value of fiat money. In January 2015, the ECB, like other central banks, attempted to solve a solvency problem linked to excessive debt accumulation with policies designed for a liquidity problem. That is like trying to treat cancer with an aspirin regimen.

The confiscation of capital through artificially negative interest rates in Europe was just a more drastic version of what was happening in the U.S. since it lowered interest rates to zero during the financial crisis. While deflation posed a greater threat in Europe, in the U.S. it was a mirage despite deluded claims by members of the Federal Reserve that inflation is too low. Real world prices of goods and services increased dramatically over the past decade; only economists claim otherwise, which is another reason why the last person you should ask about the economy is an economist.

Low yields in the U.S. have confiscated enormous amounts of money from American consumers. As Christopher Whelan of Kroll Bond Rating Agency writes: "ZIRP [zero interest rate policy] has reduced the cost of funds for the $15 trillion asset U.S. banking system from roughly half a trillion dollars annually to less than $50 billion in 2014. This decrease in the interest expense for banks comes directly out of the pockets of savers and financial institutions."[14] In other words, banks are paying out hundreds of billions of dollars less in interest as a result of the Fed's repressive policies. In fairness, this is not a one-way bet; consumers also pay lower mortgage rates. But ZIRP and QE have clearly benefited borrowers while punishing savers.

While economists believed that interest rate repression would stimulate economic growth and reduce inflation, it did nothing of the sort. Instead, it suppressed economic growth and unleashed epic financial asset inflation while doing little to reduce inflation in goods and services. The latter only looks tepid because the government measures it in ways that have little to do with the real world. Fed apologists can use all the excuses in the world, but there is only one of two ways to explain this: rank incompetence or a willful desire to distort the facts.

Negative interest rates in Europe are a symptom of policy failure and a violation of the laws of capitalism. The same is true of persistent near-zero rates in the United States and Japan. Invisible rates render it impossible for fiduciaries to generate positive returns for their clients, insurance companies to issue policies, and savers to entrust their money to banks.[15] They are a symptom of failed economic policies, not some clever device to defeat deflation (which for the most part doesn't yet exist or pose a serious threat) and stimulate economic growth. These policies are mathematically doomed to fail regardless of what economists, who are merely failed monetary philosophers practicing a soft science, purport to tell us. The fact that European and American central banks followed the path of Japan with virtually no objection represents one of the most profound intellectual failures in the history of modern economic policy.

While the global economy is facing a solvency problem linked to excessive debt accumulation, the world's central banks are pursuing policies designed for a liquidity problem. As noted above and discussed further below, the only solutions in this known universe for a solvency problem are inflation, currency devaluation or default (the other possibility, extremely high rates of growth, is unrealistic). Since none of these real-world solutions is politically palatable—no leader on today's world stage has the courage to propose them and would be voted out of office by selfish and short-sighted constituents if he/she did—central banks are left creating huge doses of debt since equity can't be conjured out of thin air. But all of this debt is just exacerbating the solvency problem and failing to solve the liquidity problem, pushing global markets closer to crisis.

Out-of-Control Global Debt

The global economy cannot generate enough income to service and/or repay the debts it has already incurred or, for that matter, the incalculable trillions of dollars of future promises politicians have made. In this respect, the United States is just a microcosm of the rest of the world. As Figure I.4 illustrates, debt has grown much faster than the economy in the United States since the early 1980s. Furthermore, the gap between the growth rate of debt and the growth rate of the economy has accelerated over the past two decades, which guarantees that the economy can never hope to catch up and generate enough income to pay the interest or the principal on the debt.

In September 2014, the Geneva-based International Centre for Monetary and Banking Studies published a study entitled "Deleveraging? What Deleveraging?" where it reported that, "[c]ontrary to widely held beliefs, the world has not yet begun to delever and the global debt-to-GDP is still growing, breaking new highs."[16] The report was written by the highly respected economists Vincent Reinhart of Morgan Stanley, Lucrezia Reichlin of the London School of Business, Luigi Buttiglione of Brevan Howard Capital Management LP, and Philip Lane of Trinity College in Dublin. Going further, the report's distinguished authors warned that, "in a poisonous combination, world growth and inflation are also lower than previously expected, also—though not only—as a legacy of the past crisis."[17]

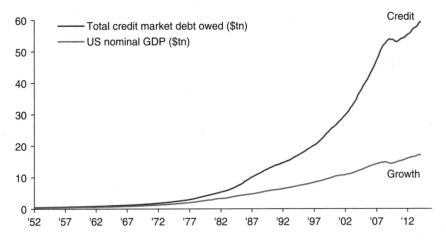

Figure I.4   Debt Has Grown Much Faster Than the Economy in the U.S. Economy
SOURCE: BofA Merrill Lynch Global Investment Strategy, Federal Reserve Bank, DataStream.

The authors showed that, excluding the leverage of financial companies worldwide, debt was equivalent to 212 percent of global GDP, up 38 percent since 2008. Debt was equivalent to roughly 264 percent of GDP in the U.S., 257 percent in Europe, and 411 percent in Japan. While debt was rising, global growth was falling. The six-year moving average of the world's potential growth rate fell to below 3 percent postcrisis from about 4.5 percent before the crisis, no doubt largely due to the much higher level of debt weighing on economies. When increasing amounts of financial and intellectual capital are devoted to servicing debt, growth is bound to suffer (see Figure I.5). Further, the authors point out: "Deleveraging and slower nominal growth are in many cases interacting in a vicious loop, with the latter making the deleveraging process harder and the former exacerbating the economic slowdown. Moreover,

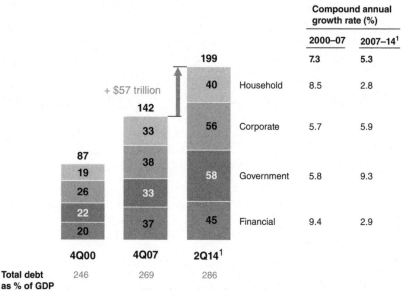

Global stock of debt outstanding by type
$ trillion, constant 2013 exchange rates

				Compound annual growth rate (%)	
				2000–07	2007–14[1]
			199	7.3	5.3
+ $57 trillion			40 Household	8.5	2.8
	142				
	33		56 Corporate	5.7	5.9
87	38				
19			58 Government	5.8	9.3
26	33				
22	37		45 Financial	9.4	2.9
20					
4Q00	4Q07	2Q14[1]			

Total debt as % of GDP   246   269   286

[1] 2Q14 data for advanced economics and China; 4Q13 data for other developing economics.

NOTE: Numbers may not sum due to rounding.

Figure I.5 Global Debt Has Increased by $57 Trillion since 2007, Outpacing World GDP Growth
SOURCE: Haver Analytics, national sources, *World Economic Outlook*, IMF; BIS; McKinsey Global Institute analysis.

the global capacity to take on debt has been reduced through the combination of slower expansion in real output and lower inflation."[18]

This disturbing picture was confirmed several months later by The McKinsey Global Institute. In a report entitled "Debt and (Not Much) Deleveraging," McKinsey reported that between 2007 and 2014, global debt had grown by $57 trillion to $199 trillion, raising the ratio of global debt-to-GDP by 17 percentage points. Developing countries have accounted for half of this growth; government debt has soared (by $25 trillion) and private sector deleveraging has been limited. Households in the U.S., UK, Spain, and Ireland had deleveraged somewhat, but elsewhere they had not. In particular, as noted earlier, China's total debt quadrupled from $7 trillion in 2007 to $28 trillion by mid-2014, fueled by real estate and shadow banking, and China's total debt as a percentage of GDP exceeded that of the United States (but honestly, who knows how bad China's opaque debt figures really are?). McKinsey summed up the last five years of the global economy: "[i]t is clear that deleveraging is rare and that the solutions are in short supply."[19] Actually, it is not solutions that are in short supply but rather the political and moral courage to implement them.

Both the McKinsey and the Geneva reports illustrate beyond a shadow of a doubt the unsustainable and dangerous path on which the global economy is set. Even worse, the policy mechanisms that brought the world to this point largely destroyed the market's ability to send meaningful pricing signals to market participants. Since the crisis, central banks have been the largest buyers of government bonds, distorting the market's normal supply/demand dynamics and "snapping the antenna" off the bond market in the words of economist Dr. Philippa Malmgren.[20] Governments have distorted the price of benchmark bonds as well as the price of money and made it virtually impossible to determine the natural rate of interest or inflation.

Untamed Derivatives

One of the primary forms that global debt has assumed in the modern economy is the derivatives contract. AIG blew up because it wrote too many derivatives contracts on collateralized bond obligations that held billions of dollars of subprime mortgages. But the derivatives threat in the market in 2008 was much broader and deeper than that—there were roughly $60 trillion of credit default swaps that were written on a wide variety of underlying obligations that brought the financial system to its knees.

Seven years later, despite efforts to tame the derivatives beast, these instruments of financial mass destruction still pose an existential threat to the global finance sector. One of the stated aims of Dodd-Frank was to address the "too big to fail" problem in the financial industry. Unfortunately, the legislation left in its wake a much more highly concentrated financial industry with fewer firms that are no longer "too big to fail" but actually "too big to save." One of the primary ways in which they are "too big to save" is by holding hundreds of trillions of dollars of derivatives on their balance sheets whose true risks their managements don't understand (because if they did understand these risks, they wouldn't allow their institutions to hold them).

The Bank for International Settlements reported that the notional amount of outstanding over-the-counter derivatives stood at $630.1 trillion at December 30, 2014.[21] The "gross market value" of outstanding derivatives contracts, which measures the cost of replacing them at prevailing market prices and the maximum loss that market participants would suffer if all counterparties failed to perform, increased over the second half of 2014 from $17 trillion in June to $21 trillion at the end of December 2014.[22] A third measure of derivatives exposure, "gross credit exposure," which adjusts gross market values for legally enforceable bilateral netting agreements but does not take account of collateral posted with respect to the contracts, rose to $3.4 trillion at the end of December 2014 from $2.8 trillion in June 2014.[23] In a moment, we will see why the "gross market value" and "gross credit exposure" figures, which are large enough to shatter the financial system in the next crisis, are important but still don't tell the whole story.

The Office of the Comptroller of the Currency tracks the exposure of U.S. banks to derivatives and reported that just four large U.S. banks (JPMorgan, Bank of America, Citigroup, and Goldman Sachs) carried a combined $220.4 trillion of derivatives on their books at the end of December 2014. This figure dwarfed their combined $769.2 billion in equity capital by multiples ranging from 151 at Bank of America to an astounding 565 at Goldman Sachs (see Table I.4).

Table I.4   Exposure of U.S. Banks to Derivatives ($ in billions)

Bank Name	Shareholders' Equity	Total Assets	Total Derivatives	Ratio of Total Derivatives/ Shareholders' Equity
JPMorgan Chase Bank NA	$232.0	$2,573.1	$63,683.3	275x
Citibank National Assn	$210.5	$1,843.0	$56,295.8	267x
Goldman Sachs Bank USA	$82.8	$856.2	$46,778.6	565x
Bank of America NA	$243.8	$2,104.5	$36,726.3	151x

SOURCE: 2014 Annual Reports; Office of the Comptroller of the Currency Quarterly Report on Bank Trading and Derivatives Activities Fourth Quarter 2014.

Since then, these banks have reduced their derivatives books by several trillion dollars each, but their derivatives exposures still remain dangerously large. Excluded from this list is the world's largest known purveyor of derivatives, Deutsche Bank AG, which as of late 2015 held $60 trillion of derivatives contracts on its books. Deutsche Bank may well pose the single biggest systemic risk of any financial institution in the world.[24] This is because it suffers from severe management, operational, and regulatory deficiencies that have gone unremedied for more than a decade. These problems finally burst into the open in July 2014 when *The Wall Street Journal* disclosed that the Federal Reserve Bank of New York's concerns about the bank had been growing for years.

On December 11, 2013, Daniel Mucca, a New York Fed senior vice president responsible for supervising Deutsche Bank, wrote the following to the bank's senior management: "Since 2002, the FRBNY has highlighted significant weaknesses in the firm's regulatory reporting framework that has remained outstanding for a decade. Most concerning is the fact that although the root causes of these errors were not eliminated, prior supervisory issues were considered remediated and closed by senior management." He added that financial reports produced by the bank "are of low quality, inaccurate and unreliable. The size and breadth of the errors strongly suggest that the firm's U.S. regulatory reporting structure requires wide-ranging remedial action." The New

York Fed had voiced concerns about the quality of the data reported in 2002, 2007, and 2012. The letter said that the bank had made "no progress" at fixing previously identified problems and examiners found "material errors and poor data integrity" in its U.S. public filings, which are used by regulators to evaluate its operations. Mr. Mucca added that the shortcomings amounted to a "systemic breakdown" and "expose the firm to significant operational risk and misstated regulatory reports." The bank's external auditor, KPMG LLP, also identified "deficiencies" in the way the bank's U.S. entities were reporting financial data in 2013 according to an internal email reviewed by *The Wall Street Journal.*

As heartening as it is to hear that the Fed is on the case, the real question is how six years after the financial crisis an institution holding enough derivatives to blow up the global financial system could be permitted to operate with financial controls that would force a corner drug store out of business. People have asked how Bernie Madoff was able to escape the attention of regulators for so many years, but in that case regulators never flagged the fraud that was occurring under their noses. In the case of Deutsche Bank that—to repeat—holds enough derivatives on its books to blow up the world, regulators repeatedly flagged problems but failed to either require them to be fixed or to rein in the bank's operations in order to protect investors and the system. This is simply inexcusable.

Not only has the issue of concentration risk in the financial system been inadequately addressed, but it was exacerbated by the extinction of several large firms during the financial crisis and a new regulatory regime that blindly favors size over flexibility while allowing derivatives risk to fester right under regulators' noses. This is one more example why that White House official wanted me to explain to the people advising President Obama that relying on regulators to police derivatives is going to end in tears.

Those who like to downplay the risks of derivatives, all of whom are grossly conflicted because they have an economic interest in the instruments' continued growth, argue that focusing on notional derivative contracts exaggerates the risks they pose. They argue that systemic risk should be measured in terms of the lower "gross credit exposures," which, as noted above, stood at $21 trillion at December 31, 2014. Even this number, however, should make the hair stand up on the back of the neck of anyone who understands how these instruments work. But focusing on anything other than the larger notional amounts of outstanding derivatives demonstrates a basic failure to understand how modern markets operate.

James Rickards, who among his many accomplishments was brought in to help restructure the insolvent Long Term Capital Management hedge fund after it blew up after using too much leverage and too many derivatives in 1998, explains why the much larger notional figures are the relevant ones to focus on in terms of evaluating risk:

> In complex systems, shorts are not subtracted from longs—they are *added* together. Every dollar of notional value represents some linkage between agents in the system. Every dollar of notional value creates some interdependence. If a counterparty fails, what started out as a net position for a particular bank instantaneously becomes a gross position, because the "hedge" has disappeared. Fundamentally, the risk is in the gross position, not the net.[25]

In other words, lower "total gross credit exposure" or "gross market value" are relevant when it doesn't matter, i.e., when markets are functioning normally. In a crisis, as Mr. Rickards explains, counterparties either will be unable and/or unwilling to perform and the volume of broken contracts will overwhelm these institutions and render them instantly insolvent.

Financial markets are complex systems. They exhibit exponential rather than linear change because their constituents are interlinked and interdependent; any change in one component affects all of the other components in the system. Since financial markets involve human actors, they involve an additional, unquantifiable factor: the issue of trust. A market is ultimately built not on a foundation of money but on a bedrock of trust, which Francis Fukuyama defined as "the expectation that arises within a community of regular, honest, and cooperative behavior, based on commonly shared norms, on the part of other members of the community."[26]

Debt instruments are contracts in which two parties agree to undertake certain obligations to each other. If they fail to fulfill those obligations, each of them can pursue legal remedies against the other in a court of law. The problem with such a regime is that the pursuit of such remedies takes years while the failure to meet one's obligations can inflict immediate damage from which a party can never truly recover. Furthermore, in the event of a systemic crisis, the financial wherewithal to make the other party whole may not exist.

In 2008, the world caught a glimpse of what happens when financial counterparties lose trust in each other as well as confidence in the system. Many of them refused to meet their obligations under all types of financial contracts including derivatives contracts. This led the entire system to the brink of collapse. The financial system has placed itself in an extremely vulnerable position by allowing more than $600 trillion of derivatives contracts, including at least $16 trillion of credit default swaps as of December 31, 2014, to proliferate in the hands of a small group of firms.

Efforts have been made to tame credit derivatives, but these efforts largely miss the mark. The primary focus has been to move derivatives trades onto clearing houses that can provide regulators with greater transparency[27] as well as to establish collateral requirements and similar rules. The problem with this approach, as I noted in the first edition to this book, is that clearing houses can inadvertently become new "too big to fail" institutions if they run into financial trouble during a crisis and are themselves deemed to pose systemic risk. If a clearing house were to experience financial trouble and become unable to meet its obligations, there would be an enormous temptation to bail it out in the name of financial stability; this would merely replace one "too big to fail" institution (the banks) with a new one (the clearing house). Furthermore, as discussed in Chapter 7, significant volumes of derivatives trades are still being conducted beyond the scope of regulatory scrutiny.

Credit default contracts on subprime mortgages rendered AIG insolvent and forced the U.S. government to bail out the insurer. The volume of outstanding credit default swaps is much lower today than on the cusp of the financial crisis. The notional volume of single-name credit default swaps declined from $25.1 trillion in 2007 to $10.8 trillion in mid-2014.[28] The notional volume of multi-name credit default swaps has also decreased significantly from $20.1 trillion in 2007 to $8.6 trillion in mid-2014 (most of these are swaps on index products such as high yield bond or loan indices). Nonetheless, these volumes still dwarf the capital of dealers and the $2.3 trillion of total capital in the high yield bond and bank loan markets in 2014.[29] If counterparties were to become unwilling or unable to perform again, all bets would be off. The system remains overleveraged and unprepared for another crisis for which the only response would appear to be a blanket government guarantee of the obligations of the institutions carrying these trillions of dollars of derivatives on their books.

These risks are far from theoretical. In 2013—a mere five years after the collapse of Lehman Brothers and near-collapse of AIG, the latter of which would have constituted an extinction-level-event for the global financial system—JPMorgan lost more than $6 billion on trades involving credit default swap bets on high yield bond indices in the incident infamously known as the "London Whale." This multi-billion loss happened right under the nose of the bank's CEO Jamie Dimon, widely believed to be the best risk manager in the business. This illustrates that even those considered to be the smartest guys in the room don't understand derivatives, which are highly complex and specialized instruments.

Furthermore, this unfortunate episode demonstrated once again that credit derivatives markets are thinly traded and highly illiquid and volatile; when market conditions deteriorate, counterparties become unable or unwilling to perform and create systemic dislocations that sink the values of the securities underlying derivatives contracts. In point of fact, despite their large notional volumes, credit default swap markets have always been (and will remain) extremely illiquid as investors learned during the 2008–2009 crisis when relatively low trading volumes led to huge moves in the credit spreads of troubled firms such as Bear Stearns and Lehman Brothers as described in Chapter 7.

Rather than reducing systemic instability, credit derivatives significantly increase systemic fragility and render illiquid underlying cash markets far more prone to large price swings not only in a crisis but in normal market conditions. This volatility and potential for loss (particularly in leveraged portfolios) has been disguised since 2009 by central bank-distorted markets. When the next market dislocation arrives, as it inevitably will, these derivatives will again earn their reputation as the "weapons of mass financial destruction" that Warren Buffett bestowed on them (although that has not prevented the Oracle of Omaha from investing in them extensively himself!).

Market Corruption

While the financial system is now populated by fewer "too big to save" institutions, it also appears that these firms are "too big to jail." But the real story is that our government lacks the wherewithal to enforce its own laws.[30] The highly concentrated nature of risk in the financial system is more problematic in view of the inability of regulators to rein in institutions' bad behavior. Some of the world's largest banks have engaged in serial violations of the law and paid large fines while being given multiple waivers shielding them from the loss of their banking licenses while virtually none of the corporate executives who committed the deeds in question have been punished criminally. Deutsche Bank's ability to keep regulators at bay is just one example of the corruption of markets.

After the savings-and-loan crisis of the early 1990s, over 1,000 executives were prosecuted and more than 800 convicted. While some of these prosecutions, such as Michael Milken's, were politically motivated and unjust, the lion's share were appropriate. After the 2008 financial crisis, which unlike the savings-and-loan mess posed a true systemic threat, virtually none of the individuals who participated in the decisions that caused systemic harm has been prosecuted.

Speaking as a highly experienced attorney and market practitioner as well as a citizen, this breeds disrespect for the law and the government that is obligated to enforce the rules of fair play. As *The Economist* writes: "If banks have been involved in acts serious enough to qualify for billions of dollars in penalties, then a few more executives must surely have committed a crime."[31] Surely the crimes did not commit themselves, nor did they materialize out of thin air; they were the result of deliberate actions on the part of highly educated and presumably intelligent individuals who deserve to be punished. The fact that they were not punished is a profound regulatory and moral failure that weakens the financial system.

In his classic study of financial bubbles, *Manias, Panics and Crashes: A History of Financial Crises*, Charles Kindleberger pointed to a common characteristic of speculative booms: "Commercial and financial crises are intimately bound up with transactions that overstep the confines of the law and morality, shadowy though these confines be. The propensities to swindle and be swindled run parallel to the propensity to speculate during a boom."[32] In May 2015, the government entered into another in a long line of settlements with a group of large financial institutions: a $5.6 billion settlement for the manipulation of exchange rates in the foreign currency exchange spot market. This was just the latest in a series of instances in which individuals working at the heart of the financial system violated the law but nobody went to jail. This settlement followed a similar one involving the manipulation of LIBOR by some of the same institutions.

As part of the settlement, the SEC decided to give another waiver to these institutions that would allow them to conduct business as usual despite the fact that they were repeat offenders. This did not sit well with one SEC Commissioner, Kara M. Stein, who is a frequent target of *The Wall Street Journal*'s editorial page for being too tough a regulator. In this case, however, Ms. Stein should be applauded for speaking out; she should remind us of Brooksley Born, the former chair of the CFTC whose warnings about the risks of lax derivatives regulation were dismissed by The Committee to Save the World in 1999.

Ms. Stein dissented from the grant of the waivers to UBS, Barclays, Citigroup, JPMorgan Chase, and the Royal Bank of Scotland, pointing out that this was Barclays' third waiver since 2007, UBS's seventh waiver since 2008, JPMorgan's sixth waiver since 2008, Citigroup's fourth waiver since 2006, and Royal Bank of Scotland's third waiver since 2013. She wrote that, "[a]llowing these institutions to continue business as usual, after multiple and serious regulatory and criminal violations, poses risks to investors and the American public that are being ignored. It is not sufficient to look at each waiver request in a vacuum."

She pointed out that UBS's waiver in the earlier LIBOR case was expressly conditioned on no further violations. That condition was violated by its conduct in the foreign exchange case, yet another waiver was granted. She continued: "It is troubling enough to consistently grant waivers for criminal misconduct. It is an order of magnitude more troubling to refuse to enforce our own explicit requirements for such waivers. This type of recidivism and repeated criminal misconduct should lead to revocations of prior waivers, not the granting of a whole new set of waivers. We have the tools, and with the tools the responsibility, to empower those at the top of these institutions to create meaningful cultural shifts, yet we refuse to use them." In conclusion, she wrote, "I am troubled by repeated instances of noncompliance at these global financial institutions, which may be indicative of a continuing culture that does not adequately support legal and ethical behavior. Further, I am concerned that the latest series of actions has effectively rendered criminal convictions of financial institutions largely symbolic. Firms and institutions increasingly rely on the Commission's repeated issuance of waivers to remove the consequences of a criminal conviction, consequences that may actually positively contribute to a firm's compliance and conduct going forward."

Large institutions that repeatedly break the law have come to see multibillion dollar fines as another cost of doing business. They may complain about them publicly, but until their senior executives are made to pay the ultimate price—the loss of their jobs or their freedom—little is going to change. This may sound harsh, but the systemic harm resulting from the manipulation of markets as important as LIBOR and foreign exchange is profound.

Years ago, the senior executives of Salomon Brothers lost their jobs after it was discovered that Treasury auctions were manipulated on their watch; and we don't need to be reminded what happened to Drexel Burnham Lambert, Inc. and its visionary leader Michael Milken after he was alleged to have violated laws much less serious than the manipulation of major markets like interest rates and currencies. Today the consequences of law-breaking have been gutted due to regulators' fears of destabilizing large institutions during an epic credit bubble, something that Charles Kindleberger warned about. We should heed that warning and stiffen our spines against the fraud in our midst before it drags down the system with it. Manipulating markets is not business as usual and should not be tolerated; it should be punished severely before it inflicts harm from which the system can't recover.

The Geopolitics of Appeasement

In 2008 the world was facing an economic crisis, but at least the geopolitical situation was relatively stable. That is no longer the case in 2016. Inexcusable foreign policy failures by the Obama administration have left the world a shambles.

The only thing worse than being led by a president lacking the knowledge, experience, and character to lead a great nation is to surround that leader with advisors with similar limitations. But rather than a team of rivals, Barack Obama assembled a confederacy of dunces in Joe Biden, Hillary Clinton, Susan Rice, and John Kerry, a group that supported his worst foreign policy instincts and choices. Principled and competent members of the foreign policy team like Leon Panetta, Robert Gates, General Stanley McChrystal, and General David Petraeus left the administration early. As a result of chronic mismanagement of foreign affairs by the Obama team, the global hegemony of the United States has been profoundly weakened since the financial crisis. It will take decades for America and its allies to recover.

As Charles Krauthammer writes: "For all the sublimity of art, physics, music, mathematics and other manifestations of human genius, everything depends on the mundane, frustrating, often debased vocation known as politics (and its most exacting subspecialty—statecraft). Because if we don't get politics right, everything else risks extinction."[33] The Obama administration has gotten virtually nothing right when it comes to foreign policy. In the hands of President Barack Obama and his foreign policy staff, statecraft has been a series of abdications of American power and appeasements of America's enemies throughout the world. It is virtually impossible to name a single place on the globe that is more stable at the end of Mr. Obama's two terms in office than when he entered in January 2009.

The geopolitical stage deteriorated to such a dangerous extent under Mr. Obama that the United States is facing existential risks that didn't exist during the financial crisis. Many of the forces creating these risks were simmering under the surface in 2008, but they were so badly mismanaged by the Obama administration that one could reasonably ask whether the errors were intentional. After all, even incompetence is supposed to have its limits. But with this administration, that was not the case. Sunni–Shia conflict and radical Islamic terrorism are hardly new phenomena. Nor are Russian aggression in Eastern Europe or Chinese incursions in the South China Sea. Yet the responses to these destabilizing threats on the part of Mr. Obama, Mrs. Clinton, and the rest of this foreign policy team were so incompetent as to beggar reason.

In November 2008, Americans elected an untested one-term Senator with no foreign policy experience and a desire to set a different course from his predecessor, George W. Bush. Unfortunately, that course was based on an ill-advised retreat from America's leadership role in a world where anti-American and anti-Western threats were intensifying. There were certainly lessons to be learned from the foreign policy mistakes of Mr. Bush. Tragically, Mr. Obama and his team learned the wrong ones. Much of the country was rightly dissatisfied with the state of the country as George W. Bush ended his tenure and Mr. Obama offered the promise of "hope and change." But as President Obama approached the end of his second term, "hope and change" had dissolved into the ugly remnants of a sluggish and overindebted economy; record levels of inner city black-on-black violence and minority unemployment; a profoundly weakened American presence abroad; and direct threats to America and its allies from radical Islamic terrorists As disturbing as were the domestic policy failures of the Obama years, the foreign policy failures were potentially catastrophic.

The world grew far more dangerous in the years after the financial crisis than at any time since the end of the Cold War. This situation was exacerbated by a lack of resolute American leadership to counter rising threats from Iran, ISIS, Russia, and China. By late 2015, Iran was closer to achieving nuclear capability than ever before while solidifying its control over much of the Middle East after signing a one-sided (in its favor) nuclear deal with the Obama administration that was opposed by a majority of Congress and the American people. Russia occupied Ukraine and was threatening all of Eastern Europe while establishing a military presence in the Middle East for the first time to bolster Iran and Syria. China was asserting itself aggressively across the South China Sea. And ISIS was breeding home-grown terrorism throughout the West while carving a swathe of antediluvian horror across the Mideast. Make no mistake—these are not only geopolitical risks but economic and market risks.

Even those who were unhappy with the aggressive foreign policy of George W. Bush must conclude that things went from bad to worse under Mr. Obama. To some of us, Mr. Obama's belief that mullahs in Iran, jihadists in the Mideast, and Russian and Chinese leaders would succumb to his charms was dangerously naïve and completely delusional. But in our wildest dreams, even Mr. Obama's sharpest critic could not have imagined that this president would inflict as much damage on American interests as he has done during his time in the White House.

As his administration advanced, Mr. Obama managed foreign policy based on the assumption that what he regards as his superior intellect, knowledge, and judgment (for which, by the way, there is not a scintilla of objective evidence) superseded irrefutable and mounting evidence that his policies were producing results at odds with his own statements and the best interests of the American people. The worse the evidence became, the more he pursued the same damaging policies (an approach he shared with the nation's central bankers). We need only look at the facts on the ground to see the ruins of Mr. Obama's arrogant misconceptions.

Iran

In what will likely serve as his gravest foreign policy failure (unfortunately it is difficult to choose among so many disasters), the Obama administration entered a deal that will provide Iran with the opportunity to gain fast-track nuclear capability while freeing the country from crippling economic sanctions. The National Military Strategy of the United States is a report issued by the Chairman of the Joint Chiefs of Staff to the Secretary of Defense every year outlining the strategic aims of the armed services. The 2015 report, which was delivered in June 2015, described Iran as follows: "[Iran] is pursuing nuclear and missile delivery technologies despite repeated United Nations Security Council resolutions demanding that it cease such efforts. It is a state-sponsor of terrorism that has undermined stability in many nations, including Israel, Lebanon, Iraq, Syria, and Yemen. Iran's actions have destabilized the region and brought misery to countless people while denying the Iranian people the prospect of a prosperous future."[34] Despite this warning from its highest ranking military official, the Obama administration agreed to a nuclear deal that gives the country a largely free path to nuclear capability after 15 years without limiting its support of terrorism or threats against Israel and the U.S.

The administration's desperation for a deal despite Iran's continued support for global terrorism and aggression in the Middle East would lead one to believe that the United States rather than Iran was in the weaker negotiating position. Yet as Karim Sadjadpour, an Iran expert at the

Carnegie Endowment, wrote during the negotiations: "Iran is the one hemorrhaging hundreds of billions of dollars due to sanctions, tens of billions because of fallen oil prices and billions sustaining the Assad regime in Syria....And it's Ali Khamenei [Iran's Supreme Leader], not [U.S. Secretary of State] John Kerry, who presides over a population desperate to see sanctions relief."[35] With the Iranian currency plunging, inflation skyrocketing and the economy shrinking under the pressure of international sanctions, and with a bipartisan Congress pushing to further tighten the sanctions to increase the pressure on Iran in early 2015, Mr. Obama loosened the sanctions and injected billions of dollars into the Iranian economy while conceding in advance Iran's right to enrich uranium.

Then, as the June 30, 2015, deadline approached (and passed), Mr. Obama and Mr. Kerry dismissed as "rhetoric" repeated incendiary statements by Mr. Khamenei and a vote by the Iranian Parliament rejecting demands that any agreement provide for inspections of Iran's military facilities and immediate sanctions relief. In other words, while Iran was publicly stating that it had no intention of complying with any agreement (interspersed with calls of "Death to America" and for the destruction of Israel), Mr. Obama and Mr. Kerry continued to negotiate in good faith. Two weeks later, when a final agreement was reached, it allowed Iran to produce as much nuclear fuel as it wishes after 15 years, to limit inspections of its military facilities, to retain a significant number of its centrifuges, and to inspect its own Parchin nuclear site through a secret side deal with the International Atomic Energy Agency that was not disclosed to Congress (in violation of the law).

The agreement did not prevent Iran from entering new weapons deals with Russia, which it did before the ink was even dry on the agreement, or stop supporting terrorism. Iran was granted roughly $150 billion of sanctions relief that even the Obama administration admitted would be used in part to support Iran's proxies Hamas and Hezbollah in their attacks against Israel. Reports indicated that Hezbollah had 120,000 rockets and missiles trained on Israel at the time the Iran deal was going to be signed by Mr. Obama, but that was apparently an insufficient threat to dissuade the president from moving forward from funding a group sworn to wipe America's ally and the only democracy in the Middle East off the face of the earth.

The Iran deal was opposed by large majorities of both the Senate and the House of Representatives. While the Obama administration blocked any formal vote in the Senate (an act of epic moral and political cowardice), only 42 of 100 senators supported the deal. On September 11, 2015, the House of Representatives held a formal vote to approve the deal that was defeated by an overwhelming 269–162 majority. Numerous public opinion polls showed that an overwhelming majority of the American people objected to the deal. Nonetheless, Mr. Obama decided he knew better and moved ahead. It is impossible to recall another time in American history when a president so openly flouted the opinions of a majority of Congress, the country's citizens, and its closest allies to appease a sworn enemy.

As Congress was registering its disapproval of the deal, Iran's Supreme Leader was telling the world that Israel would not exist in 25 years, another in a series of inflammatory speeches repudiating any claims by the Obama administration that the nuclear deal would create a rapprochement between Iran and the West. Mr. Obama, of course, claimed that he was too sophisticated to believe such threats. The world also learned the same week that Congress rejected the deal that Russia had been secretly mounting a major military build-up in Syria to back the Iranian puppet regime of Bashar al-Assad, leaving the Obama administration scrambling to explain away another foreign policy debacle of its own making. And when the International Atomic Energy Agency (IAEA) issued its final report on Iran's nuclear program as part of the deal in late 2015, it reported that Iran had not cooperated and had withheld key information required by the agreement. It is clear that Mr. Obama signed an agreement that only one party intends to honor, and that party is not Iran.

In entering the Iran nuclear deal, the Obama administration violated two clauses of the Constitution. It did so because it knew it could not enter the agreement by lawful means. First, it breached the Treaty Clause, which requires the president to submit major foreign policy agreements that constitute treaties to the Senate for two-thirds approval. Article II, Section 2 of the Constitution states that the president "shall have Power, by and with the Advice and Consent of the Senate, to make Treaties, provided two-thirds of the Senators present concur." Knowing it lacked the requisite 67 votes to approve this agreement, Mr. Obama deemed the agreement to be an "executive agreement" that would only bind Mr. Obama and not subsequent presidents. In fact, only 42 members of the Senate supported the deal, 25 votes short of what would be necessary for a treaty. Of course, even if a subsequent president repudiates this unlawful agreement, the sanctions relief cannot be reversed.

The Obama administration also violated the Take Care Clause of the Constitution. Article II, Section III holds that the president must "take Care that the Laws be faithfully executed." In May 2015, both houses of Congress passed by overwhelming majorities, and the president signed into law, H.R. 1191, the Iran Nuclear Agreement Review Act of 2015 (the "Review Act" also known as the "Corker-Cardin Bill") that provided for congressional oversight of the nuclear deal. The Review Act required the president to submit to Congress the text of the deal as well as all "annexes, appendices, codicils, side agreements, implementing materials, documents and guidance, technical or other understandings, and any related agreements, whether entered into or implemented prior to the agreement or to be entered into or implemented in the future." The administration violated this language by failing to provide to Congress the side agreements between Iran and the IAEA that provided, among other things, that Iran would be permitted to inspect its own Parchin nuclear site (the agreement Iran breached in late 2015). So in addition to violating the Constitution, Mr. Obama broke his word to Congress by failing to provide these side agreements.

In a further end-run around Congress and the American people, the Obama administration allowed the deal to be brought to the United Nations Security Council for approval before even bringing it to Congress, giving Vladimir Putin and Xi Jinping the first word on the agreement.

President Obama's deal with Iran ignored the legitimate concerns of Israel, Egypt and Saudi Arabia and led these traditional American allies to seek new alliances and, in the case of the latter two, their own nuclear weapons capability. While the Israeli Prime Minister tried to explain to Mr. Obama that "the enemy of my enemy is my enemy," the Middle East will now be governed by the adage "the enemy of my enemy is my friend." Such arrangements are fragile and unstable. Obama's dismissive treatment during his administration of Israel, the only democracy in the Middle East and a steadfast ally, has been a national and moral disgrace as well as a profound strategic blunder that weakens the influence and interests of the U.S. not only in the Middle East but throughout the world. This treatment most likely emboldened several Jewish members of Congress to vote in favor of the Iran nuclear deal, shamefully selling out their constituents and their principles. When you openly mistreat one of your most important allies, your other allies question your reliability and your character.

The Republican minority in Congress also has to answer for failing to stop this deal. When Harry Reid was the Majority Leader of the Senate, he was willing to toss aside years of tradition and ignore the filibuster rule in order to force through Obama judicial nominees that were being blocked by the Republicans. For some reason, Republican Majority Leader Mitch McConnell was unwilling to do the same with respect to the much more important Iran deal. Had he been willing to do so, this unlawful and dangerous agreement would have been blocked. While Mr. Obama deserves the blame for the Iran agreement, he had many co-conspirators in Congress.

With respect to Iran, Mr. Obama believes he knows something that every other expert in the world does not, but he is profoundly mistaken. For some mysterious reason he believes that the mullahs, who repeatedly tell the world that they intend to destroy the United States and Israel, don't mean what they say. Perversely, Mr. Obama is more prepared to trust Iran's leaders than Americans who disagree with him, respected American foreign policy experts, members of Congress and America's long-time allies.

The world cannot afford the luxury of Mr. Obama's arrogance and delusions. With or without an agreement, Iran will continue to move forward with its nuclear program; the world should be making it more difficult to do so rather than dropping $150 billion in its lap to fund radical Islamic terrorism and attacks on Israel through its proxies Hamas and Hezbollah.

Mr. Obama's conduct is deserving of the admonition Winston Churchill delivered to Neville Chamberlain after he appeased Hitler at the Munich Conference in 1939: "You were given the choice between war and dishonor. You chose dishonor and you will have war." When the United States learned about Iran's nuclear plans in 2003, the appropriate response was an immediate land and sea blockade of the country and the imposition of the strictest possible economic sanctions. That remains the only appropriate response. You cannot reason with madmen and those who believe they can are reckless fools who place the world at risk. Mr. Obama and the Democrats who supported the Iran nuclear deal have committed a treasonous error for which they will have to answer to the American people and the world in the years ahead.

ISIS

While Iran poses the gravest threat to global stability in the Middle East, it is hardly the only one. The premature departure of American troops from the Middle East without Status of Forces Agreements in place to satisfy outdated Obama campaign promises that no longer fit the facts on the ground unleashed a simmering Shia-Sunni war as ISIS assumed the mantle of Al Qaeda, obliterated the border between Iraq and Syria, and ignited a reign of satanic terror across the region.

The Chairman of the Joint Chiefs warned that violent extremist organizations such as ISIS "are working to undermine transregional security, especially in the Middle East and North Africa. Such groups are dedicated to radicalizing populations, spreading violence, and leveraging terror to impose their visions of societal organization. They are strongest where governments are weakest, exploiting people trapped in fragile or failed states. In many locations, [these groups] coexist with transnational criminal organizations, where they conduct illicit trade and spread corruption, further undermining security and stability."[36] But Mr. Obama characteristically thought he knew better and arrogantly dismissed ISIS as the "JV team" of terrorists. How sadly was he mistaken.

ISIS uses social media and the Internet to inspire home-grown terrorists throughout the world, creating a random threat that is virtually impossible to defend against. Shortly before the July 4th holiday in 2015, the FBI reportedly broke up a number of plots to attack U.S. targets by homegrown ISIS-inspired terrorists. Shortly thereafter, FBI Director James Comey told Congress that the FBI had active ongoing investigations in all 50 states related to similar threats and that he was uncertain how long the FBI could continue to prevent all of these plots from succeeding. It did not take long to find out. A few days after Mr. Comey's warning, four marines were shot and killed in an attack by an ISIS-inspired home-grown gunman on a military recruiting office in Chattanooga, Tennessee.

In August 2015, it was disclosed that American Kayla Mueller, who was held hostage by ISIS and ultimately killed, was raped and tortured repeatedly by ISIS leader Abu Bakr-al Baghdadi during her captivity. Besides demonstrating that any claims that ISIS is guided by Islam or any religion is a farce, this report confirmed the nature of an enemy that is actively recruiting people inside the United States and around the world to kill Americans and other Westerners. On the day this news was released, President Barack Obama was found on a golf course in Martha's Vineyard rather than back in the Oval Office with his military advisors planning an appropriate military response to this desecration of an innocent American woman and American values. His golf partner was another former Democratic president and the husband of his former Secretary of State and presumptive Democratic presidential nominee, who helped shape the foreign policy that facilitated the formation of ISIS. She was off raising money from wealthy liberals vacationing on the island.

This was how the leader of the free world—the man who is asking Americans to trust his judgment on issues of existential importance such as Iran gaining access to nuclear weapons—conducts himself in wartime. I have no doubt that Dwight Eisenhower, Ronald Reagan, or George W. Bush would have been in the Oval Office in shirt and tie demonstrating to the American people and the world how to respond to unspeakable attacks on an innocent American woman. And when it came to speaking about ISIS, Mr. Obama was more concerned about offending the vast majority of non-radical Muslims who reject ISIS than calling out radical Islam as the enemy of all civilized people. In view of this type of behavior, should anybody be surprised that the 44th president of the United States is leaving the world in shambles as he prepares to leave office not a moment too soon?

Mr. Obama's "JV team" comment came back to haunt him in 2015. ISIS operatives unleashed two terrorist attacks in Paris in 2015, the first on the offices of the satirical magazine *Charlie Hebdo* in January that killed 12 and the second on several sites in Paris in November, killing at least 130 people and wounding hundreds more. The Paris attack came shortly after ISIS claimed responsibility for planting a bomb on a Russian civilian airliner flying out of Egypt, killing all 224 people aboard. Then on December 2, 2015, two ISIS-inspired American radical Islamic terrorists killed 14 and wounded 21 in an attack in San Bernardino, California, the worst terrorist attack on American soil since 9-11. These attacks on Western targets were in addition to constant attacks on civilians in

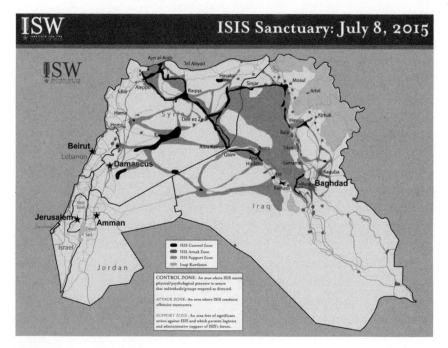

Figure I.6 The "JV" Team

SOURCE: Harleen Gambhir, "ISIS's Global Strategy: A Wargame," Institute for the Study of War, 2015, available at http://understandingwar.org/sites/default/files/ISIS%20Global%20Strategy%20 –%20A%20Wargame%20FINAL.pdf.

the Middle East, Africa, and Asia. ISIS did not exist at the time of the 2008 financial crisis; six years later it poses an existential threat to the United States, Europe, and much of the Middle East.

Russia

Behind Iran and Syria lurks the destabilizing influence of Russia and its ambitious leader Vladimir Putin. Russia is an economically weak nation that has been able to punch well above its weight due to Mr. Putin's ability to bully and manipulate spineless Western leaders. As noted in The National Military Strategy of the United States of America 2015, Russia "has repeatedly demonstrated that it does not respect the sovereignty of its neighbors and it is willing to use force to achieve its goals. Russia's military actions are undermining regional security directly and through proxy forces. These actions violate numerous agreements that Russia has signed in which it committed to act in accordance with international norms, including the UN Charter, Helsinki Accords, Russia-NATO Founding Act, Budapest Memorandum and the Intermediate-Range Nuclear Forces Treaty."[37] In 2014, Russia invaded Ukraine and was hit with severe economic sanctions that nonetheless failed to temper its aggression. Those sanctions should be significantly intensified until Russia changes course.

Rather than exploit the economic weakness caused by these sanctions and the simultaneous collapse in oil prices so important to the Russian economy, however, the United States and Europe failed to follow through with additional measures and allowed Russia to remain in Ukraine and threaten other Eastern European countries that would like to draw closer to NATO economically. They then allowed Russia to extend its aggression into the Middle East shortly after the Iran nuclear deal was signed. In the ultimate appeasement of Putin, the Obama administration allowed Russia to start calling the shots with respect to the Syrian civil war after signing the Iran nuclear deal.

Mr. Putin knows a weak mark when he sees one, and Mr. Obama and the current European leadership rank among the weakest marks in history. As described more fully below, seeing an opening in the Middle East due to the Obama administration's weakness, Mr. Putin stepped in and built a military presence in Syria in league with Iran shortly after the Iran nuclear deal was signed. Claiming to fight ISIS but focusing on bombing American-backed Syrian rebels, Mr. Putin changed the balance of power in the region by teaming with Iran to buck-up the regime of the genocidal Bashar al-Assad. This worked to the detriment of American interests while the Obama administration acted like war is a video game that can be fought from 30,000 feet. Russian aggression around the world is likely to accelerate without a radical change in American policy. Mr. Putin will be very sorry to see Mr. Obama's second term come to an end.

Syria

Mr. Putin has toyed with Mr. Obama in Syria. Mr. Putin intervened in Syria after the so-called "red line" on chemical weapons drawn by the American president was erased by a war-weary and selfish American public and Congress. Mr. Putin negotiated an agreement whereby

Syria's chemical weapons would be shipped to Russia, an agreement that only a naïve former community organizer could possibly believe would actually be enforced. Mr. Putin subsequently increased Russia's military presence in Syria right under the nose of the Obama administration in order to bolster the Assad regime. Not even a year after the bogus chemical weapons deal, Syrian president, Iranian puppet, and serial *genocidaire* Bashar al-Assad was again gassing his people to death (when he wasn't butchering them with barrel bombs) while the West stood silent in complicity.

But matters deteriorated much further in Syria after the Iran deal was completed. It turned out that Russia and Iran were waiting for Mr. Obama to sign on the dotted line before descending on Syria to back their ally Mr. Assad and move against his opposition, which included not only ISIS but American-backed rebels. Under cover of fighting ISIS, Russia established its first Middle Eastern military base and turned its guns primarily on the rebels backed by the United States. This humiliation of Mr. Obama occurred days after he met with Vladimir Putin at the United Nations in New York. Mr. Putin acted like the cat who swallowed the canary as the amateurish American president started to figure out a few days later that he had been played for the small-time community organizer he remains. Mr. Obama tried to talk his way out his embarrassment by claiming that Mr. Putin was spreading himself too thin, but anyone with a functioning frontal cortex realized what had happened. American appeasement had created an opening for Iran to take over Syria and Russia to displace America at the center of Middle Eastern politics, an enormous strategic blunder that will cause incalculable damage to American and Israeli interests for years to come.

Furthermore, by mid-2015, Syria's civil war had unleashed the largest refugee crisis since the Second World War as a result of Mr. Obama's incompetence. And this was no mere refugee crisis: it was an opportunity for ISIS to plant its operatives among the Syrians fleeing Assad and let them gain entry to Europe and the United States. With limited ability to screen these refugees, well-intentioned Western countries were exposing themselves to potential terrorists as another unintended consequence of failed foreign policy. Once again, leading from behind was leading to horrific consequences in a world that cries out for American leadership. Europe and the United States were left to wrestle with the potential inflow of millions of Syrian refugees while the Middle East went up in flames. Mr. Putin had once again read the U.S. president for an appeaser-in-chief unwilling to assert American power in a strategically vital region of the world.

China

China is asserting its hegemony throughout the South China Sea, angering its Asian neighbors and mocking the so-called "tilt to Asia" that Mr. Obama and former Secretary of State Hillary Clinton announced during Mr. Obama's first term. The Chairman of the Joint Chiefs warns that, "China's actions are adding tension to the Asia-Pacific region.... [I]ts claims to nearly the entire South China Sea are inconsistent with international law. The international community continues to call on China to settle such issues cooperatively and without coercion. China has responded with aggressive land reclamation efforts that will allow it to position military forces astride vital international sea lanes."[38]

Of more economic importance, China is forging a new Silk Road across Asia, Africa, and the Middle East (and even parts of South America) while the U.S. pretends to be engaged in "nation building at home" (President Obama's words) but is actually allowing its cities to burn as inner city murders skyrocket, police shootings of civilians escalate, and 50 years of failed progressive policies lead minorities to lose all hope in the system. China's Silk Road will forge valuable commercial ties across the world while America moves forward into the twenty-first century without a coherent industrial or geopolitical strategy (see Figure I.7).

China has major economic and demographic problems, including a debt bubble that began to burst in 2014. China is a paper giant and does not have the ability to outcompete a competently managed United States. But that is not stopping it from forging major commercial ties in the fastest growing regions of the world while Western democracies are mired in their own debt and entitlement woes. The United States needs to stand up to Chinese aggression to maintain its important role in Pacific trade and strategic arrangements. There may also be a role for the United States to play helping China navigate its economic, social and environmental challenges while containing China's hegemonic aggression.

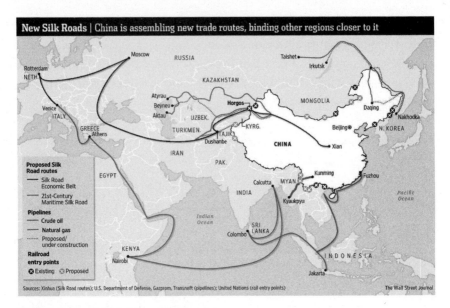

Figure I.7   China's New Silk Road
SOURCE: From the article, "China Sees Itself at Center of New Asian Order" by Jeremy Page, *The Wall Street Journal,* November 9, 2014.

But it will require strong, creative, and visionary American leadership to accomplish this while harboring no illusions regarding China's geopolitical aspirations. That will require regime change at home.

Economic cooperation and collaboration between the United States and China could create enormous opportunities for both countries while also providing a strategic counterweight to Russian aggression. Helping China deal with its ruined environment presents one of the best business opportunities of the twenty-first century for Western companies and governments. Rather than allow Russia to become China's economic partner, the U.S. should play that role. That would be a far more meaningful "tilt to Asia" than the feeble efforts initiated by the Obama administration.

The Obama Doctrine

Just as economics is an intellectual human construct, so is foreign policy. As Charles Krauthammer writes, "Fairly or not, politics is the driver of history. It will determine whether we will live long enough to be heard one day. Out there. By them, the few—the only—who got it right."[39]

Rarely has a president gotten foreign policy as consistently wrong as Barack Obama, with consequences that will damage economies and markets by increasing global instability for generations to come. While central bankers were destroying the global economy with their economic policies, the Obama administration allowed the geopolitical sphere to spin out of control.

A deliberate policy on the part of the Obama administration to retrench America's strategic presence abroad in order to focus on liberal policy initiatives at home left the world in chaos.[40]

Mr. Obama and his administration believe that climate change poses a more immediate existential threat than radical Islam. He actually said that the climate change conference in Paris, held shortly after radical Islamic terrorists butchered 130 people in that city, was a repudiation of terrorism, suggesting he might actually believe that radical Islamic terrorists share his frame of reference about the importance of the environment. This comment alone encapsulates how detached and deluded he is on the subject. Mr. Obama's obsession with climate change at the expense of fighting terrorism is a major intellectual and strategic error because it fails to distinguish between long-term and short-term threats. Climate change causes environmental damage over extremely long periods of time while terrorism poses an immediate existential and strategic threat. If the United States and other nations don't snuff out the immediate threat posed by ISIS and radical Islamic terrorism, Western civilization may not survive long enough to have to worry about the long-term damage caused by climate change. That may sound alarmist but it would be wise to take seriously the words of those who say they want to destroy us. All it would take is for one of them to get their hands on a nuclear, chemical, or electronic pulse weapon to change the world as we know it. Climate change is being aggressively addressed by governments and businesses around the world, but only the government can defend the nation. Mr. Obama's failure to establish a proper sequence of priorities with respect to these two threats demonstrates his unique unfitness for the office to which he was elected.

Mr. Obama also believes that foreign governments and actors will alter their policies if the United States accommodates their territorial aggressions, substituting narcissism and a profoundly misplaced intellectual arrogance for an understanding of how the world really works. This worldview is based on a flawed understanding of history and *realpolitik*;

it is little more than an ideological affectation and exercise in wish ful-fillment. Radical Islamic terrorists, mullahs, and men like Vladimir Putin or Xi Jinping will not alter their ideologies or behavior based on the magical thinking of a former community organizer. Throughout history, such individuals and groups consistently demonstrate that they will act in their own self-interest unless they are deterred by force. They do not share Western values or modes of thought.

As George Mason University Professor Colin Dueck writes, "[a]s a general rule, foreign governments or transnational actors do not feel obligated to alter their basic policy preferences or to make unwanted concessions on their own simply because an American president is accommodating, restrained, or articulate. That is not how international politics works. If the interests, goals, and priorities of other national governments align with those of the United States on specific issues, then those governments will cooperate with Washington on those issues. If not, they won't. Either way, whether we like it or not, the goals and priorities of foreign governments are defined by those governments, not by the president of the United States."[41] Mr. Obama approached the world with no foreign policy experience and a basic misunderstanding of geopolitics and leaves behind a much more dangerous world that poses enormous risks to both citizens and investors.

America must reject the Obama foreign policy doctrine. As described in more detail in Chapter 10, the United States must restore military spending that was cut by the budget sequester. America must then commit the necessary military resources—including ground troops—to defeat ISIS in the Middle East and restore stability to the region that it abandoned without a Status of Forces Agreement. It must defend—not close—all of its borders. America must confront and limit Russian aggression rather than be intimidated by paper tiger Vladimir Putin, who opposes NATO and American interests around the world. Russia is an economically and demographically weak state that can be contained with strong leadership. China's aspirations in the South China Sea must also be contained; China's economy is also a paper tiger and America has the power to maintain its strong role in the Pacific if it acts forcefully and creatively. The United States must start acknowledging that it has strategic and ideological enemies and start calling them by name. Political correctness has reduced public discourse in this country to weak-minded and intellectually vacuous onanism. This is the fault of academic, business, and political leaders who refuse to stand up for sacrosanct principles such as freedom of expression and liberal discourse and a mainstream media that exults in shallowness and rewards the loudest instead of the most constructive and intelligent voices.

The United States is the most diverse and open society in the world. The greatest threat to those qualities is the closed-mindedness of progressive ideologues who believe they know more than the rest of us and should substitute their flawed historical and moral judgments for those of experienced and realistic people who actually understand how the world works. We are at war with radical Islam and involved in an intense geopolitical competition with Russia and China that could turn into war if America doesn't revamp its foreign policy to defend American interests and values.

Radical Islam is led by Iran, not ISIS; ISIS is a symptom of the global disease of jihadism that weak Western leadership allows to fester. Iran, in turn, is backed by Russia and China. We need to connect the dots and deal with these threats. Barack Obama has repeatedly demonstrated through his words and deeds that he doesn't understand any of this although he thinks that he does. Few individuals have inflicted as much damage on the power and prestige of the United States as Mr. Obama. That is why he has the dubious distinction of chairing The Committee to Destroy the World.

We Are On an Unsustainable Economic Path

Denial is not a strategy for policymakers citizens, or investors. Yet that is precisely the strategy all three constituencies are pursuing as existential challenges to the global economic system metastasize. When a system is on an unsustainable path, it is certain to experience a change in conditions—the only question is when that change will occur and how severe it will be. The problems I have outlined are serious but they can be addressed by new leadership. The global financial system is resilient and can make the adjustments to deal with unsustainable debt expansion and inadequate economic growth. But it is less resilient than it should be and the adjustments are going to be painful. And we are running out of time.

There are only four ways to repay the monstrous level of global debt that now exists:

1. Currency debasement;
2. Inflation;
3. Default; or
4. Growth.

The first three options are variations on the same theme: debt will not be repaid in constant dollars and lenders will lose money. Since debt has run so far ahead of growth since the financial crisis, the fourth option, growth, is no longer available. Investors who understand this and react appropriately will profit enormously.

Central bankers admit as much while politicians and Congress fiddle while the economy burns. The Committee to Destroy the World repeatedly states that it wants to increase inflation. Yet while printing money around the clock is inflating asset prices, this type of inflation is not reflected in official government statistics. This causes central bankers to maintain policies that don't achieve their goals but lead to many unintended consequences.

The first play that central bankers ran shortly after the financial crisis was to lower interest rates to zero. The next play was to monetize trillions of dollars/yen/euros/yuan of debt through various bond purchasing and quantitative easing schemes. But all of these policies failed to ignite the type of economic growth and inflation that was intended although they triggered massive financial asset inflation and devalued other fiat currencies against the U.S. dollar. The next play will involve further currency debasement through additional quantitative easing programs that will leave global investors wrestling with the realization that the fiat currencies in which their investments are denominated are collapsing in value. There are a number of ways for investors to deal with this challenge that are discussed in Chapter 11 of this book.

America Must Make a Choice

The American people have a choice. Our economic and political leaders have failed miserably in every respect. They have set the United States on a course for economic and geopolitical disaster. Unelected central bankers are destroying the economy while Congress does nothing. With every passing day, debt, derivatives, and foreign policy cowardice move us closer to the brink of another crisis—except this time the tools to stabilize the system are much more limited.

America is populated by spoiled citizens who expect entitlements without responsibility, spoiled investors who expect high returns without risk, and spoiled politicians who expect to be re-elected without delivering responsible policies or, if they aren't re-elected, believe they are entitled to expensive sinecures where they can sell favors to the highest bidder.

Americans must demand change or they will have nobody to blame but themselves when they can no longer pay their bills or defend their borders. We have a choice between a productive future and crisis. We have chosen an unproductive future and are guaranteed crisis unless we stand up and hold our leaders accountable now.

Make no mistake about it—we are on the road to another financial crisis that will make the last one look like a garden party. The policies of The Committee to Destroy the World guarantee such a result. The world is far more leveraged than it was before the financial crisis. Central banks have shot all of the arrows in their quiver and can only launch further QE programs that haven't worked in the past and won't work in the future. Unlike 2009, central banks are no longer in a position to come to the rescue the next time stock markets start to collapse.

When that happens, investors can expect the value of all of their financial assets to collapse—stocks, bonds, commodities, real estate, and collectibles. Unlike the last time that happened in 2008 and 2009, the central bankers they worship will prove to be broken idols who truly destroyed not only the world but the dreams of those who foolishly counted on their wisdom and intellect.

The first edition of this book was written to explain what needed to be done to avoid the situation we are in. This second edition is now being published to urge people to demand change and to help investors and citizens prepare for the crisis that is coming as a result of the continuing failures of our leaders and policymakers.

A Few Words about This Book

While I initially welcomed the opportunity to update this book to reflect the events since its initial publication in 2010, I quickly realized that rewriting is more difficult than writing from scratch. I have done my best to maintain the flow of the original text while insuring that the book can stand on its own as reflective of the state of the financial world in early 2016. I have done my best to revise all of the chapters where needed. My readers will have to determine whether I succeeded or not.

The Committee to Destroy the World proceeds on the assumption that the closely linked disciplines of finance and economics are fields of thought that involve the humanities as much as they do the sciences. As the world becomes increasingly interconnected and networked, the boundaries between finance and other disciplines are disappearing. The key mechanism that facilitated this process is the digitalization of finance. Digitalization breaks down knowledge into its constituent parts and dissolves barriers between structures and disciplines to an unprecedented extent. When everything can be reduced to a 1 or a 0, as can be done today with computers, the barriers between different objects is much easier to overcome. This allows previously disparate areas to merge with one another. Modern economics is living proof of this and includes disciplines from mathematics and the hard sciences such as biology, physics, and chemistry (in quantitative finance) to psychology (in behavioral finance) and history and sociology. The humanities play an essential role in understanding markets, as the following pages are intended to demonstrate.

The forces that shape markets are essentially human, and great investors tend to be those individuals who think like great historians or cultural critics because they understand how to read human nature. Ultimately, human beings and not machines guide the economy. I have had the privilege of learning from some of the greatest investors of our generation. Great investors have the ability to read the *Zeitgeist* and form a coherent worldview (which shapes their investment thesis). Part of the problem with today's investment world is that too little of the world's money is driven by humanists while too much is guided by technocrats enslaved by computer programs or other short-term oriented strategies that are completely divorced from the rhythms of the sea of humanity.

Unless otherwise noted, the chapters below appeared in the first edition of the book and have been revised as needed to reflect changes that appeared since publication of the first edition.

The Committee to Destroy the World proceeds as follows:

The Introduction you've just read is a new chapter written for this second edition entitled "The Committee to Destroy the World," which describes the state of the world seven years after the financial crisis. Suffice it to say that while economic conditions are as fragile as they were in 2007, geopolitical conditions are more dangerous than at any time since the Cold War. As I demonstrated, this is largely due to a series of economic and foreign policy errors by the Federal Reserve and the Obama administration.

Chapter 1 is entitled "The 2008 Crisis–Tragedy or Farce?" It explores the characteristics of modern economies and markets that contributed to their instability and caused the financial crisis that permanently wounded world capitalism. I also discuss the policy decisions, systemic malaise, and global threats that will inevitably trigger the next crisis.

Chapter 2 is entitled "The Death of Capital" and attempts to develop a working definition of capital. The key quality that must be understood about capital is that it is a flexible process, not a fixed structure or category. As a process, it is inherently unstable. Capital died in the fall of 2008 because it was misunderstood and therefore mismanaged. In order to be sustained, it must first be understood.

Chapter 3 is entitled "Capital Ideas" and discusses some important aspects of capital and capitalism through the prism of the work of four of the world's great economic thinkers: Adam Smith, Karl Marx, John Maynard Keynes, and Hyman Minsky. Despite manning two opposite ends of the ideological spectrum, Smith and Marx offer much-needed insights into the basic processes of economic behavior that are too often overlooked by those charged with overseeing the world's capital. Keynes and his best interpreter, Hyman Minsky, offer deep psychological insights into the processes by which capitalist systems create instability. My reading of these thinkers is highly selective and may be deemed idiosyncratic by some readers, but at its core seeks to isolate the common themes that each of them stress in trying to diagnose what ails the system that offers the last best hope on earth for sustained prosperity. After reading their work, we should begin to understand why it is long past time that we start to live the phrase "moral economy."

Chapter 4 is entitled "Empty Promises" and discusses the death of the promise in modern finance. At its core, capitalism is a system built on promises. Capital died when economic actors stopped believing in each other's promises. Debt, which is the primary force that drives capitalist economies and distinguishes them from other forms such as socialism, is a promissory structure. Lenders need to believe that borrowers will keep their promises, and vice versa. Chapter 4 explores this complex relationship.

Chapter 5 is entitled "Financialization" and discusses one of the most important economic phenomena of the last several decades, the "financialization" of the U.S. economy. Financialization is the process whereby speculation came to dominate productive investment and debt came to replace equity in all types of capital structures. While globalization gets all the press, financialization is every bit as important in understanding the changes that occurred over the past two decades.

Chapter 6 is entitled "From Innovators to Undertakers" and was substantially rewritten for this second edition. Chapter 6 describes one of the manifestations of the massive increase in indebtedness that contributed to the 2008 financial crisis: private equity. Private equity began as an innovative industry in the 1970s and 1980s, forcing large corporations to increase efficiency and maximize shareholder value. By the mid-1990s, unfortunately, private equity had outgrown this function and became primarily a speculative activity that generated enormous fees for private equity firms and their Wall Street sponsors while saddling Corporate America with loads of debt. Moreover, the key premise that underlies private equity investments—that investing in private firms inures management from the pressures of public ownership and provides a long-term perspective to grow businesses—is starkly contradicted by the industry's egregious fee structures, short-term oriented business practices and mediocre (at best) risk-adjusted returns. That said, many private equity firms learned from their mistakes and changed their business models after the financial crisis, morphing into asset management firms. For the most part, they stopped buying large companies in highly leveraged transactions and instead shifted to providing growth capital to businesses. The large, publicly-traded public equity firms also adopted compensation schemes that better align their executives' compensation with their shareholders, minimizing the conflicts of interest that plagued their businesses in their early stages as public companies. The long-term damage private equity has imposed on the U.S. and British economies will be felt for years to come, but the industry has stopped leveraging up the economy at the rate it was previously doing so.

Chapter 7 is entitled "Welcome to Jurassic Park" and delves into derivatives with a special focus on credit derivatives, the financial instruments that were at the center of the 2008 financial crisis. Credit default swaps, the primary form of such derivatives, played a key role in the failures of Bear Stearns, Lehman Brothers, and AIG. Moreover, credit default swaps are truly what Warren Buffett termed "weapons of mass financial destruction" because of the perverse incentive structures they create that encourage creditors to force companies into bankruptcy. Derivatives are, for the most part, a hotbed of speculation for wealthy institutions and should be strictly regulated. By late 2015, a small number of closely linked institutions held roughly $650 trillion of derivatives contracts, posing a significant threat to financial stability. The solution of moving the trading of these instruments onto clearing exchanges will not come close to eliminating the risk they pose to systemic stability.

Chapter 8 is entitled "The Road to Hell" and discusses how the legal system aided and abetted the financialization of the U.S. economy through establishment of a "fiduciary culture" that privileges short-term investment goals over long-term investment goals. This fiduciary culture acts as a smokescreen that enables society to place the wrong values on the wrong activities and outcomes. The result is a society in which value is consistently destroyed and dross treated as gold. This chapter also discusses how the professional investment industry is a mechanism for destroying wealth rather than creating it. Enslaved by wrong-headed theories that markets are efficient and portfolios should be diversified into areas such as private equity, modern portfolio theory is profoundly flawed. Moreover, modern portfolio theory fails to understand that divisions between debt and equity are blurred by modern financial technology and clings to artificial distinctions that lead to liability mismatching and massive investment losses. It is time for these ideas to be revised.

Chapter 9 is entitled "Finance after Armageddon." It made a series of proposals for changes in the current regulatory regime that were necessary to prevent a replay of the financial crisis. It was based in large part on the April 2008 issue of my newsletter *The Credit Strategist* entitled "How To Fix It," which ruffled a lot of feathers by calling for reforms of many established Wall Street practices. Many of these proposals ended up being adopted but some were not and there is a high likelihood that many of the abuses that led to the death of trillions of dollars of capital in 2008 will reoccur. As soon as the U.S. government stepped in and rescued Wall Street from itself, the financial industry fought against important regulatory changes that threatened its profits but were designed to protect society from speculation and risk-taking. The Obama administration and members of Congress caved in to intense lobbying pressure and largely backed off truly effective derivatives regulation although they stuck to their guns on other measures such as increasing bank capital, limiting the ability of federally insured banks to speculate, and compensation reform. Unfortunately, the failure to rein in derivatives could still render all other reforms moot. Chapter 9 offers an unexpurgated version of the types of regulation that are needed to address the two most important defects of the financial system that led to crisis: the increasing opacity of modern financial practices; and the domination of speculation over productive investment.

Chapter 10 is a new chapter written for this second edition entitled "Unfinished Business" and discusses additional monetary, fiscal, and legal policy changes that need to be made to set the U.S. economy on a more productive course. I provide a comprehensive tax reform plan, a plan to set the federal budget on a more sustainable path, and a proposal to change the composition of the Federal Open Market Committee.

Chapter 11 is another new chapter written for this second edition entitled "How to Save Yourself." It provides advice for investors regarding how to invest in what is certain to be a far more challenging environment than the post-crisis bull market. I also discuss my own hedge fund, The Third Friday Total Return Fund, L.P., which has been delivering superior returns for the last eight years and where I invest a lot of my own money.

Chapter 12 is the "Conclusion—'This Is Later.'" The financial markets and geopolitical worlds have changed significantly over the last five years; unfortunately, they have not changed for the better, which occasioned the need to issue the stark warnings repeated throughout this second edition.

CHAPTER 1

The 2008 Crisis—
Tragedy or Farce?

I n 1852, Karl Marx wrote that history tends to repeat itself—the first time as tragedy, the second as farce.[1] Nowhere has this warning about man's compulsion to repeat his mistakes been more frustrating to witness than in the world of finance. When it comes to finance, there is only one certainty: Mistakes will be repeated again and again until their perpetrators lose their minds, their jobs, their money, or all of the above. The worst part is that professional perpetrators will lose all of their clients' money as well as their own. If the working definition of insanity is repeating the same mistake over and over again while getting the same bad result, then Wall Street is a living exemplar of an insane asylum. Not only do Wall Street, policymakers, and regulators repeat their mistakes, they always manage to commit larger, more expensive and more reckless ones each time around.

While driving to work at the Beverly Hills offices of the investment bank Drexel Burnham Lambert, Inc. early one morning in February 1990, I wasn't thinking about Marx's dictum. But by the time I drove home that afternoon (earlier than planned), I was living it. The last thing I expected that day was to be called into a meeting and told that one of the most powerful firms on Wall Street was going to declare bankruptcy later that day. I was blown away. At the time, Drexel had all of $3.5 billion in assets and was the biggest underwriter of junk bonds in the world. At the time, it all seemed like a very big deal.

Less than 20 years later, what happened at Drexel seems like small potatoes. In September 2008, Lehman Brothers Holdings, Inc., became the first large investment bank to fail since Drexel, except it was 200 times larger than my former employer with a $600 billion balance sheet. Lehman conducted business with virtually every significant financial entity in the world and its collapse threatened the stability of the global economy.

But Lehman Brothers was only the tip of the iceberg. The Bush administration and the Federal Reserve were simultaneously facing an even bigger threat that required their immediate attention: the potential collapse of insurance giant American International Group (AIG). Just a couple of days later, the government was forced to step up and bail out AIG with $85 billion of capital to avoid what would have likely been an extinction-level-event for the global financial system had AIG been allowed to go under. AIG sported a $1 trillion balance sheet and had seen fit to sell trillions of dollars of credit insurance on subprime mortgages without properly understanding or pricing their risk.

The Death of Capital

In the immediate wake of Lehman's bankruptcy and AIG's near-demise, capital died. Economic activity came to a grinding halt around the world. Financial markets collapsed. Lenders stopped lending. Counterparties refused to honor their obligations. The global financial system faced its most severe crisis since the Great Depression as the flow of capital ceased. Figures of economic authority in both the public and private sectors lost all credibility. Reassuring words offered by Federal Reserve Chairman Ben Bernanke and Treasury Secretary Hank Paulson rang hollow. President Bush seemed to be hiding in the White House bunker. And other important financial firms were literally facing extinction.

Goldman Sachs and Morgan Stanley, once considered among the strongest financial institutions in the world, were pushed to the brink of failure by speculators in the thinly traded credit default swap market who were able to raise the firms' borrowing costs with trades involving relatively small amounts of capital. Merrill Lynch, once known as the "Thundering Herd," was revealed to be the "Dundering Herd" under the incompetent leadership of Stanley O'Neal and had to be sold over- night to Bank of America in a hasty transaction that raised myriad legal and ethical questions whose niceties were brushed aside during the heat of the crisis. The U.S. government was forced to play whack-a-mole as it veered from one crisis to another and ended up engaging in a prolonged and unprecedented series of direct and indirect interventions into the economy that ended up costing trillions of dollars and continue to have enormous and largely negative repercussions to this day.

The world learned a very hard lesson: financial markets are built on nothing more than a thin tissue of confidence and the belief that prom- ises and commitments will be kept. Tragedy or farce, call it what you will, this crisis was the real deal. People were angry. They shook their heads and asked, "How could things have come to this?" They should have been asking instead, "How could we have reasonably expected things to turn out otherwise?"

Those of us who warned that markets were heading for a fall had been dismissed as Cassandras, just as we were treated when we issued similar warnings during the Internet Bubble that led to a spectacular crash in stocks and the credit markets in 2000–2001. When this book was originally published in 2010, the immediate crisis appeared to be over and a veneer of stability had returned to the financial markets. But the underlying economies on which markets must ultimately depend remained structurally weak, and the path toward sustained economic growth was still out of reach. Two years after the crisis, policymakers were still wrestling with how to restore financial stability. And seven years later, they have still not succeeded; the global financial system remains highly fragile. In order to forge a sustainable future, we need a better understanding of the sources of instability that caused the last financial crisis and are leading us straight into another one.

The reasons why we are heading toward another crisis are obvious and irrefutable. Since 2009, fiscal and monetary policy have failed to address the underlying problems that led to the 2008 financial crisis: too much debt and too little economic growth. The post-crisis market and economic recoveries were almost exclusively the result of an unprecedented explosion of debt around the world. By the end of 2014, global debt had grown to roughly $200 trillion, an amount that can never be repaid. Posing additional systemic risk is roughly $650 trillion of derivatives sitting on the balance sheets of the world's largest financial institutions. While debt grew by more than 40 percent in the six years after the financial crisis, the economy only expanded by 18 percent during that period. The disparity between economic growth and debt growth demonstrates that the world is losing the ability to generate the income necessary to service its growing debt burden. Something is going to have to give.

There are only four ways to repay debt: currency devaluation; inflation; default; or growth. Since the rate of growth required to generate the income necessary to service the current stock of debt is higher than can reasonably be expected, that option is no longer feasible. That leaves the other three options, all of which are versions of the same outcome—repayment of debt at less than its face amount in constant dollars. This leaves policymakers and investors facing difficult choices in the years ahead. And the longer the day of reckoning is delayed, the more difficult those choices are going to be.

Seeds of Instability

The Committee to Destroy the World explores three key characteristics of modern economies and markets that contributed to their instability and ultimately caused the crisis that permanently wounded world capitalism in 2008 and have, if anything, accelerated since then.[2] These characteristics are the following:

Finance Dominates Industry. The financial markets have overtaken the industrial and manufacturing sectors as the dominant force in the global economy. The financial sector has grown much faster than other sectors of the economy over the last few decades. Since 1970, the financial sector's share of national income in the U.S. and U.K. has more than doubled.[3] Finance, which I define as applied economics, dominates not only the economy but culture, politics, science, and virtually all human endeavors. Finance dominates industry and manufacturing as the motive force of modern Western economies.[4] Some historians, such as the eminent French historian Fernand Braudel, argue that the dominance of finance is a sign of a civilization's waning power. Whether that will prove to be the case for the United States and Europe remains to be seen.

Markets Are Governed by Flawed Intellectual Assumptions. Despite overwhelming evidence to the contrary, the financial system is structured on the assumptions that markets are efficient and investors are rational. Both assumptions are patently false. Furthermore, the laws that govern investor behavior require them to focus on narrow short-term economic considerations at the expense of long-term economic and social factors that would contribute to a more equitable and, in the long run, wealthier global economy. Many current investment strategies are based on concepts such as diversification and correlation that need to be revised in light of technological changes that have altered market structures. The work of great economic thinkers such as Adam Smith, Karl Marx, John Maynard Keynes, and Hyman Minsky should be reread to revise our understanding of capital to reflect the fact that capital is a highly unstable process (as opposed to a static object) that must be managed and regulated far more effectively than it has been in the past.

Speculation Trumps Productive Investment. As a result of the rise of finance and misguided regulation of the financial services industry, a disproportionate amount of financial and intellectual capital is devoted to speculation rather than to productive investment. As the size and importance of the financial sector increased during the three decades leading to the financial crisis, the deregulated financial industry created incentives for capital to be directed to unproductive activities such as housing and leveraged buyouts of twilight industries that needed to be retooled rather than weighed down with new debt. By the mid-2000s, massive amounts of capital were used to leverage up the balance sheets of dying businesses such as newspapers and automobile manufacturers in what could only generously be termed a lost cause and might truly be deemed a farce (in Marx's sense of the word). Had that capital been devoted to more productive uses, far fewer jobs might have been lost and fewer factories might sit idle today.

Since the financial crisis, a tidal wave of regulations has been unleashed to try to redress these problems. While these regulations left the U.S. financial sector nominally better capitalized than before the crisis, they did not address the hundreds of trillions of dollars of derivatives that still sit on these institutions' balance sheets and pose a systemic risk that few people truly understand and virtually nobody wants to discuss honestly. These regulations also left the U.S. financial system more concentrated, more rigid, and less liquid. This leaves markets more vulnerable to financial accidents and more prone to crisis.

A Word on Speculation

Speculation is one of the most important concepts discussed in this book. Speculation describes economic activities that do not add to the capital stock or increase the productive capacity of the economy. Instead, financial speculation involves economic activity that is not intended to create lasting economic value but is merely intended to generate short-term financial profits. Whether or not such activities are *intended* to be productive is another question, but by and large economic actors do not pay attention to such questions in their quest for immediate gratification. The growth of finance has contributed to a deeply unfortunate trend in Western societies in which an incalculable amount of intellectual and financial capital is devoted to activities that do not contribute to the productive capacity of the global economy or to the improvement of the human condition.

Speculation is hardly new to the U.S. economy. As Lawrence E. Mitchell describes in his book, *The Speculation Economy*, speculation is hard-wired into the legal structure of American business. Professor Mitchell dates this phenomenon back to the end of the nineteenth century.

It was only during the last few years of the nineteenth century that business distress combined with surplus capital searching for investment opportunities, changes in state corporation laws, and the creative greed of private bankers, trust promoters and the newly evolving investment banks created the perfect storm that shifted the production goals of American industry from goods and services to manufacturing and selling stock.[5]

The type of speculation that Professor Mitchell describes is endemic to the very capital structure of the American corporation. "Waves of watered stock created by the giant modern corporation brought average Americans into the market for the first time. The instability of these new securities and the corporations that issued them provided enormous opportunity, both intended and not, for ordinary people and professionals alike to speculate, leading sometimes to mere bull runs and sometimes to widespread panic."[6] The instability inherent in corporate capital structures is a microcosm of the systemic instability described by Hyman Minsky in his "financial-instability hypothesis," a subject discussed in Chapter 3 of this book. The important point to understand is that speculation leaves room for capital to make mischief. Rather than finding a home in productive uses, speculative capital nests in areas where it sits and festers, creating imbalances that later come home to roost.

The great economic historian Charles Kindleberger defined "pure speculation" as "buying for resale rather than use in the case of commodities, or for resale rather than income in the case of financial assets."[7] This is a polite description of what is colloquially known as the "Greater Fool Theory," which gained an increasingly prominent role in financial markets during the series of expanding bubbles that characterized the U.S. economy and financial markets over the past 30 years. Buying on the basis that someone else will come along and pay more for your assets became a national pastime in the U.S. housing market in mid-2000s, and returned in full force to both public and private equity and debt markets during the post-crisis, central bank-fueled bull market that began in 2009.

Since the financial crisis, speculation assumed a new form as the global economy began to cannibalize itself. In the public sector, the

Federal Reserve's unconventional "quantitative easing" policy led it to purchase trillions of dollars of debt issued by the United States Treasury and other agencies of the U.S. government. Between 2009 and October 2014, the Federal Reserve purchased more than $4 trillion of Treasuries and agency securities that are currently sitting on its roughly $4.5 trillion balance sheet. This policy was copied by Mario Draghi's European Central Bank, which launched its own $1.1 trillion bond purchase program in early 2015, just a few months after Haruhiko Kuroda's Bank of Japan announced an even more radical program in October 2014 that included the purchase not only of Japanese Government Bonds but stocks and ETFs.

These programs are designed to lower interest rates on the theory that low interest rates will stimulate economic activity. But while they undoubtedly lowered interest rates and inflated stock and bond markets around the world, they utterly failed to create sustainable economic growth. Instead, consumers and businesses reacted to lower interest rates in ways that central bankers did not expect. Consumers opted to save rather than spend, while businesses devoted their capital to stock buybacks rather than expansion and hiring. The best laid plans of central planners fell completely flat once again.

This is most apparent in Corporate America. Since the financial crisis in 2009, U.S. corporations repurchased more than $2 trillion of their own stock. In many cases, they borrowed large amounts of money to do so, weakening their balance sheets in the process. These repurchases accelerated as stock prices rose, completely belying the argument that corporations are savvy buyers of their own stock who only buy when their stock is cheap. In fact, they generally do the opposite and buy more stock as the price rises. For the most part, they are responding to the incessant demands of institutional shareholders as well as executive compensation schemes that reward managers for boosting stock prices in the short-term regardless of the negative long-term consequences.

Economies that eat their own are doomed to perish. I am unaware of any race of cannibals that has thrived in the history of mankind. Eventually cannibals run out of victims. Rather than cannibalistic economic policies, the world hungers for pro-growth policies. These policies exist; what is lacking is the political and moral courage to carry them forward.

Financialization

In addition to the destabilizing characteristics of modern markets and economies described above, a series of changes within the actual business of finance were key contributors to systemic instability whose only logical outcome was the 2008 financial crisis and future crises. All of these changes come under the common heading of financialization, which in its broadest sense speaks to the increasingly dominant role that finance assumed in Western economies in the decades leading to the financial crisis. These features, many of which were addressed by new post-crisis regulations, included the following:

- The transition of financial institutions, in particular banks, from deposit-taking and lending institutions into risk-taking institutions.
- The increasing utilization of debt instead of equity as a source of capital at all levels of the private and public sector.
- The growth of an unregulated "shadow banking system" that consists of a nexus of private equity funds, hedge funds, money market funds, nonbanks such as GE Capital, and special purpose entities such as collateralized debt obligations (CDOs) and structured investment vehicles (SIVs) that moved control of the money supply beyond the reach of central banks.
- Dramatic changes in the short-term money markets that included the utilization of riskier assets in products that were marketed as low risk such as money market funds.
- The explosion of credit derivatives, structured credit products and other derivative financial instruments that supplanted cash securities.
- Enormous growth in the private equity business.
- Increased reliance on mathematical models to govern investment decisions.[8]

These pre-crisis changes were all manifestations of three trends: an overall shift in economic activity away from production in favor of speculation; toward opacity and away from transparency; and toward debt and away from equity. The result was an emphasis on business and investment practices that increased the tolerance for risk and dramatically increased the instability of the financial system.

Post-crisis, many of these destabilizing trends were addressed. Money market funds were reformed to reduce the risks they took in the period leading up to the crisis. Large banks are no longer permitted to risk their own capital to the extent they did before the crisis thanks to the Volcker Rule. U.S. banks are much better capitalized and much less leveraged than in the period prior to the crisis (the same cannot be said of European banks, which remain dangerously leveraged). SIVs were largely outlawed. More disturbingly, little has been done to address the potential threat posed by derivatives. While many consider the largest institutions "too big to fail," it would be more appropriate to consider them "too big to save" since the volume of derivatives they hold is unthinkably large and nobody can genuinely claim to know what will happen. The only statement that can be made with certainty is that in the event of a crisis, a significant number of the counterparties to these derivatives contracts will not be in a position to meet their obligations, triggering a daisy-chain of defaults that would threaten the solvency of the highly leveraged global financial system.

The singular failure of post-crisis policy is the inability of the global system to grow via equity rather than debt. As a result, the system is more fragile than ever. In *The Committee to Destroy the World*, financialization is understood as the process whereby the credit system makes increasing amounts of capital available for speculative rather than productive economic activity. Financialization is supported by lax regulation and a blind belief that markets will always make optimal capital allocation decisions. In 2008, the American economy led the global economy into what one astute observer described as "a crisis of financialization . . . a crisis of that venturesome new world of leverage, deregulation, and financial innovation."[9] Despite the heavy hand of regulation that came down on the financial system after the crisis, financialization remains a potent force in the economy and broader society.

The financialization of the U.S. economy was facilitated by two broad trends. First, as noted, regulatory and other business policies favored financial speculation over production. This took the form of accounting and tax laws that favored debt over equity and also permitted companies to disguise their true financial condition. As a formal matter, this favoring of speculation led to a system governed by formal rules that fictionalized the depiction of economic reality. These rules included:

- Accounting conventions that bear little relationship to reality (for example, the treatment of stock options and the allowance of non-GAAP earnings adjustments that grossly inflate corporate earnings).
- Accounting and tax rules that privilege debt over equity.[10]
- Tax rules that favor a small class of entrepreneurial capitalists so disproportionately that it created an American oligarchy to rival the Russian one that grew up in the shadow of the fall of the Soviet Union (including but not limited to the "carried interest" tax break that favored the earnings of the private equity and hedge fund industries).
- A proliferation of complex financial products that purported to reduce risk but actually increased it on a systemic basis (the first instance being portfolio insurance that contributed to the 1987 stock market crash and the latest manifestation being credit insurance in the form of credit default swaps that pushed several large financial institutions into insolvency).

The denouement of the deregulatory orgy came in two parts: the 1999 repeal of The Glass-Steagall Act of 1933 that originally prevented commercial banks from entering businesses thought to be unduly risky; and the Securities and Exchange Commission's disastrous 2004 relaxation of net capital rules limiting the amount of leverage that the major investment banks could assume on their balance sheets.

Citigroup, Inc. was one of the main promoters of Glass-Steagall repeal under its former Chairman Sandy Weill; within a decade it was a ward of the state. The megabank spent the decade following Glass-Steagall repeal (under the chairmanship of former Treasury Secretary and proponent of Glass-Steagall repeal Robert Rubin, who joined the bank a wealthy and respected figure and departed a decade later much wealthier but far less respected) failing to combine its various businesses; breaking securities and banking laws in the United States, Japan, and elsewhere; forming multibillion dollar off-balance-sheet entities to conceal liabilities from the prying eyes of regulators, credit rating agencies, and investors; playing a key role in championing the Internet bubble through the offices of, among others, the disgraced telecommunications analyst Jack Grubman; and losing tens of billions of dollars in ill-advised mortgage and corporate loans before being forced to come hat in hand to the U.S. government for multiple bailouts. It took less than four years for three of the firms that joined Citigroup in lobbying to be allowed to break the leverage barrier in 2004—Bear Stearns & Co., Inc., Lehman Brothers Holdings, Inc., and Merrill Lynch & Co., Inc.—to blow themselves up with their newfound powers. These rule changes were based on intellectually flawed rationalizations that were given establishment imprimaturs by Nobel Prize winners and a radical free-market ideology that gained a blind following after the collapse of a Soviet system that failed based on its own deficiencies, not as a result of the genius of the American economic system.

The second facilitator of financialization was the U.S. legal system. One could fill the Library of Congress with books describing the flaws of the U.S. legal system. For the purposes of understanding the death of capital in 2008, however, there is one particular area of American jurisprudence that has been particularly damaging: the law governing fiduciary duty. Over the past century, the U.S. legal system developed a body of law governing the conduct of fiduciaries that privileges the short-term economic interests of a company's shareholders over the long-term, non-economic interests of society. This resulted from the adoption of what is referred to as the "agency approach" to the corporate governance challenge of aligning the interests of shareholders and management in public corporations. The agency approach promoted the view that the best way to align the interests of corporate managers and shareholders is to align their financial interests, and established that the primary or sole purpose of corporations is to maximize shareholder returns within the confines of the law.[11] As a result of this ideology—and it is nothing other than an ideology, because it is simply a human thought-construct—corporate managers and boards of directors are legally required to place the interests of shareholders ahead of those of creditors, labor, the environment, and other parts of society that are arguably equally deserving of consideration.[12]

One of the most pernicious consequences of the imposition of a narrow profit maximization motive on corporate boards of directors was the flood of private equity transactions that consumed the public equity markets in the United States beginning in the 1980s and continuing through the eve of the financial crisis. The concept of maximizing value for shareholders was used by corporate raiders, leveraged buyout artists, and other private parties to wrest control of numerous public corporations from the hands of public shareholders. In the early days of the private equity industry in the 1970s and 1980s, this arguably pressured public company managements to improve efficiency and productivity and contributed to better management and business practices. Unfortunately, by the mid-1990s and continuing through the beginning of the 2008 financial crisis, this morphed into little more than substituting debt for equity on corporate balance sheets and diverting untold billions of dollars into private hands at the expense of public shareholders. Moreover, the going-private phenomenon imposed an enormous opportunity cost on the U.S. economy in terms of lost jobs, reduced research and development (R&D), and meaningfully lower productive investment in America's future. But it was sanctioned by the view that shareholders of public corporations were entitled to obtain the highest possible value for their stock (and the belief that the market for corporate control is the most effective way of delivering that result).

Since the financial crisis, a new manifestation of this phenomenon arose: the rise of "activist investors," who are just a more respectable version of the corporate raiders and "greenmailers" of the 1980s. These "activists," who with rare exceptions (such as Nelson Peltz) never ran an operating business themselves, force companies to raise their dividends and buy back large amounts of stock (often with borrowed money) in order to meet their obligation to "maximize shareholder value." Even the venerable Warren Buffett joined forces in 2014 with the Brazilian private equity firm 3G to purchase large companies like Heinz and Kraft and is now resorting to "rationalizing" operations through thousands of job cuts in order to "maximize" shareholder value. This is just another version of cannibal capitalism, and growth through subtraction is unlikely to provide the kind of expansion of employment, R&D and capital spending that will add to GDP in the years ahead. It is dangerous to believe that rising stock prices (which can drop as easily as rise) are an economic panacea especially when they are driven higher by cheap debt and cost cutting rather than higher productivity and sustainable revenue growth. All too often the forces that drive up stock prices exact a terrible toll on other parts of the economy that are not properly factored into the thinking of the institutions whose short-term interests are allegedly being served when activists drive up the value of their stockholdings.

The narrow reading of fiduciary duty that was adopted by U.S. courts may seem to be consistent with the interests of traditional laissez-faire capitalism, but is, in fact, directly contrary to the teachings of Adam Smith and other theorists of capital, as the following pages explain. Moreover, the development of the law of fiduciaries has had a questionable effect on corporate creativity and social conduct. It provides legal justification for short-sighted investment and business strategies that diminish the productive capacity of the economy while encouraging speculative activity that harms businesses and communities. The non-shareholder interests that are deliberately pushed to the side by fiduciaries—the rights of workers, the health of the environment, the long-term contributions made by corporations to their communities in supporting social and educational programs—are at least as important in building a robust economy as maximizing value for shareholders in the short term. There is not and never has been anything preordained in this interpretation of the law. Instead, this interpretation of the duties of corporate managers was a dubious intellectual and moral choice that must be challenged in order to develop a more just society and a healthier and more productive economy.

The Corruption of Moral Sentiments

There is another crucially important reason why we need to question traditional economic and legal thinking to understand how markets continue to get things so terribly wrong intellectually, strategically, and morally. In 2008, as in earlier crises, the markets were victims of a lowering of ethical standards and a thorough corruption of moral sentiments. This was hardly the first time such lapses occurred; this behavior followed a familiar pattern in which conduct that in earlier periods was clearly considered illegal, immoral, or simply feckless somehow became accepted as conventional behavior that was widely practiced, acknowledged and tolerated.

In the Internet bubble, one example of this type of conduct was the participation of research analysts in marketing initial public offerings of newly minted Internet companies that had few prospects for success. Securities laws were supposed to prevent such behavior, yet even the largest and ostensibly most reputable investment banks deployed their analysts in this manner. After the Internet bubble burst, high-tech companies engaged in a new set of shenanigans when they began repricing or resetting the dates on stock options for their top executives. Leading up to the 2008 crisis, questionable but widely known behavior was less a matter of breaking the law than violating common sense: the use of egregious amounts of leverage by virtually every participant in the financial markets (individuals, non-financial corporations, investment banks, hedge funds, private equity firms, commercial banks) in every financial activity imaginable from home ownership to the most arcane trading strategies.

These dangerous borrowing levels were in no way illegal; in fact, they were expressly sanctioned by the government. We already noted the changes in net capital rules that were implemented in 2004 by the Securities and Exchange Commission that allowed five large investment banks to increase their borrowings, ultimately pushing the leverage ratios of some of the firms that subsequently failed from 12-to-1 to over 30-to-1 (meaning that a mere 3 percent drop in asset values could render them insolvent—and in at least three cases that we know about, it did). This leverage was used to increase the short-term profitability of these firms with little regard to the long-term risks involved because their executives were compensated based on asymmetric schemes whereby they profited greatly if their firms made money but also remained obscenely wealthy even if their firms failed. As a result, firms like Bear Stearns and Lehman Brothers were left in the hands of modern-day Captain Ahabs like Richard Fuld and James Cayne who could afford to watch their ships sink while retaining enormous personal wealth. Everybody knew how leveraged these firms were in 2006 and 2007 but virtually nobody spoke up to warn of the possible dangers to the financial system posed by their creaky capital structures. Markets are based on incentives. In the years leading up to the 2008 crisis, the incentive structures of Western financial markets became totally corrupted. The types of excesses seen in the last two bubbles dwarfed those of the Gilded Age or the Reagan Years. America did not suffer simply an economic crisis; it also suffered a moral crisis.

Since the financial crisis, however, we learned that the largest institutions engaged in and continue to engage in illegal and unethical conduct on what can only be considered a systemic scale. While it should surprise nobody to learn that there was widespread wrongdoing associated with the mortgage business that fed the Housing Bubble that was a proximate cause of the financial crisis, pervasive lawbreaking among the financial elite also extended to manipulation of the London Interbank Offered Rate (Libor), the lifeblood lending rate of the financial markets, the foreign exchange markets, the credit default swap market, the Treasury market, and the most extensive insider trading scandal in Wall Street history. These violations spanned the period prior to, during and after the financial crisis and included not only serial but repeat offenses by virtually every major financial institution in the world. The violations demonstrate that there is something seriously rotten at the heart of modern finance. While institutions pled guilty to criminal charges, virtually no senior executives were held to account for these crimes. One might be tempted to believe that these acts were committed in a vacuum, but unfortunately they were perpetrated by highly educated executives who knew better. The fact that individuals went unpunished breeds deep cynicism for the law and disrespect for the institution of finance.

Low Rates and Lax Rules

It was within the context described above that the economic forces that were building for years pushed the global financial system to the brink of insolvency in 2008. In an operative sense, the two proximate causes of the crisis were years of loose monetary policy and recklessly lax financial regulation, both of which were driven by free market ideologies that grew ascendant during the Reagan/Thatcher years.

Beginning in 1981, global interest rates began a long-term secular decline that continued through the financial crisis of 2008 (and the post-crisis period). These low rates pushed up asset values and financed higher debt-financed consumption funded by countries running current account surpluses whose exchange rates were tied to the dollar. Moreover, debt and consumption growth came to exceed income growth, a situation that was unsustainable. At some point, people have to pay for what they consume, and have to be able to repay their debts. Or so it would seem. As the United States recovers from the measures that were required to avoid a complete collapse of the global banking system in 2008, it is facing years of sustained high structural unemployment, below-trend economic growth, and huge deficits as far as the eye can see.

The financial world that almost collapsed in 2008 was far different from the world that was shocked by the U.S. stock market crash just two decades earlier in 1987. Financial markets were light years more technologically advanced this time around. Portfolio insurance, which contributed to the 1987 stock market crash, was primitive in comparison to the derivative weapons of mass destruction that brought the markets to their knees two decades later. Unfortunately, neither regulation nor traditional investment practices sufficiently adapted to this new regime. The explosive growth of the financial sector in Western economies created a single, interconnected global market for money and credit that no longer operated according to the old rules. Instead of being governed by sovereigns, the world came to be ruled by currencies and interest rates that were no longer confined by national boundaries. Two closely linked manifestations of the emergence of finance as a dominant force led to tears. First, the invention of credit derivatives, so-called insurance products, facilitated speculation on an unprecedented scale. Second, the banking system became supplanted by its shadow, a parallel universe of financial institutions that operated outside the control of regulators while concealing their true financial condition from investors, regulators, and lenders.[13]

Free market ideologies justified and reinforced the ascendancy of finance, but failed to adequately account for the radical changes that technology and globalization wrought in the fabric of the markets. Supply-side economics, which called for lower taxes and less government involvement in the economy, failed to account for the pro-cyclical nature of human behavior and the necessity to rein in the basic human instincts of greed and fear. Financial thinking on the part of investors as well as regulators failed to reflect the underlying changes in the markets and the economies whose goods they trade.

Western capitalism transformed over the past 30 years into one dominated like no time in history by financial markets where financial instruments are traded rather than manufacturing markets where goods are produced. In this phase of capitalism, every economic object is reduced to some type of marketable or tradable financial instrument. The accumulation of wealth is no longer based on the production of hard or tangible assets; today's wealth is dominated by intangible forms that financial technology renders interchangeable and readily tradable on the world's financial markets. The result is a global economic system that is constantly shifting below our feet. Most of the time, those shifts are incremental and manageable. But at other times, change speeds up, or changes that have been occurring over time suddenly accelerate and present a new set of economic conditions to which we have to adapt quickly. At these moments, the markets move in ways that change the course of history. Black Monday 1987 was one of those days. In 2008, we saw several such days when the stock market moved in 1,000-point arcs and credit markets froze up as though nobody would ever make another trade or extend another loan. While changes in markets themselves affect the course of history, they importantly reflect changes occurring in the world outside the markets, the most important being those wrought by the minds of men.

By the time the crisis of 2008 materialized, finance, and the rules ostensibly designed to protect finance from itself, were woefully unprepared to manage a system that had changed profoundly from the world in which the rules were written. In a world of feedback loops that operate with exponential rather than linear force, and where discontinuities are woven into the fabric of market reality, traditional investment and regulatory theories were rendered anachronistic. One explanation for what was happening is that a digital world was playing according to analog rules. Another explanation is that a globalized world was operating according to local rules. The crisis revealed that time-honored modes of thinking about concepts such as risk needed to be retrofitted to new realities. Most important, investors needed to start coming to terms with the fact that markets are not efficient and investors are not rational. How could investors be presumed rational when their thinking failed to reflect the radical changes that were occurring in markets and societies around the world?

The Global Liquidity Bubble

Abundant global liquidity gave investors a plethora of opportunities to invest based on these flawed beliefs over the last three decades. Investors who understand how to read the business cycle, which is heavily influenced by global liquidity flows, flourished in recent decades. Beginning in the mid-1980s, the world became awash in capital as a result of a series of historic economic shifts that created enormous trade and capital imbalances throughout the global economy. These shifts were accompanied by advances in financial technology that facilitated the creation of new forms of money to soak up this global liquidity. After capital became untethered from gold in the early 1970s, there was literally no limit to how much capital could be created. As a result, too much capital killed capital.

Two broad economic phenomena in the years leading up to the financial crisis illustrate the financial debacle that ensued in 2008. First, the growth of debt consistently exceeded the growth of underlying Western economies. Figure 1.1 illustrates the inexorable growth in debt in the United States over the past several decades. In the United States, total debt as a percentage of GDP grew from 255.3 percent in 1997 to 352.6 percent in 2007.[14] It should also be noted that, for the first time, debt levels beginning in the early part of the 2010s began to constitute as great a percentage of GDP as they did during the Great Depression.[15]

This accumulation of debt was facilitated by the ability of financiers to literally create liquidity out of the air through financial innovations

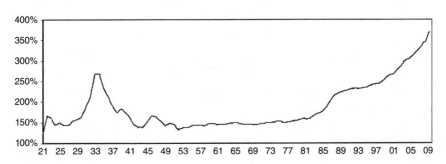

Figure 1.1   United States Total Debt as Percent of GDP
SOURCE: Bridgewater Associates, Inc.

such as collateralized debt obligations (which packaged up trillions of dollars of individual mortgages, automobile loans, corporate bonds or bank loans, and other types of debt) and credit default swaps (a form of insurance on debt instruments such as bonds and mortgages). As new forms of capital were spawned, debt began to grow at an extremely rapid and ultimately unsustainable pace.

As significant as the growth of debt was prior to the financial crisis, the explosion of debt after the crisis was simply breathtaking. It is both mindboggling and inexcusable that business and government leaders are not more outspoken about the dangers posed by the suffocating burden debt is placing on the global economy; they are clearly too invested in the current system to challenge a status quo that threatens to deliver another crisis to our door in the near future. Their silence is a profound betrayal of their obligations as public servants and citizens.

Second, in the years leading to the financial crisis, an increasingly globalized financial system married excess savings in developing countries with a dearth of savings in developed countries. This devil's bargain of borrowing and lending created dependencies that ultimately grew into pacts of mutual financial destruction that, in terms of their threat to global stability, came to replace the Cold War nuclear weapons pacts of a generation earlier.[16] As a result, emerging market economies accumulated trillions of dollars of dollar-denominated debts with insufficient resources to repay them.

Neither of these phenomena—massive global liquidity and money flows between developed and developing countries—could be maintained without the business of finance, whose transformation further increased instability. A world in which physicists made it possible for competing powers to blow the physical world to smithereens by splitting the atom was rendered financially unstable by financial engineers deconstructing financial instruments into 1s and 0s and then recombining them into highly leveraged lethal weapons. With far more capital than could reasonably be put to productive use, the world's largest investors began to direct these explosives into highly speculative activities that were disguised in one of two ways. Some of these speculative activities were hidden in plain sight, like the equity and credit markets where asset prices exceeded all reason and new standards of valuation were cooked up by so-called experts to try to justify "new,

new things."[18] Other activities were hidden in the "shadow banking system," a complex web of nonbanking institutions whose holdings and true financial condition were deliberately concealed by the largest financial institutions in the world from the eyes of regulators and investors.

The immediate result was the near collapse of the global economic system and the world's financial markets in 2008. The long-term result is prolonged and entrenched government involvement in previously lightly regulated capitalist economies and years of sluggish post-crisis economic growth that is likely to persist even if economies can be weaned off government support (something that appears to be increasingly unlikely with every passing quarter of disappointing post-crisis growth). Trillions of dollars of capital were directed to speculative activities such as derivatives trading, leveraged buyouts, and other investments that added little or nothing to the productive capacity of the economy in the pre-crisis years. In the post-crisis years, trillions of dollars were directed to various types of cannibalistic activities such as stock buybacks and quantitative easing that failed to ignite organic economic growth, leaving economies more indebted and less vibrant than before. These funds were wasted, and they are lost forever. Even in a perfect world, much of this new capital would have undoubtedly found its way into unproductive uses. But a more proactive fiscal policy regime could have directed capital to areas that are both productive and life-enhancing such as education, medical and scientific research, infrastructure improvement, and projects to improve the environment. It may not be too late, but it is getting awfully late in the game. Economies urgently need to start implementing pro-growth policies that can start directing capital to areas where they can stimulate growth.

The less-than-optimal allocation of capital was the logical result of a series of miserable policy choices. Monetary policy was strongly pro-cyclical rather than countercyclical and tended to favor debt over equity and speculation over production. Other regulatory policies that governed the financial markets during this period—capital standards, accounting rules, tax laws—led the financial sector to conduct business in a manner that exacerbated rather than limited risk. Economic actors respond to incentives and that is what they did. Rather than leading financial institutions to ease credit during boom periods and tighten credit during downturns, policy led institutions to do just the opposite. This had the unintended and destabilizing effect of intensifying cyclical changes in the economy. Rather than leading individuals and institutions to save for a rainy day and create a cushion to permit them to survive economic downturns, these policies led them to spend when they should have saved and borrow when they should have repaid debt. The result was that capital was scarce when most needed and abundant when least needed and least able to be put to productive uses.

Too much money chasing too few goods is supposed to be inflationary, but the normal processes that cause inflation were moderated over the past three decades by technological changes and the entry of billions of low-cost workers from the developing world into the global economy. These changes suppressed labor costs and gravitated against rising inflation during most of this period. But these disinflationary forces are receding while financial assets experienced an unsustainable inflationary boom since the crisis. By the same token, too much money chasing too few productive opportunities is bound to lead to speculation. Bad money supplants good money; debt supplants equity. This is the classic crisis of capitalism that Karl Marx predicted, except that instead of products seeking out new markets, finance capital itself became the product looking for new outlets. Unfortunately it found all too many willing buyers of whatever new products Wall Street could cook up.

The credit crisis was the logical result of the proliferation of debt (and the substitution of debt for equity in virtually every kind of capital structure imaginable) that was eating away at the stability of the United States' most important financial, legal, and social institutions for decades. The U.S. banking system finally collapsed in 2008 under the weight of trillions of dollars of bad loans that never should have been made in the first place. These loans were the deliberate result of decisions made by individuals who personally profited from them at a societal cost that will be calculated for decades to come. It may look like the mess was cleaned up, but it only looks that way. In addition to the trillions of dollars that were flushed down the drain, the opportunity costs are incalculable. The collapse of America's financial markets in 2008 was an outward sign of the potential beginning of the end of U.S. global hegemony. The crisis in financial markets demands that policy makers engage in a radical rethinking of the mantras of free market ideology that have misled U.S. economic and legal policy for the past several decades.

A Crisis of Confidence

In human terms, what triggered the credit crisis and resulting collapse in financial markets was a loss of confidence on the part of virtually every institution and investor of significance. The financial system is based on trust. Financial actors of all sorts—both individuals and institutions—lost trust in each other by the end of the summer in 2008. As a result, they stopped doing business with each other on the most basic level. Banks stopped making loans, and stock and bond traders refused to trade with each other. It took historic and unprecedented government actions to restore this trust. The kind of trust that allows markets to function builds up over many years, yet it is very fragile and can evaporate overnight. Once lost, it is very difficult to regain. The fact that markets began to recover in March 2009 should not be taken as a sign that the past can be forgotten.

The question that should be on the minds of all investors going forward is what could trigger another crisis. The answer is that it will be the same thing that caused the last crisis—a loss of confidence in the system and central bankers. Central bank policies that stopped the global financial system from collapsing failed to create the conditions for long-term prosperity and caused many negative unintended consequences. Rather than stimulate spending, low interest rates led economic actors to increase savings. Rather than leading to higher growth, monetary policy led to slower growth. Rising stock prices fed by easy money distracted investors from these disturbing truths, but sooner or later reality will smack them over the head. When it does, there will be another crisis of confidence and markets will fall—and they will fall hard.

The crisis created other sinister long-term consequences. The flawed financial products and investment strategies that were responsible for what happened originated in the hearts of Western capitalism—the towers of Wall Street and the City of London. The crisis of confidence that resulted from the failure of borrowers to meet their obligations can be laid directly at the feet of the largest financial institutions and gatekeepers in the world, and all of these are Western-based. As a result, confidence in the Western model of capitalism suffered a body blow. The credit rating agencies and investment and commercial banks that promulgated the subprime mortgage debacle were profoundly discredited intellectually and morally by their conduct.

The fact that this occurred during a period when U.S. foreign policy isolated the world's dominant economic power from its traditional allies and rightly or wrongly made it the target of hatred among large sectors of the world population may be a historical accident or may be suggestive of broader historical trends. The Obama administration's profoundly misguided attempts to apologize for American power only made matters worse when the world learned that America could no longer be counted on as a reliable ally or global leader. The United States exited the first decade of the twenty-first century far weaker than it entered it. And rather than blaming others, the financially and militarily most powerful country in the world needs to look within and figure out how to do better.

We are still tallying the total damage from the credit crisis, but the final cost will be tens of trillions of dollars. But this capital wasn't lost—it was murdered. As much as we should blame failures of human character and emotion (greed and fear), we must also blame failures of human intellect (stupidity). The most highly educated segment of our population—the PhDs, the MBAs, the JDs—made inexcusable errors of judgment, raising legitimate questions about the utility of such degrees when they fail to include a modicum of common sense and, more important, common decency in their curricula. As the holder of more than one of these degrees, I am highly aware of their shortcomings.

There is a huge difference between being educated and being smart. The credentialed individuals that continually lead the world into one crisis after another—which includes The Committee to Destroy the World—are of two types. The first lacks the type of real world experience that teaches humility and allows them to make smart decisions. The second are political animals who serve their own interests rather than those of the people who appointed or elected them. Either way, their pedigrees conceal hollow cores that are revealed by the catastrophic consequences of their work. Until the world learns to value honest dissent and outside-the-box thinking over the moral cowardice of groupthink and consensus, we will continue to be guided by people who may be educated but who aren't remotely smart.

This is why nothing seemed amiss to most people while the world was going mad in the years leading up to the crisis. We had Ben Bernanke assuring everyone that plunging housing prices in the mid-2000s would not cause a crisis. And institutions like the International Monetary Fund demonstrated its ignorance of financial markets by pompously (and cluelessly) claiming that "growing recognition that the dispersal of credit risk by banks to a broader and more diverse group of investors… has helped make the banking and overall financial system more resilient."[18] In fact, some of us who were actually trading in those markets were warning that risk was not being widely dispersed but was in fact being more concentrated among a limited number of investors. But those of us who issued such warnings were sharply criticized and often ostracized. Errors of intellect and judgment were endorsed by some of the most respected business and government leaders in the world. Alan Greenspan in particular repeatedly made public comments endorsing policies that in retrospect turned out to be extremely reckless. At the time, however, these policies were part of an economic orthodoxy that few were willing to question. From an economic standpoint, this orthodoxy overlooked the important role that asset prices play in the economy as well as the increasing role that debt was playing in the growth of the economy. It also failed to account for concepts such as discontinuity, path dependency, and feedback loops that can wreak havoc on an economy and markets. The failure to include these considerations in economic analysis led to fatal deficiencies in policy.

Lionized by some, Greenspan's reign as Federal Reserve chairman should be judged by history as an abject failure of policy and intellect. Greenspan himself felt compelled to admit that his worldview was flawed when, early in 2009, he told Congress that he had relied on his belief that financial actors would act in their own best interest while failing to understand that individual self-interest is often contrary to the public interest. In an exchange with Representative Henry Waxman, Greenspan admitted that "those of us who have looked to the self-interest of lending institutions to protect shareholders' equity—myself especially—are in a state of shocked disbelief." Waxman responded by saying, "In other words, you found that your view of the world, your ideology, was not right, it was not working." The former chairman responded, "Absolutely, precisely [perhaps the clearest answer Greenspan had ever given to Congress]. You know, that's precisely the reason I was shocked, because I have been going for 40 years or more with considerable evidence that it was working exceptionally well."[19] Had he been a student of Hyman Minsky instead of Ayn Rand, Greenspan would not have made such a fatal error.

In 1986, Minsky warned that, "the self-interest of bankers, leveraged investors, and investment producers can lead the economy to inflationary expansions and unemployment-creating contractions. Supply and demand analysis—in which market processes lead to an equilibrium—does not explain the behavior of a capitalist economy, for capitalist financial processes mean that the economy has endogenous destabilizing forces. Financial fragility, which is a prerequisite for financial instability, is, fundamentally, a result of internal market processes."[20] By ignoring the internal processes that led to an unsustainable buildup of low-cost debt, central bank policy under Greenspan fueled a false prosperity. Coupled with tax and other economic policies that were aimed at rewarding speculative rather than productive investment, the result was a gutting of the United States' economic base and a mortgaging of its future.

Unfortunately, Mr. Greenspan's successors learned little from his mistakes. While Ben Bernanke was rightfully praised for taking actions that prevented a complete collapse of the financial system during the financial crisis, he perpetuated these policies long after they were justified. His pre-crisis policies and failure to see the Housing Crisis unfold are also serious marks against him. His successor Janet Yellen and the rest of the Federal Reserve Governors kept interest rates at zero for far too long and engaged in a series of quantitative easing moves that failed to create sustainable economic growth. Yet rather than change course, they kept doubling down on these failed policies, leaving the Federal Reserve's balance sheet swollen with debt, financial markets starved of liquidity and reliable price signals, the economy rife with massive misallocations of capital, and the global economy awash in trillions of dollars of debt that can never be repaid.

The best face that can be put on this policy approach is that the Federal Reserve views the global economy as stuck in a simmering crisis from which it will miraculously emerge if policy is left loose enough for long enough to allow growth to re-ignite. But that is a false hope. A more realistic assessment is that the Federal Reserve is run by a group of former tenured economics professors who never managed a business or sat on a trading desk and have little understanding of how the real world works. Rather than prompt people to spend, low interest rates led people to save money. Rather than promote sustainable economic growth, QE loaded the world with trillions of dollars of debt that is suffocating growth. The world is heading toward another financial crisis when markets figure out that these policies will never produce their intended results.

Why Finance Matters

Students of history understand that the consequences of these errors are not merely theoretical. When I am asked by young people what course of study they should follow if they want to pursue a career in finance, I tell them to study History, Psychology (preferably mass psychology), Philosophy, and Economics in that order. History is the best education for people interested in learning about markets because it teaches how the world reacts to change—and change is the only constant in markets. As Winston Churchill famously said: "The further backward you look, the further forward you can see."

In *The War of the Worlds*, a history of the blood-soaked twentieth century, historian Niall Ferguson argues very persuasively that economic volatility coincides with social instability. He defines economic volatility as "the frequency and amplitude of changes in the rate of economic growth, prices, interest rates, and employment, with all the associated social stresses and strains."[21] Professor Ferguson makes a strong case that "ethnic conflict is correlated with economic *volatility*. A rapid growth in output and incomes can be just as destabilizing as a rapid contraction. A useful measure of economic conditions, too seldom referred to by historians, is volatility, by which is meant the standard deviation of the change in a given indicator over a particular period of time."[22] He explains (in words that sounded eerie written on the eve of the 2008 financial crisis and echo even more disturbingly after witnessing the chaos wrought in America's inner cities and around the world by years of failed Obama administration foreign and domestic policies) that:

> Economic volatility matters because it tends to exacerbate social conflict. It seems intuitively obvious that periods of economic crisis create incentives for politically dominant groups to pass the burdens of adjustment on to others. With the growth of state intervention in economic life, the opportunities for such discriminatory redistribution clearly proliferated. What could be easier in a time of general hardship than to exclude a particular group from the system of public benefits? What is perhaps less obvious is that social dislocation may also follow periods of rapid growth, since the benefits of growth are very seldom evenly distributed. Indeed, it may be precisely the minority of winners in an upswing who are targeted for retribution in a subsequent downswing.[23]

Even the least historically minded among us need not be reminded that World War II and the Holocaust followed the Great Depression. In 2016, the geopolitical situation is more unstable than any time since the end of the Cold War largely due to the deliberate decision of the Obama administration to abdicate America's leadership role in the world.

The world is certainly far more dangerous than during the financial crisis. Russia's incursion into Ukraine threatens Eastern Europe, NATO, and the post-World War II balance of power on the European Continent. China is asserting its hegemony in the South China Sea in a provocative manner. As a result of America's retreat from Iraq without a Status of Forces Agreement, the Middle East is now experiencing a Sunni-Shia war and the rise of radical Islam, including the rise of ISIS and the revival of Al Qaeda. Syria is a charnel house as Bashar al-Assad commits genocide on his own people, triggering the largest refugee crisis since the Second World War. He is actively supported by Russia and Iran in the wake of Barack Obama's decision to enter a strategically and morally indefensible deal with Iran that will provide the world's largest state supporter of terrorism a clear path to nuclear weapons by 2030. Terrorists are attacking Western cities like Paris with impunity while Mr. Obama and his former Secretary of State Hillary Clinton worry more about offending the vast majority of Muslims who are not terrorists than calling out those Muslims who are running around murdering people. This is the fractured state of the world in the age of Obama.

Back at home, the southern border of the United States is a sieve while the Obama administration refuses to enforce America's immigration laws and allows sanctuary cities to harbor illegal immigrants who break the law. America's inner cities are home to intolerable levels of poverty and out-of-control gun violence after five decades of failed progressive policies that are long overdue for reassessment. But honest dialogue about the causes of this violence are suppressed by political correctness that refuses to admit that it is primarily driven by blacks killing other blacks due to pathologies deeply embedded in their own communities. Black youth unemployment was over 30 percent in 2015 while 72 percent of black children and 53 percent of Hispanic children were born to unmarried women and 40 percent of all children were born to unmarried women in America in 2015 while a majority of all mothers under 30 are not living with the fathers of their children. The Obama administration lowered eligibility requirements for welfare payments and Social Security disability payments while pushing his failing healthcare plan on the American people. The results are rising levels of dependency that will result in rising budget deficits over the rest of the decade as the true trillion-dollar costs of ObamaCare start materializing. The fabric of American society is crumbling as economic change accelerates and we allow ourselves to be governed by policies that didn't work in the past and aren't going to work in the future.

As bad as things were at the end of George W. Bush's presidency in 2008, they are considerably worse after nearly two terms at the hands of Barack Obama. The global economy is as fragile as in 1999 or 2007—years that preceded market meltdowns and recessions; the geopolitical landscape resembles 1910 or 1939, years that preceded major global wars; and America's inner cities recall the Days of Rage of the 1960s. Our business and political leaders are fiddling while America is burning down. Without a radical course change, America and the world are headed for serious trouble.

The past has much to teach us about the consequences of ill-advised economic and foreign policies, but we needn't search very far to see the damage that has been wrought. Our mistakes have exacted an incalculable human cost on the citizens in this country and abroad. Millions of people lost their homes and their jobs as a result of the subprime mortgage debacle. Toward the end of 2009, the official jobless rate in the United States was more than 10 percent and the number, when underemployed and discouraged workers were included, was over 17 percent. The real unemployment figure was probably in the vicinity of 20 percent. Economic hardship and the stresses unemployment causes led families to break up and addiction and suicide rates to rise. At the end of 2009, one in eight Americans was receiving at least some of his or her nutrition from food stamps, including one in four children. Communities around the country were destroyed by house foreclosures. Plant closures by the automobile industry devastated the American heartland. The social fabric of an already fraying society was badly damaged.

Six years after the crisis, things looked better but they were not as good as they looked. The unemployment rate in June 2015 had dropped to 5.3 percent, down from a peak of 10.8 percent in 2009 at the worst point of the post-crisis recession. U6, which includes discouraged and underemployed workers, was down to 10.5 percent from 17.1 percent at the same point in 2009. But if we look deeper, the job market is still in very bad shape. There are more people out of the workforce than at any time since the late 1970s. The labor participation rate was only 62.6 percent in June 2015, the lowest level since the 1970s, meaning that almost 100 million able-bodied Americans were unable to find full-time employment. If the job participation rate in June 2015 was the same as it was when Barack Obama took office in January 2009, the unemployment rate would be closer to 2009 levels. The Federal Reserve refuses to acknowledge that the low labor participation rate is an indication that there is a structural rather than a cyclical unemployment problem that is not susceptible to monetary remedies. Instead, in the absence of meaningful fiscal policy initiatives, the Fed keeps its foot on the gas of low interest rates and keeps praying for the best. Prayers work best in church and synagogue; their efficacy in the economy remains unproven.

Global Threats Require Systemic Stability

The world desperately needs a healthy financial system as it faces unprecedented strains on its resources, rising geopolitical tensions, and challenges to human survivability in the twenty-first century and beyond. Finance should not be treated like just another national pastime that is followed through the media like baseball or cricket. And the financial markets are not the economy, even though they play one on television. The markets are the lifeblood of human civilization. They are the organizations that enable us to feed and clothe and heal our fellow humans, and abusing them is no different than abusing ourselves and risking our future. Like the capital they shepherd, markets must be nurtured and protected, not abused and neglected and left to the offices of greed and fear.

Any serious book about markets today must be written with a consciousness of the significant challenges facing the human species as it enters the twenty-first century. There are many fine books on finance, but today's world calls for something more. Finance needs to be understood as the force driving most of the social, political, ecological, and spiritual trends at work in the world. Unfortunately, many of these trends pose long-term threats to our species. Fixing the global financial system is not only an economic imperative—it is arguably a requirement for the survival of mankind. One telling example will suffice to illustrate what is at stake.

The world is facing a growing trend toward aging populations. Some countries like Russia and Japan are facing demographic disasters in the years ahead as their populations are projected to plunge in size. The costs of dealing with this inexorable demographic phenomenon dwarf the trillions of dollars that were spent by governments to prevent a global depression in 2008. Table 1.1, developed by the International Monetary Fund,[24] shows how much each country spent on the financial crisis as a percentage of its GDP, compared to how much each country is projected to spend as a percentage of its GDP to deal with the cost of its aging population. The latter so far exceeds the former as to render the amounts spent on the financial crisis almost trivial in present value terms.

Table 1.1   Net Present Value Impact on Fiscal Deficit of Crisis Compared to Age-Related Spending as a Percent of GDP

Country	Crisis	Aging	Age-Related Spending/Crisis Spending
Australia	26%	482%	18.5x
Canada	14	726	51.9
France	21	276	13.1
Germany	14	280	20.0
Italy	28	169	6.0
Japan	28	158	5.6
Korea	14	683	48.8
Mexico	6	261	43.5
Spain	35	652	18.6
Turkey	12	204	17.0
United Kingdom	29	335	11.6
United States	34	495	14.6
Advanced G-20 Countries	28	409	14.6

SOURCE: www.imf.org/external/np/pp/eng/2009/030609.pdf.

The column on the far right side of Table 1.1 divides projected age-related spending by crisis spending to show how future age-related spending is going to swamp crisis-related spending. For example, in the United States, age-related spending will amount to 14.6 times the amount that was spent on the financial crisis! Coincidentally, in all of the G20 countries, average age-related spending will also amount to approximately 14.6 times the cost of the financial crisis.

What Table 1.1 shows is that the United States and other G20 countries were facing forbidding financial challenges even before they had to step in with trillions of dollars of emergency funds in 2008. In other words, if we think we are facing fiscal challenges now, just wait until we get a few years down the road.

Moreover, beyond the example of aging populations and the cost of managing the financial crisis, there are other long-term threats to human survival, some of which require serious and immediate attention where a healthy global financial system will have to play an essential role.[25]

These threats, which are listed in Table 1.2, are by their very nature unpredictable and have the potential to trigger extreme impacts—in short, they are examples of the Black Swans that Nassim Nicholas Taleb brought into popular consciousness that have been circling in the skies above us throughout history. They are among the threats that mankind must confront and overcome in order to preserve its future.

If one adds the costs of addressing these issues (which are enormous but incalculable) to those found in Table 1.1, the potential magnitude is overwhelming. A negative outcome with respect to any of these potential crises would be a game-changer, resulting in exponential rather than linear damage: environmental catastrophe, a world war, a global health crisis, or a collapse of civil authority. These are precisely the type of discontinuities that the vast majority of investment strategies are unable to hedge against.

The world is going to have to search high and wide for the resources to deal with these threats. But even if it can find the resources, it will not be able to deliver them if the global financial system remains an unstable house of cards. A strong and stable financial system will be the bare minimum required to deal with these threats, and we don't have such a system today. Moreover, such a system will have to be managed by men and women who possess not only raw intelligence and intellectual creativity but wisdom, real-world experience, and moral courage. Our finance-driven world, unfortunately, rewards only the first two of these attributes, and its failure to value the last three is nothing short of catastrophic.

Table 1.2   Future Black Swans?

Environmental degradation and climate change

Nuclear proliferation

Terrorism

Population imbalances

An increasing gulf between rich and poor

Ethnic conflict

A pandemic such as AIDS, SARS, or something worse

World hunger

People like Brooksley Born, the former chairperson of the Commodities Futures Trading Commission, whose advocacy for regulating the growing market for financial derivatives fell on deaf ears in the 1990s, are only recognized for their courage in speaking truth to power after the damage they sought to prevent is done. We need more Brooksley Borns and fewer Alan Greenspans, Lawrence Summers, and Robert Rubins, the men who rejected her recommendation to regulate derivatives based on rigid ideology rather than an understanding of the facts. The most highly celebrated individuals in public life repeatedly fail us, yet they are celebrated by a complicit and superficial financial and political media. Individuals in positions where they can make a difference in the world need to be smarter, wiser, and more courageous than their predecessors, very few of whom were willing to speak out or exercise their influence to upset the status quo. Just as polities get the leaders they deserve, societies get the financial systems they deserve. We must look inward to examine the deeply embedded cultural values and intellectual assumptions that consistently lead economic actors of all types—investors, regulators, corporate executives—to conduct themselves in a manner that places the stability of the financial system, and therefore of society, at risk.

The global economy and financial markets have yet to face the disruptive challenge of unwinding the massive amounts of stimulus that the world's governments injected after the crisis in order to prevent a global depression. Seven years after the financial crisis, it remains very difficult to foresee how stimulus can be withdrawn without triggering serious market volatility. While many pundits were claiming throughout the 2013–2015 period that that the global economy was on the cusp of a self-sustaining recovery, there was in fact no evidentiary basis for making such a claim. "Self-sustaining" presumably means "without the support of central banks," and markets have not experienced a single minute of existence without massive central bank support since the financial crisis. Accordingly, there has never been a basis for making any claim for a self-sustaining recovery since the crisis.

If economic growth is insufficient to fund not just ongoing deficits but the repayment of the trillions of dollars of debt already incurred, withdrawal of stimulus can only lead to slower or negative growth. One alternative is that stimulus simply won't be withdrawn in any meaningful way, creating a situation in which massive government deficits will continue to grow as far as the eye can see. The U.S. federal deficit will soon pass $20 trillion and the annual cost of servicing that deficit will likely hit $1 trillion in the first half of the next decade; thus far, this cost has been mercifully suppressed by the low interest rates engineered by the Federal Reserve. But while mercy may have its limits, markets do not.

The only reason the financial system has not yet collapsed under its own weight is because interest rates have been maintained at zero since the financial crisis, but sooner or later investors will insist on a positive return on their capital. And when that happens, all hell will break lose. If the dollar was not the global reserve currency, an objective observer would view the U.S. balance sheet as resembling that of a country heading for a sovereign debt default. Other countries that defaulted on their debt did not have the privilege of issuing debt in the global reserve currency, but eventually the United States will no longer enjoy that advantage unless it radically changes its ways.

The American political system—and that includes both politicians and voters—shows little stomach to make the kinds of tough choices that can provide a realistic alternative to a bleak future. The consequences of adding trillions of dollars of debt to America's balance sheet are certain to be profoundly negative. The resulting imbalances are likely to include a weaker currency and higher inflation as well as many other unanticipated problems that will be disruptive to economic and social stability. Whatever course is chosen to deal with this debt, the ramifications are going to be highly disruptive to economic and social conditions as we know them today. For that reason, it is more urgent than ever that radical systemic reforms be instituted as soon as possible to provide the necessary margins of safety before the inevitable instability lands on our doorstep.

CHAPTER 2

The Death of Capital

C apital is a powerful and complex phenomenon that many thinkers have struggled to define over the centuries. The statement that
capital died in 2008 is intended to mean that after years of being
misunderstood, abused, and wasted, capital stopped flowing around
the world and became totally frozen in place. The manifestation of its
death was the abrupt slowdown in economic activity that occurred in
September 2008, around the time the U.S. investment banking firm
Lehman Brothers declared bankruptcy and the U.S. government was
forced to prop up AIG with $85 billion of loans (which ultimately rose
to $170 billion in assistance).

One of the most graphic illustrations of the cessation of economic
activity that occurred in late 2008 is what happened to the Baltic Dry
Index, a daily measure of global shipping activity.[1] Figure 2.1 shows this
index falling off a cliff in September 2008, signaling the sudden collapse of global economic activity as capital flows came to a standstill.
This index was considered to be a leading indicator of global economic
activity at the time and measured the price of moving the world's raw

Baltic Dry Index

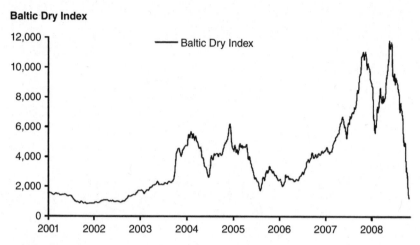

Figure 2.1 Capital RIP September 2008
SOURCE: Bloomberg.

materials around the globe. By the end of 2008, nothing was moving around the globe. Capital had indeed died.

One of the key characteristics of capital is that it is a process and not a structure, a category, or an object. Capital is a process because it is the embodiment of the human relationships that generate economic activity. Those relationships can be ones of equality or inequality (almost always the latter), but they are relationships nonetheless. A relationship involves some type of connection in which two or more parties interact and affect the behavior of the other. In the autumn of 2008, the world saw a temporary but complete breakdown in those relationships.

In the first decade of the twenty-first century, capital came to have virtually no connection with the underlying social relations that generate economic value. As the embodiment of the economic value created by human labor, capital has always maintained an indirect relationship with the actual act of wealth generation, so this is not a new phenomenon. But the distance between capital and wealth generation became attenuated beyond all previous bounds by the changes wrought by modern finance. The very concept of capital—not to mention capital itself—was devalued by modern financial practices. Rather than a precious resource used to improve the human condition through the provision of jobs, health care, education, and the like, capital was further alienated from these social purposes than in earlier historical periods.

The world experienced the death of capital that had built up for decades due to a combination of counterproductive political and economic forces. In the autumn of 2008, in the wake of the bankruptcy of Lehman Brothers and the near-collapse of AIG, capital froze, and with it the functioning of the global economy when longstanding forces coalesced into an overpowering wave of debt and disillusion. Capital was ultimately thawed out by a blowtorch of massive government stimulus and support, but its transformation into a phenomenon completely disembodied from its generative sources remained in place.

Capital was placed on life support by the emergency measures taken by the world's wealthiest governments and central banks. These entities threw trillions of dollars at the symptoms in order to temporarily restart the flow of capital around the globe. But the measures taken in late 2008 and early 2009 to keep the patient alive were only temporary and had deleterious long-term effects. The most harmful ones included a massive build-up of global debt and the ongoing devaluation of fiat currencies. In order to return capital to permanent health instead of merely the walking dead, new long-term economic policies must be put into place. But those policies cannot be implemented without a thorough understanding of what capital is and how it functions. In order to be properly managed and regulated, capital must be understood in view of its true nature as a process rather than an object and in view of changing market conditions and market structures. The very fact that capital died in the first decade of the twenty-first century suggests that those charged with shepherding it did not understand its intrinsic nature.

How did modern capitalism manage to place capital on the endangered species list? After all, modern society had ostensibly developed far more advanced tools to manage risk—particularly man-made risk—than ever before in its history. Computer technology and mathematical ingenuity were presumably designed to protect the financial system from precisely the disruptions that it suffered in 2008. Instead, in the ultimate irony, tools implemented to reduce risk ended up increasing it—to reckless and systemically threatening levels. Students of capitalism have long known there is something inherent in the nature of capital that renders it unstable. But what is it exactly that makes capital so difficult to manage?

The Four Essential Characteristics of Capital

Coming to a working definition of capital that reflects its real-world complexity is an imposing task. But avoiding it would be like performing an autopsy without touching the corpse. If the academics who have exercised such undue influence on markets have taught us anything, it is that markets work in theory but not in practice. Accordingly, capital needs to be understood as it really is, not as we imagine it to be. That is why we cannot leave the definition to the professors; the job must be done by practitioners, meaning investors who take the field every day to do battle in flesh-and-blood markets. In order to define capital, we must combine theory and practice into a formulation that reflects the real world.

Because capital is a process, it remains in constant motion. Below are the four characteristics of capital that are essential to a proper understanding of how it functions in the actual markets where money is made and lost every day.

Capital as It Is, Not as We Want It to Be
1. It is a process, not a structure, an object, or a category.
2. It is constantly changing form.
3. It is a construct of the human mind.
4. It is unstable.

The Oxford English Dictionary describes financial capital as "the accumulated wealth of an individual, company, or community, used as a fund for carrying on fresh production; *wealth in any form used to help in producing more wealth*" (emphasis added).[2] "Wealth in any form used to help in producing more wealth" is the key to understanding capital because it describes a process, not an object or a structure or a category.

Capital Is a Process

First and foremost, capital is a living, breathing phenomenon. It is an expression of the human relationships that generate economic value. Just as these relationships are dynamic in nature, so is capital. Static capital is dead capital.

Without human labor producing it, capital cannot come into being. Both the creation of capital and the investment of capital originate in human relationships. For this reason, labor must be understood as another form of capital.[3] Labor is exchanged for other forms of capital in the form of commodities (such as food, clothing, and shelter) or in the form of money. In today's knowledge economy, intellectual labor is the most valuable form of capital. The analysis of capital as the product of labor is well-rehearsed. What is less appreciated is the fact that invested capital is also representative of human relationships.

The world's financial markets are driven by investments made on behalf of institutions that represent charities, universities, labor unions, and municipalities. Their investments are made to support the basic human needs of their beneficiaries—education, healthcare, retirement, and disability payments if individuals lose their ability to work. When we speak about the public utility function that certain parts of the financial system are designed to serve, such as banks, we are speaking about these institutions' function to provide for the betterment of human life. This function originates in the most basic economic act, the labor that creates capital. Capital is always one step removed from that labor, which was one of Karl Marx's keenest insights (as I discuss in Chapter 3). But today capital has become so many steps removed from labor that it has lost its essential character as the stimulating force behind improving human life. We cannot understand capital until we understand that it originates in human labor and that it has become more alienated from labor than perhaps ever before in history.

The most important attribute of capital as it functions in the real world is that because it is a process, it is a relationship and not a category, an object, or a structure. In other words, it is not static. Capital is anything that can be exchanged for any other form of capital—money, property, or labor. In the modern world, increasing amounts of capital are intangible in form such as patents, trademarks, copyrights, and other forms of intellectual property, as well as contract rights such as derivative financial instruments. Accordingly, the forms in which capital are represented have become increasingly complex. Finally, because capital is by its very nature a representation of something else, it is an indirect expression of the value of the underlying thing it represents.[4]

Capital Constantly Changes Form

Another essential characteristic of capital is that it has the potential to change form. Capital is chameleon-like. This is related to what is called its liquidity function. Illiquid capital is an oxymoron. In order for something to be considered capital, it must have the potential to be turned into another form of capital, such as goods (food, clothing, housing), labor (which creates goods or money), or money (which purchases goods and labor). Turning one form of capital into another is perhaps the most important characteristic of capital; this characteristic is often taken for granted (particularly by investors), always at an enormously painful, even financially fatal, cost. Many long-term investors learned this lesson about liquidity the hard way in 2008. People joke about John Maynard Keynes' remark that the market has the ability to remain irrational longer than an investor can remain solvent, but the great economist's point was a deadly serious one.

In the period before the financial crisis, many institutions that viewed themselves as long-term investors and followed the "endowment model" of investing failed to properly plan for the liquidity that they would need to fund their day-to-day operations.[5] Companies go bankrupt because they run out of liquidity and are unable to pay their bills even if the value of their assets as shown on their balance sheets exceeds the face amount of their liabilities (although they quickly discover that the value of their assets plunges if they file for bankruptcy). One of the keys to long-term investment survival is living to play another day, and liquidity crises are the single biggest threat to that ability.

Capital Is a Human Construct

Capital is also not something that is found in nature or subject to natural laws like physics and mathematics. Capital is a construct of the human mind. It is the tangible or intangible product of human labor, but as already noted it can also be human labor itself that can be exchanged for another form of capital (property or money, for example). As a human construct, it is a product of human perception. Capital only has value to the extent economic actors (human beings, or entities or organizations controlled by human beings) are prepared to place a value on it. This means they are willing to exchange it for another form of capital they believe to be of equal (or lesser) value. The concept of value introduces the psychological or subjective component of human nature into the mix. Value is a highly unstable concept that is constantly subject to changing human perceptions. While minions labor away in markets around the world each day purporting to place precise values on different types of securities and financial instruments, the only certainty about these values is that they are wrong. Values are changing constantly (the image of the blinking computer screen aptly captures this phenomenon) as the assumptions and circumstances used to determine value are adjusted. While this may seem an obvious point to make, the world's financial markets operate as though there is a Holy Grail of value that is constantly within reach. Nothing could be further from the truth. Chasing value is like chasing a mirage. Capital is the economic form of that mirage.

Capital Is Unstable

These three essential attributes of capital lead to one inevitable conclusion—capital tends toward instability rather than stability. A process that can change form and is subject to human perception is hardly a candidate for stability. And that is exactly what we find throughout history: Capital is a highly unstable concept. This quality remains poorly appreciated, and as a result, capital remains poorly regulated and managed. If we can come to a better understanding of capital, how it lives and how it dies, we can hope to corral it to better uses.

How Capital Dies

Once we understand what capital is, we can also understand how it ceases to exist. Capital's essential quality is change. When capital loses the ability to change, it dies. This is another way of saying what was said above: Capital must remain in motion at all times or retain the potential to be in motion. Static capital is dead capital. Unrelated, unconnected, or isolated capital is dead capital. When investors speak about "dead money" or "dead capital," they are speaking metaphorically about an investment that is neither generating a return nor likely to generate a return in the foreseeable future. The reasons for this are legion; the primary one is that it can't be turned into another kind of asset that can generate a return. When Western capitalism came to a grinding halt in the fourth quarter of 2008, capital stopped living and breathing. Capital literally and figuratively stopped moving and changing.

Because it is a relationship, capital requires at least two parties to bring it to life. This is where markets come into being. Capital requires some type of mechanism of exchange, initially of information about capital and ultimately of capital itself. Understanding market information requires market participants to share certain intellectual and moral assumptions. The parties do not have to like each other, they do not have to trust each other, but they have to be able to agree on the value of something and believe that the system in which they are acting will enforce their bargain. There must be some kind of meeting of the minds, which is a human and social phenomenon. So we see again that at the all-important level of exchange, where capital creates value, capital is a social construct. Capital dies when it loses its human and social content and context. Inhuman capital is dead capital.

Capital Is Misunderstood

It is apparent from observing the evolution of financial markets that too few people in positions of influence properly understand what financial capital is, how it functions, and how it should be managed and regulated. That is not to say that many of these same people have not figured out how to make money, in some cases enormous sums of it. But making money and understanding capital are two entirely different accomplishments. Society's confusion of wealth with talent and intelligence is only one of the illusions that needs to be dispelled in order to establish more stable markets and a more just society. But understanding capital is quite another matter. This lack of understanding is what led to capital's temporary demise in 2008 and the economic and human chaos and suffering that ensued. It is also why capital virtually always provides less than optimal returns to its holders. The failure to understand capital is why all types of societies, whether they call themselves capitalist, socialist, communist, or some variation thereof, operate well below their full economic potential.[6] It is also why all economies, in particular those that call themselves capitalist, remain highly unstable even in the so-called "age of advanced risk management" (a term that gives all oxymorons a bad name).

Among other lessons, the financial collapse of 2008 demonstrated that the U.S. economic system was not built on stable and enduring intellectual and moral underpinnings. Instead, it was built on an ideological and intellectual house of cards on top of which was constructed an economic house of cards. Financial Armageddon finally arrived in 2008, as a number of market observers (myself included) had predicted, as a result of noxious regulatory and business trends that had gone unchecked for decades. The external manifestations of these trends were excessive leverage at all levels of the financial system and a highly politicized and profoundly ineffective regulatory scheme. These were symptoms of a profound misunderstanding of capital, the basic building block of economies, and an equally deep failure to understand markets, the places where capital is exchanged. There was no appreciation of the fact that capital is an unstable social phenomenon, or that eradicating the relationship between capital and the labor that creates it was bound to have serious (and potentially catastrophic) consequences. The nature of capital was badly misunderstood by its practitioners and guardians, and the result was a near-death experience for the Western banking system and the free markets themselves. The trends that caused the 2008 crisis are still in place and in many cases are worse today than a decade ago. *The Committee to Destroy the World* was written as a kind of post-mortem on a financial system that is now trying to be come back to life but is being pulled back into the grave by stupidity, blindness and avarice. A healthy capitalist system only stands a chance of being resurrected if those in positions of influence can come to understand how the *corpus economicus* really functions in a radically changing and unstable world.

The Failure of Risk Management

Ironically, the incessant march toward financial instability occurred in a world that had claimed to master risk. In 1992, Peter Bernstein wrote what is still rightly considered to be a modern classic on the subject of finance, *Capital Ideas*. Bernstein's book was widely admired for its insightful discussion of the academic theories that laid the groundwork for the revolution in finance that led to the development of derivative products, portfolio management techniques, and what many believed to be the advanced management of risk. In an early passage, Bernstein wrote the following:

Today investors are more keenly aware of risk, and better able to deal with it, than at any time in the past. They have a more sophisticated understanding of how financial markets behave and are capable of using to advantage the vast array of new vehicles and new trading strategies specifically tailored to their needs. Innovative techniques of corporate finance have led to more careful evaluation of corporate wealth and more effective allocation of capital. The financial restructuring of the 1980s created novel solutions to the problems arising from the separation of ownership and control and made corporate managers more responsive to the interests of shareholders.[6]

Investors and regulators came to believe—falsely as it turned out—that new products such as securitization and credit derivatives were effectively dispersing risk throughout the global financial system where it could better be absorbed. In fact, they were doing precisely the opposite. Bernstein's imprimatur regarding the ability of the new tools of finance carried a great deal of weight within the financial industry; unfortunately it was profoundly misplaced.

The risk management techniques praised by Bernstein relied on advanced computer programming power to better capture relationships between the prices of different securities and markets and to more accurately measure the correlation among different securities and asset classes. The intellectual assumptions underlying such risk management approaches, however, included reliance on two basic premises that were completely unfounded: first, markets are efficient; and second, investors are rational. Beyond these erroneous assumptions lay other flawed theories, such as the belief that diversification of portfolios would protect investors from losses and that relying on historical performance serves as a valid basis for forecasting future price movements. Among other errors, all of these assumptions failed to adequately account for low-probability high-impact events (what have come to be known as "Black Swans" thanks to the insights of Nassim Nicholas Taleb). Accordingly, risk management models assumed normal distributions of events and did not stress test for so-called "fat tails" that have occurred with increasing regularity during the past 20 years. This turned out to be a fatal omission.

Another problem was that the models guiding investors failed to evolve to reflect the increasingly networked nature of financial markets, which created a situation in which the actions of a single large financial institution can have a systemic impact. The technical term for such effects are "network externalities," which means that market developments will induce different firms to react in similar ways rather than act independently. Thus, the financial condition of an individual company proved to be an inadequate measure of systemic risk, and systemic disturbances increased the riskiness of individual companies that on their own may have looked stable. Finally, such risk management techniques sought to apply the laws of mathematics and physics to financial markets, which are socially and economically driven worlds that do not operate according to physical laws. Markets tend to be irrational; subjecting them to the rational laws of science is unlikely to lead to meaningful results. The damage wrought from such intellectual confusion was extreme.

Four years later, in an enlightening 1996 book on the subject of risk, *Against the Gods*, Bernstein sounded a warning about undue reliance on some of the forecasting tools he had praised in *Capital Ideas*:

> Likeness to truth is not the same as truth. Without any theoretical structure to explain why patterns seem to repeat themselves across time or across systems, these innovations provide little assurance that today's signals will trigger tomorrow's events. We are left with only the subtle sequences of data that the enormous power of the computer can reveal. Thus forecasting tools based on nonlinear models or on computer gymnastics are subject to many of the same hurdles that stand in the way of conventional probability theory: the raw material of the model is the data of the past.[7]

And of course the history of financial markets since Bernstein wrote *Capital Ideas* and *Against the Gods* belies any rational observer's optimism about the ability of investors to properly utilize and profit from scientific, computer-driven risk management tools. In the last two decades alone, there have been five severe disruptions in the credit markets—four manageable ones in 1990–1991, 1994, 1998, and 2001–2002, and the truly catastrophic collapse in 2007–2008 that required unprecedented governmental intervention. Even though the financial system emerged basically intact from the first four of these debacles, it clearly gained little wisdom about the risks it was running. In fact, each succeeding market crisis revealed that the financial system had increased its risk profile after the previous one. The underlying causes of instability were left unaddressed, and the imbalances bred by increasing global debt levels were increasing. The world repeated that pattern after the 2008 financial crisis.

One clear lesson of episodes such as the junk bond/savings and loan scandal of 1990–1991, the Long-Term Capital Management crisis of 1998, and the credit crisis of 2001–2002 was that neither investors nor regulators learned very much from their mistakes. That, or they were too brainwashed with free market and risk management mantras to open their minds to the possibility that the conditions of underlying instability were worsening. In their blindness, they continued to cling to flawed assumptions and blatant misunderstandings about the basic ways in which markets work and the nature of capital itself. Even after the near-death experience of the 2008 financial crisis, these errors persisted and the world moved closer to another crisis caused by too much debt. A system that is unwilling to question its assumptions is unlikely to be prepared for the adverse consequences that result from them.

The risk management ideology lauded in *Capital Ideas* exercised an enormous influence on the thinking of market practitioners, politicians, and regulators throughout the 1990s and early 2000s. This was extremely unfortunate because confidence in mankind's ability to master risk was profoundly misplaced. Moreover, the almost religious belief that computers and mathematical models could master risk and that regulation was increasingly unnecessary came at the worst possible time in history in terms of man's ability to inflict damage on the economic system, because radical changes in human economic and political arrangements were occurring.

At the beginning of the 1980s, Ronald Reagan and Margaret Thatcher entered office a year apart and led the ideological charge in favor of free markets. By the time Ronald Reagan left office in 1988, Soviet-style communism was coming apart and the Chinese version was tossed aside by Deng Xiaoping in favor of a market-based economy. Less than a year after Ronald Reagan left the presidency, he watched the fall of the Berlin Wall that he had implored Mikhail Gorbachev to tear down. The victory of capitalism over communism that Reagan led was complete.

It is all too rare when external events validate a political ideology, but that is what occurred when the Berlin Wall fell, the Soviet Union split apart, and China embraced capitalism. This historic endorsement of free markets validated capitalism throughout the world, overlooking the fact that communism collapsed under its own weight as much as from the so-called genius of capitalism. Nonetheless, the fall of communism was an unequivocally positive development for mankind. Billions of people around the world began to taste economic freedom for the first time. But the collapse of one flawed system was accompanied, particularly in the United States and the United Kingdom, by a virtually blind adoption of another flawed system: unfettered free market capitalism—a belief in the ability of the markets to cure all ills and to effectively manage all risks.

During this period, Alan Greenspan was anointed the high priest of free market capitalism as chairman of the Federal Reserve. Many books have already been written criticizing his ostensible adherence to free market dogma,[8] yet it should not be overlooked that Greenspan's own Federal Reserve was all too willing to bail out markets on numerous occasions. Greenspan was more than prepared to toss out the window his free market principles in the face of true or perceived systemic risk. The bailout of Mexico in 1994, the Asian financial crisis of 1997–1998, Russia's debt default in 1998, Long-Term Capital Management's collapse in 1998, the Enron and WorldCom frauds in 2001, the 2001–2002 credit market collapse—in each of these cases, Greenspan's Federal Reserve intervened in the markets in one form or another. It did so either by lowering interest rates or directly or indirectly intervening in financial markets. Greenspan's frequent exercise of the central bank's lender of last resort function stood as a constant warning (for those who wanted to heed it) that the free market was not as free as it was cracked up to be, and that if allowed to continue functioning as it was, it would end up cracking up. Sadly, we came to discover in 2008 that the Soviet Union wasn't the only empire capable of being driven into insolvency and instability by the potency of the free market.

But despite the fact that the world's most esteemed central banker's actions did not live up to his free market reputation, the political and thinking classes continued to worship free markets (and Mr. Greenspan). The Glass-Steagall Act, which separated commercial and investment banking, fell by the wayside in 1999 under the lobbying of Citigroup, the now failed financial supermarket that spent the late 1990s and first decade of the 2000s engaged in combining its different businesses while committing a series of ethical, legal, and financial breaches that should have shamed its executives and board members rather than lifting them higher and higher in public esteem.

Once the barrier between deposit-taking and risk-taking institutions fell, the next step was to eliminate regulations that limited the amount of leverage that these newly empowered investment banks could employ in their businesses. In 2004, the Securities and Exchange Commission, under heavy lobbying from the leaders of two firms that survived 2008 after agreeing to turn themselves back into commercial banks (Morgan Stanley and Goldman Sachs) and three that did not (Merrill Lynch, Lehman Brothers, and Bear Stearns), decided to lift the 12-to-1 limit on balance sheet leverage on the large Wall Street investment banks. Few questioned the wisdom of these moves and most praised the freeing of the financial industry from rules that were considered archaic and antigrowth. A few Cassandras suspected that the old rule was necessary to prevent Wall Street from destroying itself. But proponents of what turned out to be a suicide pact argued that Wall Street would lose business to London and other jurisdictions that permitted higher leverage, and the race to the bottom was on. By the time the walls came crashing down, several of the largest investment banks sported debt-to-equity ratios in excess of 30 to 1. When the public learned how leveraged these firms had become, regulators and politicians began tripping over themselves to express their shock that gambling had been allowed at Rick's Cabaret. But by then it was too late—the chips were called in, and the casino stopped extending credit to even its best customers.

To the bitter end, however, free market acolytes continued to carry forward the belief that risk was conquered and the markets could handle whatever came their way. In early 2007, shortly before the financial markets almost collapsed, Bernstein published a sequel to *Capital Ideas*, which he titled *Capital Ideas Evolving*. He should have named his new book *Capital Ideas Devolving,* for the net result of these ideas turned out to be the near obliteration of the Western financial system. On the eve of financial Armageddon, Bernstein wrote:

It may sound ironic, but as investors increasingly draw on Capital
Ideas to shape their strategies, to innovate new financial instruments,
and to motivate the drive for higher returns in relation to risk, the
real world itself is on a path toward an increasing resemblance to the
theoretical world described in *Capital Ideas*. Subsequent pages repeat
that observation on more than a few occasions. Baloney those ideas
were not.[9]

It is too late for Bernstein to retract that last sentence, but I
will be presumptuous enough to do it for him. For if the financial
world has come to resemble anything, it is the aftermath of the
attack of the Martians in H.G. Wells' *The War of the Worlds*. Never
have so many technically overeducated but morally undereducated
people done so much damage to so many. The models and products
that were developed to conquer risk instead turned on their inventors and destroyed them. The finance professors who concocted
portfolio theory, the Black–Scholes model, credit default swaps, and
collateralized default obligations did little more than demonstrate
the truth of the adage, "Markets work in theory but they don't work
in practice."

Even worse, the post-World War II economic model that served
as the basis of so much apparent prosperity had morphed into an edifice of debt and delusion. This model took a sharp turn for the worse
in the 1980s, when debt assumed a much greater role in all levels of
the U.S. economy. The ideological and intellectual assumptions that
supported rampant debt growth and the triumph of speculation over
production turned out to be profoundly flawed in their basic pre-
cepts.[10] As always happens in markets, which are primarily driven by
emotion, the pendulum swung too far. Free markets required prudent regulation, and computer technology and quantitative thinking
couldn't free the world from the demons of risk. In order to understand how the Western financial system destroyed itself, and to place
this system back on a sound economic track, the post-World War II
understanding of markets and capital must be revised. New answers are
needed. The best place to start looking for them, as the next chapter suggests, is by rereading some great philosophers who happened to write
about economics.

CHAPTER 3

Capital Ideas

One of the great ironies embedded inside the structure of all complex systems is that they sow the seeds of their own demise. Such is the case for modern economies and bull markets. The collapse of the Western financial system in 2008 demonstrated beyond a shadow of a doubt that there are internal contradictions embedded in how modern capitalist societies organize themselves. The free market mantras that permitted lightly regulated financial industries to conduct business in reckless and self-serving ways over the three decades leading up to the crisis were thoroughly discredited by the need for Western governments to bail out their largest financial institutions.

The seeds of destruction were primarily ideological; they grew out of widely accepted but flawed ways of thinking about capital, economic growth, and financial regulation. Instead of basing economic growth on a modified free market model that privileges concepts such as equity, transparency, production, and prudent and limited regulation, those in positions of influence chose a radical free market path of debt, opacity, speculation, and wholesale deregulation. There were two problems with this approach. First, the United States does not have a genuine free market; government regulation and crony capitalism play an enormous role in distorting incentives and interfering with the free market. Second, this regime was based on the radical error of pretending that markets are efficient and investors are rational when precisely the opposite is true.

The choices did not have to be as stark as that—there is a middle ground that can serve the interests of all economic stakeholders. But the pendulum clearly swung too far in favor of the radical free market model. And after the financial crisis, the results lay in ruins all around us: insolvent banks, disenfranchised workers, impoverished state, local, and federal governments, a poisoned planet, embarrassed regulators, hypocritical and corrupt legislators crying for retribution between visits to the campaign feeding trough on Wall Street, and a public that lost trust in government. A capitalist system inherently prone to booms and busts became even more prone to disequilibrium. In order to understand what happened and in order to rebuild a more resilient system, we must dig deeply into basic economic principles and reevaluate them.

There are many influential economic thinkers whose work would greatly benefit market participants. In order to better understand the death of capital in 2008, four particular thinkers are worthy of extended discussion—Adam Smith, Karl Marx, John Maynard Keynes, and Hyman Minsky. But these thinkers need to be approached in a way that transcends economics. Three of the seminal works of economic theory that are examined in this chapter—*The Wealth of Nations* (1776); *Capital* (1867); and *The General Theory of Employment, Interest and Money* (1936)—are best considered intellectual performances that far exceed the discipline of economics and qualify as both great literature and great philosophy that have influenced intellectual debate in a variety of disciplines for generations. Each of these works has been analyzed and debated endlessly in academic and policy circles for years and continues to provide rich material for thinkers in a variety of disciplines. This is a tribute to the genius of their authors and the fact that the concepts discussed in these works are subject to multiple interpretations and misinterpretations.

What follows is a highly selective if not idiosyncratic reading of the aspects of these seminal thinkers that ties together their interpretations of some of the key characteristics of capital, capitalism, and markets. It is my contention that these intellectual giants provide insights into the nature of capital that are largely misunderstood by investors, regulators, and policymakers. The result is that little progress has been made in effectively managing the boom and bust nature of free market capitalism, which in turn has caused capitalism to fall far short of reaching its full potential to contribute to the growth and welfare of human society.

The first two thinkers, Adam Smith and Karl Marx, stand at opposite sides of the ideological spectrum yet share an enormous amount of common ground. These philosophers remain two of the most insightful students of capitalism long after their work began to influence the world. Adam Smith saw capitalism as a force for good, while Marx saw it as a cause of conflict and abuse. Their work provides important insights into the characteristics that render capital inherently unstable and crisis-prone. What follows is not intended to be a complete discussion of these two complex thinkers; rather, it is an attempt to draw out some of their key ideas as they affect the modern understanding of financial markets.

Smith and Marx speak to several of the key intellectual and moral underpinnings of our economic collapse. Both men describe markets governed by complex human relationships that at their basic level are strongly affected by people seeking social approbation. They also make powerful statements about the fact that human economic interactions, and the relationships between money and goods, are highly mediated. In discussing these two thinkers, I hope to illuminate some of the forces that drive economic actors to behave in certain ways that are ultimately very harmful to the long-term interests of society. By better understanding the profound truths that Smith and Marx described, we can hopefully address some of these flaws more effectively as we work to design a more productive economic system that serves the interests of all of us, not just the most privileged among us.

The last two thinkers wrote more recently and were particularly prominent in recent discussions surrounding the financial crisis of 2008. John Maynard Keynes and his most important modern interpreter, Hyman Minsky, understood the psychological aspects of capitalism as well as anybody who ever studied the system. In fact, Keynes may best be considered the greatest psychologist of economics, a mantle that Minsky assumed in warning of the dangers of financial instability. By focusing on the ways in which economic actors react to their environment, both men not only demonstrate great insight into human behavior but provide a road map for investors and regulators charged with navigating financial markets. Students of Minsky were undoubtedly the best prepared to recognize the unstable financing structures that led to the 2008 crisis, how these structures developed, and why such structures are endemic to the nature of capitalism and remain a serious threat.

The United States spent the last four decades—the 1980s, 1990s, 2000s, and now the 2010s—with an increasingly leveraged economic system whose primary occupation was to conceal declining productivity and weakening profitability from the eyes of investors and regulators while enriching a small elite.[1] By the end of the Bush II administration, the United States faced the most serious economic downturn since the Great Depression of the 1930s as its banking system lay broken and major industries such as housing and automobile manufacturing were on the verge of total collapse. The policies followed during the Obama administration and other governments around the world to set the global economy on a path of sustainable economic growth utterly failed to right the ship. It is necessary to analyze the deep structures of capital and capitalism in order to understand what happened and chart a new pathway to recovery. There is no better place to start such a study than the work of Adam Smith.

Adam Smith and the Tyranny of Crowds

When Adam Smith wrote about markets, he pictured in his mind the markets he walked in the streets of the eighteenth-century Scottish cities where he grew up (Kirkcaldy), attended school (Glasgow), and made his career (Edinburgh). These were smelly, bustling street markets filled with a huge assortment of physical goods and characters drawn out of a Charles Dickens novel. The historian Fernand Braudel gives us a vivid picture of the types of markets that Adam Smith experienced every day, filled with:

> [a] varied and active proletariat: pea-shellers, who had a reputation for being inveterate gossips; frog-skinners, . . . porters, sweepers, carters, unlicensed pedlars of both sexes, fussy controllers who passed on

their derisory offices from father to son; secondhand dealers, peasants and peasant women recognizable by their dress, as were respectable townswomen looking for a bargain, servant-girls who had worked out, so their employers complained, how to make something out of the shopping-money (to shoe the mule, *ferrer la mule* as they said); bakers selling coarse bread on the marketplace, butchers whose displays of meat encumbered the streets and squares, wholesalers . . . selling fish, butter and cheese in large quantities; tax-collectors. And everywhere of course were the piles of produce, slabs of butter, heaps of vegetables, pyramids of cheeses, fruit, wet fish, game, meat which the butcher cut up on the spot, unsold books whose pages were used to wrap up purchases. From the countryside there also came straw, hay, wood, wool, hemp, flax, and even fabrics woven on village looms.[2]

The overwhelming features of these markets were the smells, the sounds of people and animals, humans moving to and fro, the interaction among butchers and bakers and tradesmen buying and selling their goods. Smith had a very specific conception of what markets looked like and how the people in them behaved. Such markets still exist today, primarily in less developed countries but also in some developed countries where they remain quaint reminders of how people used to live. They are colorful emblems of the basic human relationships that remain the foundation of all economic exchanges.

Of course, the markets that drive economic activity today look very different. Physical markets of the type that Adam Smith knew are largely a sideshow or curiosity in modern Western societies. The markets that fuel modern global economies do not involve the trading of physical goods. They are largely antiseptic, electronic arenas where the only strong odors arise from the excesses of the night before. The primary commodities exchanged in modern markets are electronic bytes that represent stocks, bonds, mortgages, corporate bank loans, and currencies or, increasingly, complex derivative contracts that represent an interest in these financial instruments. To the extent there is a strong physical dimension to the proceedings, it is found in the impressive appearance that the technology that facilitates this trading assumes in the form of long rows of traders and their sleek computers and electronic computer screens. The sight is indeed impressive but has virtually no representational relationship with the underlying economic objects that are being exchanged. Unlike the street markets in eighteenth-century Glasgow or Edinburgh, the buyers and sellers rarely deal with each other face to face. Instead, they speak on the telephone or e-mail or text each other. Their communication is highly mediated; it is, to a large extent, impersonal and disembodied. This does not mean that their relationship is completely bereft of personal contact, but there is a great deal of truth to the concept that the age of gentlemanly capitalism has passed. The real question is whether the age of human capitalism has gone with it. The answer to that question is a resounding no.

Every day, on electronic trading floors around the globe, trillions of dollars of trades are effected on the basis of verbal agreements that are only later solidified into binding written contracts. A trader's word is literally his or her bond. A simple "you're done" is sufficient to signal that a trade is complete, whether that trade is for a million or a billion dollars of value. Despite the fact that the relationships between buyers and sellers as well as the goods they are trading are largely disembodied, a remarkably small percentage of trades end up being seriously disputed. Part of the reason for this is that technology allows for discussions between traders to be recorded. Another reason is far more elemental—nobody will deal with a trader who doesn't keep his or her word, and word circulates very quickly about who is trustworthy and who is not in the tight-knit trading community. There are protocols that have developed over time that must be followed if traders are going to be able to make a living. All of the computer terminals in the world can't erase the crucial human element that lies at the bottom of every single trade. This is one reason that Adam Smith has a great deal to teach us.

Adam Smith, of course, is best known as the author of what many people consider to be the bible of capitalism, *An Inquiry into the Nature and Causes of the Wealth of Nations* (1776). But two decades earlier, he wrote an arguably more important book, a treatise on moral philosophy entitled *The Theory of Moral Sentiments* (1759). In his earlier book, Smith sought to lay out the basis for moral conduct in human society and argued that people's concern for the opinions of others ultimately leads them to act in moral and civilized ways. In Smith's worldview, the process by which men develop a moral sense is very similar to the manner in which they develop markets. Both institutions—human society and human markets—are the result of human beings interacting with each other in ways that make them feel good about themselves by fulfilling their own needs. Just as the desire to fulfill material needs leads to the exchange of goods and hence the development of markets, the desire to fulfill emotional needs leads men and women to be sensitive to the views of others and thereby to develop a moral sense. Neither the markets nor the morals they develop are perfect; in fact, both are constant works-in-process that are flawed, subject to emotion, and unstable. Over time, Smith believes that the process of developing and refining a moral sense leads to the formation of order in morality and markets that is superior to other forms because it fulfills human needs better than other forms. In other words, Smith argues that such a system is not only a realistic description of how men and women behave, but it is an optimal system. That does not mean, however, that these systems can simply be allowed to operate without laws or institutions. Rather, Smith was searching for the optimal institutional framework in which people's innate qualities could be put to the best use. Taking people as they were (or, as he saw them, warts and all), Smith was trying to design a world that would make people the best they could be.[3]

In *The Wealth of Nations*, Smith famously wrote that "[i]t is not from the benevolence of the butcher, the brewer, or the baker, that we expect our dinner, but from their regard to their own interest."[4] Yet Smith's project was not to unconditionally praise an "invisible hand"[5] of self-interest guiding free-market behavior, but to identify those institutions and processes that could provide human beings with the best opportunity to act in constructive, decent, and moral ways. He believed that a free market in which men and women could demonstrate their worth by exchanging goods and services was among the most important of those institutions. The freedom to earn a living through exchange would, in Smith's view, give individuals the best opportunity to avoid the types of dependency on others that leads to immoral behavior.

Smith's view that people base their conduct on their concern for the opinion of others is wholly relativistic. As such, it provides both wisdom and warning. The wisdom comes from Smith's recognition that human beings are strongly driven by social approbation. We desperately want to feel that we are part of a group that accepts us. And the first step to accomplishing that is understanding how others feel about us.

From the first words of *The Theory of Moral Sentiments*, Smith focuses on our concern for the feelings of others. "How selfish soever man may be supposed, there are evidently some principles in his nature, which interest him in the fortune of others, and render their happiness necessary to him, though he derives nothing from it, except the pleasure of seeing it." He continues, "[t]hat we often derive sorrow from the sorrow of others, is a matter of fact too obvious to require any instances to prove it." The way we try to understand how other people feel is to put ourselves in their place. "As we have no immediate experience of what other men feel, we can form no idea of the manner in which they are affected, but by conceiving what we ourselves should feel in the like situation." Continuing, Smith writes, "That this is the source of our fellow-feeling for the misery of others, that it is by changing places in fancy with the sufferer, that we come either to conceive or to be affected by what he feels."[6]

In order to judge the feelings of others, Smith tries to establish an objective standard (similar to the "prudent man" rule discussed in Chapter 8 of this book) that he terms the "impartial spectator." It is from the standpoint of this impartial spectator that others should be judged:

> We conceive ourselves as acting in the presence of a person quite candid and equitable, of one who has no particular relation either to ourselves, or to those whose interests are affected by our conduct, who is neither father, nor brother, nor friend either to them or to us, but is merely a man in general, an impartial spectator who considers our conduct with the same indifference with which we regard that of other people.[7]

In Smith's world, all moral judgments rely on the judgment of this independent man.[8]

As the scholar Dennis Rasmussen points out, Smith understood that undue concern with the opinions of others could "lead to a corruption of people's moral sentiments, selfishly motivated appeals to others' self-interest, and a good deal of ostentation."[9] Social approbation does not always bring out the best in people. Too often, people worship the wrong idols. Smith's statement that undue admiration for the rich is the source of the corruption of our moral sentiments, which is found at the beginning of this book, speaks an uncomfortable truth that should be posted on the entryway of every financial institution and government building in the world. Smith's philosophical project is aimed at fashioning a just society out of the fact that people are unduly concerned with the opinions of others, and that these opinions steer them to admire the wrong moral attributes in other people. But instead of simply identifying this as a flaw, Smith attempts to use worship of the rich and powerful as a basis for fashioning a more just society.

Smith believes that a commercial society is particularly well-suited to such a project. In a commercial society, people are dependent on one another to work together to meet their needs. They generally cannot meet their needs alone (even Thoreau ventured into Concord from Walden Pond regularly to replenish his stores). For this reason, people have a strong incentive to work together and depend on each other. As Dennis Rasmussen writes, for this reason Smith believed that "commerce encourages traits like reliability, decency, honesty, cooperativeness, a commitment to keeping one's promises, and a strict adherence to society's norms of justice."[10] In Smith's view, it is incumbent upon people in a market society to conduct themselves in a moral way in order to be able to participate in and benefit from commercial activity.[11] It is in people's interest to engage in good behavior because that will better help them fill their needs.

Of course, Smith was striving for an ideal, and commercial life is not so simple. The warning concealed in Smith's words comes from his failure to identify any independent moral standard as the basis for human conduct. Instead of basing morality on natural law, religion, or reason, Smith argued that moral conduct originates entirely in human beings' feelings or sentiments. The rules of morality result from feelings, not vice versa. Smith writes:

> It is thus that the general rules of morality are formed. They are ultimately founded upon experience of what, in particular instances, our moral faculties, our natural sense of merit and propriety, approve or disapprove of. We do not originally approve or condemn particular actions, because, upon examination, they appear to be agreeable or inconsistent with a certain general rule. The general rule, on the contrary, is formed by finding from experience that all actions of a certain

kind, or circumstanced in a certain manner, are approved or disap-
proved of....Those general rules...are all formed from the experience
we have had of the effects which actions of all different kinds naturally
produce upon us.[12]

These feelings are not only our own—they are what we imagine
others would feel watching our conduct. "If we saw ourselves in the
light in which others see us, or in which they would see us if they
knew all, a reformation would generally be unavoidable. We could not
otherwise endure the sight."[13] By making the opinions of others the
standard by which we judge ourselves rather than some independent or
objective moral standard, we risk surrendering ourselves to the madness
of crowds. After all, history has demonstrated repeatedly that groups are
particularly susceptible to flawed thinking.

There is a dark side to this concurrence-seeking ethos that has
played itself out throughout history. It lies at the heart of the type of
herd thinking that causes phenomena such as investment bubbles and,
in its most pernicious form, genocide. In his classic study, *Groupthink*,
Irving Janis identified strong consensus-seeking behavior as one of the
main causes of defective decision-making in classic policy disasters such
as the Kennedy and Johnson administrations' actions with respect to the
Vietnam War and the Bay of Pigs.[14] The desire of members of a group
to be accepted by others, which lies at the heart of Adam Smith's theory
of moral sentiments, tends to silence dissenting voices, limit the airing of
unpopular views, and lead to poor decision-making.

Permitting the opinions of others to govern important human
activities is a highly problematic enterprise. It is another version of conceding all wisdom to the free market. But crowds, and markets, often
get things terribly wrong; in point of fact, they often act irrationally.
Smith observed that human behavior and institutions evolve through
the interaction of human beings attempting to satisfy their emotional or
economic needs. However true this may be as a matter of fact, it need
not be dispositive as a matter of prescription. Some human impulses
are contrary to the health of the larger community, even deviant and
dangerous. Greed and fear, two human drives that govern a great deal
of market behavior, are directly contrary to the operation of healthy
markets and a productive economy if they are not properly reined in.

Adam Smith described how men and markets develop and believed that markets could be designed with the proper governing institutions to contain man's worst instincts. One of the purposes of *The Committee to Destroy the World* is to evaluate the failure to develop the right kinds of institutional structures to manage the tyranny of crowds.

Smith wrote a long time ago, but the world has not passed him by. In many ways, the world is still trying to catch up to him. We are still trying to design the proper institutions and markets that will allow man's best attributes to flourish while governing the demons of his nature. Recent events demonstrate that the dark side of human nature—greed, fear, arrogance, stupidity—remains a formidable foe that places humankind's welfare at risk at regular intervals. The social approbation that Smith identified as the primary basis of man's moral sentiments still drives many peoples' behavior, especially their economic behavior. Sadly, free markets are all too imperfect governors of human behavior. The unfortunate truth is that financial crises, which are occurring with increasing, not decreasing, frequency are the result of deeply embedded traits of human nature and recurring failures to regulate our worst instincts. Two-and-a-half centuries after Adam Smith, mankind still needs to be protected from itself.

One of the frustrating lessons of markets is that investors continually ignore Groucho Marx's sage advice not to join any club that would accept them as members. Financial markets should often be avoided entirely, but investors cannot help themselves when they see everyone around them clamoring to participate. Today's markets are obviously far different from the more intimate ones that Smith walked in eighteenth-century Kirkcaldy, Glasgow, and Edinburgh. The products and economic actors he described—butchers and bakers, pin and woolen coat makers—vividly captured his frame of reference. Smith had personal, first-hand interactions with the men and women hawking their wares in these teeming and chaotic markets that somehow organized themselves into institutions that made food, clothing, and other goods available to Scottish society.

Today, the trading of goods has been replaced by the trading of bytes, and the personal relationships that defined mercantile relationships in the eighteenth century are abraded by technology and radical changes in the forms that capital assumes. But at the heart of these markets still lie the personal and social relationships between human beings that Adam Smith identified as the central feature of all human institutions. It is incumbent upon us today to take his wisdom and apply it to the new outward forms that markets assume with the understanding that the essential inward forms that drive markets are still governed by human relationships.

The Fallacy of Composition

Another aspect of Adam Smith's view of how moral sentiments develop raises another set of challenges for promoters of free markets. Smith's description of men developing their moral senses in *The Theory of Moral Sentiments* tells a story of trial and error:

> In order to produce this concord [of sentiments], as nature teaches the spectators to assume the circumstances of the person principally concerned, so she teaches this last in some measure to assume those of the spectators. As they are continually placing themselves in his situation, and thence conceiving emotions similar to what he feels; so he is as constantly placing himself in theirs, and thence conceiving some degree of that coolness about his own fortune, with which he is sensible that they will view it. As they are constantly considering what they themselves would feel, if they actually were the sufferers, so he is constantly led to imagine in what manner he would be affected if he was only one of the spectators of his own situation. As their sympathy makes them look at it in some measure with his eyes, so his sympathy makes him look at it, in some measure, with theirs, especially when in their presence, and acting under their observation: and, as the reflected passion which he thus conceives is much weaker than the original one, it necessarily abates the violence of what he felt before he came into their presence, before he began to recollect in what manner they would be affected by it, and to view his situation in this candid and impartial light.[15]

Rather than beginning from a set of general rules, the rules of morality are developed from the experience of observing other people and accepting and rejecting the reactions to these observations. This is very similar to Smith's description of how markets develop in *The Wealth of*

Nations, as Professor James R. Otteson argues very persuasively in *Adam Smith's Marketplace of Life.* Professor Otteson writes that Smith's view of human nature:

> [S]hows human morality to display four central substantive characteristics: it is a system that rises unintentionally from the actions of individuals, it displays an unconscious and slow development from informal to formal as needs and interests change and progress, it depends on regular exchange among freely associating people, and it receives its initial and ongoing impetus from the desires of the people who use it. But this account also adheres to a framework that . . . has the central elements of a system of unintended order modeled on an economic market.[16]

This process of observation and imitation leads human beings to adapt their behavior over time into modes that allow them to work together and build a functioning society. It is a process that is basic to many complex living systems.

In fact, Smith's view of the development of human morality is very similar to the process of self-organizing criticality described by Stuart Kauffman in his brilliant book on the organization of complex systems, *At Home in the Universe.* Kauffman argues that:

> Laws of complexity spontaneously generate much of the order of the natural world. . . . We have all known that simple physical systems exhibit spontaneous order: an oil droplet in water forms a sphere; snowflakes exhibit their evanescent sixfold symmetry. What is new is that the range of spontaneous order is enormously greater than we have supposed. Profound order is being discovered in large, complex, and apparently random systems. I believe that this emergent order underlies not only the origin of life itself, but much of the order seen in organisms today.[17]

Kauffman then describes some of the broad processes of natural life that he believes are echoed in economic systems.

> Life, then, unrolls in an unending procession of change, with small and large bursts of speciations, and small and large bursts of extinctions, ringing out the old, ringing in the new. If this view is correct, then

the patterns of life's bursts and burials are caused by internal processes, endogenous and natural. These patterns of speciations and extinctions, avalanching across ecosystems and time, are somehow self-organized, somehow collective emergent phenomena, somehow natural expressions of the laws of complexity we seek. . . . No small matter these small and large avalanches of creativity and destruction, for the natural history of life for the past 550 million years has echoes of the same phenomena at all levels: from ecosystems to economic systems undergoing technological evolution, in which avalanches of new goods and technologies emerge and drive old ones extinct.[18]

His conclusion is that "the fate of all complex adapting systems in the biosphere—from single cells to economies—is to evolve to a natural state between order and chaos, a grand compromise between structure and surprise."[19] If this is, in fact, the way societies and markets evolve—and there is a great deal of evidence that this is the case—then these insights are extremely important for our understanding of financial crises, our approaches to managing them, and our hopes of preventing them or at least of mitigating the permanent damage they inflict.

Financial markets in a capitalist system are marked by constant change and adaptability at every level of operation. The creation of new financial products is often a response to a market inefficiency that can be exploited for profit. Sometimes that market inefficiency results from regulation, and other times from changes in the nonfinancial economy. But market changes begin with the actions of individual economic actors who are seeking to solve a problem and, in a capitalist system, earn a profit at the same time. Individual economic actors behave based on their view of their own self-interest. There is a strong pro-cyclical, or path dependent, character to this activity. This is the essence of capitalism. Smith's and Kauffman's views of human processes and markets seem to describe the type of pro-cyclical behavior that sows the seeds of financial crises.

The problem is that this regime runs into something known as the "fallacy of composition," which teaches us that the sum of individual decisions often does not add up to a beneficial result for the system as a whole. In fact, individual decisions that can be shown to be rational when considered individually often tend to lead to disastrous results when aggregated. Again, these results should not be surprising; in fact, they are predictable if you know where to look for the warning signs. In economic terms, this phenomenon is closely associated with pro-cyclical behavior, which reinforces the existing direction of economic forces and markets. The classic example of the "fallacy of composition" was described by John Maynard Keynes in *The General Theory*, where he described how the rational behavior of individuals reducing their spending during an economic downturn will exacerbate that downturn and potentially lead to a depression (this is famously known as "the paradox of thrift"). In a market in which individuals are free to make their own decisions based on their self-interest, decisions based on rational individual profit motives (which are generally reasonably short-term in nature) ultimately tend to lead to instability rather than stability when they are aggregated. In certain respects this is also the great lesson of the economist Hyman Minsky, who taught that stability breeds instability. When the economy and the financial markets appear to be stable, it is perfectly rational for investors to feel that it is prudent to take more risk. The problem lies in the fact that everybody tends to increase their risk appetite at the same time, which raises overall systemic risk to dangerous levels. In fact, history demonstrates repeatedly that risk at any time should only be increased cautiously because many other people are likely to be increasing theirs at the same time, magnifying the overall risk context in which the individual decisions are being made.

Investment contrarians fancy themselves capable of separating themselves from the crowd and investing in an anticyclical manner. In today's world, however, where investments are driven by computerized money flows and quantitative investment strategies, it has become more difficult than ever to separate oneself from the crowd logistically even if one can do so psychologically. Larger investment portfolios, in particular, are captive to market movements unless they exercise extraordinary vigilance in spotting pro-cyclical market behavior and structure their investments in a manner that allows them to liquidate positions easily. As 2008 demonstrated, few large portfolios are capable of doing so, which explains the similarity in negative performance that occurred during that *annus horribilis*. Only investors who were able to spot market excesses born of pro-cyclical investment behavior that were going on for years were able to defend themselves against the inevitable downward correlation of all asset classes that occurred when the markets could no longer sustain excessive valuations and leverage.

Karl Marx and the Origins of Opacity

It is unfortunate that many conservative thinkers dismiss the work of Karl Marx due to the damage it has caused in the hands of tyrants because it has a great deal to teach us about the system he criticized. There is a deep and bitter irony in the fact that this deep reader of man's economic nature—and arguably the most astute interpreter of capitalism despite the tragic misreadings his work has engendered— sits at the opposite end of the ideological spectrum from Adam Smith. But a careful reading of Adam Smith and Karl Marx shows that these two thinkers share much more than is commonly believed. As we pick up the pieces of a world economy that was almost destroyed by the credit crisis of 2008, Marx's stinging comment about history repeating itself first as tragedy and then as farce mocks capitalism's compulsion to repeat the mistakes of the past. Marx's economic theories are highly complex and go far beyond the concept of class struggle for which he is best known. Indeed, it would be difficult to discuss the death of capital without addressing one of capital's most important critics. Despite the proclivity on the part of conservative economic and political commentators to dismiss Marx as a crackpot, his writings offer profound insights into capitalism and capitalist processes. In fact, his work attracted more mainstream attention in the wake of the financial crisis.[20]

For the purposes of understanding how Western capitalism came to consume itself at the dawn of the twenty-first century, there are few better places to retreat than the writings of Marx. Three of Marx's insights are particularly worthy of note.

1. Marx's conception of capital as a process and not a static object, which renders capitalism a system filled with contradictions that render it highly dynamic and unstable.
2. Marx's conceptualization of money and monetary forms as fetishes— indirect expressions of underlying social and economic relations whose meaning is obscured and distorted by their mediation through the form of money in its increasingly complex and derivative forms.
3. Marx's insight that value is a highly changeable and unstable concept.

All three of these concepts bear on the increasingly complex forms that money assumed in the late twentieth and early twenty-first century. The more complex and opaque that forms of money became, the more unstable concepts of value (both economic and moral) also became. And with unstable value came not only unstable markets but a highly unstable economy.

Capital Is a Process, Not a Thing

Marx's major work, *Capital*, is a tough go for most modern readers. Perhaps the best way to approach this monstrously large and convoluted work is as a major intellectual and literary achievement that happens to discuss economics. One of Marx's recent biographers, Francis Wheen, suggests why this is appropriate: "By the time he wrote *Das Kapital*, [Marx] was pushing out beyond conventional prose into radical literary collage—juxtaposing voices and quotations from mythology and literature, from factory inspectors' reports and fairy tales, in the manner of Ezra Pound's *Cantos* or Eliot's *The Waste Land*. *Das Kapital* is as discordant as Schoenberg, as nightmarish as Kafka."[21] He could have added that the book is as encyclopedic and apocalyptic as the American masterpiece, *Moby Dick*. Just as Herman Melville's masterpiece swept away most of the American fiction that preceded it, *Capital* redefined most earlier economics treatises; after *Capital*, capitalism and economics never looked the same. The image that most often comes to mind when one thinks about Marx's description of capitalism in *Capital* is the "dark Satanic mills" described by the iconoclastic English poet and artist William Blake in his poem of the early 1800s, "Jerusalem." In Marx's vision, capitalism is a dark and evil force capable of metamorphosing from one form into another while enslaving the individual. In fact, one of capitalism's greatest strengths (and instabilities) is its flexibility, its ability to adapt to changing circumstances of history, politics, or geography.

One of Marx's key economic insights is that capital is a process and not a static object.[22] He describes capital variously as "value in process," "money in process," and "money which begets money."[23] As such, capital is constantly moving, constantly changing form, and therefore unstable. Marx writes that "[i]t comes out of circulation, enters into it again, preserves and multiplies itself within its circuit, comes back out of it with expanded bulk, and begins the same round ever afresh."[24] In Marx's formulation, the key characteristic of capital is that it is both money and commodity. "It [capital] . . . always remains money and always commodity. It is in every moment both of the moments which disappear into one another in circulation. But it is this only because it itself is a constantly self-renewing circular course of exchanges."[25] Marx terms commodities a form of "use value" (because they can actually be used or consumed to meet human needs such as hunger), while money is considered a form of "exchange value" (because it can be exchanged for other things of value but cannot itself be consumed to meet human needs).

Because capital assumes both the form of money and the form of commodity in Marx's world, it is an extremely complex phenomenon. Capital spends its existence moving between these two forms—money and commodity—in order to play its multiple roles in the economy. (At one point, Marx writes, "Capital is money; capital is commodities."[26]) As money, it is used as a mechanism of exchange, while as a commodity it is used in its physical form. The transition between these two forms is what we can think of as the liquidity function, and the degree to which the liquidity function is operating smoothly is taken as one indication of the health of markets and the economy.

Yet, as we saw from reading Adam Smith, liquidity can be a misleading sign of health. Just because economic actors are providing liquidity does not mean that the assumptions underlying their actions are justified. As individuals, they may be acting on assumptions that are perfectly reasonable with respect to their individual goals and aspirations. But when these atomized actions are aggregated, they alter the context in which those actions are taken and alter the original assumptions. Marx teaches us another way of understanding how the best laid plans of individuals can turn into the madness of crowds; he offers us a different angle into the "fallacy of composition." At times, the provision of liquidity is based on flawed understandings or assumptions about the relationship between capital's roles as money and commodity. Or, put another way, assumptions about the equivalence of the value of capital as money and capital as commodity are incorrect. Since most forms of exchange in an economy are mediated through the form of money, they are indirect and subject to distortion. This is what Keynes means when he says that "much can happen between the cup and the lip." Economic actors are dealing with inherently unstable referents precisely because they are referents and not the things in themselves (that is, the underlying commodities). And there is no way to avoid this existential condition.

Those who approach the markets from a quantitative standpoint and attempt to model market moves would do well to keep in mind Marx's fluid view of capital. The value of any financial instrument stays fixed for only a theoretical moment in time (basically the moment at which another party buys it), and stock or bond prices are merely approximations of what the underlying economic referent is worth. This is why economics is better thought of as philosophy or art than science or mathematics, and why even a proper understanding of these latter two disciplines must include a healthy dose of the former two. The presumption of precision that market pundits bring to bear on their predictions of market behavior is highly misleading and renders most market predictions mere palaver.

Our Fetish about Money

In Marx's formulation, money or exchange value (which again is just one form of capital) is itself a highly complex phenomenon. Man reduces different commodities to money in order to be able to exchange different commodities for each other. Money in this sense is a great equalizer or leveler of value. Money looks like a fixed object but represents something far more complex and dynamic. In Marx's world, money represents what he variously describes as "congealed labor" or "social hieroglyphics." What he means by this is that money is the tangible expression of the value that society places on the labor that created the commodity that is represented by money.[27] In this sense, labor is itself a form of capital, as noted in Chapter 2.

Marx developed the concept of the "fetishism of commodities" (der Fetischcharakter der Ware) to describe the manner in which commodities are transformed into money. Marx explains that "the products of labor become commodities, social things whose qualities are at once perceptible and imperceptible by the senses."[28] The relationships between human beings as economic actors exchanging goods assume the form of relations between physical objects. Marx continues.

[T]he existence of the things *qua* commodities, and the value-relation between the products of labor which stamps them as commodities, have absolutely no connection with their physical properties and with the material relations arising therefrom. There it is a definite social relation between men, that assumes, in their eyes, the fantastic form of a relation between things. In order, therefore, to find an analogy, we must have recourse to the mist-enveloped regions of the religious world. In that world the productions of the human brain appear as independent beings endowed with life, and entering into relation both with one another and with the human race.[29]

Money, the form that all economic exchanges ultimately assumes, is opaque; rather than reveal the underlying social relations that create value, it obscures them.

David Harvey, one of Marx's best modern readers, writes that "the way things appear to us in daily life can conceal as much as it can reveal about their social meaning."[30] Elsewhere, Harvey writes, "[m]oney and market exchange draws a veil over, 'masks' social relationships between things. This condition Marx calls 'the fetishism of commodities.' It is one of Marx's most compelling insights, for it poses the problem of how to interpret the real but nevertheless superficial relationships that we can readily observe in the market place in appropriate social terms."[31] The Polish philosopher Leszek Kolakowski elaborates, writing that "[t]his process whereby social relations masquerade as things or relations between things is the cause of human failure to understand the society in which we live. In exchanging goods for money men involuntarily accept the position that their own qualities, abilities, and efforts do not belong to them but somehow inhere in the objects they have created."[32] Fetishism, according to Kolakowski, describes "the inability of human beings to see their own products for what they are, and their unwitting consent to be enslaved by human power instead of wielding it."[33]

Marx was highly aware of the contradictory nature of the reality of economic life captured in the concept of fetishism. In *Capital*, he writes that "[i]t is ... just this ultimate money-form of the world of commodities that actually conceals, instead of disclosing, the social character of private labor, and the social relations between the individual producers."[34] In other words, the relationships between the individuals who created the commodities are expressed in the form of the commodities themselves. As a result, the underlying relationships—their meaning, their value, both economic and social—are obscured.

In a financial world of increasing opacity, where money assumes increasingly complex and derivative forms, Marx's insight deserves special attention. The crisis of 2008, where we discovered that the balance sheets of financial institutions were buried in complex financial derivatives whose value turned out to be highly unstable if not completely indeterminable, was the ultimate lesson in the fetishism of commodities. Money, "the fetish character of commodities," the physical embodiment of the labor that goes into producing physical things, whether they be crops or widgets, is the primary way in which society comes to a common expression or understanding about the value of material things. Money is the common denominator to which all economic objects are reduced. But when money assumes indecipherable forms, the economic system becomes destabilized. Moreover, the stability or instability of money becomes a measure of the stability or instability of a society on other levels—social, political, and cultural.

There are two types of monetary stability that bear on this issue: the stability of the value of money and the stability of the form of money. Modern markets altered the character of both. The forms of money have grown increasingly complex, primarily though not exclusively through the growth of financial derivatives that both complicate and obscure the meaning of money. Derivatives shake the stability and meaning of money. Instead of simple expressions of debt such as bonds, we have complex and indirect expressions of value such as credit default swaps and collateralized debt obligations. As noted above and as discussed elsewhere in this book, these types of derivatives are a striking example of the fetish of commodities. Even Marx could not have dreamed of a form of money more alienated from labor than these modern financial concoctions. Instead of simple legal tender, we have complex legal contracts that impose contradictory or poorly defined obligations on the parties and in which lenders and borrowers have virtually no connection with each other. Moreover, such financial constructs are the epitome of opacity; their value is not immediately apparent but can be established only after a series of complex calculations. But even that determination is an approximation, for those calculations are themselves subject to a series of mathematical assumptions (not objective certainties) such as present value, discount rate, correlation, and so forth. As a result, the ability to reach general agreement on value is fragile and rather than being scientific becomes highly susceptible to subjective judgment.

Trillions of dollars of financial instruments—stocks, bonds, loans, currencies, and derivatives thereof—are traded daily based on verbal agreements that are only later written down into enforceable legal contracts. It is a tribute to the strength of market customs and practices that it took as long as it did for this system to break down under the weight of new financial instruments whose novel formulations were sufficiently complex to finally disrupt long-established norms of conduct.

The Instability of Value

It should be no surprise, then, that modern markets have the potential to trade with far greater volatility than we have ever seen before. In a world where financial instruments are almost ridiculously complex and increasingly divorced from their underlying economic referents, the concept of what a financial instrument is worth is thrown into question to a greater degree than ever before. The advent of derivatives in particular throws the entire question of value into doubt, creating an opportunity for buyers and sellers to disagree to a wider extent than ever before on the clearing prices for trades. Just a few years before the 2008 financial crisis, Mark C. Taylor wrote a groundbreaking book, *Confidence Games: Money and Markets in a World without Redemption*, in which he predicted the nature of the crisis that drove markets to the edge:

> As derivatives became more abstract and the mathematical formulas for the trading programs more complex, markets began to lose contact with anything resembling the real economy. To any rational investor, it should have been clear that markets were becoming a precarious Ponzi scheme. Contrary to expectation, products originally developed to manage risk increased market volatility and thus intensified the very uncertainty investors were trying to avoid.[35]

The condition described by Taylor is simply an extension, or exaggeration, of something Marx identified. There is an inherent contradiction in a system that uses money to express value at the same time that it conceals the underlying basis of that value. This creates the opportunity for the users of money to place an incorrect value on the underlying referent.

Marx understood that "[t]he possibility . . . of quantitative incongruity between price and magnitude of value, or the deviation of the former from the latter, is inherent in the price-form itself."[36] He argued that "[t]his is no defect, but, on the contrary, admirably adapts the price-form to a mode of production whose inherent laws can impose themselves as the means of apparently lawless irregularities that compensate one another."[37] Further, "[t]he price-form . . . is not only compatible with the possibility of a quantitative incongruity between magnitude of value and price, i.e., between the former and its expression in money, but it may also conceal a qualitative inconsistency, so much so, that, although money is nothing but the value-form of commodities, price ceases altogether to express value."[38] Marx's words are particularly apposite in markets in crisis where buyers and sellers are effectively on strike, such as the credit markets in 2008. The problem Marx describes—the incompatibility between value and its form of expression—is exacerbated when the form that money assumes is no longer simple stocks or bonds but far more complex derivative contracts such as credit default swaps or collateral debt obligations. Such instruments are by their very nature more difficult to value due to their inherent complexity. Their value is buffeted on a real-time basis by a variety of factors.

Take the example of a credit default swap: Its value is affected by changes in interest rates, changes in the financial condition of the underlying corporate credit, changes in the financial condition of similar corporations and of the counterparties themselves, supply and demand factors in the market for corporate credit, general economic conditions, and numerous other factors. Moreover, the obligations of the two parties to the contract are defined by a contract that is theoretically standardized but is in practice often bespoke. Accordingly, the ability to agree on the value of such complex instruments is highly compromised. This is one of the prices we pay—in some markets a very high price—for the benefits provided by instruments that are designed to reduce risk by carving it up in ways that distribute it among different market participants. When one considers the complexity of such instruments within the context of what Marx teaches us about the instability of value, one might consider it a miracle that modern markets function at all. It is also a sign of the durability of Marx's thought that he still has so much to teach us today about capital and capitalism.

John Maynard Keynes

Reading *The General Theory of Employment, Interest and Money* (1936) should be sufficient to disabuse people of the dominant thought paradigms that have guided investors into serial investment disasters in recent years. The concepts of efficient markets or rational investors are rendered mincemeat in the hands of John Maynard Keynes, who writes with a flair that few before or after have been able to match. The irony is that his great wisdom about so many aspects of market behavior has also led to such grotesquely wrong conclusions about how to solve market crises and revive troubled economies. The Keynesian prescription for recovery involves doing more of what was done in the first place to create the crisis: governments spending, printing, and borrowing more money. This may solve the immediate crisis, but it creates long-term imbalances that must be resolved at some point in the future, either through currency devaluation, inflation, or other destabilizing economic and social processes. The problem is that nobody has come up with a viable short-term alternative to the Keynesian solution that does not involve swallowing some very distasteful short-term medicine: bank and business failures, high rates of unemployment, social upheaval, and similar distresses. In the midst of a crisis, Keynes' prescription makes sense as a means of preventing immediate economic calamity. But it leaves a much bigger mess to clean up in the long run.

Accordingly, Keynesianism is best limited to a prescription for crisis management. As Hyman Minsky stresses in his seminal study of the master, "[i]n 1936, when *The General Theory* appeared, the world was in the seventh year of the Great Depression."[39] The so-called "classical school of economics" had failed to predict the coming of the depression, and Keynes' work was an attempt to come up with both an explanation of the causes and proposed solutions. Keynes developed his economic insights within the context of a global collapse of unparalleled depth and duration. The real goal of economic policy should be to minimize the types of imbalances that lead to crisis in the first place, which requires a sophisticated understanding of the processes of capital and the behavior of capitalists.

A careful reading of *The General Theory* reveals that a book considered to be one of the great economic texts of all time is as much an economics treatise as a psychological primer on how investors behave and what this means for the market as a whole. While the book is filled with its fair share of economic jargon and mathematical formulas, it is primarily memorable for its passages describing human behavior. Perhaps this is what accounts for the fact that its lasting value lies more in its psychological insights into the markets and investor behavior than in its prescriptions for economic policy management. In fact, as noted earlier, its policy prescriptions tend to promulgate economic imbalances. The proper way to employ them proscriptively to reduce the boom and bust cycles of capitalism would be to apply them in a countercyclical manner outside of the crisis context for which they are primarily designed.

Keynes argues that emotion, not reason, is what dominates investment markets. The distinction he draws between speculation and productive investment is based on this view. Keynes defines "speculation" as "the activity of forecasting the psychology of the market" and "enterprise" as "the activity of forecasting the prospective yield of assets over their whole life."[40] Unfortunately, the more developed markets become, the more speculative they become because of the fact that market participants are primarily emotional animals. "As the organisation of investment markets improves," he writes, "the risk of the predominance of speculation . . . increase[s]."[41] Capitalism is highly unstable because it is inherently prone to the imbalances resulting from the fact that capitalists are driven by emotion rather than reason. "The social object of skilled investment should be to defeat the dark forces of time and ignorance which envelop our future. The actual, private object of the most skilled investment to-day is 'to beat the gun,' as the Americans so well express it, to outwit the crowd, and to pass the bad, or depreciating, half-crown to the other fellow."[42] In other words, the primary objective of investors is not to determine the fundamental value of an investment; rather, it is to determine what other investors think the value is.

In a famous passage, Keynes compares investing to a newspaper competition in which people have to choose the six prettiest faces out of a hundred photographs:

> [P]rofessional investment may be likened to those newspaper competitions in which the competitors have to pick out the six prettiest faces from a hundred photographs, the prize being awarded to the competitor whose choice most nearly corresponds to the average preferences of the competitors as a whole; so that each competitor has to pick, not those faces which he himself finds prettiest, but those which he thinks likeliest to catch the fancy of the other competitors, all of whom are looking at the problem from the same point of view. It is not a case of choosing those which, to the best of one's judgment, are really the prettiest, nor even those which average opinion genuinely thinks the prettiest. We have reached the third degree where we devote our intelligences to anticipating what average opinion expects the average opinion to be. And there are some, I believe, who practice the fourth, fifth, and higher degrees.[43]

All financial instruments, not merely stocks and bonds, are subject to this type of beauty contest in which the goal is to pick the most average-looking girl. Keynes writes with respect to interest rates: "the rate of interest is a highly psychological phenomenon ...The long-term market-rate of interest will depend, not only on the current policy of the monetary authority but also on market expectations concerning its future policy."[44] The problem arises when all the faces look pretty or ugly at the same time. At such times, all anchors of value are lost and men are left to the vagaries of the crowd to guide their behavior. The outcome is rarely favorable for individual investors or for the market as a whole.

Keynes' famous description of the "animal spirits" that drive financial markets captures his emphasis on the emotional component that he views as central to the investment process. This famous passage is worth quoting in its entirety:

> Even apart from the instability due to speculation, there is the instability due to the characteristic of human nature that a large proportion of our positive activities depend on spontaneous optimism rather than

on a mathematical expectation, whether moral or hedonistic or economic. Most, probably, of our decisions to do something positive, the full consequences of which will be drawn out over many days to come, can only be taken as a result of animal spirits—of a spontaneous urge to action rather than inaction, and not as the outcome of a weighted average of quantitative benefits multiplied by quantitative probabilities. Enterprise only pretends to itself to be mainly actuated by the statements in its own prospectus, however candid and sincere. Only a little more than an expedition to the South Pole, is it based on an exact calculation of benefits to come. Thus if the animal spirits are dimmed and the spontaneous optimism falters, leaving us to depend on nothing but a mathematical expectation, enterprise will fade and die—though fears of loss may have a basis no more reasonable than hopes of profit had before.[45]

Finally, he writes that "human decisions affecting the future, whether personal or political or economic, cannot depend on strict mathematical expectation, since the basis for making such calculations does not exist; and…it is our innate urge to activity which makes the wheels go round, our rational selves choosing between the alternatives as best we are able, calculating where we can, but often falling back for our motive on whim or sentiment or chance."[46] As insightful as these words are, we should also remember that they were written by the man on whom modern policymakers are relying to revive the global economy. Policymakers need to understand the entirety of Keynes' message, not just the parts that they want to hear in a quest for politically expedient solutions to intractable economic problems.

Perhaps Keynes' most significant insight into human behavior involves what he termed the "paradox of thrift," the phenomenon that is a version of the "fallacy of composition" discussed earlier. Keynes did not originate this phenomenon; it appears to date back to the 1714 allegorical poem "The Fable of the Bees," which Keynes quotes from rather extensively in Chapter 23 of *The General Theory* (who says there is no place for literature in economics—even mediocre literature?). This phenomenon turns on its head all concepts of rational behavior. It also renders most market theories useless in practice. The paradox of thrift holds that if too many people seek to save rather than spend money at one time, the economy will be starved of investment and consumption and economic growth will suffer. The paradox comes from the fact that saving rather than spending is believed to be a constructive activity, yet it leads to economic harm when engaged in by too many people at the same time. This is also true with respect to investment activity. When market conditions lead too many investors to sell at the same time, markets tends to fall rapidly and in some cases collapse. Individual selling decisions may well be rational and designed to protect capital, but when too many investors make such decisions at the same time it leads to massive market losses. Few if any of the classic investment theories such as Harry Markowitz's modern portfolio theory or William Sharpe's capital asset pricing model or the Black-Scholes model effectively capture this reality (or other discontinuities, which are admittedly difficult to capture in mathematical language). Moreover, mass selling has the psychological effect of causing panic and leading to further selling, another phenomenon for which the classic investment theories fail to account.

Throughout *The General Theory,* Keynes stresses the importance of human expectations in economics. In fact, he writes that "the part played by expectations in economic analysis" was one of three "perplexities" that most impeded the writing of his great book.[47] For Keynes, expectations about the future are everything. "During a boom," he writes, "the popular estimation of the magnitude of both these risks, both borrower's risk and lender's risk, is apt to become unusually and imprudently low."[48] Human beings tend to believe that the current state of affairs will continue, although their belief is not based on anything to which they can point. "In abnormal times in particular, when the hypothesis of an indefinite continuance of the existing state of affairs is less plausible than usual even though there are no express grounds to anticipate a definite change, the market will be subject to waves of optimistic and pessimistic sentiment, which are unreasoning and yet in a sense legitimate where no solid basis exists for a reasonable calculation."[49] This leads to the uncomfortable reality that whatever the models purport to tell us, markets tend to seize up when large numbers of investors decide to sell at the same time because "there is no such thing as liquidity of investment for the community as a whole."[50]

One dramatic example of this phenomenon occurred in 1998 when the hedge fund Long Term Capital Management collapsed. Investors suddenly discovered correlations among different asset classes for which their models had failed to account. This was largely due to the fact that these correlations arose from factors such as overlapping ownership of assets by a concentrated group of institutions and hedge funds, the use of exorbitant amounts of leverage by these holders to own these assets, and other factors that even Nobel Prize winning economists failed to grasp (probably because they were Nobel Prize winners!). These factors led investors to simultaneously sell positions that in theory should not have been correlated but in practice became instantly and highly correlated. One of Keynes' great strengths is that he didn't allow mathematical formulas to distract him from the human realities of investing. Hence, the famous adage that is attributed to him, "The market can stay irrational longer than you can stay solvent." In a world heading ever deeper into insolvency, such words should ring in our ears.

Hyman Minsky

The 2008 financial crisis did a great deal to revive the reputation of Hyman Minsky. The revival was long overdue. Minsky remains a grossly underappreciated thinker, but he understood and acknowledged the importance of those who preceded him. Minsky rightly considered Keynes' *The General Theory* to be one of the most important works of modern thought: "[i]f Keynes, along with Marx, Darwin, Freud, and Einstein, belongs in the pantheon of seminal thinkers who triggered modern intellectual revolutions, it is because of the contribution to economics, both as a science and as a relevant guide to public policy, that is contained in his *General Theory of Employment, Interest and Money*."[51] Minsky's work is based on his interpretation of Keynes, and it is difficult to read one today without reading the other.

Minsky is known for his "financial-instability hypothesis," which argues that stable economies sow the seeds of their own demise. Minsky traces this idea back to Keynes' thinking in *The General Theory*. Minsky explains that "implicit in [Keynes'] analysis is a view that a capitalist economy is fundamentally flawed." He continues:

> This flaw exists because the financial system necessary for capitalist vitality and vigor—which translates entrepreneurial animal spirits into effective demand for investment—contains the potential for runaway

expansion, powered by an investment boom. This runaway expansion is brought to a halt because accumulated financial changes render the financial system fragile, so that not unusual changes can trigger serious financial difficulties. Because Keynes arrived at his views on how a capitalist economy operates by examining problems of decision-making under conditions of intractable uncertainty, in his system, stability, even if it is the result of policy, is destabilizing. Even if policy succeeds in eliminating the waste of great depressions, the fundamental financial attributes of capitalism mean that periodic difficulties in constraining and then sustaining demand will ensue.[52]

Minsky traced his "financial-instability hypothesis" to Keynes, but there is an even deeper connection that links these two men's thinking. Keynes' focus on the importance of human expectations in the face of uncertainty strongly influenced Minsky's view of how economic actors react to conditions of financial stability.

Implicit in Minsky's "financial-instability hypothesis" is the assumption that economic actors conduct themselves based on how they feel about their economic environment. When they experience a stable environment, they are emboldened to take risk; when they experience instability and hardship, they tend to act more conservatively. These are primarily psychological reactions to their experiences, an exercise of their "animal spirits" as Keynes described them. These two great economists understood that economic behavior was human behavior, and, as such, was influenced by the forces that govern human beings—feelings and emotion. This relates their work back to Adam Smith, who believed that human beings acted in a certain manner in order to gain the approval of other people. Acting in a manner that gained other peoples' approval, Smith believed, would reinforce certain types of behavior that were conducive to the development of a fair and just society. The essentially social and psychological nature of all economic behavior then calls us back to Marx's criticism of capitalism. Marx believed that capitalism would fail because it insufficiently acknowledged the social and human components of labor and instead reduced human relations through the process of fetishism to relationships between things in the form of money. These four thinkers believed that human relationships and emotions lie at the heart of all capitalist processes. As we have learned often enough over the past two decades, any system that fails to adequately account for the human element that lies at the heart of all economic activity is prone to instability and potential failure.

Hyman Minsky was largely unknown outside the world of economic professionals until the financial crisis, although some observers such as PIMCO's Paul McCulley, *The Credit Bubble Bulletin*'s Doug Noland, GMO LLC's Jeremy Grantham, and I were writing about him for several years before his work came all too vividly to life in the summer of 2007.[53] Today everybody is a Minsky disciple—or should be. Those who were familiar with Minsky's work before the crisis were in the best position to predict the credit cataclysm that occurred. Minsky should now take his place next to John Maynard Keynes as one of the twentieth century's most important economic thinkers. Like those in the pantheon he joins, his contributions were inspired by his keen insights into noneconomic areas of thought such as human psychology.

The "financial-instability hypothesis" can be summarized as follows: The better things get, the better they are expected to continue to be. Human beings tend to extrapolate current conditions indefinitely into the future. Based on the assumption that positive economic conditions will continue, people let their guards down with respect to risk, which leads them to take more of it. As each individual takes more risk, the overall riskiness of the system increases. This is not an insight into economics; it is an insight into human behavior. Minsky did not require a degree in mathematics or physics to come up with his "financial-instability hypothesis"—what he possessed was keen insight into human nature and human psychology.

Minsky expounded on his theory at greatest length in his seminal work, *Stabilizing an Unstable Economy* (1986). Minsky divided the process of risk absorption into three phases. In the first phase, which he called "hedge finance," economic actors expect cash flows from their business operations to be sufficient to meet their obligations now and in the future. In the second phase, termed "speculative finance," economic actors do not expect cash flows from operations to be sufficient to meet all of their cash payment obligations, particularly their short-term obligations. In this phase, actors must roll over existing debt in order to remain solvent. The third phase, which was given the colorful and somewhat controversial name of "Ponzi finance," involves a situation in which economic actors know that they will not be able to meet their cash obligations through operations and will have to borrow to meet them. In this phase, additional debt must be raised in order to retain solvency.[54] Ponzi finance is the dominant characteristic of the global economy today. It is a decidedly unhealthy state of affairs.

The stability of an economy is determined by the mix of these three types of financing structures within it. Hedge finance structures are subject to the risk that business operations will not generate sufficient cash flows to meet future obligations. Speculative and Ponzi finance structures are not only subject to that risk but are vulnerable to a much more significant risk that is outside the control of individual businessmen—the risk that financial markets will become inhospitable and render it difficult to roll over existing debt or raise additional debt to meet future obligations. As Minsky writes, "[s]peculative and Ponzi units must issue debt in order to meet payments and commitments. This means that they must always meet the market. Furthermore, they are vulnerable to any disruption, in the form of transitory unfavorable financing terms, that may occur in financial markets."[55] For this reason, speculative and Ponzi finance structures are far riskier than hedge finance structures, and an economy whose composition is weighted more toward Ponzi financing rather than hedge financing is prone to instability.

Large Western economies became Ponzi economies by the mid-1990s. By the mid-2000s, conditions were so Ponzi-like that it was only a question of "when," not "if" the system would succumb to internal instability. From homebuyers who borrowed more than their homes were worth based on the belief that home prices would continue rising, to private equity firms that purchased companies at exorbitant prices using debt structures that enabled them to pay interest in additional debt rather than cash, the entire financial system was engaged in one massive Ponzi scheme in the sense that Hyman Minsky used the term. This does not mean that such financing schemes were fraudulent or illegal (although in the case of the mortgage market many reportedly were). It does mean, however, that in most cases they were imprudently or even recklessly constructed.

Minsky's use of the term Ponzi should not be glossed over. Minsky responded to harsh criticism of his use of the term in a long footnote to his seminal article titled, "The financial-instability hypothesis" (1982): "[t]he type of financial relations that I label Ponzi finance is a quite general and not necessarily fraudulent characteristic of a capitalist financial structure. Financial relations the validation of which depends on the selling out of positions are a normal functioning part of the capitalist process. Furthermore, every 'bubble' or stock-market speculation in which profitability depends on the timing of entry and exit is of the nature of a 'Ponzi scheme.'"[56] Recent commentators who have brought Minsky's work back to the prominence that it deserves have devoted little attention to Minsky's terminology, but it deserves further emphasis than it has received.

Minsky's use of the term "Ponzi" in describing the type of financial structure that grew predominant in the late twentieth and early twenty-first century should not be considered disingenuous. Ponzi is not a morally neutral word. It refers to Charles Ponzi, an infamous swindler who, for a short period in 1920, employed the technique of using money raised from later investors to repay earlier investors. He was not the first and certainly not the last crook to employ such a scheme, but his name stuck to it (although Bernie Madoff has offered himself as an alternative, with the new term "being Madoff'd" starting to sneak into modern vernacular). Minsky was making a point in using such a value-laden term, and despite his seemingly innocent disclaimer about his intent, there can be no question of his disapproval:

> However, the label attached to the financing relations I identify as Ponzi is not important. What is important is whether or not such structures exist and what effect such financing has on system behavior. In particular, if Ponzi financing exists, if the extent of Ponzi financing determines the domain of instability of the economy, and if Ponzi financing is a normal adjunct of investment production, then there are normally functioning endogenous factors that make for significant instabilities.[57]

Minsky's insight about Ponzi structures is of crucial importance in understanding modern capitalism. Ponzi finance is highly unstable; it is vulnerable not only to changes in conditions of borrowers, but to deterioration in market conditions. Ponzi finance is closely associated with financial instability. Describing such a state of affairs with a term associated with a swindler should not be understood as value neutral; it is a way of suggesting that such financing structures are irresponsible and immoral, even if they are not illegal. The fact that they lead to financial instability that causes social unrest, higher unemployment, a widening of the gap between rich and poor, and other adverse consequences suggests that such financing structures should be viewed as reckless and socially damaging. In his own deadpan way, this is what Minsky was trying to tell us.

Government policies that permit Ponzi finance to flourish end up imposing an enormous burden on society. This is why an increasing number of economists take issue with former Federal Reserve Chairman Alan Greenspan's view that a central bank should not take action with respect to a sharp increase in asset prices. In fact, Minsky teaches that it is not rising asset prices per se that should trigger countercyclical policy by central banks so much as the reasons behind the rise. If Ponzi finance structures are responsible for pushing prices higher, central banks should begin tightening policy and taking other steps to counter the process. Failing to take any action in the face of sharply rising asset prices that were being fed by an orgy of leverage in the form of Ponzi finance turned out to be a catastrophic error on Greenspan's part during his term, a mistake that was repeated by his successor Ben Bernanke during the first two years of his term and, after being interrupted by the financial crisis, were again perpetuated by the Janet Yellen-led Federal Reserve and other major central banks in the post-crisis years. Minsky's "financial-instability hypothesis" also renders highly dubious concepts such as "the great moderation" that Bernanke endorsed in advocating that the economy had reached a new era of stability in the mid-2000s. Bernanke promulgated this view in a widely noted speech in 2004 and again in a 2006 speech and clung to it until 2007. A careful reading of Minsky, however, would have led Bernanke to reach just the opposite conclusion—that benign economic conditions would lead, not to further stability, but to instability. This turned out to be a profound intellectual error as it led the Federal Reserve to follow a lax monetary policy for far too long.

It is one thing when manufacturing firms collapse under the weight of their debts and other obligations; their balance sheets can be restructured and their assets sold or liquidated in the process Joseph Schumpeter described as "creative destruction." The presumption is that more productive businesses will take their place in the economy. But when financial firms run into trouble because they cannot pay their debts, a larger societal interest is harmed because of the public utility function that financial institutions play in the economy. This is particularly true in regulated industries where the government has provided an explicit or implicit guarantee. The collapse of a financial firm leads to deflationary debt destruction as capital is wiped out. This leads to a loss of confidence among economic actors that leads to the death of capital. When that occurs, governments must act through their central banks and fulfill their functions as lenders of last resort. In 2008, conditions became so desperate that the world saw its central banks and governments perform this function in previously unimagined ways.

Lessons on Capital from the Masters

Smith, Marx, Keynes, and Minsky are deserving of a much more thorough examination than they have received here. The point of this discussion of their work is to draw out some common insights that these intellectual giants offer with respect to capital and capitalist processes. First, all of them consider capital and capitalism to be highly unstable phenomena that are subject to the emotions of economic actors in the marketplace. This renders markets themselves highly unstable and subject to cycles of boom and bust. Second, the unavoidable conclusion that reading these men's work leads to is that understanding capital, capitalism, and markets requires a deep understanding of human nature, in particular the irrational and emotional side of human nature. Mathematical understanding is of limited utility when it comes to navigating financial markets because the forces that drive these markets are not mathematical or rational in nature. Third, these four thinkers believe that capitalist processes bear within themselves the seeds of their own instability and potential destruction. The innate nature of capital and capitalism involves contradictions and conflicts that lead to instability. Further, mathematical and rational thinking often leads to instability and irrational outcomes. From a practical standpoint, this means that every bull market sows the seeds of its own demise, a lesson investors forget at their own peril.

Reading these seminal thinkers then raises the question about what one should think about the fact that so much of modern finance theory and market dogma is guided by belief in concepts such as efficient markets, quantitative finance, and other rational constructs that are repeatedly contradicted by the real world experience of investors. Why do investors ignore not only the best that has been thought about markets but their own experiences, and as a result repeatedly subject themselves to catastrophic losses? The answer lies in the fact that investors, who also happen to be human beings, cannot escape their essential nature. Emotion is such a powerful phenomenon precisely because it trumps reason. Men are made to believe that the future will resemble the past, and in some respects it does. But they tend to be extremely selective about which parts of the past they choose to remember.

As with so many complex systems, markets discovered in 2007 and 2008 that the tools designed to reduce risk introduced new risks that hadn't been contemplated before. Even worse, these risks were hidden by the complex and opaque nature of the new financial instruments that were sold as risk management tools. These products contained within them the seeds of their own demise because they were not in fact new creations but just another form of capital and subject to the same laws that always govern capital. If we are to contain the madness of crowds, we need to help them understand what is driving them insane. In uncovering the answer to this question, we learn that the fault lies not in the stars but in ourselves. For while every individual rationally pursues economic goals that he believes will enrich him or her, the aggregation of those individual desires tends to lead to instability. It is no accident, therefore, that each of the four thinkers discussed in this chapter emphasizes the important role played in the markets by the "fallacy of composition." Cycles of boom and bust will remain with us as long as we remain human. Try as we might to remove the human element from economics, the dismal science remains in its essence trapped by who we are.

CHAPTER 4

Empty Promises

A t the heart of Adam Smith's admonition that society should strive to be just is the concept of debt not purely in a financial sense but also in a philosophical and moral sense. Every economic transaction involves an exchange of value between two parties. But it also involves an exchange of promises. Two parties undertake obligations to each other. One party offers something to another party, and this gives rise to an obligation by the other party to give something back. Smith was seeking to outline the types of institutional arrangements that would ensure that such exchanges are fair to both parties, or as fair as possible within the exigencies of human society. He was asking the question: What do human beings owe each other? What is a debt? What is an obligation? How do we balance the scales between people as evenly as possible?

Promises Aren't What They Used to Be

Any discussion of the modern financial system, the disarray into which it was thrown in 2008, and the threats it faces after years of failed post-crisis policies must confront the overwhelming role that debt plays in virtually all financial arrangements. Among the most significant changes in the global economy in the three decades leading up to the financial crisis—particularly in the United States and other Western economies—was the incredible increase in indebtedness at all levels of society. Between 1980 and 2008, the share of household and consumer debt alone increased from 100 percent of the U.S. GDP to 173 percent, an increase of approximately $6 trillion.[1] The debt balloon expanded until it literally burst. The growth of debt financing and the increasing sub-stitution of debt for equity in corporate capital structures and personal balance sheets became the gravamen of our age. This debt explosion accelerated after the crisis with total global debt reaching $199 trillion in 2014 according to the McKinsey Global Institute.[2] We cannot under-stand our economy or our society until we understand how central debt is both economically and culturally. In order to properly discuss debt, we need to understand the essential role that promissory arrangements play in every financial instrument or transaction known to man.

Every financial instrument involves some type of promise. Whether it is called a stock or a bond, equity or debt, an insurance policy or a pension trust, an option or a futures contract, every financial instrument involves a payment or promise of payment of money in exchange for a promise of future receipts. Sometimes that promise of future payment is contingent, as in the case of an equity security. In other cases, the promise is contrac-tually certain, as in the case of a debt obligation like a bond or a bank loan, or in the unhappy case of a life insurance contract. The primary difference between debt and equity is the degree of certainty and the time horizon (fixed or uncertain) over which that the promise will be kept.

Any type of promise implies a belief in the future. Promises are by their nature a sign of optimism. Equity promises are more contingent than debt promises, so perhaps they denote the greatest degree of opti-mism of all financial instruments. In a leveraged capital structure, all of the debt is effectively a form of equity since there is a significant risk that it will not be repaid. Equity demands a higher return than debt because of this high degree of uncertainty regarding repayment. The forms that our financial promises assume say a great deal about our expectations about the future, not only economically, but philosophically, psychologically, and culturally.

In recent years, the traditional differences between debt and equity became blurred as leverage became an increasingly dominant component of the economy's and corporations' capital structures. Financial innovation created new forms of capital such as new types of preferred stock and convertible debt that combine the attributes of debt and equity. Many derivative instruments also combine debt and equity features. High yield bonds (corporate debt obligations rated less than investment grade by the major rating agencies) are another type of security that combine the attributes of debt and equity. The high yield bond market exploded in size since its founding in the 1980s. Today, these bonds constitute a significant component of the capital structures of many U.S. and European corporations (and post-crisis are becoming more common in Asia). While they are considered debt, however, high yield bonds are not really debt at all. Instead, they are in reality a hybrid debt/equity security that is best described as "equity with a coupon" that poses a high risk of default.

This conflation of debt and equity is one reason why traditional correlations between asset classes are breaking down. While traditional portfolio theory teaches that the returns on bonds and stocks should not correlate in certain types of economic environments, recent experience demonstrates that the returns on these different asset classes in fact correlate very strongly, particularly in extreme market conditions. This should not be surprising in view of the fact that these asset classes increasingly resemble each other in their constituent parts. The different debt and equity layers of a leveraged capital structure—which describes the vast majority of corporations in the United States and Europe—should logically trade in tandem as the financial condition of the underlying business improves or deteriorates. There is no rational reason why a leveraged company's debt and equity should react any differently to positive or negative news about the business's prospects. The fact that the stock of a bankrupt company can trade above zero while its debt trades well below par value remains one of the abiding anomalies of the financial markets, one that is best explained by the adage that markets don't have to work in theory but have no choice but to work in practice.

As the forms of debt and equity have changed, so have the guises in which financial promises travel. First, as noted above, debt rather than equity became the predominant form of capital in circulation. Second, the structures in which debt appears became increasingly complex and opaque and organized in a manner that ruptured the relationship between borrowers and lenders. These changes radically transformed the economy on both a local and global level and served as both cause and consequence of profound changes in our values and expectations.

The fact that debt came to play such a dominant role in our economy says a great deal about our values and beliefs as a society. By choosing to use debt as the dominant medium of exchange, we are telling each other that we trust each other. We are saying that we will keep our promises. We are confirming that our words have common meanings, that we speak a common language, and that we follow a common set of rules. More than anything, we are also affirming our belief in the future. We are telling each other that the world will continue to prosper and grow and that we will do everything reasonably necessary to ensure that happens. Most important, we are counting on the fact that future conditions will be sufficiently robust to allow this debt to be repaid.

But the world keeps minting new debt to an amount that it can never reasonably hope to repay. In view of the inconceivably large volume of global debt that exists in 2016, the underlying code of trust on which debt is based is likely to be called into question in the years ahead, posing serious threats not only to economic but to social and cultural stability. At the heart of every debt obligation lie two promises: a lender promises to lend money to a borrower, and a borrower promises to repay that money (with interest) to the lender. In today's highly complex economy, modern debt obligations such as bonds or bank loans include an additional web of detailed legal promises known as "covenants" that govern the behavior of the borrower and the lender. These covenants require the borrower to conduct its business in a certain way as a condition for accepting the loan. For example, the borrower agrees not to incur additional debt, or not to pay dividends to its shareholders, or agrees to make regularly scheduled financial reports to the borrower. As long as the borrower keeps these promises, the lender promises to stand aside and allow the borrower to manage its affairs as it sees fit.

In 2008, Martin Wolf, the chief economic commentator for the *Financial Times*, wrote that "the central feature of the financial system... [is that] it is a pyramid of promises—often promises of long or even indefinite duration. This makes it remarkable that sophisticated financial systems exist.... Promises may not be kept."[3] Continuing, Wolf described the trillions of dollars of outstanding financial assets as "promises of future, of often contingent, receipts in return for current payment.... As the financial system grows more complex, it piles promises upon promises."[4] Promises are by their very nature uncertain in their fulfillment. Promises also contain a temporal element—they are executory in nature. As such, they are subject to the contingencies of time and human nature.

When we make a promise to another person, that person is depending on the fact that nothing will change (or change sufficiently) in the intervening time to alter our commitment and ability to keep our word. Yet the world is filled with changing circumstances that may affect our ability or willingness to keep our promises. As all of us know, the only certainty in life is change. So promises are, by their nature, highly contingent. In many respects, making a promise or accepting a promise is a great leap of faith. It denotes a commitment by the party making the promise, and trust by the party receiving the promise. In the global economy, trillions of promises big and small are made every day. While these promises are being made, circumstances both internal and external to the parties making them are changing, sometimes radically. Few of these changing circumstances make it easier for promises to be kept. Most of the time, reality is working to give people reasons or excuses to break, or amend, their promises. It is no small miracle that so many promises are ultimately kept. Large and complex financial transactions involve such a large number of complicated promises (both internal, such as the commitments of the parties, and external, such as the multifarious laws and regulations that must be satisfied) that it is miraculous that so many transactions get consummated at all.

The Digitalization of Promises

In recent years, the forms of debt, and therefore the character of our promises, have been drastically altered by the application of computer technology and advanced mathematics to traditional financial instruments such as bonds, mortgage loans, and corporate loans. The digitalization of financial information that was made possible by the computer chip ushered in a revolution in finance that profoundly altered the relationship between lenders and borrowers. The primary change it wrought was severing the personal connection that traditionally existed between the two parties to a loan. Instead of going down to the local bank and obtaining a mortgage from a banker with whom he or she has a personal relationship, today's homeowner enters a transaction with a faceless corporation. This impersonal corporate entity finances the most important financial transaction the borrower will likely enter into in his lifetime and is granted enormous power over the borrower's financial future. In effect, this regime creates a system of debts without promises, which in many respects is an oxymoron, or a system of impersonal promises, which is also a contradiction in terms. A recognition that many of the obligations created by modern finance are empty promises will help us to better understand the nature of the promises economic actors are now expected to keep, why they are harder to keep (or easier to break) than promises made in earlier times, and why this renders the financial sector increasingly unstable and vulnerable to periodic crises.

Today, all financial data is capable of being digitalized. When data is digitalized, it is reduced to 1s and 0s. This means that every financial instrument is reduced to the same basic constituent parts. The differences between various types of debt obligations, such as mortgages, automobile loans, or bank loans, are effectively erased by this process. The ramifications of this transformation of different financial instruments into their constituent elements are truly revolutionary. On a practical level, it became possible to analyze, manipulate, and stress-test voluminous amounts of financial data in relatively short periods of time. Lending decisions that used to be based, at least in part, on a personal relationship between a lender and a borrower instead came to rely on computer-based underwriting systems that substituted credit scores for human judgment. Among other things, this led to profound intellectual errors involving the use of flawed financial models that failed to consider whether the data was being tested against proper benchmarks.

The digitalization of information made possible the phenomenon that came to be known as "securitization." This process involved the bundling of hundreds or thousands of individual mortgages into special purpose entities that could then be sold to institutional investors. Securitization dramatically increased the distance between individual borrowers and their lenders. Securitizations were effected through the formation of special purpose investment vehicles (i.e., corporations or limited liabilities companies) that were normally formed in a tax-favored jurisdiction like the Cayman Islands. The capital structures of these entities were divided into different pieces (Wall Street adopted the French word *tranche* to describe these different pieces) that were piled on top of each other and given descending credit ratings from AAA to BB with an unrated bottom tranche of equity.

Figure 4.1 compares the traditional model of credit (on the top of the figure) with the much more complex securitized model of credit (on the bottom of the figure). By the time the financial engineers were done, we sure weren't in Kansas anymore.

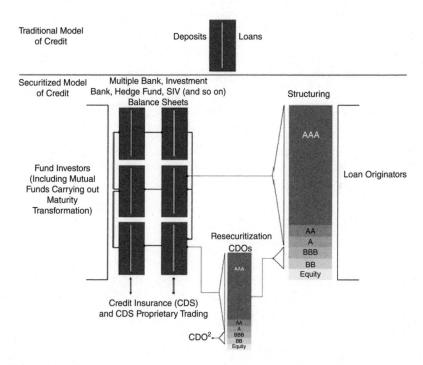

Figure 4.1   Increasing Complexity of Securitized Credit Model

Collateralized Mortgage Obligations

In the case of mortgages, these products were called collateralized mortgage obligations (CMOs). The theory behind CMOs was that a geographically diversified pool of mortgages would have a low risk of default because real estate is local in nature and heavily influenced by local economic conditions. Moreover, these entities were considered to be overcollateralized in the sense that there was believed to be more aggregate collateral (more mortgages) than necessary to repay each of the rated tranches and to produce an attractive return to the equity (bottom) tranche.

Both of these assumptions turned out to be woefully wrong. First, while real estate is local, the sale of the ultimate debt to financial institutions that are linked together in global markets eradicated the local nature of the underlying investment. Creators of CMOs should have been looking at the capital sources (i.e., the buyers of the debt issued by the CMOs), not the underlying borrowers, in seeking the protection ostensibly provided by diversification.[5] Second, the underlying mortgages turned out—particularly with respect to subprime and Alt-A borrowers—to be worth far less than their face amount during the historic housing market collapse that began in 2006. Credit insurance contracts written on these types of products rendered insurance giant AIG insolvent and in need of a government bailout in 2008.

Compared to the traditional model of credit (a simple lender/borrower relationship), the securitized model of credit introduced an enormous amount of complexity into the mix. To illustrate just how complex these concoctions became, we will first look at an example of a basic CMO and then jump to a more complicated real-world example that should make readers' heads spin.

Figure 4.2 shows the structure of a basic CMO. Very few if any such structures exist in the real world today, although in the early years of the market deals generally had a limited number of tranches like the one in the figure. CMOs are generally designed so that payments on the underlying mortgages are applied sequentially from the top tranche to the bottom tranche through the life of the deal. The bottom tranche is unrated and considered equity because it assumes the first risk of loss when mortgages in the pool default.

Tranche	Par Amount
A	$194,500,000
B	36,000,000
C	96,500,000
Z-accrual	73,000,000
	$400,000,000

Figure 4.2 Basic CMO Structure
SOURCE: Frank S. Fabozzi, *Fixed Income Analysis*, 2nd ed. (Hoboken, NJ: John Wiley & Sons, 2007), 278.

One of Wall Street's basic business principles is to introduce complexity into its products so it can obscure what it is really selling. CMOs, however, set new standards for complexity (topped only when credit default swaps came along and began to be used to provide insurance on the different tranches of CMOs, a topic discussed in Chapter 6). From the perspective of the manager of a CMO, these products often function like Rubik's Cubes due to the complex web of covenants with which they must comply. Every time the manager wants to buy or sell a new mortgage, he must run that mortgage through a complex model to insure that all of the multiple covenants governing the CMO remain in compliance.

To give readers a flavor of how complex these instruments became, Figure 4.3 shows the structure of an actual CMO issued in 1994 that issued 17 different tranches of debt.

In view of the fact that Figure 4.3 was typical of the actual types of instruments that regulators were trying to decipher in the midst of the financial crisis, it is a miracle that the system survived at all. This complexity makes it extremely doubtful that regulators can even begin to understand these types of investments before being able to determine whether they might cause systemic threats. It required several years to unwind these structures after the crisis (and many of them were still being unwound as of early 2016).

One issue with respect to all of these increasingly complex derivative concoctions is the degree of separation between the underlying borrower and the ultimate lender. As the forms of these contracts became increasingly convoluted, the relationship between borrower and lender became increasingly attenuated. Promisor and promisee (borrower and lender) basically had no relationship with each other but were instead connected through a chain of contracts that removed any

Total Issue: $300,000,000

Issue Date: 2/18/94

Original Settlement Date:
3/30/94

Tranche	Original Balance ($)	Coupon (%)	Average Life (yrs)
A (PAC Bond)	24,600,000	4.50	1.3
B (PAC Bond)	11,100,000	5.00	2.5
C (PAC Bond)	25,500,000	5.25	3.5
D (PAC Bond)	9,150,000	5.65	4.5
E (PAC Bond)	31,650,000	6.00	5.8
G (PAC Bond)	30,750,000	6.25	7.9
H (PAC Bond)	27,450,000	6.50	10.9
J (PAC Bond)	5,220,000	6.50	14.4
K (PAC Bond)	7,612,000	7.00	18.4
LA (SCH Bond)	26,673,000	7.00	3.5
LB (SCH Bond)	36,087,000	7.00	3.5
M (SCH Bond)	18,738,000	7.00	11.2
O (TAC Bond)	13,348,000	7.00	2.5
OA (TAC Bond)	3,600,000	7.00	7.2
IA (IO, PAC Bond)	30,246,000	7.00	7.1
PF (FLTR, Support Bond)	21,016,000	6.75*	17.5
PS (INV FLTR, Support Bond)	7,506,000	7.70*	17.5

* Coupon at issuance.

Structural Features

Cash Flow Allocation: Commencing on the first principal payment date of the Class A Bonds, principal equal to the amount specified in the Prospectus will be applied to the Class A, B, C, D, E, G, H, ,J, K, LB, M, O, OA, PF and PS Bonds. After all other Classes have been retired, any remaining principal will be used to retire the Class O, OA, IA, IB, M, A, B, C, D, G, H, J and K Bonds. The notional Class IA Bond will have its notional principal amount retired along with the PAC Bonds.

Other: The PAC Range is 95% to 300% PSA for the A–K Bonds, 190% to 250% PSA for the LA, LB and M Bonds, and 225% PSA for the O and OA Bonds.

Figure 4.3 Summary of Federal Home Loan Mortgage Corporation—Multiclass Mortgage Participation Certificates

SOURCE: Frank S. Fabozzi, *Fixed Income Analysis*, 2nd ed. (Hoboken, NJ: John Wiley & Sons, 2007), 278.

meaningful promissory connection from their relationship. In really exotic structures, like some of the ones that brought insurance giant AIG to its knees, credit default swaps were tied to individual tranches of collateralized debt obligations (CDOs) that themselves consisted of pools of underlying obligations in other CDOs (these are known as CDO-squareds). In such structures, the distance between the lender and ultimate borrower was so attenuated that they might as well have been circulating in different galaxies.

The distance between the individual mortgage borrower and the ultimate investor in a CMO is illustrated in Figure 4.4.

Figure 4.4 is intended to show the structure of a typical transaction. The process begins when a group of mortgages are packaged together, which occurs on the far left hand side of the diagram. Individual borrowers are aggregated into a pool of borrowers by the originator, who then sells this portfolio to a special purpose vehicle, which is the CMO itself. The CMO then sells rated tranches of debt to investors in order to fund the purchase of these assets. In the real world, these two steps basically occur simultaneously. The original borrower is found all the way on the far left-hand side of the diagram, and the ultimate lender is found all the way on the right side. We are a long way from going to the local bank to get a loan from your friendly neighborhood banker. Figure 4.4 illustrates why CMOs and other types of CDOs are the ultimate fetish instrument (borrowing from Marx's terminology). The actual CDO tranches that are sold to investors are completely untethered from the underlying human and economic obligations on which they are based, and create an enormous distance between the ultimate lenders and the actual borrowers who must repay the loans.

This raises important questions about how to determine the value of these instruments, because one of the key points about fetish instruments is that they obscure rather than reveal the relationships that support them. As discussed in Chapter 2, money is already one step removed from the commodities whose value it represents. As money assumes increasingly complex forms, its relationship with these commodities becomes increasingly complicated and obscured. The value of a stock or bond, which are just two of the virtually unlimited forms of capital in circulation today, is determined by a complex group of factors because these securities are representations of complex underlying

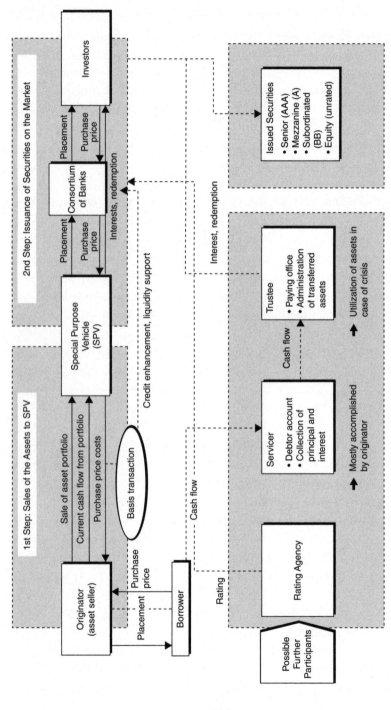

Figure 4.4 Degrees of Separation

SOURCE: Andreas A. Jobst, *Collateralized Loan Obligations (CLOs): A Primer*, London School of Economics and Political Science, Financial Markets Group, 2003.

economic relationships. As the forms of money grow increasingly complex, it becomes more and more difficult to determine their value. By the time we reach complex derivative instruments, which are sophisticated legal contracts with many moving parts, the determination of value is almost forbiddingly difficult and requires as much art as mathematics. The liquidity function, which is the ultimate arbiter of value in market economies, is strongly influenced by the form that money assumes. For this reason, complex derivatives are necessarily far less liquid than more simple forms of money like stocks and bonds.

CMOs were constructed using several assumptions that were expected to work in theory but failed miserably in practice. The first assumption was that diversification of the underlying portfolio by property type and location would minimize losses based on the belief that these varying property types would not behave the same way (in terms of price) in an economic downturn. In point of fact, virtually all real estate prices correlated downward—sharply downward—when the real estate bubble burst beginning in 2006. Why did this happen? This is where things got interesting. As noted earlier, the very fact that so many properties became securitized rendered obsolete the age-old real estate adage that "all real estate is local." Securitization rendered all real estate, regardless of its physical location, local, because its ultimate ownership became vested in CMO debt tranches owned by institutional investors. These investors were spread throughout the global financial system rather than located inside local banks whose financial fortunes were closely tied to the local communities near the properties. The money that made it possible to bid up real estate prices in local markets in states like Florida, Arizona, and California no longer originated in those states but instead came from financial centers in Europe and Asia (and even, remarkably, Iceland) where the rated tranches of CMOs were sold. The globalization of the real estate market was the logical outcome of the sundering of the promissory relationship between lender and borrower, but the ramifications were far more profound than a borrower's inability to maintain a personal relationship with his or her lender. Rather than spreading risk, securitization concentrated it among a group of electronically linked investors subject to herd-like behavior.

The second erroneous assumption used to promote CMOs was the belief that a man's house is his castle, that he will do anything to defend it (in modern times this has come to mean he will do anything to prevent being kicked out of it by his lender), and it is therefore a sound credit risk. In fact, just the opposite was true. As the economist Robert Shiller points out, "[a] home represents a highly leveraged exposure to a single, stationary plot of real estate—about the riskiest asset one can imagine."[6] Moreover, the riskiness of this asset was increased when lending standards were tossed out the window by subprime lenders who engaged in some of the most reckless lending practices one can imagine. For example, NINJA loans were extended to borrowers with no jobs, no income, and no assets; other loans were extended in amounts that exceeded the value of the underlying properties. The thought that combining hundreds or thousands of highly risky assets into one big pile of risky assets would somehow reduce overall risk actually should have been highly counterintuitive. Yet this was precisely the conclusion that was reached by teams of highly educated mathematicians who apparently were so caught up in their theories and equations that they forgot to apply any common sense to their work. One can concede, for the sake of argument, that it is a rare individual who possesses both the advanced mathematical talents required to design and analyze complex financial instruments and deep knowledge of the financial markets in which those instruments will be traded. But the firms that sold hundreds of billions of dollars of these products certainly possessed inside their walls the combination of talents that should have been brought to bear on the validity of the basic assumptions underlying the CMO financial models. But instead of acting as a series of checks and balances, the different parts of these firms appeared to reinforce reckless behavior rather than rein it in.

A third flawed assumption involved the wholesale dependence on FICO scores to measure the creditworthiness of borrowers. Moody's Investors Service and Standard & Poor's, the two agencies whose ratings were required for CMOs to sell debt to investors, used FICO scores to evaluate the creditworthiness of the underlying borrowers in these deals. FICO scores are credit rating scores that are generated by Fair Isaac Corp. of Minneapolis, Minnesota, that evaluate a person's creditworthiness. The rating agencies (as well as underwriters and investors) failed to take into account the fact that FICO scores had not been in existence during previous recessions. As a result, these scores were incapable of providing accurate predictions of consumer behavior during a sharp housing downturn. Rating agencies interpreted data without any reference to historical context. By accepting past data at its face value and failing to adjust it for changes in economic conditions, the rating agencies ended up issuing wildly flawed ratings on hundreds of billions of dollars of CMOs. The rest, as they say, is history, but history as nightmare.

HSBC Drinks the Mortgage Kool-Aid

The folly of this type of thinking was illustrated by what happened when London-based HSBC Holdings PLC, one of the world's largest banks with operations in 76 countries and territories, joined the subprime party with its 2003 acquisition of Household International, Inc. Household was a large subprime lender based in Prospect Heights, Illinois, the heart of the United States. Less than four years later, in February 2007, the 142-year-old British banking giant announced that it was adding $1.7 billion to its loan reserves to account for losses in its subprime mortgage portfolio. But that was only the beginning. Before the subprime crisis was over, HSBC would suffer many more billions of dollars of losses from the work of its clever finance doctorates.

The business that HSBC acquired from Household focused on second lien loans, sometimes known as "piggyback loans." These loans allowed a buyer to combine a bigger mortgage from a first mortgagor with a second lien from a second lender into an amount that often exceeded 100 percent of the purchase price of a home. In the event of default, the second lien holder would only be paid off after the first mortgage was satisfied. For this reason, second liens paid higher interest rates than first liens and were ostensibly more attractive to some lenders who believed they were capable of evaluating the risk. HSBC believed it was one such lender. It was wrong.

Shortly after its purchase of Household, HSBC's then Chief Executive William Aldinger (in a comment he surely came to regret) bragged that the bank employed 150 PhDs skilled at modeling credit risk. He didn't define what he meant by "risk," and clearly neither did his hard-working PhDs, because it turned out that they clearly lacked the expertise required to properly analyze subprime credit and default probabilities. By the end of the first quarter of 2009, HSBC's subprime losses reached $8.3 billion and were still running. Management admitted that the write-downs were not over either. At that point, it did not require a doctorate in mathematics to calculate the loss at an astonishing $55.3 million per PhD (assuming any of the original 150 were still around and not been fired).

The HSBC saga illustrated the risk of undue reliance on financial models. Among the problems involved in analyzing HSBC's portfolio, according to *The Wall Street Journal*, was an absence of data on loans to subprime borrowers making small or nonexistent down payments (i.e., borrowers with no equity in their homes who found it relatively easy to walk away from their loans). It turned out that HSBC was relying heavily on FICO scores. Prior to this, FICO scores had never been tested against a downturn in the housing market or against second lien loans, rendering them of limited predictive utility. Douglas Flint, HSBC's finance director, told investors that "what is clear now is that FICO scores are less effective or ineffective" when lenders are granting loans in an unusually low interest rate environment. It turns out that using FICO scores in such an environment is akin to using peak earnings to calculate and then project a corporation's future earnings, or applying the decade's lowest default rates to project future corporate bond default rates (all errors that were made by major financial industry players at various times and were being committed again by many with respect to loans to the energy industry after the financial crisis).

Actually, if you think about it, it shouldn't have required a single doctorate, not to mention 150 of them, to figure out that different credit tools were needed to build and monitor subprime loan portfolios. As Peter Bernstein noted in his book on risk, "Likeness to truth is not the same as truth. Without any theoretical structure to explain why patterns seem to repeat themselves across time or across systems, these innovations provide little assurance that today's signals will trigger tomorrow's events. We are left with only the subtle sequences of data that the enormous power of the computer can reveal. Thus, forecasting tools based on nonlinear models or on computer gymnastics are subject to many of the same hurdles that stand in the way of conventional probability theory: the raw material of the model is the data of the past."[7] The markets would see this error repeated many times over the next couple of years or, to be more precise, they would see the consequences of an error that was being committed incessantly in the financial world throughout the 1990s and 2000s materialize in frightening dimensions in the 2007–2008 time frame. And then, once the smoke cleared after that crisis, markets would see similar errors committed all over again as an epic, central bank-sponsored bull market began in March 2009 and created a massive credit bubble in energy and commodities that began to collapse in mid-2014.

A Fetish Is Not a Promise

Securitization eradicated the individual identity of borrowers and substituted a broad-based credit rating system on which investors came to rely in determining whether to purchase CDOs. It no longer mattered whether a borrower was an individual purchasing a home or a car, a corporation using the money to build a new plant or to finance the acquisition of a competitor, or a private equity firm paying too much to buy a company in order to generate transaction fees for its general partners. The individual borrower came to have absolutely no identity or meaning to the ultimate lender. There was absolutely no relationship between borrower and lender.

The securitization of financial assets such as mortgages or bank loans represented a modern manifestation of what Karl Marx termed the "fetish character of commodities," the commodity in this case being the mortgage or bank loan itself. Marx's description of the lack of relationship between the underlying economic commodity and the form in which it is traded in the marketplace (which was discussed in more detail in Chapter 2) perfectly describes a collateralized debt obligation. Any relationship between lender and borrower in such a product is completely eradicated. A collateralized debt obligation is the ultimate fetish instrument. The distance between the individual mortgage holder, the economic actor generating cash flows in the form of mortgage payments, and the lender, is about as attenuated as possible. This effectively obliterates the promissory character of the original mortgage and leaves room for all kinds of mischief that can interrupt the flow of funds and prevent repayment of the underlying debt. In more blatant situations, courts in the United States have prevented loans from being foreclosed on due to the inability of the collateralized loan obligation to prove ownership of the underlying loan. In those cases, the entity lost track of the deed to the home![8] Instruments that were designed to reduce risk by slicing and dicing it and reallocating it among parties who could pick and choose their favorite flavor instead ended up choking on a poisonous buffet.

Parties that have no relationship are in no position to make promises to each other. Financial instruments, even the debts packaged into large pools and then resold to investors in securitized form, still involve formal but depersonalized promises between the parties that created them. Adam Smith's view that the regard for the opinion of others leads them to act morally and responsibly can play no role in a system in which personal relationships have been sundered. Changing the form of these instruments devalued the promises that stand behind them. It also left the global economy holding sacks of empty promises when the debts came due.

CHAPTER 5

Financialization

O ne of the key economic phenomena of the last three decades has been the United States' transition from a manufacturer and exporter of goods to a manufacturer and exporter of dollars and other financial products such as financial derivatives. This could not have been achieved without the complicity of the nation's trading partners, particularly Japan, China, and Middle Eastern countries that needed to invest huge oil surpluses. But the phenomenal growth of finance capital that came to define capitalism over the past 30 years was accompanied by policies that favored financial market deregulation, a diminution of workers' rights and organized labor power, weakened antitrust enforcement, and corporate governance rules that placed the rights of shareholders ahead of those of all other corporate and societal constituencies. The growing dominance of finance in the world economy was an essential factor in the displacement of productive investment by speculation that culminated in the financial crisis of 2008. Finance became its own *raison d'être*, and instead of providing credit to fund capital expansion and economic growth, the financial sector's function became to expand itself.

Money Begetting Money

The term that is used to describe this phenomenon is "financialization." It is the process of money begetting money, or more broadly of capital begetting capital. Financialization, along with globalization, is arguably the defining economic force of our time. Surprisingly little has been written about this phenomenon while barrels of ink have been spilled (and continue to be spilled) on the topic of globalization.[1] The term is broadly defined as finance increasing the role it plays in virtually every facet of modern life and culture. Perhaps the most useful definition was provided by Peter Gowan, who defined "financialization" as "the total subordination of the credit system's public functions to the self-expansion of money capital. Indeed, the entire spectrum of capitalist activity is drawn under the sway of money capital, in that the latter absorbs an expanding share of the profits generated across all other sectors."[2] Gowan's definition captures the increasingly dominant role that finance assumed not merely in modern market economies in which the exchange of physical goods is increasingly supplanted by the exchange of different intangible forms of capital, but in modern culture where areas such as media, architecture, and art are increasingly permeated by monetary forms and influences.[3]

Financialization was also nourished by remarkable advances in computer technology that turned the world into a vast network of interconnected markets. All types of financial instruments are traded around the clock through these global networks, and it is the very ability to trade these economic objects 24/7/365 that had an enormous effect on their value, as well as on the stability of their value and of the values that they purport to represent. In the 1950s, President Dwight Eisenhower warned of the dangers of the military-industrial complex. Today, the world is threatened by a financial-political complex. While we still have superpowers (as well as rogue actors) capable of staring each other down with nuclear weapons of mass destruction, today we also have highly leveraged financial institutions deemed too big to fail staring down each other with complex financial instruments that are capable of unleashing incalculable economic losses and global instability.

Most important, all of these institutions are linked through a global computer network. As Professor Mark C. Taylor points out, "*the distinctive characteristic of our age is not simply the spread of computers but the impact of connecting them.* When computers are networked *everything* changes. What has occurred in the past four decades is the emergence of a new network economy that is inseparable from a new network culture."[4] In addition to the leaders of sovereign nations holding the keys to complex launch codes controlling weapons of mass physical destruction, we now have devious electronic terrorists capable of inflicting worldwide cyber-destruction on markets. As Taylor notes, "[t]he constantly changing networks that increasingly govern our lives have a distinct logic that we are only beginning to understand."[5] The same can be said of the logic with which these networks govern the markets. Without really understanding what was happening, the world surrendered its sovereignty to people capable of inflicting untold harm without firing a single weapon in the traditional sense. This is another new dimension to financialization in global financial markets.

The term financialization began to gain traction in the 1990s in the work of the political scientist Kevin Phillips. Phillips used the term in his 1993 book *Boiling Point* and then devoted an entire chapter to the subject in his follow-up work, *Arrogant Capital*, which appeared the following year. In *Boiling Point*, Phillips described financialization as "the cumulating influence of finance, government debt, unearned income, *rentiers,* overseas investment, domestic economic polarization, and social stratification."[6] He also made the point (which had been made by earlier economic historians, most notably the eminent Frenchmen Fernand Braudel) that "excessive preoccupation with finance and tolerance of debt are apparently typical of great economic powers in their late stages. They foreshadow economic decline, but often accompany new heights of cultural sophistication, in part because the hurly-burly expansion of the middle class and its values are receding. Yet these slow transitions involve real economic cost to the average person or family, and political restiveness reflects that."[7] In *Arrogant Capital*, Phillips expanded his definition of financialization to tie it to government's decreasing control over capital flows and the economy. He wrote, "finance has not simply been spreading into every nook and cranny of economic life; a sizeable portion of the financial sector, electronically liberated from past constraints, has put aside old concerns with funding the nation's long-range industrial future, has divorced itself from the precarious prospects of Americans who toil in factories, fields, or even suburban shopping malls and is simply feeding wherever it can."[8] The result of this process is a "split between the divergent real and financial economies."[9] In populist terms, financialization stands for the triumph of Wall Street over Main Street. In economic terms, it denotes a far more complex shift in the composition of economic growth in favor of financial rather than industrial capital.

An important component of Phillips' populist view of financialization is the significant political power that financial institutions exercise over U.S. society, which allows them to block reforms aimed at reining in excessive leverage and other potential systemic risks. These institutions and the individuals who manage and work in them are able to influence economic policies and structures to serve their own interests. The most significant manifestation of this power in recent decades was an incessant push toward financial deregulation, which created more opportunities for financial firms to earn profits through activities that involved increasingly imprudent risks such as increasing balance sheet leverage and reducing systemic transparency. In fact, many of the efforts of powerful financial institutions were directed at ensuring that their actions were concealed from the eyes of regulators and investors. This had the effect of ensuring that the risks they were taking were kept beyond the reach of government control.

The concealment of risk became so deeply embedded in Wall Street and Washington, D.C. that even serial scandals and the enormous financial losses and market disruptions resulting from them failed to motivate business and political leaders to deal with increasingly obvious systemic problems before it was too late to prevent the 2008 crisis. In 2001, Enron Corporation was revealed to be an empty shell that had shuffled many of its most valuable assets off of its balance sheets with the assistance of some of the largest financial institutions in the world, including Citigroup and JPMorgan. Politicians and regulators screamed in outrage as Enron's investment grade rating was revealed to be a complete sham and the company was forced to file for bankruptcy protection. But at precisely the same time this was occurring, those very same financial institutions were sponsoring even larger off-balance-sheet entities known as structured investment vehicles (known as "SIVs") to conceal hundreds of billions of dollars of mortgages, loans, and other financial assets from their investors and regulators.

This sham only came to an end in 2007 when these entities, which were recklessly financing the purchase of long-dated, illiquid, complex securities with short-term commercial paper, suffered a loss of confidence and were no longer able to refinance their short-term debt. They were forced into liquidation at great cost to their sponsoring banks and equity investors.

But even this couldn't convince Wall Street to come out into the open. At the same time these SIVs were collapsing at great reputational and financial cost to the largest financial institutions in the world, these same firms were actively building and sponsoring secretive trading platforms known as "dark pools." These were designed to facilitate high frequency trading strategies that are not only unavailable to the general public but gives these firms the ability to front run (trade ahead of) their own clients, an illegal and immoral activity that is further debased by its very secrecy. Only in the summer of 2009 did the regulatory authorities begin to step in to prevent this latest version of Wall Street's obsession with hiding its activities from the eyes of the world, but financial firms fought tooth-and-nail through their lobbyists to prevent these extremely profitable activities from being shut down. The financialization of the markets keeps merging into a kind of sanctioned deviousness.

When risk is hidden, risk-taking tends to become excessive because economic actors come to ignore the consequences of their actions. A key, and until recently often overlooked, aspect of financialization is a financial industry that devotes much of its high-priced intellectual capital not only to mispricing risk but to deliberately concealing it. This permits these institutions to sell complex products such as derivatives for more than they are worth to parties who are deprived of the information to price them properly. This can only occur because politically powerful institutions are repeatedly able to muscle regulators into maintaining a hands-off attitude toward their activities.

Power Begetting Power

In the years between the publication of Phillips' books in the early 1990s and the collapse of the financial system in 2008, the largest financial institutions in the United States worked assiduously to limit the ability of regulators to control their business activities. These were the years of so-called "prosperity" during President Bill Clinton's two terms in office through the time of the first Iraq War, and then the period after the 2001–2002 credit crisis that saw an explosion of debt and complacency with few parallels in history. The financial-political complex was successful in, among other things, repealing the Glass-Steagall Act in 1999 (which limited the ability of deposit-taking institutions to take risks) and lowering the net capital requirements of the five largest investment banks in 2004, two landmark regulatory changes that significantly heightened the systemic risks that led to the 2008 financial crisis. These risks materialized in two primary areas: derivatives and balance sheet leverage of investment banks. The time-honored complicity between K Street and Wall Street to feed the beast of speculation blew up in everybody's faces. Efforts to limit leverage at financial institutions and regulate derivatives in the aftermath of the crisis—measures that could have prevented the crisis in the first place—were actively combatted by an expensive lobbying effort by the largest financial industry firms.

The industry's attempts to block regulatory reform are as old as the industry itself. A case in point, which preceded the 1987 stock market crash, is recounted by former Federal Reserve Chairman Paul Volcker. Volcker told of his failed attempts to alter the rules governing margin requirements in 1986 in order to slow down the flood of leveraged buyouts that were worrying the central bank chairman and other policy makers. Leveraged buyers of corporations were using the target company's shares as collateral for the debt used to purchase these shares. One obvious way to limit these transactions would have been to limit the amount of borrowing that could be incurred in such situations. When Volcker made such a proposal, he ran into strong resistance from none other than former Merrill Lynch Chairman, and then-Secretary of the Treasury, Donald Regan. Volcker explained how Regan mobilized the Wall Street powers to defeat his proposal:

> [W]e played around with making a ruling to apply the margin requirement to the extent we could. Don Regan, then the Secretary of the Treasury, got practically every agency in the government to write to us saying that such a ruling would destroy America. Even the State Department wrote to us. And what the hell did the State Department

have to do with it? The administration didn't want to interrupt the M&A boom. That was partly ideology, partly whatever. We circulated the proposed ruling for comment, and suddenly this very technical question was a highly distorted front-page story in *The New York Times*. As a sheer political matter, I think it [the regulation of leveraged acquisitions] would have been almost impossible, even if you had had more conviction than I had. The intensity of the political pressure sometimes startled me.[10]

This incident was an eerie precursor to what occurred two decades later when, as previously noted, Henry Paulson, then chairman of Goldman Sachs and soon-to-be treasury secretary, led the lobbying effort to relax the net capital rules that were limiting investment banks' ability to leverage their balance sheets more than 12 to 1. Mr. Paulson, along with his colleagues from Morgan Stanley and three firms that would not survive 2008—Bear Stearns, Lehman Brothers, and Merrill Lynch—argued for this relief from balance sheet constraint on the basis that it was creating a competitive disadvantage for U.S.-based investment banks vis-à-vis U.S. commercial banks and foreign institutions. Ironically, it was the regulatory change these men sought, not the *status quo,* that came close to destroying U.S. capitalism.

The failure of three of the five firms that lobbied for net capital relief in 2004 did nothing to change the financial industry's *modus operandi.* According to *The New York Times,* on November 13, 2008—a mere month after receiving Troubled Asset Relief Program (TARP) funds—the nine largest participants in the derivatives markets (including Citigroup, which was generally acknowledged to be insolvent at the time, and Bank of America, which was about to set off a political maelstrom by allowing its newly acquired Merrill Lynch to pay out billions of dollars of bonuses after reporting an unexpected multibillion dollar loss) created a lobbying organization, the CDS Dealers Consortium. The group hired a prominent Washington lobbyist and attorney, Edward J. Rosen, to draft a confidential memorandum that was shared with the Treasury Department and Congressional leaders and played a key role in shaping the debate over derivatives legislation. Apparently, the fact that Bear Stearns and Lehman Brothers were largely driven out of business through the credit derivatives market, and that Goldman

Sachs and Morgan Stanley were placed in jeopardy by credit default swap traders (see Chapter 7), was quickly forgotten. There was nothing unusual about this; it was business as usual driven by greed. But business as usual was what pushed the financial system to the brink in the fall of 2008, and allowing the parties that benefitted the most from relaxing financial regulation to shape policy was unlikely to lead to good results.

Another area in which the financial industry was active in pushing its agenda even after it was clear that its agenda poses a danger to the financial system involves the so-called "shadow banking system" and the off-balance-sheet vehicles known as SIVs that caused hundreds of billions of dollars of losses in 2007–2008. These SIVs were deliberately designed as special purpose entities to be hidden from the prying eyes of investors and regulators. Moreover, these entities used enormous amounts of leverage to enhance their returns. The flaw in their business model was that they used short-term borrowings to finance illiquid long-term investments, and when the credit markets froze up beginning in 2007, they found they were unable to roll over their borrowings, resulting in massive defaults and losses.

Despite the obvious idiocy of such structures, the banks and other financial institutions that sponsored them were determined to go down fighting. On June 4, 2009, *The Wall Street Journal* reported[11] that a group funded by these institutions that included the Chamber of Commerce, the Mortgage Bankers Association, and the American Council of Life Insurers sent Treasury Secretary Timothy Geithner a letter urging the delay of a new rule requiring SIVs to be brought back on the balance sheets of their sponsoring institutions. This group spent millions of dollars lobbying members of Congress on the issue as well. Their concern was that the rule would require the sponsoring institutions to set aside more capital to hold these entities on their balance sheet, which is exactly what these institutions should have been doing! Next to the failure to regulate the credit default swap market, permitting SIVs to grow to the point where they threatened the stability of the financial system ranked as the most serious failure of regulation leading to the 2008 crisis. Again, there was nothing surprising about these lobbying efforts other than the fact that they once again demonstrated that key financial players and their congressional sponsors learned little from the worst crisis of capitalism in the last century.

Theories of Financialization

It is abundantly clear that financialization does not come about by accident; rather, it is the deliberate result of policy actions designed to lead an economy in a direction that favors certain interests over others. Perhaps this is why Marxist-oriented critics are the most interested in discussing the subject and the most astute in dissecting its implications. Observers who are opposed to the governing ideology of the system tend to be far more willing to look at complex issues with an eye toward genuine reform.

A far more theoretically sophisticated discussion of financialization than Kevin Phillips' is found in Giovanni Arrighi's books, *The Long Twentieth Century* (1994) and *Adam Smith in Beijing* (2007). In *The Long Twentieth Century*, Professor Arrighi, a Marxist-oriented professor of sociology, defines financialization as a pattern of economic accumulation in which profit-making occurs increasingly through financial channels rather than through trade and commodity production.[12] Professor Arrighi bases his articulation of financialization on the work of another Marxist professor, Professor David Harvey. Both Professor Arrighi and Professor Harvey are astute interpreters of Karl Marx (something Kevin Phillips certainly has never aspired to be) and interpret the shift in global economic activity from production to speculation as a process involving dramatic changes in the way that capital is accumulated and the new forms capital began to assume in the 1970s. The advent of new financial instruments and markets, such as those for derivative products, is evidence of the inherent flexibility of capitalism and capital accumulation. Indeed, as we defined capital in Chapter 2, one of its key attributes is flexibility and the ability to assume many different guises.

Harvey argues that capitalism began a historic transition in the late 1960s to a system of "flexible accumulation."[13] This was a response to the rigidities of a form of capitalism Harvey calls "Fordism," which is characterized as "rigidity of long-term and large-scale fixed capital investments in mass–production systems that precluded much flexibility of design and presumed stable growth in invariant consumer markets."[14] Flexible accumulation "rests on flexibility with respect to labor processes, labor markets, products, and patterns of consumption. It is characterized by the emergence of entirely new sectors of production, new ways of providing financial services, new markets, and above all, greatly intensified rates of commercial, technological, and organizational innovation. . . . It has also entailed a new round of . . . 'time-space compression' . . . in the capitalist world—the time horizons of both private and public decision-making have shrunk, while satellite communication and declining transport costs have made it increasingly possible to spread those decisions immediately over an ever wider and variegated space."[15] These changes are reflected in the dramatic evolution in financial markets:

> There have been phases of capitalist history—from 1890 to 1920, for example—when "finance capital" (however defined) seemed to occupy a position of paramount importance within capitalism, only to lose that position in the speculative crashes that followed. In the present phase, however, it is not so much the concentration of power in financial institutions that matters, as the explosion in new financial instruments and markets, coupled with the rise of sophisticated systems of financial coordination on a global scale. It is through this financial system that much of the geographical and temporal flexibility of capital accumulation has been achieved.[16]

New financial products and new trading systems that link markets around the world enabled the financial industry to expand (in Harvey's words, to achieve "geographical and temporal flexibility"), but they also contribute to instability. Harvey writes that "the financial system has achieved a degree of autonomy from real production unprecedented in capitalism's history, carrying capitalism into an era of equally unprecedented financial dangers."[17] To some degree, finance capitalism has always played a dual role, serving the industrial economy as well as serving itself. The question is the balance between these two roles. A healthy and productive economy is one in which finance capitalism is supporting economic activity that adds to the productive capacity of an economy to a meaningful degree. That contribution will differ at various times and in various contexts, but it is clear that the two decades leading up to 2008 saw too much of finance capitalism's intellectual and economic capital focused on speculative rather than productive activities. While significant sums of money were spent on productive activities such as scientific research and business innovation, even greater sums were squandered on speculative trading of securities and the pointless debt-financed buying and selling of businesses. These activities diverted much needed capital from productive uses that could have enhanced the underlying capacity of the economy to grow.

Arrighi builds on Harvey's work in developing the concept of financialization. He writes that "finance capital is not a particular stage of world capitalism, let alone its latest and highest stage. Rather, it is a recurrent phenomenon which has marked the capitalist era from its earliest beginnings in late medieval and early modern Europe. Throughout the capitalist era financial expansions have signaled the transition from one regime of accumulation on a world scale to another."[18] Specifically, he argues that financialization is "the predominant capitalist response to the joint crisis of profitability and hegemony."[19] In other words, financialization is capitalism's response to the persistent problem of finding new markets in which to earn profits. When manufacturing no longer is capable of generating sufficient profits, capital flows toward speculative activities in the financial realm. As Professor Arrighi describes the phenomenon, "financial expansions are taken to be symptomatic of a situation in which the investment of money in the expansion of trade and production no longer serves the purpose of increasing the cash flow to the capitalist stratum as effectively as pure financial deals can. In such a situation, capital invested in trade and production tends to revert to its money form and accumulate more directly."[20] In other words, when financialization has taken hold of an economy, finance-driven deals (transactions that do not add to the capital stock) are necessary to keep capital from dying.

The current situation of the United States economy, in which manufacturing has declined and finance dominates, is an illustration of this process. In *Adam Smith in Beijing*, Professor Arrighi describes financialization as the last (and perhaps terminal) stage in the search for profitability. He writes:

> The logic of the product cycle for the leading capitalist organizations of a given epoch is to shift resources ceaselessly through one kind or another of innovation from market niches that have become over-crowded (and therefore less profitable) to those that are less crowded (and therefore more profitable). When escalating competition reduces the availability of relatively empty, profitable niches in the commodity markets, the leading capitalist organizations have one last refuge, to which they can retreat and shift competitive pressures onto others. This final refuge is Schumpeter's headquarters of the capitalist system—the money market.[21]

By the "money market," Professor Arrighi means the markets in which money is the primary product, not money market funds and other short-term investment instruments. The post–World War II United States economy has experienced this process. Since the late 1940s, the share of national income coming from manufacturing declined by approximately two-thirds while the share attributable to FIRE (finance, insurance, and real estate) doubled. See Figure 5.1.

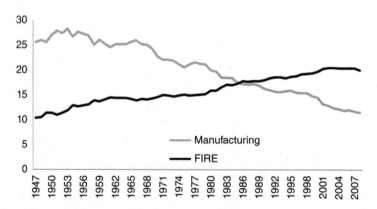

Figure 5.1   Rising Post–World War II Dominance of Finance Industry and Decline of Manufacturing, 1971–2008
SOURCE: Bureau of Economic Analysis.

The "money market" is a very broad category that in the period leading up to the 2008 financial crisis was typified in Corporate America by
the boom in leveraged buyouts (see Chapter 6), where debt was incurred
not to build new plants, purchase new equipment, or to fund research and
development projects, but simply to effect changes of ownership where
equity is purchased with debt. Arrighi bases his analysis in great part on
the detailed statistical analysis of UCLA Professor Robert Brenner, who
describes this activity very clearly in the following passage:

> In the end, there was no escaping the fact that the explosion of
> investment and consumption that drove the last phase of the U.S.
> expansion—as well as the major uptick in productivity growth to
> which it gave rise—was heavily dependent upon a historic increase
> in borrowing, which was itself made possible by a record equity price
> run-up that was powered by speculation in defiance of actual corpo-
> rate returns.[22]

In the mid–2000s, many of these transactions took the even more
egregiously speculative form of transactions in which one private equity
firm sold a company to another private equity firm, or financings in which
private equity firms loaded companies with more debt in order to pay
cash dividends to themselves. Not only did these transactions add nothing to the productive capacity of the economy, but by increasing financial
commitments without improving companies' abilities to meet them, they
rendered the financial system more unstable. As Brenner describes it:

> Rather than discovering and funding the most promising fields for
> expansion . . . the deregulated U.S. financial sector ignored the paucity
> of underlying corporate profits and drove an epoch-making *misalloca-
> tion* of funds into high-tech paper assets and, in turn, as a consequence,
> a parallel, and equally titanic, *misdirection* of new plant, equipment, and
> software into oversubscribed manufacturing and related lines, espe-
> cially information technology. The logic behind this behavior lay in
> the peculiar constraints under which financial markets operate, which
> could not be further from the fantasies of orthodox economic theory.[23]

The last sentence is Professor Brenner's way of describing private equity
fee incentives that drove many of these nonproductive transactions to

be done. These transactions were laden with large up-front fees payable to the investment bankers and private equity sponsors in order to ensure that these parties could extract their pound of flesh before the companies involved could succumb to the heavy debts thrust upon them. The rising failure rate of private equity transactions beginning in 2008 was all too predictable in view of the incentives that drove these deals to be done in the first place.

Professor Arrighi also argues, following on the work of the French historian Fernando Braudel, that financialization is "a symptom of maturity of a particular capitalist development."[24] While it is too soon to determine whether the particular brand of Western capitalism that gave birth to cycles of boom and bust has reached its zenith, it is certainly beyond dispute that the cycle that came to a resounding thud in 2008 showed its age in the dominance of finance capital in the economy through the mid-2000s. Every boom and bust cycle ends when certain features grow out of balance, and the use of leverage, derivatives, and securitization undoubtedly had grown to unsustainable levels by 2007.

· The financialization of the U.S. economy also coincided with a consumption boom that began in the early 1980s. Both phenomena were induced by extremely lax monetary policy on the part of the Federal Reserve, which created a worldwide liquidity boom. Since all of this liquidity could not be put to use in truly productive activities, much of it found its way into financial speculation and the consumer version of speculation—consumption. Consumption, particularly when it involves goods that are believed to increase in value, such as houses, collectibles, and art, should be considered another form of speculation. The increasing size of the average U.S. home, as well as the growing number of second homes and vacation properties and the purchase of multiple automobiles and other vehicles, were manifestations of the speculative aspect of consumption. Consumption grew to a record percentage of U.S. GDP during this period from the 40-year average of approximately 66 percent to 71 percent by late 2007 (see Figure 5.2).[25]

The increasing dependence of the U.S. economy on both financialization and consumption, rather than on the expansion of production, continues to haunt the U.S. economy six years after the financial crisis.

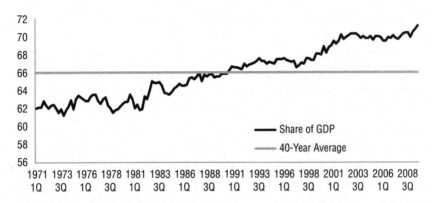

Figure 5.2 Consumption as a Growing Percentage of U.S. GDP, 1971–2008
SOURCE: Bureau of Economic Analysis.

Where financialization takes hold, the financial economy drives the real economy rather than vice versa. The result is a world replete with too much debt, too much capacity, too much labor, and central banks producing too much money as they attempt to keep the entire system afloat. This regime is unsustainable and unhealthy for long-term economic growth. History is filled with examples of financialized economies that came crashing down on the heads of their financiers and government enablers, forcing governments to resort to radical policy actions that were designed to prop up short-term growth but failed to create the proper foundations for long-term growth. Financialization is a sign that economic policies failed to create the conditions for robust organic growth. Instead, an economy that is dominated by finance capital is characterized by a dependence on debt rather than equity finance and speculative rather than productive investments. These activities result from highly distorted incentives written into the law by politicians who are directly or indirectly beholden to the agents of financialization while they are in government and after they retire into private sector sinecures. Financialization creates an insidious cycle of unproductive economic activity that must feed on itself because, creating nothing productive itself, it has nothing else on which to feed.

The Monetization of Values

It is in cultural terms that financialization may be having its greatest impact on the world. Culture is what ultimately shapes behavior. It tells people what types of conduct is acceptable. Financialization involves a process in which boundaries are broken down between the economy and other parts of society such as art, education, and the media. As boundaries between the economy and culture broke down through the processes of financialization, cultural and behavioral standards lapsed as well. Financialization taught some participants in the financial markets that anything goes. It is undeniable that regulators, legislators, and senior executives came to tolerate and even encourage behavior that in earlier eras were deemed unacceptable. Lower standards of judgment and conduct became normalized in the marketplace during the Internet bubble and the housing bubble that were symptoms of profound cultural changes that were inseparable from the process of financialization itself.

In this sense, financialization also can be understood as the "monetization of values" whereby all conduct is measured by whether it produces a profit, not whether it is economically or socially productive or consistent with high standards of law and morality. On one level, it includes legal but socially and economically unproductive behavior like leveraged buyouts that load companies with debt but result in mass layoffs, lower R&D, reduced expenditures on new plants, and large fees for private equity firms. On another level, it implicates conduct such as Wall Street analysts touting stocks they were privately trashing during the Internet bubble, or mortgage lenders extending credit to borrowers who they knew could not repay it during the housing bubble. This conduct was tolerated and even encouraged by people in supervisory positions who stood to earn enormous profits from this unethical behavior. Moreover, this conduct was an open secret in business and regulatory circles, creating a culture that tolerated illegality and immorality. Even worse, this culture was further encouraged by the public statements of business and government leaders such as Alan Greenspan, who publicly praised the wonders of computer technology and adjustable rate mortgages (the latter comment being sufficiently loony to prompt the question whether there should be age limits for certain federal employees). Complicity was rampant at every level of the financial and political system.

Valeant Pharmaceuticals

The Financialization of Healthcare

One example of the profits-over-principle ethos bred by financialization is Valeant Pharmaceuticals International, Inc. Valeant is a Canadian firm by virtue of the fact that it shifted its legal base of operations to Canada to reduce its taxes even though it operates primarily out of the United States. Valeant's business model consists of buying other drug companies in transactions financed with tens of billions of dollars of high yield debt, firing most of the target company's employees, spending virtually nothing on R&D (3 percent of revenues compared to the industry standard of 15 percent) and raising the prices of its drugs (by an average of 66 percent over the five years ending in 2015 according to Deutsche Bank Securities). This predatory behavior was rewarded with a skyrocketing stock price and media and hedge fund adulation. Valeant's stock price rose tenfold from 2010 to its all-time closing high of $263.52 on August 5, 2015. Shortly thereafter, presidential candidate Hillary Clinton started talking about skyrocketing drug prices, and the company received a subpoena from Congressional Democrats regarding its drug pricing practices. In response to rising scrutiny of these practices, the company announced on an earnings call on October 19, 2015, that it was abandoning its aggressive acquisition strategy and would limit future drug price increases to no more than 10 percent a year. Two days later, on October 21, 2015, a short selling firm, Citron Research, published a research report raising questions about the company's sales practices, including its use of a mail-order pharmacy called Philidor for which it had paid $100 million for an option to buy the entire company. Once Philidor's questionable business practices came to light, Valeant severed the relationship, and shortly thereafter, Philidor closed its doors. These events raised questions in investors' minds about the sustainability of Valeant's business model and its ability to service the $30 billion of debt it accumulated during its acquisition spree. Valeant's stock plunged by more than 50 percent to close at a 52-week closing low of $70.32 on November 17, 2015, inflicting huge losses on hedge funds and other institutional investors that had flocked into it.

In economic terms, financialization was the stage that capitalism reached at the beginning of the twenty-first century when commodity production merged with aesthetic production. The collapse of the gold standard was the first step in radically destabilizing measures of value in the global economy.[26] These forces would not have become destabilizing had prudent and non-politicized regulation been put in place to govern them. But unsurprisingly, the interests that served to profit from the new regime, the financial-political complex, used their power and influence to manipulate legislation and regulation to serve their short-term goals at the expense of the longer term interests of the system. This is an age-old story, and as the world continues to recover from the economic crisis of 2008, those forces are back at work, trying to gain advantages regardless of the longer term health of the system.

CHAPTER 6

From Innovators to Undertakers

The financialization of the U.S. economy was characterized by an enormous increase in indebtedness among corporations and consumers. Among the leading contributors to the rise in debt in the years leading to the financial crisis was the leveraged buyout boom, which represented an attempt to monetize all aspects of the business corporation. At the peak of the debt bubble that led to the 2008 crisis, private equity was the motivating force behind the leveraging of Corporate America. From 2003 through 2007, annual leveraged buyout debt issuance skyrocketed from $71 billion to $669 billion.[1] In 1980, $5 billion of capital was committed to private equity funds; by 2004, this figure had increased to $300 billion.[2] And by 2008, this number was approaching $1 trillion.[3] As with all things on Wall Street, investors and promoters took a decent idea and replicated it into oblivion.

Promoters of private equity make two primary arguments. First, they argue that private ownership obviates the so-called "agency problem," which refers to the issues that arise when the management of a public company has only a small ownership stake in the business. Harvard Business School Professor Michael C. Jensen sounded this cry in his 1989 apologia for leveraged buyouts, "Eclipse of the Public Corporation." In that article, Professor Jensen wrote: "By resolving the central weakness of the public corporation—the conflict between owners and managers over the control and use of corporate resources—these new organizations [private equity-owned businesses] are making remarkable gains in operating efficiency, employee productivity, and shareholder value."[4] In the early years of the private industry, these claims were supportable. Unfortunately, as the industry grew and became commoditized, such claims lost their validity.

Second, private equity proponents argue that private owners of corporations are in a position to take a long-term view of these businesses and make decisions free of the short-term demands of the public markets. Like many aspects of the financial markets, these arguments work in theory but fail in practice. In particular, these arguments made sense when a few pioneers were engaging in these activities but became devalued when crowds rushed in to imitate them. To the extent that the agency problem is solvable (which is questionable), public companies solved it by granting their managers generous equity ownership stakes through stock options and other performance-based compensation schemes. These forms of executive compensation not only opened the door to a panoply of new abuses, but also undermined one of the justifications for private equity. Public company executives can be incentivized in very similar ways to private company managers. Moreover, private equity funds turned out to be as susceptible to conflicts of interest as public corporations and as short-term oriented as their public company brethren.[5]

The History of Private Equity Funds

In the 1970s, private equity funds did serve an important systemic purpose by pressuring public company management teams to improve productivity and better align their interests with those of their shareholders. Private equity played an important role in the 1980s in forcing large conglomerates to rationalize their holdings and maximize shareholder value. Unfortunately, the price of this activism was a growing love affair with debt as a means of enriching shareholders in the short run. Moreover, the evidence suggests that, over time, private equity's original goal (in addition to generating profits for its partners) fell by the wayside as more entrants joined the industry. Instead of becoming an engine of innovation and change, private equity became little more than a fee vomitorium for Wall Street and a disposal site for businesses that had outlived their usefulness as public companies, components of large conglomerates, or productive contributors to the broader economy. By the mid-1990s, private equity was no longer focused on squeezing efficiencies out of stodgy businesses through superior management techniques; instead, it became focused on taking advantage of the low cost of capital to take dying businesses off the hands of owners who no longer wanted to provide them with decent burials. Private equity became the place where capital went to die.

In 1990, Hyman Minsky foretold the situation that came to pass with respect to the disproportionately influential (and negative) role played by private equity in the economy in the first decade of the twenty-first century:

> A peculiar regime emerged in which the main business in the financial markets became far removed from the financing of the capital development of the country. Furthermore, the main purpose of those who controlled corporations was no longer making profits from production and trade but rather to assure that the liabilities of the corporations were fully priced in the financial market, to give value to shareholders. The giving of value to shareholders took the form of pledging a very high proportion of prospective cash flows to satisfy debt liabilities. This prior commitment of cash meant that there was little in the way of internal finance left for the capital development of the economy.... The question of whether a financial structure that commits a large part of cash flows to debt validation leads to a debacle such as took place between 1929 and 1933 is now an open question.[6]

In 2008, a little more than a decade after Minsky's death, we learned the painful answer to that question. In the corporate sector, the 2008 financial crisis was the culmination of years of investment activity that consisted of little more than working to ensure that, in Minsky's words, "the liabilities of the corporations were fully priced in the financial market, to give value to shareholders." In other words, speculation trumped productive investment as debt was substituted for equity on corporate balance sheets in transactions whose primary purpose was not to add to the productive capacity of the economy but to generate fees for private equity firms and their Wall Street underwriters and advisers. Only secondarily were these transactions designed to generate profits that the firms could share with their limited partners after skimming their generous share off the top. And the primary use to which those returns were put was to raise more money from the same institutions to start the unproductive process all over again.

As Professor Jensen wrote in 1989, "the public corporation is not suitable in industries where long-term growth is slow, where internally generated funds outstrip the opportunities to invest them profitably, or where downsizing is the most productive long-term strategy.... In... cash-rich, low-growth or declining sectors, the pressure on management to waste cash flow through organizational slack or investments in unsound projects is often irresistible. It is in precisely these sectors that the publicly held corporation has declined most rapidly."[7] This was true in the 1980s, when large, profitable conglomerates like Chicago-based Beatrice Cos., which owned such well-known branded consumer product names as Avis, Tropicana, Playtex, Hunt-Wesson, and Samsonite, were disassembled through leveraged buyouts. Jensen's observation continued to be true 20 years later, when faltering auto giant Chrysler Corp. and auto and consumer finance giant General Motors Acceptance Corp. (GMAC) were sold to the private equity firm Cerberus Capital Management LLC when there was nowhere else to bury these businesses other than bankruptcy court. The difference between these two types of companies, however, could not be starker.

Beatrice was an $11 billion conglomerate whose individual businesses were viable but undervalued by the public stock market. Chrysler was a dying business in a restructuring industry suffering from deep structural problems and needed to be liquidated.[8] GMAC, on the other hand, was providing financing to an overburdened consumer purchasing products from two crippled industries: automobiles and housing. Cerberus Capital Management's investment in Chrysler and GMAC was a vivid illustration of how businesses that were too infirm to be sold to strategic buyers could still be unloaded on so-called "sophisticated financial buyers" due to the availability of inexpensive debt capital and the ability of private equity firms to charge huge (and completely unjustified) fees for simply completing transactions regardless of their investment merit or prospects for profitability. Cerberus was no fool, however; rather than make the entire multibillion dollar investment itself, it managed to convince other buyout firms not only to participate alongside it in an investment syndicate but to pay it a portion of any future profits if the investment worked out. (While investors in Cerberus's funds had a right to be unhappy with these two investments, investors in funds that couldn't come up with enough investment ideas on their own for their capital and decided to let Cerberus promote them should have been apoplectic.) But when firms are motivated (and compensated) based on the quantity rather than the quality of their investments, as private equity firms came to be in the 1990s and 2000s, such seemingly irrational arrangements are tolerated in the money-driven logic of Wall Street.

From Boom to Bust

Due to the fact that the early entrants in private equity were able to enjoy little competition and therefore monopoly profits, the business gained the veneer of wealth, power, and legitimacy that allowed it to grow into a major financial force. But its growing size and scale quickly erased its so-called "advantages"—immunity from the agency problem, for example. A careful analysis of the private equity industry over the last 35 years—which basically spans its entire modern history—demonstrates that private equity funds and the executives who run them create limited value either for the economy at large or for their investors. A number of individual transactions indisputably created value, but on the whole the industry has been a bust from a macroeconomic and societal standpoint. What these investors did master is the art of enriching themselves at the expense of virtually everybody else with whom they come into contact. The primary economic act that a leveraged buyout or leveraged recapitalization (which is best understood as a partial leveraged buyout) accomplishes is to substitute debt for equity on a company's balance sheet. It rarely creates new products. It rarely builds new plants. It rarely funds new research and development. And it rarely leads to the creation of new jobs or new industries. Every aspect of corporate existence is sublimated to the need to service the company's debt. As economist Robert W. Parenteau has written: "With LBOs came a surge in corporate debt that was unrelated to the expansion of the capital stock. Firms were borrowing without building much in the way of new plants and equipment. Debt obligations were being piled onto an existing capital stock that was not much more productive than prior to the LBO boom."[9]

The substitution of debt for equity was one of the leading contributors to the 2008 financial crisis due to the fact that it increased the volume of financial commitments that companies were facing as the financial markets ceased to function and the economy came to a grinding halt in the final quarter of 2008. This was a classic illustration of the "financial-instability hypothesis" outlined by Hyman Minsky, who, as we saw in Chapter 3, argued that years of economic stability would breed instability as economic actors grew increasingly complacent during calm periods and increased their risks by taking on more debt obligations. As Parenteau points out, "[e]ventually, the weight of an accelerating pace of financial commitments against little improvement in the means to increase corporate sector incomes would insure a state of rising financial fragility."[10] The private equity industry and the investors who provided it with equity and debt capital were a living example of Minsky's hypothesis as they continued to build up Ponzi finance structures in the years leading up to the 2008 crisis through the use of financing strategies and instruments that allowed them to stretch balance sheets to the furthest possible limits. (These included covenant-lite bank loans, second lien bank loans, so-called "toggle notes" that could pay interest in cash or in additional notes, and similar structures.[11]) This incessant buildup of debt, led by the private equity industry, rendered corporations increasingly reliant on functioning capital markets and their ability to access additional capital at low cost. This could only continue if lenders maintained confidence in their borrowers' promises to repay them. In other words, the entire financial system was relying on lenders remaining as complacent about repayment in the future as they had been during the period when excesses were building. As we saw in Chapter 4, the death of the promise rendered this an extremely dubious proposition.

The private equity business began with a small number of firms and outsized returns. It is difficult to imagine today, in a world filled with multibillion dollar private equity funds, that the pioneers of the industry, Kohlberg Kravis & Roberts (KKR), started out raising money on an ad hoc basis in 1976 after Bear Stearns, the firm at which its principals were working, turned down a proposal to set up a separate unit to do leveraged buyouts. In 1978, KKR raised the first known private equity fund with a specific mandate to sponsor public-to-private transactions; the fund was all of $30 million in size. Initial investors included Allstate Insurance Co., Teachers Insurance, and Citicorp's venture capital fund. KKR's 1979 acquisition of Houdaille Industries for $355 million marked the first sizeable modern public-to-private buyout of a public company. It employed 13 percent equity and 87 percent debt. The pace of public-to-private takeovers picked up steadily after that. Between 1979 and 1982, the number of these transactions increased from 16 to 31, and the average value of deals rose from $64.9 million to $112.2 million. In the late 1970s and early 1980s, leveraged buyouts of public companies made sense because many public companies were trading below replacement value (i.e., it was less expensive to purchase the company's stock than to try to rebuild the assets from the ground up).

Wall Street is a funny place. It touts originality but flourishes by copying the ideas of others. In the case of leveraged buyouts, it took one spectacular deal to open the floodgates for the private equity business. In 1982, a small buyout firm in New Jersey run by former Treasury Secretary William Simon and his partner Ray Chambers, Wesray Capital Corporation, purchased Gibson Greeting Cards from RCA Corporation for $80 million. The firm invested a mere $1 million of its own money in the deal and borrowed the other $79 million. A year later, Wesray sold 30 percent of the company in an initial public offering that valued Gibson Greetings at an extraordinary $330 million. This was better than the alchemists had done turning dross to gold in the Middle Ages. This transaction attracted hordes of copycats to the business. New private equity funds sprung up overnight around the United States. New commitments to these funds grew from a mere $0.5 billion in 1982 to $1.9 billion in 1983 and $14.7 billion in 1987. A new industry was born. Anybody who had studied business history would have known that the result would be an all-too-predictable crowding-out effect whereby too much capital would depress returns for all but a few firms.

By the time 2000 rolled around, the industry was grossly overpopulated with too many firms chasing too few targets, many of which had already been through one or more cycles of private ownership. Like many things on Wall Street, a good idea was taken to such extremes that it became a very, very bad idea. Private equity claimed that its *raison d'être* was the failure of public company management teams and boards of directors to maximize value for their shareholders. In the early days of the private equity industry, the targets of going private transactions were typically inefficiently run public corporations whose top executives were failing to maximize the value or efficiency of their companies' assets. Many large conglomerates that were constructed in the 1960s and 1970s were disarticulated in the 1980s and 1990s by private equity firms that were able to wring efficiencies out of bloated overhead structures and inefficient managements. But soon the hunter came to resemble the prey. Early returns among the pioneers of private equity were high largely because there was little competition. The early industry leaders—KKR; Forstmann, Little & Co.; Wesray; Gibbons, Green, van Amerongen & Co.; and others—were able to generate returns of 30 percent or more partly due to the fact that they did not have many competitors when they were buying companies in the 1980s and early 1990s. By the mid-1990s, however, the market was populated by hundreds of private equity firms that were attracted to the high returns and fees earned by these early industry leaders. The entrance of multiple competitors turned a once extremely profitable industry into a much less profitable industry, if not for private equity firms than certainly for their limited partners. It also turned into an enormous source of profits for Wall Street, which cheered on the growth of the private industry with all of its financial and political might.

As the business became increasingly overcrowded, Wall Street adopted the auction process as the most efficient way in which to sell corporate properties. This was extremely positive for sellers and disastrous for buyers because it drove the prices of corporate assets through the roof. In an auction, the winner quickly became the loser as it immediately became the owner of a property for which it had likely overpaid by a considerable margin, particularly in periods when debt capital was cheap (which covered most of the 1990s and 2000s). Moreover, winning an auction required very little acumen on the part of private equity firms; it does not take any special skill to pay more than the next guy for a company. Accordingly, as the years progressed, acquisition multiples continued to climb to uneconomic levels. The race to the bottom was run by professionals whose skills were untested by adverse market conditions and whose qualifications as stewards of corporate assets were based primarily on their academic achievements and their ability to navigate benign fundraising markets (both with investors and lenders). Few boasted track records of managing businesses through difficult business cycles. The table was set for Armageddon.

Private Equity Fees: The New Agency Problem

Just as some pundits have described hedge funds as a compensation scheme rather than an asset class, the same could be said about private equity. Private equity firms mastered the art of charging fees with respect to virtually every activity in which they engage. In fact, prior to the financial crisis and the passage of Dodd-Frank, private equity firms charged their investors for practically everything they did short of going to their gold-plated bathrooms (high-priced attorneys reserved that right for themselves). Private equity firms charged fees on the money they raised, on each transaction they completed, on each portfolio company they monitored, on each financing or merger and acquisition transaction their portfolio companies completed, and on each portfolio company they sold. One would think that the management fees they charged on the money they managed would adequately compensate them for these activities, but apparently those fees (a more than generous 1.5 to 2 percent per year) were simply for the privilege of being allowed entrance to the club.

A simple example will suffice to demonstrate the egregiousness of these fees. When Dollar General Corp., the chain of discount stores taken private by KKR and Goldman Sachs, filed for a $750 million initial public offering of stock in 2009, it was required to disclose the fees the company was paying its two private equity sponsors. It turned out that Dollar General had paid KKR and Goldman Sachs a "success fee" of $75 million for buying it in 2007; $13 million in additional "monitoring fees" over the next two years; and would be paying them a final $64 million upon completion of the offering to terminate the monitoring relationship. In other words, KKR and Goldman Sachs soaked Dollar General for $152 million in fees in addition to the management fees (presumably 1.5 to

2 percent per annum) and performance fees (presumably 20 percent above a hurdle rate) they were earning from their funds. Some portion of these fees may have been shared with these firms' limited partners, but that information was not disclosed. Nonetheless, this $152 million didn't come out of nowhere; whatever portion (if any) that was not rebated to limited partners came out of the pockets of the same investors who were already paying management and performance fees. Moreover, Dollar General happened to be one of the very few large, private equity transactions of the 2005–2007 vintage that flourished sufficiently to be able to issue public stock in 2009. Most other large deals struggled yet still paid similarly large success fees, monitoring fees, and whatever other fees could be cooked up to their private equity sponsors. In every case, these large fees contributed to the weakening of balance sheets and enriched private equity sponsors at the expense of creditors and limited partners. In view of the fact that private equity returns are far less attractive than advertised even before risk-adjusting them (see the next section), it would seem that limited partners should have closed down this feeding trough long ago.

Yet not until the passage of Dodd-Frank and the requirement that private equity firms register as investment advisers did these practices come to an end. Since the financial crisis, these regulatory reforms and more aggressive negotiating by private equity limited partners have effectively eliminated these egregious fees. But the question that should have been asked much earlier is what were these private equity managers doing to earn these fees in addition to their hefty management fees? The answer is that they were doing nothing other than what they were being paid to do in the first place: managing their limited partners' investments.

The inappropriateness of these fees is demonstrated by a simple comparison with another group of managers that is hardly reluctant to charge high fees: hedge fund managers. A hedge fund charges a management fee (normally between 1 and 2 percent) plus a performance fee (normally 15 or 20 percent of the profits). If, in addition, the hedge fund were to charge an additional fee on every stock or bond transaction into which it entered, that would be considered egregiously unfair to investors. Yet that is closely analogous to the additional fees that private equity firms charged with respect to monitoring their portfolio companies, or arranging financing or merger transactions for their portfolio companies. For some reason, private equity limited partners were convinced they should pay these additional fees, but it strains credulity to come up with a reasonable basis to justify this practice when they were already being charged hefty management and performance fees.

In 2015, a study done by Oxford University and the Frankfurt School of Finance & Management found that private equity firms charged an aggregate of $20 billion of these fees to 600 companies over the last two decades, including companies that failed such as Texas-based Energy Futures Holdings Corp., which paid $666 million of fees to KKR & Co., TPG, and Goldman Sachs.[12] This is why it is not surprising that one study found that the actual fees paid to private equity firms amount to as much as 6 percent per year.[13]

Also in 2015, the California Public Employees' Retirement System (CalPERS) reported that the difference between its returns were 19 percent before subtracting fees and 12 percent after subtracting fees on its private equity investments over the last 20 years.[14] Such large percentage fees are *prima facie* evidence that private equity firms consistently abuse the special position of trust they hold as fiduciaries to their limited partners. These fees amount in aggregate to billions of dollars that reduce the value of portfolio companies and represent a direct shift of wealth out of the pockets of their investors and into the pockets of the private equity firms' principals. Another study concluded that two-thirds of expected income for private equity firms comes from fixed revenue components that are not sensitive to investment performance.[15] In other words, private equity firms have structured their businesses to reward themselves handsomely regardless of the outcome of their investments, which directly contradicts the private equity mantra that the interests of shareholders and management should be aligned. So much for solving the agency problem!

One further word should also be said about the industry's high management fees. A 1.5 to 2 percent fee on the tens of billions of dollars that the private industry raised has a deeply corrupting influence on general partners because it amounts to so much money that it renders performance-based fees far less important. Private equity firms managing multibillion dollar funds are assured of gargantuan compensation regardless of whether or not their deals are successful, creating a clear conflict of interest between themselves and their limited partners. The payment of additional fees for monitoring portfolio companies or arranging financings or add-on acquisitions for them further exacerbate this conflict. A much more equitable arrangement would involve much lower fixed management fees, no additional fees for carrying out the necessary tasks of managing the portfolio companies, and a 20 percent performance fee with high water marks and claw backs. Such a fee structure would not only appropriately incentivize private equity firms to perform but also properly reflect their limited contribution to economic growth.

Accordingly, instead of solving the agency problems inherent in public companies, the typical private equity fee structure introduced a slew of new problems. It didn't have to be that way. But human nature being what it is—and Wall Street being the kind of place it is—it was perhaps inevitable that the abuses that private equity was designed to cure would sneak back in through the back door. The combination of high management fees on invested and committed capital, additional fees for managing portfolio companies, and a significant share of the profits from selling portfolio companies established a strong incentive for private equity firms to raise as much money as possible, put it to work as quickly as possible, and then pay themselves a dividend or sell these companies at a profit as quickly as possible. Most significantly, even if the third part of this triad was not accomplished, the private equity firm profited handsomely merely from raising a fund and investing the money quickly regardless of the quality of those investments.

The behavior of the largest private equity firms in the period leading up to the 2008 crisis conformed to this pattern as they raised the largest possible funds and put their capital to work as quickly as possible in some of the largest and most questionable private equity deals on record. Examples include the $29.9 billion buyout of casino giant Harrah's Entertainment, Inc., by a private equity group led by Apollo Management L.P. and Texas Pacific Group (which ended up in bankruptcy); the $17.6 billion purchase of Freescale Semiconductor, Inc. by a group of private equity firms that included The Blackstone Group, The Carlyle Group, Pereira Funds, and Texas Pacific Group; and KKR's and Clayton Dubilier's purchase of U.S. Foodservice at an actual multiple of EBITDA of more than 18 times (despite intellectually insulting attempts to convince investors that the multiple was much lower). While private equity firms used to take years to invest their funds, some of the largest funds raised by Bain & Company and The Blackstone Group in that period spent as much as half of their funds (which amounted to billions of dollars) within the first year of raising them.

In late 2009, a large group of institutional investors began organizing to fight back against the egregious fees being charged by private equity firms. A group of 220 investors with about $1 trillion invested in the asset class joined together to demand that private equity firms adopt a framework of best practices and align their interests more squarely with their investors. The new group was called the Institutional Limited Partners Association and focused on the panoply of fees that they were being charged in addition to the basic management and performance fees. This was the first step in ending the practice of private equity firms charging multiple sets of fees for effectively doing the same thing: managing their funds. The irony of such a demand should not go unremarked. Private equity transactions—leveraged buyouts—are based on the rationale that public corporations inadequately align the interests of managers and shareholders. Leveraged buyouts are intended to better align those interests as well as improve operational efficiencies in the business.

One would think that the private equity firms pursuing such strategies (or giving them lip service since few leveraged buyouts in recent years were done to improve productivity) would apply the same principles to their own businesses. Instead, they did the opposite. They disenfranchised their limited partners by providing them with limited transparency and liquidity while extracting huge fees that are unjustified by the risk-adjusted returns they offer (as well as basic standards of fairness and decency). Of course, nobody was putting a gun to the heads of the largest pension funds and endowments in the world to invest in these funds, but these institutions were placed under enormous peer pressure by the propaganda machine that was built up by the private equity industry and their consultants. A better educated investor community was finally becoming less tolerant of the abusive treatment that private equity firms had been doling out to their investors for decades.

The Myth of Private Equity Returns

In November 2015, the California Public Employees' Retirement System reported that its private equity investments had produced an annualized return of 11.1 percent since 1990 compared with an annualized total return of 9.4 percent for the S&P 500.[16] It trumpeted this return as the highest among all of its asset classes but it left out one important fact—it was reporting nominal and not risk-adjusted returns. On a risk-adjusted basis, these returns were arguably inferior to those produced by the S&P 500 and many other investments it could have made. Furthermore, a modestly leveraged investment in the S&P 500 over that period would have produced far superior risk-adjusted returns.

The quality of private equity returns is a topic that deserves more public attention than it has received. Like all investment returns (and statistics generally), private equity returns are subject to manipulation and interpretation. They are significantly affected by the timing of when investments are made and when they are sold, which is not always entirely within the control of the private equity general partner and therefore not necessarily a fair measure of performance. Moreover, public market conditions play an enormous role in determining the success or failure of private equity investments since the outcome of these investments is usually dependent on conditions in the public markets. Accordingly, measuring private equity performance must take into account timing and coincident market conditions as well as factors such as liquidity, leverage, and fees to come to a meaningful conclusion. Unfortunately, there is little evidence that any of these considerations are taken into account when investors evaluate these returns and render their decisions about whether to invest in this asset class.

If private equity returns were subject to the type of scrutiny that all investment returns should be subject, it is highly questionable whether any but a small portion of them would prove to be particularly attractive. Most important, all investment returns must be risk-adjusted in order to be properly evaluated. In the case of private equity returns, risk adjustment means reflecting the fact that these investment funds are highly concentrated, highly leveraged, extremely illiquid, and subject to inordinately high fees. In order to properly compare them to other types of returns in a fair manner, one has to make sure that these characteristics of private equity are fully accounted-for in the return calculation. In the case of private equity returns, there is little evidence that this is done. Instead, investors tend to look at nominal numbers and leave with the impression that private equity outperforms many other asset classes. This simply isn't the case.

A similar argument was made in an important comprehensive study of corporate capital structures in the United States in the 1980s and

1990s that concluded the following: "The investors in LBO funds might be thought smart money, but this identification is not self-evident. Returns of 30 percent sound good until one recognizes that a bet on the S&P 500 consisting of one part equity and five or ten parts debt would have done better, given the trend of equity prices. Institutional investors who are prepared to sell their shareholdings in the market to LBO organizers who then reap substantial fees from the same institutions for underperforming a (leveraged) benchmark does not meet a minimal test of smart money."[17] In an age when consultants and investors place a special emphasis on "Sharpe ratios" (which measure the excess return generated per unit of risk taken) and other risk metrics, it would seem a fairly elementary proposition that returns from private equity should be risk-adjusted.

A typical leveraged buyout fund suffers from a number of risks that fiduciaries are taught to frown upon—concentration risk (funds are generally invested in a limited number of portfolio companies compared to a public equity fund); liquidity risk (portfolio companies must be sold in private corporate transactions or in initial public offerings of stock rather than in public markets); and leverage risk (portfolio companies are purchased using significant amounts of leverage, particularly in the years approaching the 2008 financial crisis, and again in 2014-15). Accordingly, when a private equity firm advertises that it has earned compounded annual return of 15 percent over its lifetime, that number needs to be understood (and adjusted downward) in the context of the concentration, liquidity, and leverage risks that were taken to obtain that return.[18]

A simple illustration drawn from a 2005 study of private equity returns by Steve Kaplan of the University of Chicago Graduate School of Business and Antoinette Schorr of MIT's Sloan School of Management will suffice to demonstrate the complexity of the task.[19] Between March 1997 and March 2000, an investment of $50 million in the S&P 500 would have grown to $103.5 million, a return of 26.8 percent. A private equity fund investing $50 million and realizing $100 million after fees during that same period would have generated an internal rate of return (IRR) of 26 percent. The three-year period immediately following paints a completely different picture. A private equity fund investing $50 million in March 2000 and realizing $50 million in March 2003 would have returned 0 percent, but would have grossly outperformed the

S&P 500 during that period, in which a $50 million investment would have shrunk to $29.5 million. This lesson in absolute versus relative returns should be kept in mind when evaluating all money managers, including private equity firms. But the analysis is even more complex than that, because a truly accurate analysis of returns would have to dissect the specific investments that a private equity firm makes, the amount of leverage it employs in each investment, the manner in which it treats its limited partners with respect to transparency and fees, and other factors. Investing in the public markets is much simpler and more transparent, even in hedge funds that also suffer from agency problems due to their fee arrangements.

Even with these qualifications, it is highly questionable whether any but a very few private equity firms have earned their keep. Most of the studies of private equity returns have concluded that private equity returns are no better than the returns that an investor could obtain from investing in the public stock market using similar amounts of leverage. Investors in private equity funds pay a high price in terms of liquidity and fees for the right to become members of the private equity club. But a closer look at this club suggests that membership does not have its privileges. In fact, after 2008, investors in private equity did well to recall the old Groucho Marx joke that says that a person should be wary of joining any club that would invite him or her to become a member. Private equity clubs share some of the attributes of roach motels (once you enter, it takes years to exit) and high-end luxury vacation home clubs (the exit fees may be painful, they require a lot of upkeep, you are partners with a lot of difficult people, and there may be little money left at the end).

The most damning broad-based study of private equity returns was performed in 2008 by two European professors, Ludovic Phalippou of the University of Amsterdam Business School and Oliver Gottschalg of HEC Paris.[20] Professors Phalippou and Gottschalg evaluated 1,328 mature private equity funds and found that performance estimates identified in previous research and used as industry benchmarks are overstated. They summarize their conclusions as follows: "We find an average net-of-fees performance of 3 percent per year below that of the S&P 500. Adjusting for risk brings the underperformance to 6 percent per year. We estimate fees to be 6 percent per year." With respect to benchmarks, the authors found that "it is basically impossible for investors to benchmark the past performance of funds with information reported in prospectuses. These documents contain only multiples and IRRs.... We show... that average IRRs give upward biased performance estimates. In addition, IRRs cannot be directly compared to the performance of, say, the S&P 500 over the same period." They also pointed out that while many investors told them they were satisfied with private equity returns because they had "doubled their money," the average fund duration was 75 months (6.25 years); in comparison, the average public stock market portfolio returned on average 1 percent per month between 1980 and 2003, which would have produced a better return than a doubling of an investor's money over that period. The authors also offered possible reasons for private equity underperformance (and investors' acceptance of it), including the possibility that investors "might attribute too much weight to the performance of a few successful investments"; and the possibility that "investors have a biased view of performance because performance is generally reported gross of fees and... fees [are] larger than for other asset classes." Finally, the authors pointed out that some investors such as pension funds and government-related entities may have noneconomic motives for investing in private equity such as stimulating local economies. Unfortunately, in view of ugly pay-for-play scandals that occurred in California, New York, and other states, it appears that the non-economic motives for investing in certain private equity funds were hardly benign.

About the only independent study (that is, a study not financed by the private equity industry itself) that argues in favor of private equity outperformance was one conducted by Professor Gottschalg and Professor Alexander P. Groh of the Montpelier Business School in France in 2006.[21] This study, however, was narrowly based and focused on only 133 U.S. buyouts between 1984 and 2004 and compared this limited universe to a simulated portfolio of equally leveraged investments in the S&P index. This study claimed that the 133 buyouts outperformed the public market by 12.6 percent per annum gross of all fees. Based on the fact that this study only looked at a very small number of the buyouts done during the 20-year period in question and compared them to a simulated selection of S&P 500 companies, it is difficult to conclude very much from it. Moreover, this study says very little about the returns of private equity funds since it focused on individual private equity transactions. It was a theoretical exercise that has little application to the real world where investments are made and money is earned and lost.

The 2008 financial crisis demonstrated several of the inherent flaws of the private equity industry. This is unfortunate because an industry that is designed to be sheltered from the vagaries of the public markets should have been better positioned to survive such a market downturn. The fact that the private equity industry fared so poorly during the crisis revealed that its original character as an asset class that was designed to be a superior form of long-term ownership of capital assets failed. The losses generated by firms in 2008 wiped out years of positive returns and strongly suggested that previous years' returns, to the extent they were based on unrealized gains and subjective valuations of portfolio companies, were illusory. The industry wants to have it both ways; it wants to be judged on long-term performance but be compensated on short-term performance. Those goals are at odds with each other. After the financial crisis, most firms (even the elite performers) were far under water in terms of earning their performance fees and some faced large cash claw back liabilities resulting from losses that ate up profits from performance fees earned on companies that were bought and sold at a profit in earlier years. The results from 2008 damaged the long-term track records of virtually every private equity firm in existence, making it harder for them to conceal the true mediocrity of the industry's returns and more difficult to justify its very existence. This contributed to many of them shifting their business models away from private equity toward more stable asset management businesses in the years that followed. Over time, their track records improved as their portfolio companies recovered and some firms took advantage of market conditions to make timely investments in beaten down companies. But their failure to anticipate the crisis and the losses suffered as a result tarnished their reputations as the smartest guys in the room.

Men Behaving Badly

The behavior of private equity firms is usually a reliable indicator of the stage a credit cycle has reached. The less productive their behavior, the more likely the cycle is reaching its late stages. Two types of transactions in which private equity firms repeatedly engage during the late stages of credit cycles tend to indicate that credit is mispriced, the credit cycle is far advanced, and debt investors should be running in the other direction from bond and loan offerings involving private equity-owned borrowers.

The first type of transaction that investors should avoid is the infamous "dividend deal," in which a private equity-owned firm borrows money to pay a dividend distribution to its owners. The debt raised in these transactions is not used to enhance the business of the borrower in any way, for example, by building additional facilities, funding research and development, creating new products, or hiring new workers. The money instead is paid out to the private equity sponsor in order to reduce the capital it originally invested in the business. This practice is contrary to the *raison d'être* of private equity, which is supposed to be based on overcoming an important aspect of the agency problem, specifically, the potential conflicts of interest raised when the owners and management of the company have only a small ownership stake in the enterprise. While the private equity firm generally maintains a significant ownership position after a dividend transaction, the amount of money it has at risk in the business is significantly reduced if not eliminated.

Dividend transactions are particularly noxious to the health of lenders, who are left lending money to a company whose owners are in possession of a free "call option" on any appreciation in the value of the business but are also in a position to walk away without losing money if the business begins to falter under the weight of its new debt. The only potential limitation on these dividend deals is the law governing fraudulent transfers, but these are relatively easily avoided.[22] Many companies that have paid dividends to their private equity sponsors over the years have subsequently gone bankrupt, leaving their lenders with large losses and their private equity sponsors feeling no pain.[23]

The second practice that indicates that the credit cycle is entering its terminal stages is the phenomenon of private equity-owned companies being sold by one buyout firm to another. Some firms, like Simmons Company (the mattress manufacturer) or General Nutrition Companies, have been sold numerous times between buyout firms. Simmons Company, in fact, is a company that fell into bankruptcy after paying a large dividend to one of its private equity owners during the course of being bought and sold seven different times by buyout firms over a period of two decades.[24] One of the purposes of a leveraged buyout is supposed to be to wring efficiencies out of a business that was previously publicly held. Accordingly, there is little rationale for a private equity firm purchasing a company that has already been retooled by another private equity firm (or several) since there should theoretically be few efficiencies left to capture. The real reason such deals are done, of course, is to generate fees for private equity firms. The selling firm is able to generate a "realization event" that triggers a "transaction" fee and allows it to return capital to investors, while the buying firm is able to pay itself a transaction fee on the purchase. The wonder is that lenders continue to finance such transactions, which are done at higher and higher multiples of cash flow and contribute little to economic growth. The question investors and lenders should be asking when they see such deals is why no strategic buyer is interested in buying these companies at a higher price than another private equity firm. The answer to that question is the reason why investors should avoid lending to these companies and be asking private equity firms why they can't find something better to buy than somebody else's used merchandise.

Private Equity and Cheap Debt: Birds of a Feather Flop Together

The private equity industry could not have flourished without access to investors willing to pay its egregious fees. But there is another group of investors who have been more than willing over the years to lend their capital to this industry at rates that offer nothing close to an appropriate return for the risk: junk bond and leveraged loan investors. Without investors willing to grossly underprice risk, the private equity business never would have reached its enormous size and scope.

The story of Michael Milken and Drexel Burnham Lambert, Inc., has been told many times (mostly inaccurately), and this is not the place to repeat it. Suffice it to say that Mr. Milken never intended the market he founded to be used to finance the types of change-of-control transactions in which private equity specializes. In the early days of the junk bond market, Drexel Burnham financed new businesses and new technologies such as Turner Broadcasting System, Inc. (CNN), McCaw

Cellular Communications (cellular telephones), Circus Circus Enterprises and other gaming companies that now comprise modern Las Vegas, and many other productive projects that contributed to the growth of the economy. By the time Mr. Milken was forced to leave Drexel Burnham to fight highly politicized government charges against him (that alleged conduct that pales in comparison to the wrongdoing that has occurred in the succeeding two decades), private equity was beginning to become an unproductive force in the financial markets and Mr. Milken was advising companies to issue equity, not debt. But the many copycats on Wall Street that saw the profits that Drexel Burnham generated from the junk bond business had no interest in heeding Mr. Milken's warning. The leveraging of the United States had started apace.

KKR became the dominant private equity firm of the 1980s on the back of Drexel Burnham's junk bond financing engine. The relationship culminated in the ill-advised buyout of RJR Nabisco (completed without Mr. Milken's involvement), which boasted a novel security called "increasing rate notes" that ultimately threatened to blow up the tobacco maker. KKR and its investors were able to escape (barely) from this transaction with their capital intact, and KKR was able to console itself with the enormous fees it paid itself while taking a reputational beating in the press from which it never fully recovered. The RJR Nabisco deal showed Wall Street at its egotistical, greedy worst, and the years that followed did little to dispel the view that private equity dealmakers and their Wall Street amanuenses were interested in little but lining their own pockets at the expense of everyone else.

Drexel Burnham was not so fortunate and ultimately succumbed in February 1990 to the pressures of a government investigation that began in 1986 (extremely poor management of the firm didn't help either). But the rest of Wall Street took up the mantle of junk bonds and continued to feed the private equity monster. In the wake of Drexel's bankruptcy, LBO transactions plunged from $75.8 billion in 1989 to $17.9 billion in 1990 and $8 billion in 1992 as the savings and loan crisis and a deep recession slowed deal activity to a halt. But soon merger activity reignited, with M&A activity increasing from $100 billion in 1992 to almost $600 billion in 1996. During that period, the number of completed deals increased from 3,500 to 6,100. This increase in transactional volume was part of the deconstruction of American conglomerates, a process that many view as having contributed to productivity improvements and operating efficiencies in U.S. business.

There is another view, however. A great deal of evidence shows that most mergers do not lead to efficiencies and enhanced productivity but instead lead to job cuts and constitute admissions that companies can't generate internal growth. Moreover, there is very little strategic impetus or justification for most private equity transactions. As noted above, private equity became a dumping ground for businesses that no longer fit inside conglomerates and could find no strategic purchaser or partner. The high cost of capital involved in leveraged buyouts suggests they are an extremely inefficient way for an economy to recycle its garbage, although outright liquidation or downsizing may be no more efficient. Accordingly—and this is borne out by the declining condition of American industry today—it might be more appropriate to view the statistics describing the merger boom of the 1990s as an augur of negative economic things to come.

In the early twenty-first century, a new kind of cheap financing became the main facilitator of leveraged buyouts—leveraged loans purchased by collateralized loan obligations (CLOs). While leveraged loans had been around since the 1980s, they only developed into a tradable security in the 1990s with the introduction of prime rate mutual funds, hedge funds that were willing to invest in them, and the creation of CLOs. Figure 6.1 shows the growth of this market through the late 2000s.

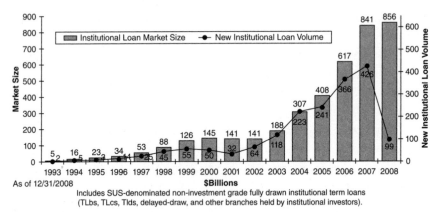

Figure 6.1   Institutional Leveraged Loan Market Size

The market exploded with the advent of CLOs, a type of collateralized debt obligation that holds leveraged loans as its primary form of collateral. Banks began to shape loans to these borrowers to conform to CLOs' specific structural needs, and a marriage made in heaven was born. Figure 6.2 shows the explosion in the CLO market and how it almost perfectly tracked the growth in the leveraged loan market.

By the mid-2000s, private equity firms dominated the market for leveraged loans and were able to dictate the terms on which such loans were offered. Pricing on these loans was based on the London Interbank Offered Rate (Libor), which is the rate at which banks loan money to each other in the London banking market. The price of a loan was based on the spread (number of basis points or hundredths of a percentage point) above Libor that a borrower is required to pay on a loan. As the market became increasingly overheated in the mid-2000s, spreads tightened and private equity firms were able to borrow at very low rates (Libor plus 125 to 250 basis points) and also negotiate extremely favorable covenants that gave them a great deal of latitude not previously accorded borrowers. These covenants, which were described in Chapter 4, allowed these borrowers to incur additional debt, pay dividends, and engage in many other activities that were contrary to the interests of lenders. The low cost of this financing, which generally came to less than 5 percent, enabled many transactions to be completed that could not have been done had money been more expensive. Alternatively,

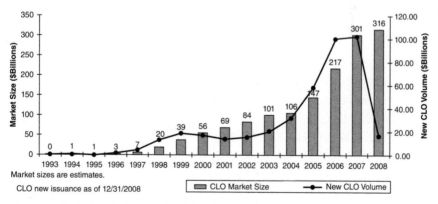

Figure 6.2 Historical Growth of the CLO Market.

low-cost financing allowed private equity firms to pay higher prices for companies than strategic buyers who were no longer able to finance at lower rates than private companies (in part due to the costs associated with the Sarbanes-Oxley Act of 2002).[25]

While the CLO market fell dormant for a couple of years after the financial crisis, it returned with a vengeance in 2011–2012 courtesy of the cheap money policies of the Federal Reserve and the ingenuity of Wall Street's leveraged finance bankers. In 2014, more than $100 billion of CLOs were issued and the leveraged loan market was again breaking records for new issuance while covenant-lite loans were the rule rather than the exception. In fact, new variations of covenant-lite loans were so extreme as to render bank debt almost unrecognizable in terms of the weak protections it provided lenders. But one thing that had not returned to its previous peak was leveraged buyout activity. For the moment, at least, the era of the mega-buyout was dead.

This was due to several factors. First, the disappointing returns and large losses generated by the huge buyouts of the mid-2000s (including in particular the bankruptcies of KKR's buyout of Energy Future Holdings and Apollo's and TPG's buyout of gaming giant Caesars Entertainment)[26] did serious damage to some private equity firms' reputations and convinced them to focus on smaller targets. In addition, the Federal Reserve and other banking regulators began pressuring banks to reduce their loans to highly leveraged companies, discouraging them from extending loans above a certain leverage threshold (generally 6.0x EBITDA/Interest coverage). This significantly reduced the appetite for highly leveraged transactions although a few were still financed by firms that are not federally insured institutions like Jefferies & Co.[27]

But there was another reason why buyout activity has waned. As the stock market continued to rally to high valuation levels, strategic buyers were better able to compete for target companies against private equity firms and use their own high stock prices as currencies to outbid them. Unlike the 2000s, private equity firms were no longer able to overpay since they could not borrow unlimited amounts of money. Instead, corporate buyers became the new buyout artists and unleashed a massive acquisition wave that was financed with huge amounts of low cost debt and bloated stock prices courtesy of the Federal Reserve.

These changes led the largest private equity firms to dramatically alter their business models in the years following the financial crisis. Following the model of The Blackstone Group L.P., which established a formidable and well-balanced business that includes private equity, investment banking, real estate and asset management, the other large firms followed suit. Today, private equity represents a much smaller part of the businesses of these companies. Furthermore, they reformed their compensation structures to better align the interests of their general partners with those of their public shareholders. For the most part, their general partners now take only *de minimus* salaries (by Wall Street standards) and earn virtually all of their income through dividends, although in some cases they are paid slightly larger dividends than public shareholders due to dual class share structures. This is a major improvement, however, over the original compensation structures that existed at the time these firms went public. The general partners have succeeded in creating enormous fortunes for themselves, but at least they are now eating their own cooking.

Private Equity Goes Public: A Study in the Oxymoronic

The very idea of a private equity firm going public is deeply ironic. While investing in the stock of private equity firms was a poor investment for the first few years after they went public, it proved to be a great investment since stock markets recovered from their post-crisis lows of March 2009. And while these novel ownership structures opened multiple cans of worms in terms of creating conflicts of interest for the owners of these firms, these conflicts appear to have been resolved to the satisfaction of shareholders. The real lesson that the public ownership of private equity firms has taught is one that I learned when I was involved in managing the Drexel Burnham Employee Partnerships during the 1990s: Investing at the bottom of a credit cycle can be enormously profitable.

The Drexel Burnham Employee Partnerships held private equity securities in many of the leveraged buyouts that were underwritten by Drexel Burnham Lambert, Inc. during the 1980s. My firm began managing this portfolio at the nadir of the 1991–1992 credit crisis triggered by the collapse of the savings and loan industry and the bankruptcy of Drexel Burnham. The high yield bond market was in disarray and high yield bond prices and private equity values were severely depressed. But as the economy recovered, I watched the value of these securities recover as we worked to maximize the value of the portfolio. This taught me an invaluable lesson: When markets recover from a credit crisis, the value of leveraged securities skyrocket. I watched that happen again 20 years later to the depressed assets held by publicly traded private equity firms as well as to their own stock prices. In addition to huge capital gains that investors garnered from investing in all but one of these firms (Fortress Investment Group, LLC's stock has yet to recover), they were paid handsome dividends along the way. This is a lesson that investors should keep in mind when the next credit crisis hits as it inevitably will.

KKR completed the first major public offering of a private equity investment fund in Europe in May 2006, listing KKR Private Equity Investors L.P. (KPE) on the Euronext exchange in Amsterdam. The manner in which this offering was handled illustrates why these offerings ran into early trouble. KPE increased the size of its offering from $1.5 billion to $5.0 billion due to strong demand, but the shares themselves received a lukewarm reception, traded down on the opening, and have never traded above the $25 per share offering price. Naturally, the firm rewarded itself with €70 million of advisory fees immediately upon being listed, not only shifting a significant chunk of money from the pockets of the public shareholders to insiders but also signaling to investors that going public would not change the general partners' practice of charging exorbitant fees every chance they could. (What other type of public company would have the gall to reward its executives for going public with such an egregious fee?) Within two months the stock had dropped to less than $22 per share, hurting the chances of any other private equity firm pulling off a similar offering. (See Figure 6.3.)

KKR's goal of listing its stock in the United States took three more years to realize. On June 24, 2009, KKR announced plans to have KPE, which was then trading at about $5.00 per share, purchase 30 percent of KKR's parent company. This was KKR's second attempt

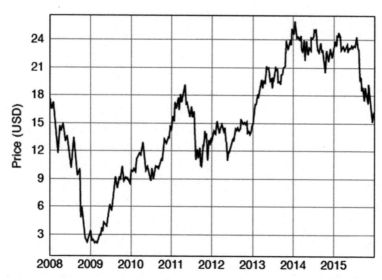

Figure 6.3 KKR & Co. (KKR) Stock Prices, December 31, 2007, through December 31, 2015
SOURCE: Bloomberg.

to bring the parent public through some type of backdoor offering, the first attempt having failed during the financial crisis in 2008. KKR finally accomplished its goal of becoming a public company on October 1, 2009, with the completion of a merger between KKR and KPE. The new company was renamed KKR & Co. In the merger, KPE received interests representing 30 percent of the outstanding equity in KKR, and KKR's owners and employees retained the remaining 70 percent. In the period between the June 2009 announcement of the merger between KPE and KKR and the final merger, the price of the KPE units rose 65 percent to over $9.00 per share (the overall stock market was enjoying a strong rally at the time). By June 1, 2015, KKR stock had recovered with the rest of the market to $22.71 and was paying an 8 percent annual dividend, but by December 31, 2015, it had fallen to $15.59.

KKR earlier brought public another investment entity, KKR Financial Holdings LLC (KFN), in June 2005 at $24.00 per share. KFN was a real estate investment trust (REIT) that was turned into an entity

primarily invested in collateralized loan obligations (CLOs). Through
KFN's CLOs, KKR was able to purchase large chunks of the bank loans
that were used to finance KKR-sponsored leveraged buyouts (as well as
loans of other private equity deals) during the height of the LBO boom
in the mid-2000s and thereafter. KFN turned out to be KKR's biggest
public embarrassment since the RJR Nabisco buyout until the bankruptcies of Energy Future Holdings in 2014 and Samson Resources in
2015. Between the time of its IPO on June 23, 2005, through December
9, 2009, KFN stock declined by approximately 80 percent due to a
combination of poor loan selection, difficult market conditions, and the
difficulties facing the private equity business. (See Figure 6.4.)

KFN never recovered its IPO value of $24.00 per share. It was
ultimately acquired by KKR in 2014 at a price of roughly $12.00 per
share. Some investors, including readers of *The Credit Strategist* who
were advised to purchase the stock when it was trading below $2.00 per
share, made out like bandits, however. KFN now serves as the foundation of KKR's growing asset management business.

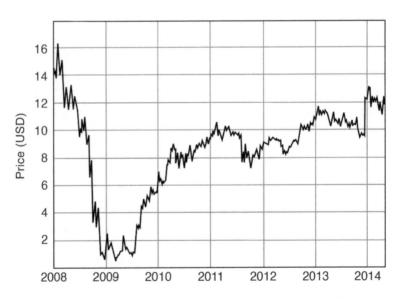

Figure 6.4   KKR Financial Holdings, LLC (KFN) Stock Prices, December 31,
2007, through April 30, 2014
Source: Bloomberg.

The Blackstone Group L.P. was the first of the large private equity giants to announce a public offering in the United States. Blackstone filed its public offering plan with the Securities and Exchange Commission in March 2007. The prospectus it filed was lengthy, highly convoluted, and disclosed little real information about the company's operations, a sure sign to wise investors that it should be avoided. This offering came just a few weeks after Fortress Investment Group LLC completed its initial public offering in February of that year. Fortress's IPO was a huge (albeit short-lived) success, with its shares rising 68 percent on the first day of trading. Fortress was both a private equity and hedge fund manager, with about 60 percent of its assets devoted to leveraged buyouts. The offering made instant billionaires of its principals and, according to *The Wall Street Journal*, "had other hedge funds and private-equity managers scrambling to their calculators, gazing over their own potential worth if they were to follow the lead of Fortress and become public."[28] The bloom quickly came off the rose, however, and Fortress's stock has been the worst performing private equity stock since it was issued at $18.50 per share in February 2007. As of December 31, 2015, it was trading at only $5.09 per share and had lost more than 70 percent of its IPO value (not to mention nearly 85 percent of its peak trading value of over $33 per share reached in April 2007), and even traded at under $1.00 per share on several days during the last week of 2008 before closing at $1.00 per share on December 31 of that year. (See Figure 6.5.)

Despite mild protests from some of Blackstone's limited partners, who were perhaps coming to realize that a public offering might sacrifice their interests to those of the firm's principals, the firm made an unseemly rush to complete its offering in June 2007 just as members of Congress and the media were catching on and began calling for regulators to scrutinize the deal more closely. And stock market investors, thinking they were being let in on some kind of inside deal by being allowed to invest in Blackstone, piled into the IPO. The stock, which was issued at $18 per share, closed at slightly over $35 per share at the close of trading on the first day, June 22, 2007. Blackstone Chairman Stephen Schwarzman was worth $10 billion on paper and his archrival Henry Kravis was surely tearing out what was left of his hair at having been beaten to the public market trough in the United States. At the time—June

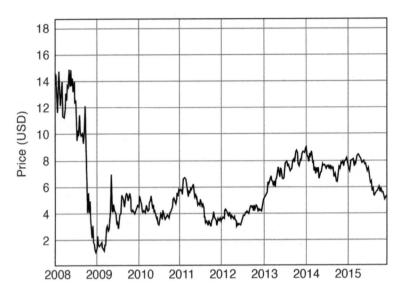

Figure 6.5   Fortress Investment Group LLC (FIG) Stock Prices, December 31, 2007, through December 31, 2015
Source: Bloomberg.

2007—I observed in *The Credit Strategist* that the Blackstone offering would undoubtedly signal the top of the market and that Blackstone stock would prove to be a terrible investment.[29] *Barron's* also presciently called the Blackstone IPO the top of the private equity market. But the firm's competitors were not to be easily deterred when they saw that Blackstone's principals were able to monetize billions of dollars of their ownership interests in their firm. (See Figure 6.6.)

Since the financial crisis, Blackstone has become the dominant private equity firm in the world and a powerhouse in all of its businesses including the predominant global real estate investment firm. As of June 1, 2015, its stock was trading at $42.42 per share and paying an 8.5 percent annual dividend, though it fell back to $30 by the end of 2015.

Next up at the plate was Leon Black. His firm, Apollo Management L.P., completed a convoluted backdoor merger into a public shell corporation in Europe called AP Alternative Investments L.P. in November 2007. For a long time, this deal was a money-loser for public shareholders, with the stock declining by more than 60 percent between

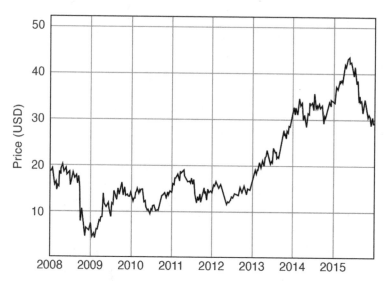

Figure 6.6   The Blackstone Group L.P. (BX) Stock Prices, December 31, 2007, through December 31, 2015
Source: Bloomberg.

its offering in November 2007 and December 9, 2009. This stock also had the dubious honor of spending much of late 2008 and early 2009 trading at under $2.00 per share. Smart investors would have bet on Mr. Black, however.

Meanwhile, Apollo Global Management (APO) finally went public in the U.S. in 2011. As of December 31, 2015, Apollo stock was trading at $15.18 per share, down from a high of $35.72 per share on January 6, 2014. (See Figure 6.7.) Apollo, which reportedly was in desperate straits at the depths of the financial crisis, was founded by three former Drexel Burnham executives, so it is not surprising that it was able to realize the value of its deeply distressed assets. One reason for the sharp decline in Apollo's stock price since 2014 may be the firm's abusive treatment of creditors in several deals, including its ill-fated leveraged buyout of Caesars Entertainment. Apollo, along with Texas Pacific Group, significantly overpaid for the gaming giant. Moreover, shortly after the deal was consummated, the financial crisis sent the gaming industry into a sharp decline. When it became obvious that Caesars would be unable to pay its debts by

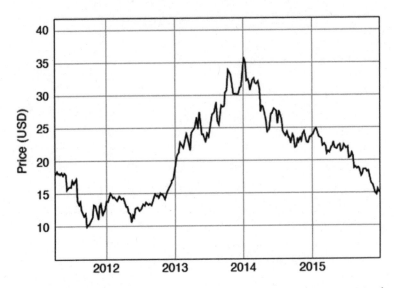

Figure 6.7   Apollo Global Management LLC (APO) Stock Prices, March 29, 2011, through December 31, 2015
SOURCE: Bloomberg.

2011, Apollo and TPG should have initiated a series of debt-for-equity exchanges to reduce the company's debt load. Instead, they engineered a series of highly questionable transactions designed to salvage their equity at the expense of creditors, triggering billions of dollars of losses for lenders, unleashing lawsuits against the firms and their principals, and severely damaging both firms' reputations. As a result, many lenders were left questioning Apollo's willingness to honor its obligations and stopped financing Apollo's private equity transactions, increasing the firm's cost of capital in other leveraged buyouts. The bankruptcy court overseeing the Caesars' bankruptcy appointed a bankruptcy examiner to investigate the transactions arranged by Apollo. The $6 billion that Apollo and Texas Pacific invested in the deal appears to be a total loss.

After the Apollo offering, the window for these deals closed for several years until The Carlyle Group L.P. went public in late 2012 and Ares Management LLC went public in 2014.

Taxing Labor as Capital

One of the truly unfortunate ways in which public policy encourages private equity activity is the favorable tax treatment of the "carried interests" of private equity firms. The "carried interest" tax creates an enormous incentive to engage in leveraged buyouts and increase the debt burden of American corporations; one would think this would be precisely the types of activity that policymakers would want to discourage. Yet like so many policies that are dictated by special interests and flawed economic thinking, the private equity industry was granted a tax break that has little intellectual, economic, or social policy justification.

Carried interests represent the share of the profits (generally 20 percent) that a private equity general partner is paid when it sells a portfolio company and realizes a gain. Due to manipulation on the part of clever tax lawyers and accountants, as well as lobbying by the Private Equity Council, the industry's mouthpiece, the private equity industry garnered capital gains treatment of its carried interest profits for many years. After the Bush administration lowered the tax rate on capital gains to 15 percent, private equity firms' principals were able to pay a much lower tax rate on the fruits of their daily labor than any other worker in the United States was required to pay on his or hers. This unjustifiably favorable tax treatment was not only poor public policy that contributed to the widening gap between rich and poor in our society, but it generated disrespect for the tax system through its obvious unfairness. It was another example of the corruption of our moral sentiments

A similar tax regime was introduced in the United Kingdom as well. In 1998, then Chancellor of Exchequer Gordon Brown introduced tax relief to encourage new business investment. Known as "taper relief," it lowered the capital gains tax on business assets, which were defined to include private equity carried interests. This regime was even more egregious than in the U.S. The capital gains tax rate was lowered from 40 percent (which was clearly too high) to an almost irrelevant 10 percent, provided that the assets were held for 10 years (this period was subsequently lowered first to four years in 2000 and then to an almost laughable two years in 2002).[30]

There is a significant distinction between a carried interest, for which a private equity partner makes no investment of capital, and an investment by a private equity general partner in his fund or directly in a portfolio company. To the extent that any individual, including a private equity partner or executive, makes an investment of capital in a company and later makes a profit upon the sale of the company, he is entitled to capital gains treatment. But carried interests do not represent an investment of the private equity principal's capital—they represent an investment of his labor. And labor is taxed—and has always been taxed—at higher ordinary income rates.[31] There is no intellectual justification for taxing one type of labor—a private equity partner's carried interest—as a capital asset when all other forms of labor are not taxed as capital assets. The fact that the private equity industry was able to convince the tax authorities, who ultimately answer to the U.S. Treasury and Congress, to allow this treatment is deplorable.

When Congress was threatening to begin taxing carried interests at ordinary income rates, a number of private equity chieftains hiked up to Capitol Hill to lobby against this change in an unseemly show of greed. Among the arguments they trotted out was one that struck an especially insincere chord: They argued that taxing them at the same rate as every other American would make them stop taking risks. Considering that 60 percent or more of the income of private equity firms is generated by fees that are unrelated to the outcome of their investments, and that the individuals making these arguments already possessed personal wealth beyond the dreams of most Americans, this argument ranked among the most appallingly cynical and intellectually vacuous to ever disgrace the halls of Congress. Sadly, our intellectually bankrupt and morally corrupt Congress bought these arguments and the private equity industry was successful in buying off repeated attempts to repeal this egregious gift to the least deserving 1 percent.

The carried interest tax break is less important in reducing the taxes of private equity executives of publicly held private equity firms. For the most part, these firms compensate their senior executives through dividend payments on their stock that are taxed at the lower long-term capital gains tax rate. Nonetheless, this egregious tax break is long past its sell-by date and should be eliminated once and for all.

Calling Dr. Kevorkian?

The true toll that private equity has exacted from the U.S. economy will not be known for decades. A mind is a terrible thing to waste, and too many minds have been squandered on the types of financial engineering to which private equity is devoted. While many of the brightest and most promising students attending U.S. universities are attracted to the exorbitant compensation offered by private equity firms and the investment banks that cater to them, American society and the entire world would be far better served if these promising young men and women became scientists and teachers. Instead, as the U.S. economy struggles to recover from the 2008 financial crisis, the corporate landscape remains littered with the carcasses of overleveraged companies that were seduced by the siren song of private equity profiteers.

According to the research firm Preqin, one-year returns for the private equity industry fell by 27.6 percent in 2008, the nadir of the financial crisis. But that hardly tells the full story of the damage these investors wrought, since private equity firms were not required to mark their assets to market in any meaningful way for decades. Only in July 2011 did the SEC require private equity firms to register as investment advisers under the Investment Advisers Act of 1940, which subjected them to new rules regarding how they value their assets and how they charge fees to their limited partners. During the financial crisis, even as they were losing hundreds of billions of dollars, private equity groups required investors to invest an additional $148 billion of cash under previous commitments in 2008 with virtually no prospects of investing it profitably while distributing back only $63 billion.[32] The outlook for 2009 was even bleaker; hundreds of billions of dollars were locked in partnerships that required further capital contributions from damaged limited partners even while the opportunities for making leveraged investments were slim or none. Rather than a source of funds for investors and a source of liquidity for financial markets, the private equity business spent itself into exhaustion and inflicted significant systemic damage while doing so. It would take several years, and the Herculean efforts of the Federal Reserve, to bail out private equity investors.

The damage wrought by the crisis was enormous and despite recovery in asset values since the market's low in 2009, many public pension funds remained seriously underfunded after the financial crisis. The California Public Employees' Retirement System (CalPERS), the nation's largest pension fund, announced a 23.4 percent loss for the fiscal year ended June 2008, a drop in value of $56 billion to $180.9 billion. It also reported that its returns from private equity were in the bottom 1 percent of its peer group with a 5.8 percent return for the past 10 years (compared to a median peer return of 9.6 percent for the period).[33] The California State Teachers' Retirement System (CalSTRS), the nation's second largest pension fund, lost 25 percent for the fiscal year ended June 2008 as well, losing $43 billion in assets to fall to $118.8 billion in size.[34] Among the largest contributors to these losses were private equity investments, although virtually every asset class (including public equities) plunged in value over the last half of 2008. Major universities like Harvard and Yale that championed the so-called "endowment model" of investing and endorsed the private equity ideal (long-term investment inured from the short-term focus of public markets) were also severely damaged by private equity losses in their endowments in 2008.

Unlike public equities and fixed-income portfolios, however, private equity portfolios left these and other institutional investors stuck with illiquid holdings and commitments to fund similar investments in a climate in which private equity investments were virtually impossible to make due to the lack of leveraged buyout financing. Some private equity firms allowed their investors to back out of these financing commitments, while others begged their investors to honor their obligations. In the meantime, most of 2009 passed without new investments being made. Instead, these firms spent most of their time propping up their existing portfolio companies, negotiating with creditors, and trying to figure out how to justify their existence now that their business model had been definitively revealed to be a "heads-we-win, tails-we-still-win-but-our-investors lose" proposition. Since the end of the financial crisis, there have been a limited number of multibillion dollar leveraged buyouts. The biggest profits were earned by firms "doubling down" on their own or their competitors' bad investments and investing new capital into bankrupt or troubled companies such as Lyondell Chemicals. Once again, the lesson is that those who can read credit cycles and ride them out or invest at precisely the moment when everyone else is panicking can earn enormous profits.

As signs of market stress began to materialize, some of largest firms began to shift their business models from leveraged buyouts to asset management just before the full force of the financial crisis hit. Apollo Management L.P., Texas Pacific Group, The Blackstone Group (through its acquisition of then-troubled asset management firm GSO Capital Partners L.P.), Bain Capital, LLC's credit affiliate Sankaty Advisors, LLC (which was already an experienced debt investor) and KKR (through KKR Financial Holdings, LLC) all loaded up on leveraged loans in early 2008 using large amounts of borrowed money and significant amounts of their limited partners' capital. Apollo even managed to convince CalPERS to give it $1 billion to invest in leveraged loans in a separate account. These firms generally followed the same formula, borrowing approximately 75 percent of the purchase price of the loans in which they invested. They thought they were getting a steal buying these loans at 25 percent discounts to par, licking their chops at the desperation of the banks that were unloading these albatrosses. Apparently they did not suspect that the banks' willingness to finance their investments in these loans was not a sign of their strong relationships with these institutions but rather an indication of the banks' desperation to shrink their balance sheets as credit markets were collapsing around them. For once, the banks took the clever private equity firms for a ride. In the second half of 2008 the loan market came apart, with the average price of a leveraged loan dropping by approximately 35 to 40 percent, wiping out the private equity stake's holdings in these loans. By then, many of these firms' limited partners had reached the limits of their tolerance for the so-called "privilege" of belonging to the private equity clubs that would have them as members. It would take years for these investments to recover in value as private equity firms morphed into large asset management firms and reduced their reliance on leveraged buyouts.[35]

Private Equity: The Damage Done

While leveraged buyouts started with the legitimate purpose of increasing corporate efficiency, by the mid-1990s they were little more than a speculative activity that generated fees for Wall Street and private equity sponsors. Instead of feeding innovation and creativity, which even the ultimately overblown venture capital-funded Internet bubble accomplished to some extent (bringing us companies such as eBay, Amazon.com, and others), the private equity machine simply provided a market for changes in corporate control that substituted debt for equity on corporate balance sheets. Capital that could have been used for research and development, new buildings, jobs, or funding innovative new products was instead consumed by interest payments. The opportunity cost in terms of financial, physical, and intellectual capital is incalculable. Private equity is where capital went to die, and it managed to bury too many bodies with the full complicity of virtually every constituent of the financial system.

But the indictment of private equity doesn't stop there. The influence of these firms in terms of the fees they pay to financial institutions and the political influence they exercise on Capitol Hill altered the incentives that drive the financial world and deeply corrupted the moral sentiments of our entire society. Private equity was instrumental in forging a financial ethos that favors the interests of the individual over those of the group, debt over equity, and speculation over production. It managed to perpetuate tax laws that led to the overleveraging of the U.S. economy as well as unjustifiably favorable tax treatment of its own profits that helped create an American oligarchy and contributed to the growing gap between rich and poor that threatens long-term social stability. As such, history should rightly look back on private equity as a deeply pernicious influence that contributed to the decline of U.S. financial and moral hegemony in the world.

The growing corporate sector indebtedness that was a defining feature of financialization was driven by the going private boom that began in the late 1970s and gained momentum in the 1980s. This phenomenon was rationalized by arguments that promoted return on equity (increasing shareholder value) at the expense of all other measures of value in a capitalist economy. The blind pursuit of shareholder value argued that the sole purpose of management is to maximize the short-term return to shareholders. Other considerations—the fair and equitable treatment of labor; sound environmental policies; enhancing the long-term health of the enterprise and surrounding community—were sacrificed at the altar of shareholders' demands for immediate gratification. This view dovetailed perfectly with the free market ideology that grew dominant during the 1980s when President Ronald Reagan and Prime Minister Margaret Thatcher reigned over the Western world and helped drive the Iron Curtain into submission (although the Communists inflicted much of the damage on themselves).

Into the breach stepped the private equity industry. Over the past 40 years, private equity gathered an inordinate amount of capital and power. The result was a leveraging up of the U.S. economy and soon thereafter of Western European economies. Now Asia is on the radar screen of these financiers. What has followed? The private equity industry's lobbyists will tell us, flying in the face of common sense and substantial evidence to the contrary, that industry has become more efficient and productive. But there is little question that crucial activities such as research and development have suffered tremendously at the hands of these owners. Rather than building businesses, the lion's share of private equity firms have made servicing debt the new Holy Grail of corporate management. They strip their portfolio companies of excess employees and assets in the name of efficiency instead of developing new products or adding new jobs or facilities or anything else of significance to the productive capacity of the economies in which their portfolio companies operate. They transferred an enormous amount of wealth from the pockets of public shareholders and their own limited partners into their own pockets. Due to the egregious fee schemes they foisted on their investors, this has not even had the desired effect of transferring wealth back into the pockets of institutional investors who saw it disappear from their public equity portfolios. Instead, private equity managers got rich at the expense of every other party with whom they interacted in the economic system. The private equity industry has inflicted so much damage on the economy in terms of draining resources and wealth away from productive uses that it is doubtful that the United States will ever recover what it has lost. Rather than proving to be the innovators that reawakened U.S. enterprise, private equity turned out to be the undertakers that buried a good part of it.

Reform of Private Equity Firms

Private equity would never have inflicted so much damage on the economy had it been subject to a modicum of sensible regulation. Fortunately, some of the reforms that I recommended in the first edition of this book were adopted to subject this industry to greater oversight.

Registration as Investment Advisers

Private equity firms were able to operate under the regulatory radar for too long in the United States and the United Kingdom. Until the financial crisis, there was little discussion in the United States of requiring these firms to register as investment advisers under the Investment Advisers Act of 1940, as amended (the "Investment Advisers Act"). As a result, despite following strategies that were identical to those offered by many hedge funds that were registered, these firms were operating in a regulatory black hole that allowed them to follow their own set of rules. In contrast, hedge funds that were registered under the Investment Advisers Act were subject to strict rules governing how they valued their investments and how they charged fees to their investors.

With respect to nonpublic securities, registered hedge funds were required to justify their valuation methodologies not only to their independent auditors but also to the Securities and Exchange Commission, which has the power to bring enforcement actions and to refer matters to the U.S. Justice Department for criminal action if abusive practices are found. Private equity firms faced no such restrictions and were free to value their holdings subject only to the scrutiny of their limited partners. These partners were generally unwilling to challenge these valuations since doing so would only depress the value of their investments. This is why so many private equity valuations should be viewed with a grain of salt (and a tumbler of Johnny Walker Red)—they are merely opinions until they are tested in the marketplace. In 2008, private equity investors discovered not only how illiquid some of these investments were, but also that previous elevated valuations were figments of their general partners' imaginations. This is one reason that private equity returns were never as high as they were purported to be even before adjusting them downward for liquidity and leverage.

There was no good reason why private equity firms, which controlled hundreds of billions of dollars of capital, ever should have been exempt from registration. Moreover, there was no rationale for treating them differently than hedge funds and other investment management organizations that were required to register under the Investment Advisers Act. Fortunately, regulators woke up to these realities after the financial crisis and required private equity firms to register as investment advisers, subjecting them to regulatory oversight for the first time.

Predictably, the SEC has reported that based on its initial series of inspections of the industry, it has found numerous violations of the law. In that light, the enforcement actions taken against KKR and Blackstone described below are hardly surprising. The question is whether investors will more aggressively demand fair treatment from an industry that has enriched itself at their expense for decades.

Fee Reform

Among the most significant consequences of subjecting private equity firms to the registration requirements of the Investment Advisers Act was to improve disclosure of their opaque and abusive compensation practices. The fact that investors allowed themselves to be charged excessive fees for so long by their private equity managers remains one of the more inexplicable phenomena in today's investment world. As it turned out, regulatory oversight of private equity fees revealed some practices that crossed over from the aggressive to the illegal, resulting in enforcement actions and the repayment of fees to investors.

The Investment Advisers Act requires full disclosure of returns and fees by private equity firms and gives investors the tools to evaluate their managers in a meaningful way. This was one of the most compelling reasons why I argued in the first edition of this book that private equity managers should be registered as investment advisers and subject to the rules governing the reporting of returns and the disclosure of fees. In view of the fact that private equity firms generally receive commitments to hold on to investors' capital for long periods of time (5 to 10 years) while hedge funds have much shorter commitment periods and are required to return capital typically on an annual basis (with some exceptions for less liquid strategies that resemble private equity), private equity firms' exemption from such disclosure rules made little sense from a policy standpoint.

Private equity firms' fee structures are egregiously unfavorable to clients (and, the same could be said of many hedge funds' fees, which is why they are required to be registered). There are few investment strategies that involve truly unique skills that merit a management fee of higher than 1.0 percent per year, or a performance fee of higher than 15 percent per year. Moreover, managers should be paid performance fees only after their investment returns exceed market performance or the rate of inflation. Accordingly, performance fees should only be payable above a hurdle rate. Investors should be paying for real performance, not fortuity. In no case should performance fees be paid for negative returns (for example, losing less money than a negative benchmark does not merit a performance fee although there have been instances where such fees have been paid). Performance fees should be used to reward absolute, not relative performance. Paying for negative performance is simply adding insult to an investor's injury and is the surest way to build distrust on the part of investors. Finally, all performance fees should be subject to both high water marks and claw backs in the event that earlier years' profits are wiped out by poor performance in later years. Managing other people's money is a privilege, not a right, and should be treated as such.

If investors were able to ascertain more information about certain investment strategies that have attracted enormous amounts of capital in recent years but have also consistently been at the center of market dislocations, it is unlikely they would invest in them. As noted above, private equity returns are far less attractive than advertised when they are properly risk-adjusted. Other nonpublic market strategies like distressed debt have similar return profiles. What is most disturbing about these opaque strategies is that they tend to follow the reverse-Black Swan model—they report decent returns when markets are rising based on unverifiable valuations of their holdings and then implode when the markets collapse as they did in 1998, 2001, 2002, and 2008. Investors get tagged with huge losses and are invariably blocked from withdrawing their remaining assets from the fund while their managers keep their previously earned fees. It has always been a point of curiosity why institutional investors are not more disturbed by reading the names of their private equity and hedge fund managers on the list of the Forbes 400 while they continue to earn mediocre returns generated by these men (they are all men).

It came as no surprise, therefore, that the private equity industry's fee practices raised serious legal problems for the industry when they were finally examined by regulators after the financial crisis. The SEC lambasted the industry for its fee and expense practices, saying that inspections of more than 150 private equity firms found widespread

abuses, including hidden fees and shifting of expenses onto fund investors without adequate disclosure. The enforcement actions were likely
just beginning in 2015.

In June 2015, KKR & Co. agreed to pay $30 million to settle
charges that it improperly allocated more than $17 million in expenses
to investors that should have been paid by its own executives and clients
who were invested in certain co-investment vehicles. KKR repaid
fund investors $18.7 million to cover misallocated fees plus interest
and paid a $10 million penalty. The SEC alleged that KKR charged
"broken-deal" costs (i.e., expenses incurred with respect to deals that
were not consummated) to its flagship private equity funds instead of
assigning them to co-investment vehicles comprised of KKR's executives and some large KKR clients. Andrew J. Ceresny, director of the
SEC's enforcement division, said, "Although KKR raised billions of
dollars of deal capital from co-investors, it unfairly required the funds
to shoulder the cost for nearly all of the expenses incurred to explore
potential investment opportunities that were pursued but ultimately
not completed." Naturally, as so often happens in these cases, KKR
settled the charges without admitting or denying guilt and promised
not to do it again.

In October 2015, The Blackstone Group entered into a similar settlement in which it paid $39 million to settle SEC charges that it failed
to sufficiently disclose to investors that in a few instances it had charged
monitoring fees for periods after it no longer retained an ownership
stake in portfolio companies. It also failed to disclose certain discounts
it received on legal services that were "substantially greater" than those
received to its funds. As usual, Blackstone paid the fine and promised not
to do it again.

These settlements disclosed that the private equity industry did not
miss an opportunity to turn over every rock in their universe to charge
investors every conceivable fee known to man. They also put the industry on notice that it will no longer be able to overcharge investors with
impunity, a change that is long overdue.

Of course, investors have a responsibility to protect themselves. In
July 2015, CalPERS, the country's largest pension fund ($305 billion),
and CalSTRS, the country's second largest pension fund ($191 billion),
admitted that they failed to track the fees they paid to their private

equity managers over a period of more than 20 years.[36] These revelations were, to say the least, highly embarrassing considering the tens of billions of dollars of private equity investments involved and the fact that the funds did not know how much they paid to their managers in "carried interest" since they started investing with them. At the end of the day, regulators can't protect investors if they aren't prepared to take some basic steps to look out for their own interests.

CHAPTER 7

Welcome to Jurassic Park

I n addition to being an enormously entertaining movie, *Jurassic Park* (1993) is a cautionary tale of technology gone wild. The film, and Michael Crichton's novel from which it was adapted, are modern twists on the ancient Prometheus myth and Mary Shelley's nineteenth-century horror story *Frankenstein*, in which an obsessed Dr. Victor Frankenstein dared to play God and created a monster that destroyed everything most dear to him. Misusing technology is an age-old tale that visited Wall Street in 2008 with dire results.

In one scene in *Jurassic Park*, the scientists who are brought to the park to evaluate its progress and safety for its insurers and financiers get into a heated debate over lunch with the park's founder, Dr. John Hammond, about the merits of trying to fool with Mother Nature. They had just witnessed a velociraptor devour a cow in a matter of seconds in a display of savagery that, among other things, renders them uninterested in their meal. Dr. Ian Malcolm, a professor of chaos theory (brilliantly played by the actor Jeff Goldblum) begins shouting at Dr. Hammond that he is tempting fate by blindly using technology without respecting its potentially destructive power:

225

The problem with the scientific power you've used is it didn't require any discipline to attain it. You read what others had done and you took the next step. You didn't earn the knowledge yourselves, so you don't take the responsibility for it. You stood on the shoulders of geniuses to accomplish something as fast as you could, and before you knew what you had, you patented it....Your scientists were so preoccupied with whether or not they could that they didn't stop to think if they should.[1]

The hubris involved in creating extinct creatures out of the DNA stored in amber buried deep in the earth is an apt metaphor for the derivatives technology that was unleashed on the financial world through the creation of credit default swaps. The ruins of the imaginary Jurassic Park serve as a vivid image of a damaged financial system once credit defaults swaps and other exotic derivative instruments backfired on their inventors in 2008. The fact that the film came out at roughly the same time that a group of investment bankers from JPMorgan created these new types of financial instrument simply lends some irony to the history of one of the greatest self-inflicted wounds in financial history.[2]

Isla Nublar

Financial derivatives are very odd animals. As Edward LiPuma and Benjamin Lee point out in a brilliant theoretical discussion of derivatives in their book *Financial Derivatives and the Globalization of Risk*, derivatives are a unique form of capital. Unlike currencies, derivatives do not gain their value or legitimacy from the backing of any government or any precious metal.[3] Unlike bonds or bank loans, derivatives do not draw their value directly from an underlying obligor (in other words, the company whose financial condition will determine whether they will be repaid). Instead, a derivative is a hybrid creature whose value is drawn from two entirely separate sources. In this discussion, we will focus on credit derivatives in their most common (and potentially noxious) form: credit default swaps (CDS).

Financial derivatives are the ultimate (so far—there will undoubtedly be further applications of computer technology to financial instruments) example of the literal deconstruction of financial instruments. The importance of the ability to deconstruct financial instruments through computer technology cannot be overemphasized; it transformed the nature of financial assets by turning them into immaterial objects of untold complexity. The digitalization of information was a key step in the process of financialization because it broke down the boundaries between different disciplines and modes of communication. Computers create the ability to reduce language and symbols into the common language of 1s and 0s in a manner that disguises or blurs differences in meaning between different types of underlying objects or forms.

Derivatives could not exist without the type of computing power that developed over the past three decades. Digitalization takes one thing—a financial instrument (a bond, stock, mortgage, loan, and so on)—and turns it into another thing: another financial instrument (a derivative). This transformation reveals the fact that these instruments are really just different combinations of the same constituent parts, much like humans and animals are different combinations of DNA or each component of the periodic table is a different combination of electrons and protons. This has tremendous ramifications for the way in which financial market participants come to view the world. It is also an enormously destabilizing force because it separates the tradable instrument from the underlying reference instrument, just as securitization in the credit markets sunders the promissory relationship between the borrower and the lender. As relationships between things that were previously connected become further separated or mediated, the opportunity for the confusion of meaning and disruption of relationships increases.

Credit derivatives disassemble bonds, loans, and mortgages into their constituent parts and then reassemble them into new configurations that can be sold to different investors (or speculators) with different risk appetites. Derivatives are the financial version of splitting the atom or dissecting the human genome. Just like nuclear weapons draw their potency from the ability of scientists to split the atom into its constituent parts, derivatives derive their power from the ability to separate financial instruments into 1s and 0s, the constituent parts of money. The problem with deconstructing a debt instrument into its constituent parts is that it abstracts the new instrument—the derivative—from its underlying or reference obligation in a manner that attenuates the relationship between lender and borrower and vests economic power over the ultimate borrower in the hands of a party that has little or no knowledge about or interest in the actual business or economic fate of this borrower.

To describe this product in the language of Karl Marx, a credit derivative like a credit default swap is the quintessential fetish instrument because it is the result of a process whereby an underlying financial instrument (a bond, bank loan, or mortgage) is deconstructed into its constituent parts and then reassembled or reconfigured into a new form that has no resemblance to the economic forces that created it. In most cases, investors who buy or sell derivatives are speculators who have no interest in or understanding of the underlying instrument or the social relations that brought it into being. This is a far more radical state of alienation than simply saying that we are no longer getting our mortgage from our neighborhood banker. The relationship between lender and borrower, the two parties to a promise, has become so attenuated as to become almost spectral. Derivatives are the ultimate manifestation of disembodied financial relationships controlled by forces that are difficult to identify or control.

Highly mediated forms of finance such as securitization and derivatives impose enormous barriers between underlying financial instruments or securities and the forms in which they are traded. When every financial object is capable of being transformed into something else, all financial instruments are revealed to be, in their essence, the same. This chameleon-like quality introduces a degree of instability into the system that did not exist before derivatives technology came to dominate markets. This instability arises from the fact that the identity and character of individual financial objects such as stocks, bonds, or mortgages can be transformed into different types of objects. Just as the ability of a traditional convertible bond to be exchanged for stock drastically changes the way it is valued compared to a nonconvertible bond, the ability of a traditional corporate bond to be pooled with other bonds into a collateralized bond obligation (CBO) or expressed in terms of a credit default swap alters its value in multiple ways by changing its liquidity and other characteristics. For investors, this raises profound questions regarding asset allocation and other traditional theories of portfolio management that some of us have long questioned. For instance, the very concept of asset classes must be called into question in view of the ability of derivatives to turn one type of security into another type of security. Such questions have enormous asset allocation consequences that are just beginning to be explored by thoughtful money managers and regulators.

Credit default swaps are legally enforceable insurance contracts in which two parties enter into an exchange of promises with respect to an underlying financial obligation, for example, a bond, bank loan, or mortgage. Neither of these parties is required to have any legal relationship (for example, a preexisting ownership relationship) with the company that issued the underlying obligation. In fact, the presence of a preexisting relationship is the factor that separates speculative derivatives positions from hedged derivatives positions. The latter involves parties who already have an ownership interest in the underlying obligation and are using the derivative to protect themselves from losses, while the former involves parties with no such ownership position who are merely betting on price movements in order to earn a new profit. Another component of the value of a derivatives contract is found in the parties who enter into the contract. Their financial condition and ability to fulfill their promises are keys to the outcome of the contract into which they have entered.

The contractual nature of derivative instruments is essential to their understanding.[4] As contracts, derivatives share certain important similarities with other credit instruments such as mortgages, bank loans, and bonds. Wherever they circulate in the economy, they must return to their point of origin for redemption (i.e., payment). Once the contract is satisfied, it disappears from circulation. As we saw in Chapter 4 discussing mortgage derivatives, the disembodied nature of these contracts can cause serious practical problems, for example, when it becomes impossible to identify who holds the mortgage on a home because the mortgage contract was sold into a large mortgage pool and cannot be tracked. Unlike the underlying cash obligations on which derivatives are based, derivatives are disembodied from the flesh-and-blood borrowers whose economic performance determines their ultimate value.

An essential component of a derivative contract's value is based on the parties' ability to enforce their rights within a system of laws. There are two aspects of enforceability. First, theoretical or legal enforceability is based on the specific language of the derivatives contract. The contract sets forth the respective obligations of the parties and the consequences of failing to meet them. Second, practical enforceability is wholly dependent on the ability of the parties undertaking financial obligations under the contract to fulfill them. In theoretical terms, a legally unenforceable promise made by a solvent party is worthless, while in practical terms a legally enforceable promise made by an insolvent or unwilling counterparty is an empty promise. Both the theoretical and practical aspects of enforceability must be present for a derivatives contract to be fulfilled.

The second component of value in a credit default swap contract is the underlying security itself. Changes in the price of this security play a determinative role in the value of the derivatives that are based on them. The indirect nature of a derivative obligation—the fact that its value is determined by reference to something outside of itself—renders it unusually complex and inherently unstable because it is subject to variables beyond the control of the parties to the contract. Moreover, unless regulatory or other legal limits are placed on the ability to issue derivatives with respect to an underlying obligation, there is no theoretical limitation on the volume of derivative contracts that can be written with respect to a specific underlying obligation. This raises particularly important systemic questions with respect to credit derivatives and credit default swaps specifically, which are discussed in detail in the following section.

At times during the 2008 financial crisis, it seemed as though the fiscal and monetary authorities were not going to be able to stop the markets from collapsing. The reason for this feeling of helplessness was not simply the volume of selling that was raining down on the markets, but the fact that it was difficult to identify the source of selling and the reasons for selling. This was particularly true with respect to credit instruments such as mortgages, bonds, and bank loans, the prices of which were driven to levels that made no rational sense unless one truly believed that the end of the world was at hand.

What was not apparent to market observers (in particular the media) was that selling pressure was being generated in the parallel universe of the credit derivatives markets, which were completely opaque and unregulated and whose prices were largely hidden from the media and the public. Price discovery—the term traders use to describe the point at which buyers and sellers come to a meeting of the minds—became a matter of shooting darts in the dark because there were no benchmarks against which to measure value. This was because the traditional benchmarks—the prices of cash credit instruments—were being driven by the shadow prices of their derivatives, whose markets were concealed from view and driven by mathematical formulas that had little or no relation to the real world in which these obligations were functioning and affecting real flesh-and-blood human beings. When the distance between lender and borrower became so attenuated as to become akin to that between a body and its ghost, it was not unreasonable to fear that regulators and governments would not be able to put the genie back in the bottle again.

More frightening is the fact that the spectral world of derivatives is not subject to the physical limitations of the underlying obligations to which they refer. The parallel universe of credit derivatives dwarfs the cash obligations with respect to which they are written. In the most widespread type of credit derivative and the one that will occupy most of our attention here—credit default swaps—the market grew to more than $60 trillion in size on the eve of the 2008 financial crisis, far greater than the volume of cash obligations it was insuring. The sheer size of this market came to exercise an enormous and often perverse influence on the world of cash credit obligations. Like Frankenstein, the creature who turned on and ultimately destroyed all that mattered most to his master, credit default swaps created horrific unintended consequences for borrowers and lenders.

The New DNA of Finance

At its core, a credit default swap is an insurance contract in which one party (the seller of protection or insurance) promises to pay the other party (the buyer) in the event that an underlying financial obligation (normally a bank loan, bond, mortgage, or pool thereof) defaults. The seller/insurer pays the buyer/insured an amount of money that will compensate for the loss. Most economists and educated market practitioners agree that using a credit default swap to hedge an existing holding of a credit instrument is a rational and socially and economically valuable and useful activity.

A couple of simple examples will demonstrate the idea behind credit default swaps.

The first example involves bonds of Microsoft, Inc. (MSFT), a financially sound company:

> Institution A owns $10 million of MSFT bonds. The bonds are trading at par (100). It is concerned that changes in interest rates may cause the price of these bonds to drop and wants to buy insurance against such an event. It goes to Institution B to purchase that insurance. The cost of such insurance is 150 basis points per year for $10 million of insurance for a five-year period, or $150,000 per year. This amount is paid annually pursuant to a standard contract known as an International Swap Dealers Association (ISDA) contract.

In addition, the buyer of protection is required to post some amount of collateral with the seller to insure his ability to make future premium payments. The collateral amount is determined by a combination of factors that includes both the credit quality of the buyer/insured as well as that of the underlying instrument. One of the reasons that the credit default swap market was able to explode in size was that collateral requirements were relatively small prior to the 2008 crisis.

Collateral is a much bigger issue with respect to our next example, a financially distressed company like General Motors Corp., in the months before it filed for bankruptcy in early 2009. In the case of a failing company, default insurance is much more expensive to purchase because the likelihood of default is very high (the insurer is highly likely to be making good on his promise to make the insured whole for his loss). The buyer of protection is required to post more collateral, and the cost of insurance includes a large upfront payment as well as large annual payments. Most of the premium, however, is captured in the large upfront payment.

> Institution A owns $10 million of General Motors bonds. The bonds are trading at 20 cents on the dollar. It is concerned that General Motors may default on these bonds and wants to buy insurance against such an event. It goes to Institution B to purchase that insurance. Because the odds of General Motors defaulting are very high, Institution B demands both an upfront payment and an annual premium for this insurance. The upfront payment is 45 points, or $4,500,000, and the annual premium is $500,000, for a five-year period. This insurance agreement is documented in a standard contract known as an ISDA contract.

One might inquire why an investor would pay such an exorbitant amount for default insurance. The answer is that he wouldn't. Trades of this type occur among speculators, not investors looking to hedge existing positions. Holders of General Motors bonds or loans who were worried about credit losses arranged to hedge (or sell) their positions much earlier, when credit insurance was still cheap. At the point where large upfront payments are involved, speculators have taken over and are placing bets on the timing of default and the likely recovery value on the swap contracts.

These examples illustrate the differences between the pricing on credit default swaps for distressed borrowers and for healthy borrowers. In fact, one might ask whether there is a need for credit default swaps on healthy borrowers, and this is where the distinction between hedging and speculation comes into play. Many investors must mark-to-market their investments on a current basis, and other investors are not required to do so. Increasingly, the investment world has moved to a mark-to-market model in which institutional investors require their investment managers to value their assets on a current basis. In recent years, this trend has been accentuated by the explosive growth of hedge funds and changes in accounting rules aimed at increasing systemic transparency.

Marking-to-market is a complex issue and a two-edged sword. In the case of short-term oriented investors such as hedge funds, marking-to-market is an appropriate requirement. If an investor has a short-term time horizon, he should be required to value his assets on a current basis. But in the case of banks, which are in the business of making long-term loans on assets that are often illiquid, or long-term investors such as pension funds that are trying to match long-term liabilities with long-term bond holdings, marking-to-market may not be appropriate. Nonetheless, there is growing sentiment that mark-to-market accounting should be used more broadly in the financial world. As a result, an increasing number of investors feel the need to hedge their investment holdings, particularly longer dated ones; and one of the primary tools for doing so in the fixed-income world is credit derivatives, and specifically credit default swaps. The primary risk involved in investing in a high-quality investment grade bond is interest rate risk rather than credit risk. Accordingly, the holder of a Microsoft bond is primarily concerned about price changes in the bond resulting from changes in interest rates, not radical changes in Microsoft's financial condition. A credit default swap is a useful way to hedge this risk. The value of the credit default swap will change as the value of the underlying Microsoft bond changes in response to changes in interest rates (or, if there are significant changes in Microsoft's credit quality, to those changes as well). As a result, the investor will be able to counterbalance losses or gains in the underlying Microsoft bond with corresponding gains or losses in the credit default swap contract on those bonds. This hedging function is eminently reasonable and serves an important and useful purpose in financial markets.[5]

The problem with these instruments arises from the fact that they are untethered from the underlying bonds and there is no practical or theoretical limitation on the amount of credit default swaps that can be written with respect to any given underlying bond, loan, mortgage, or pooled instrument. In practice, this means that if there are $2 billion of outstanding General Motors bonds, the amount of credit default swaps that can be written on those bonds is not limited to $2 billion. It can be $20 billion, or $200 billion, or $2 trillion. The net exposure (in other words, the actual amount of money at risk when offsetting trades are removed from the system) may be much less than the outstanding face amount of credit default swaps, but there is no systemic or regulatory limitation on the amount of these instruments that can be written by market participants. This is how the credit default swap market grew virtually undetected to over $60 trillion in size by early 2008 and came to threaten the very viability of the global financial system. And as noted in the Introduction, it is the notional (gross) rather than the net exposure that matters in a crisis because that is precisely the time when counterparties are unable or unwilling to perform their contractual obligations with respect to these instruments. That is what happened in 2008, triggering the crisis.

There are far more complex variations of credit default swaps. These are easier to understand if one keeps in mind that they are intended to be insurance against losses on underlying obligations. One such example is a credit default swap written on a single tranche of a collateralized debt obligation (CDO) that holds pools of residential mortgages. These were discussed earlier in this book (see Chapter 4). In this example, a credit default swap is written with respect to specific tranches of a collateralized mortgage obligation (CMO) in order to provide insurance for an owner of that tranche's bonds against a default of those bonds. For example, if a holder of one of the 17 tranches in the CMO shown in Figure 4.3 in Chapter 4 wanted protection against a default on his bonds, which would result if enough of the underlying mortgages held by the CMO defaulted, he would ask a financial institution to sell him protection in the form of a credit default swap. Depending on whether the tranche in question was considered healthy or distressed, he might pay an upfront premium plus an annual premium (for a distressed junior tranche) or just an annual premium (for a healthy senior tranche). This would provide him protection if the CMO ran into trouble and defaulted.

Finally, there is an even more complicated variation, known as a credit default swap written on a synthetic CDO. A synthetic CDO holds a pool of other credit default swaps on underlying bonds, loans, or mortgages (rather than owning the underlying bonds, loans, or mortgages themselves). In other words, a synthetic CDO does not own a pool of individual bonds or loans or mortgages but instead is a counterparty to credit default swap contracts on underlying bonds, loans, or mortgages. Like other CDOs, this type of CDO is financed through the sale of different tranches of rated debt. Holders of these different tranches can buy insurance against potential losses on these tranches by buying protection through credit default swaps. Alternatively, speculators (those who don't own the underlying tranches) can place bets on whether the underlying tranches will increase or decrease in value. Needless to say, such instruments are highly complex, extremely illiquid and difficult to unwind in market dislocations.

Warning Signs

By early 2006, the credit derivatives market was already spinning out of control. In any other industry, there would have been more than enough embarrassment to go around when it was discovered that a huge percentage of credit default swap trades had not been properly accounted for by Wall Street's back offices. As of September 30, 2005, the number of trade confirmations that were outstanding for more than 30 days stood at 97,000. Assuming an average trade size of $5 million, this meant that trades with a nominal value of $485 billion, in the words of *The Wall Street Journal*, "lacked detailed confirmations—a problem that has left banks and brokerage firms uncertain who owes what to whom."[6] In a speech to the Global Association of Risk Professionals in early 2006, then New York Federal Reserve President Timothy Geithner stepped into the fray and read Wall Street the riot act about cleaning up its mess.

> The post-trade processing and settlement infrastructure is still quite weak relative to the significance of these markets.... The total stock of unconfirmed trades is large and until recently was growing considerably faster than the total volume of new trades. The time between trade and confirmation is still quite long for a large share of transactions. The share of trades done on the available automated platforms is still substantially short of what is possible... firms were typically assigning trades without the knowledge or consent of the original counterparties. Nostro breaks, which are errors in payments discovered by counterparties at the time of the quarterly flows, rose to a significant share of total trades. Efforts to standardize documentation and provide automated confirmation services has lagged behind product development and growth in volume ... the assignment problems create uncertainty about the actual size of exposures to individual counterparties that could exacerbate market liquidity problems in the event of stress.

Wall Street, however, is not subject to embarrassment. The profit motive trumps everything else. So the large derivative trading firms promised to clean up the mess, and all was forgiven by the stern-faced Mr. Geithner and his regulatory brethren. The fact that Wall Street was unable to account for such a large portion of credit default swaps should have been a stark warning that trouble lay ahead. Little did anyone appreciate the depth of the problem or the risk it posed to the financial system. The monster was about to eat Manhattan.[7]

Dinosaurs Turn on Their Makers

Credit default swaps create a structure in which lenders are so alienated from the flesh-and-blood labor of the businesses that are responsible for repaying them that the traditional relationship between borrower and lender is not only sundered but in certain circumstances rendered adversarial. One of the dirty little secrets about credit default swaps is that they create in the buyer of protection (the insured) a strong economic incentive to see the borrower fail; in many cases, a default produces the highest possible payout and highest rate of return for the buyer of insurance. In this way, credit default swaps create perverse incentives for the parties that enter into them. Credit default swaps can create strong economic incentives for investors to root for businesses to fail because failure constitutes a "credit event" that triggers payment under the derivatives contract. Moreover, because the volume of credit default swaps can dwarf the amount of a company's outstanding debt, the derivatives market rather than direct lenders can determine the fate of a debtor. This means that the parties calling the shots are not those who have an interest in the underlying business, the employees or the communities affected by whether a company can ultimately restructure its debts. Instead, power is vested in the hands of credit default swap holders who do not own the underlying debt instruments but who have instead merely placed bets, usually with very little money down, on the future of flesh-and-blood businesses. From a public policy standpoint, this raises serious questions about the proper role of debt and derivatives markets in the economy.

The somewhat perverse phenomenon of creditors rooting for the demise of their borrowers in the credit default swap market has been termed the "empty creditor" phenomenon by Professor Henry T.C. Hu of the University of Texas Law School.[8] Professor Hu describes an empty creditor as "someone (or some institution) who may have the contractual control but, by simultaneously holding credit default swaps, little or no economic exposure if the debt goes bad." In fact, "if a creditor holds enough credit default swaps, he may simultaneously have control rights and incentives to cause the debtor firm's value to fall." This concept gives a modern meaning to Karl Marx's concept of alienation. Marx was speaking about the alienation of labor, but today the alienation of labor has been transformed into the alienation of capital. This type of alienation between borrower and lender can have an insidious effect on borrowers by making it more difficult for them to reorganize their debts.

The advent of credit default swaps creates a situation in which lenders can hedge their exposure to borrowers so effectively that they prefer to see their debts repaid by their counterparty rather than by the borrower itself. Such payment will come more quickly and is preferable to waiting for the borrower to pay after a lengthy bankruptcy or restructuring process. Accordingly, credit default swap buyers are incentivized to see borrowers fail. So-called "basis packages," in which investors own both a bond and a credit default swap related to that bond, are often structured to deliver a higher return if the borrower files for bankruptcy, thereby forcing a payout on the credit default swap contract at the time of the bankruptcy filing (as opposed to the end of the bankruptcy reorganization process, which can take months or years). Rather than leading lenders to participate in a consensual out-of-court restructuring that generally imposes much lower costs on the borrower, this regime pushes borrowers into highly expensive bankruptcy proceedings that create little economic value for anybody but bankruptcy attorneys and restructuring advisors. In the hands of speculators who have no interest in the ultimate survival of the business (if they even know what the business is and what it does), businesses are reduced to empty carcasses whose bones are more likely to be sold in liquidation than emerge as viable going concerns with new, deleveraged balance sheets.

In the period leading up to the 2008 crisis, this economically unsound phenomenon was exacerbated by the fact that many debts were incurred in private equity transactions where much of the value was skimmed off into the hands of private equity sponsors through management, monitoring, and transaction fees rather than into the hands of the limited partners who represent endowments and foundations and other tax-exempt organizations. The combination of these factors led to a voiding of the value of leveraged companies into the hands of financial speculators. The government, through the bankruptcy process or, in the event of a systemically important company, through a bailout, was left to clean up the mess.

George Soros has written persuasively on the asymmetric incentives that credit default swaps introduced into the financial system. Soros views these flaws as sufficiently profound to call for these instruments to be banned unless the purchaser of credit insurance owns the underlying instrument. In an essay in *The Wall Street Journal*, he wrote the following:

> Going short on bonds by buying a CDS contract carries limited risk but almost unlimited profit potential. By contrast, selling CDS offers limited profits but practically unlimited risks. This asymmetry

encourages speculating on the short side, which in turn exerts a downward pressure on the underlying bonds. The negative effect is reinforced by the fact that CDS are tradable and therefore tend to be priced as warrants, which can be sold at anytime, not as options, which would require an actual default to be cashed in. People buy them not because they expect an eventual default, but because they expect the CDS to appreciate in response to adverse development. AIG thought it was selling insurance on bonds, and as such, they considered CDS outrageously overpriced. In fact, it was selling bear-market warrants and it severely underestimated the risk.[9]

Soros outlines what happens when you fool with Mother Nature. First, credit default swaps offer limited risk and unlimited reward when used to make negative bets on credit. Second, investments in credit default swaps require far too little collateral, which allows a small amount of capital to affect the market (something that remains true even after post-crisis reforms increased collateral requirements). This disconnection with the real economy is what raises concerns about the role that derivatives play in today's markets. The problem with this, as LiPuma and Lee point out, is that speculative derivatives positions (i.e., those not being used to hedge an underlying position) do not appear to involve productive labor, the organization of activities that have any real connection with material resources, the output of goods or services, or the satisfaction or promotion of further productive output.[10] As a result, these instruments can be used to speculate on credit without the speculators being sufficiently at risk to cause them to think twice about the potential systemic risks they may be posing. For these reasons, Mr. Soros' argument for banning naked default swaps is compelling.

Bear Stearns: First Casualty

The collapse of Bear Stearns in 2008 illustrated some of the systemic risks that unregulated trading in credit default swaps created. Speculators were able to take aim at the firm's stock and credit default swaps and engage in a variety of short-selling strategies in an effort to profit from price changes (a drop in the stock price, or an increase in its credit default swap spreads) without any regard for the real-world consequences of their behavior. The rating agencies then stepped in and threatened to lower the company's credit rating based on these manipulative price movements, rendering the company incapable of financing itself. The inner workings of the credit default swap market were able to produce changes in Bear Stearns' borrowing costs that battered the firm's financial condition and contributed to its demise.

Bear Stearns met its maker in March 2008. At the time (and at all times), broker dealers had extensive counterparty exposure to each other. Each firm places limitations on how much overall exposure it is willing to have to another firm. If one trading desk has a certain amount of exposure to another firm, it will limit how much exposure other desks can have to that same firm. As a result, each firm has a limited ability to write credit default swaps on another firm's credit. At the time, these limitations were even tighter because of the building crisis. Since firms had to limit their exposure to Bear Stearns, every time a firm was asked to increase its exposure to the firm by writing another credit default swap, it raised the price. In an illiquid market, these price increases were disproportionately large. This led Bear Stearns' credit default swap spreads to spiral out of control. In effect, the internal workings of the credit default swap market caused Bear Stearns' collapse to become a self-fulfilling prophesy by rendering Bear Stearns' cost of funding so expensive as to render the firm incapable of financing itself. Without the ability to finance itself, a broker dealer like Bear Stearns had to close its doors (or sell itself to someone like JPMorgan Chase & Co. for a nominal amount).

In the case of Bear Stearns, sharp increases of its credit default swap spreads in the period leading to its takeover by JPMorgan Chase signaled to the media and markets that the firm was experiencing financial trouble. During the week of March 10, 2008, Bear Stearns' one-year credit default swaps spreads suddenly spiked to nearly 1,000 basis points, a level that rendered the investment bank incapable of financing itself or running its business profitably. A financial institution uses money as its raw material, and when the price of its raw material is driven up by a factor of 10 virtually overnight, it is effectively priced out of business. This is exactly what happened to Bear Stearns. Figure 7.1 shows the dramatic spike to unsustainable levels to which Bear Stearns' credit default swap spreads were driven before the company was sold to JPMorgan Chase & Co.

THE BEAR STEARNS COMPANIES INC., 5 Year CDS

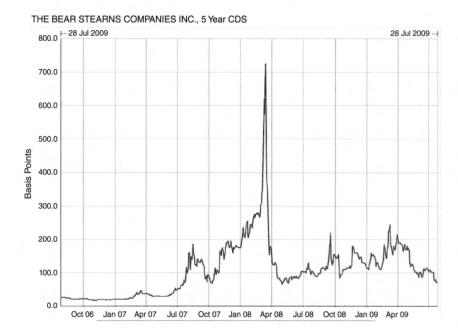

Figure 7.1 Bear Stearns' Death by CDS
SOURCE: Goldman Sachs, July 2009.

An investment bank and trading firm requires low-cost overnight funding in order to profitably hold trading inventory, and these levels were telling the marketplace that Bear Stearns could no longer borrow at reasonable rates if at all. This was a far more important indication of financial distress than the firm's stock price, which was also plunging at the time.[11]

Credit default swap spreads, because they are quoted in real time, are believed to be the most accurate and timely indicia of a borrower's credit quality. Unfortunately, there are several flaws with the concept of depending on the credit default swap market to determine the fate of important financial firms. Bear Stearns maintained active trading relationships with virtually every other financial institution in the world. Its failure would have caused severe disruption throughout the financial system (much as Lehman Brothers' bankruptcy six months later actually did). The credit default market was completely unregulated. A few trades and a relatively small amount of capital were capable of moving spreads by an inordinate degree. A major financial institution and the entire financial system were effectively held hostage by a credit default swap market in which participants could place large bets with relatively modest amounts of capital (the collateral requirements for these trades were far lower than stock margin requirements). Moreover, the market was highly illiquid (that is, a relatively small volume of trades was capable of having a disproportionately large effect on Bear Stearns' spreads). As a result, a relatively small number of traders, and a relatively small amount of capital, were likely responsible for widening Bear Stearns' credit default swap spreads to levels that suggested that the firm was at imminent risk of failure.

In March 2008, swap traders were operating with extremely limited information and mostly working based on rumor and innuendo. There is nothing more opaque or subject to rapid change than a trading house's balance sheet. Moreover, there was credible evidence that some of the firm's competitors were participating in, or at least encouraging, what amounted to a "bear raid" (excuse the pun) on the firm through the credit default swap market. In Wall Street parlance, a bear raid involves a group of speculators acting together to raise doubts about the viability of a company and profiting from that firm's failure by selling short its stock (or, in this case, its bonds and other credit instruments). Since credit default swaps at the time were effectively unregulated, there was nothing Bear Stearns could do to stop the speculation and its sale to JPMorgan Chase (at the behest of the U.S. government) for $2 per share (later adjusted to $10 per share.) At its peak in January 2007, the stock had sold for as much as $171.50 per share (which was undoubtedly far more than it was worth). Bear Stearns was hardly a poster child for risk management, but being victimized by credit default swap speculators was an unfortunate ending for a storied Wall Street firm.

American International Group (AIG)— Second Casualty

Credit default swaps reappeared as weapons of financial self-destruction six months later at insurance giant American International Group (AIG). AIG was once the pride of the global insurance industry. The company morphed into a multifaceted financial institution that was part hedge fund, part investment bank, part asset management company, and part insurance company. Unfortunately, the firm came to be dominated by a group centered in London and Connecticut known as AIG Financial Products. This group of financial engineers came to believe that AIG's AAA balance sheet empowered it to write infinite amounts of insurance on investment grade-rated risks without ever asking what would happen if those credit ratings were questioned. By the middle of 2007, the company had insured a reported $465 billion of investment grade securities. But this exposed the company to two types of risks with respect to credit ratings. The first was that the ratings on all of the AAA securities that it was insuring had to stay AAA. The second was that its own investment rating had to remain AAA. Unfortunately, AIG came to learn that these were the same question, and the answer was not the one it expected to hear.

In September 2008, AIG found itself facing approximately $27 billion of collateral calls on $62.1 billion of credit default swap contracts on synthetic collateralized mortgage obligations. A synthetic collateralized mortgage obligation is a pool of credit default swaps on different tranches of underlying pools of mortgages. These assets are typical of those that lay at the heart of the financial crisis. They were highly complex, illiquid mathematical constructs that few people understood (least of all, apparently, the people at AIG that were purporting to insure them) and few institutions wanted to own, which is why so much effort was made to lay off their risk. They travel in the guise of securities, yet they are not securities in the traditional sense of the word. In fact, as the world came to learn much to its dismay, that term is the quintessential oxymoron—whatever these constructs are, they are the farthest thing in the world from secure. They have little to do with the fundamental credit quality or earnings quality of a company or an economic entity or actor. They merely reference some other entity that references some other entity and so on in an endless daisy chain to hell.

Yet in this case, the reason for AIG's crisis lay not in these monstrosities but in itself: AIG was about to lose its own highly coveted AAA rating. On Friday, September 12, 2008, Standard & Poor's placed AIG on negative credit watch, suggesting that loss of its coveted AAA rating was imminent. The insurance giant didn't have to wait long to learn what "imminent" meant in the midst of a financial crisis. Just three days later, on Monday, September 15—the same day that Lehman Brothers filed for bankruptcy—Standard & Poor's and the two other major credit rating agencies, Moody's Investors Service and Fitch Ratings Service, downgraded the long-term credit rating of AIG. The game was up. For many companies this might be bad news, but it would not trigger corporate destruction. However, AIG's credit default swap agreements included a clause that required the insurance giant to post additional collateral if it lost its AAA rating. Such a provision is not particularly unreasonable or even unusual; if a party's credit quality deteriorates, it is reasonable for those doing business with it to ask for additional assurance that they will be repaid. In the case of AIG, however, this clause triggered a requirement to post $27.1 billion of additional collateral with respect to the synthetic collateralized mortgage obligations in question. But AIG simply did not have that kind of cash lying around in its vaults. Obviously, nobody at AIG ever envisioned a ratings downgrade.

The U.S. government was faced with little choice but to step in and provide AIG with the cash to make these collateral payments. AIG was much larger and more interconnected with the rest of the global financial system than Lehman Brothers, whose bankruptcy was shaking the financial system to its core. As I warned in *The New York Times* on September 16, 2008, AIG's failure would have been an extinction-level event for the global financial system, triggering cross defaults on all of AIG's other contracts (derivative and otherwise) around the world.[12] It would also have set off a maelstrom of defaults among the thousands of financial counterparties around the world that were depending on AIG or other parties for payments in order to meet their own obligations.

It remains an interesting question whether the U.S. government solved the problem in the right way. The credit rating agencies could have been told to back off and maintain AIG's AAA rating (although that would have been unlikely to fool the market, and AIG's own credit default swap spreads probably would have widened significantly and driven the company into insolvency). Alternatively, the U.S. government could have simply stated that it would stand behind all of AIG's financial obligations, effectively lending AIG the U.S. government's AAA rating. While there was no express legal authority for such a move, the Federal Reserve had little trouble invoking its emergency powers at other times during the crisis in the name of systemic stability.[13] This approach would have avoided the necessity of the U.S. Treasury coming up with what ultimately became approximately $175 billion in support for AIG (although the government ultimately earned a $23 million profit on its investment). The market was willing to accept U.S. government guarantees on other failed institutions such as Fannie Mae and Freddie Mac, so it likely would have been satisfied with one on AIG. But whether or not the bailout could have been done more effectively, the authorities clearly did the correct thing by stepping in and preventing AIG from failing. The real tragedy (and farce) is that AIG found itself in that position in the first place through the irresponsible issuance of hundreds of billions of credit default swap obligations.[14]

The fact that the failure of Lehman Brothers and the near-failure of AIG occurred at virtually the same time was a sign that the financial markets had ceased to function. Capital died. The damage soon spread to two other firms that were considered by most observers to be well-managed and well-capitalized: Goldman Sachs and Morgan Stanley. During that same week in September 2008, credit default swap traders had their way with these companies as well. To place the following numbers in context, remember that Lehman Brothers filed for bankruptcy on Monday, September 15, (and was obviously rumored to be in trouble in the days leading up to that date). The five-year credit default swap spreads for Goldman Sachs moved from 200 basis points on Friday, September 12, to 350 basis points on Monday, September 15, and then to 620 basis points two days later on Wednesday, September 17 (by then the government had announced an $85 billion rescue package for AIG). Morgan Stanley saw even more ominous widening in its spreads, from 250 basis points on Friday, September 12, to 500 basis points on Monday, September 15, to 997 basis points on Wednesday, September 17. Wall Street was devouring its own. At these spreads, no firm could finance itself profitably for very long. Goldman Sachs and Morgan Stanley moved quickly to raise billions of dollars of new equity capital from outside investors in order to bolster their balance sheets and were granted bank holding company status by the U.S. government in order to obtain further protections.

The Bond Insurers—Third Casualty

Another group of companies that were ruined by their exposure to credit default swaps with serious systemic ramifications were the bond insurers led by Ambac Financial Group and MBIA, Inc. Both of these companies started out in the business of insuring municipal bonds. Since managing municipal bonds requires very little intellect or imagination, municipal bond insurance is a business that really should not exist. Municipal bonds rarely default; managers who invest in those that do are in the wrong line of work, but that is a story for another day. As the margins in that business shrunk, Ambac and MBIA looked for greener pastures and found them in the world of structured products. They could not have moved from a more mundane and simplistic product (municipal bonds) to a more arcane and complex one (collateralized debt obligations). As a result, they were poorly equipped intellectually and institutionally to deal with their new business. Nonetheless, like AIG, they were clever enough to discover (in another example of why we should not confuse education with smarts or the ability to make money as an investor) that they could use their own AAA ratings to begin insuring the AAA tranches of CDOs.

As in the case of AIG, this strategy was wholly dependent on the rating agencies continuing to maintain their AAA ratings on the bond insurers as well as on the underlying securities in the senior tranches of CDOs. And as with AIG, the rating agencies pulled rugs out from under both Ambac and MBIA. On January 17, 2008, Moody's placed Ambac's AAA credit rating on watch for possible downgrade. This was well after it was apparent to everyone other than Moody's that the mortgages in the CDOs insured by Ambac were defaulting in record numbers. Moody's cited Ambac's announcement that it expected to record a $5.4 billion pretax ($3.5 billion after-tax) mark-to-market loss on its portfolio of credit default swaps written on CDOs for the fourth quarter of 2007, including a $1.1 billion loss on certain asset-backed CDOs. Moody's stated with a straight face that "this loss significantly reduces the company's capital cushion and heightens concern about potential further volatility within Ambac's mortgage and mortgage-related CDO portfolios." When you read news releases like this, you really don't know whether to laugh, cry, or throw the telephone out the window.

Fortunately, some smart investors had already seen the writing on the wall and had shorted the bond insurers' shares.

Moody's announcement followed by a few days the issuance by Ambac's competitor, MBIA, of 14-percent AA-rated notes in a desperate attempt to salvage its AAA credit rating. At the time, the 14-percent coupon was 956 basis points higher than U.S. treasury notes of the same maturity, the rate that CCC-rated companies were paying at the time. Clearly there was a serious disconnect between what Moody's was saying about the company's credit rating and how the market was viewing MBIA's financial prospects. Apparently 14 percent was the new AA interest rate for bond insurers that had chosen to enter the credit derivatives market to insure mortgage securities! MBIA was in serious straits, with exposure to bonds backed by mortgages and CDOs of $30.6 billion, including $8.14 billion of CDO-squareds (CDOs that own pieces of other CDOs). The death-knell for the bond insurers' new business model was sounded.

The downfall of the bond insurers was a potentially catastrophic event for the Wall Street firms that were underwriting hundreds of billions of dollars of CDOs. These firms not only relied on Ambac and MBIA to insure the AAA-tranches of these deals, making them easier to sell to gullible buyers, but also counted on this insurance to protect themselves from losses on the huge amounts of this paper they couldn't sell and ended up purchasing to get these underwritings done. Over the coming months, these firms would work with New York Insurance Commissioner Eric Dinallo and others to reduce their exposure to CDOs, and the bond insurers ultimately survived in wind-down mode. But another piece of the financial model that led the markets to the edge of the cliff was carried out in a body bag.

Taming the Beasts (Regulating Credit Derivatives)

Fortunately, events have proved that the financial system will not go the way of Jurassic Park, at least not yet. But the obvious question once the smoke cleared was how to regulate the credit default swap market and the rest of the derivatives market to avoid a repeat of 2008. Similar questions were raised in the commodities pits about commodities derivatives contracts, which were blamed for the spike in oil prices to over $140 per barrel in 2008 and the subsequent plunge to under $40 per barrel in the midst of the global financial crisis that followed. The fact that the credit default swap market grew to over $60 trillion in size and then pushed the global financial system to the brink of collapse ranks as one of the greatest regulatory failures of the modern financial era. The fact that regulators were cowed (or conned—pick your poison) by Wall Street into allowing credit default swaps to become the monster that ate Manhattan was inexcusable.

While credit default swaps have shrunk significantly in size since the financial crisis, they remain large enough to constitute a potential time bomb inside the financial system that could blow up any time. As long as naked swaps are allowed to be written, no firm is safe from a bear raid. A new approach to regulating these beasts is sorely needed. There are a number of practical solutions to the threat they pose. As noted previously, some respected investors like George Soros recommend outlawing credit default swaps unless the purchaser owns the underlying instrument being insured. Certainly a strong argument can be made that naked credit default swaps—those in which the derivative buyer or seller does not own an interest in the underlying instrument—should be barred. Opponents of such a ban argue that these instruments improve market liquidity for the underlying instruments, but practitioners will tell you that these arguments are dubious. Prior to the financial crisis, high yield corporate bond and bank loan market liquidity was already drying up due to the migration of trading from cash markets to derivatives markets. Large sums of capital had migrated away from cash markets into the derivatives market, making less capital available for trading the underlying instruments and significantly decreasing liquidity in those markets.

Since the crisis, overall market liquidity (both cash and derivative markets) has deteriorated further due to the advent of Dodd-Frank to the point where it is raising serious concerns about what will happen during the next serious market event. By 2015, dealers' corporate bond inventories were down 70 percent from pre-crisis levels, rendering the high yield bond market less liquid than ever. The credit derivatives markets have also become significantly less liquid though still large enough to pose a systemic threat. Outstanding credit default swaps declined to roughly $20 trillion by the end of 2014 from over $60 trillion during the financial crisis. This is still large enough to dwarf the capital of the financial system. Furthermore, a number of firms that were active in this market announced in 2014 that they were exiting the market for single name and index credit default swaps.

The real arguments supporting naked credit default swaps are mercenary; these are opaque, difficult-to-price instruments from which Wall Street earns large profits. Wall Street is not a public utility—it is a profit-seeking engine whose primary purpose is to generate money for itself. The more complex and opaque the instrument, the easier it is for Wall Street to fool investors (even supposedly smart money investors like hedge funds and large institutions) and mark up these instruments to earn outsized profits from selling and trading them.

Proposals to regulate credit derivatives after the crisis generally focused on the following three areas:

1. Requiring these instruments to be listed on an exchange.
2. Monitoring counterparty risk.
3. Increasing collateral requirements.

Listing these instruments on an exchange was intended to enhance transparency, while increasing collateral requirements was designed to limit speculation by forcing participants to have more skin in the game. While combining these measures with rules limiting financial institutions' leverage may reduce systemic risk, they still leave unanswered the overriding policy question of whether society wants so much intellectual and financial capital devoted to speculation in naked credit default swaps and other non-productive activities. Banning such naked swaps could make capital available for more economically productive lending activities if the proper incentives (such as investment tax credits or accelerated depreciation deductions) were offered. While such a reform should be part of a far more comprehensive economic program, it points to the fact that if regulation were to limit opportunities for speculation, it might increase the chances that money could find its way into more productive activities.

Listing Credit Derivatives on an Exchange

Listing and trading credit default swaps on an exchange even with enhanced counterparty disclosure may be better than doing nothing, but falls short of what is needed to protect the financial system against another blow-up. In fact, plans to trade complex financial instruments on exchanges, which include provisions requiring enhanced counterparty disclosure, tends to distract policymakers from comprehensive solutions while allowing the powers on Wall Street to keep minting money at the expense of everyone else. The argument that this approach will improve transparency is a red herring since it relies on the ability of regulators and other non-specialists to decipher highly complex financial instruments. Giving these individuals greater access to information on credit default swaps is a far cry from handing them the tools to be able to understand them and the risks they pose. This is analogous to arguing that making quantum physics textbooks widely available will allow the average person to construct a nuclear power plant. The inspection staffs at the Securities and Exchange Commission and FINRA repeatedly demonstrate their inability to conduct competent inspections of firms engaged in far less complex investment schemes than those involving derivatives. How can we expect regulators to suddenly understand complex financial instruments without providing them with the necessary training to understand them? This is a highly dubious proposition. Greek is still Greek to somebody who only speaks English. Despite the best intentions, it is a virtual certainty that government work will never attract the type of talent necessary to untangle abuses that clever traders can construct in the credit derivatives area. Requiring these trades to be effected on an exchange simply passes the buck from legislators to regulators. And regulators will never be up to the task.

Furthermore, moving these instruments onto an exchange does nothing to eliminate the moral hazard regime whereby risks are socialized and gains are privatized. In fact, such a solution is likely to exacerbate the likelihood that such a regime will expand to new parts of the financial sector. Thus far, the "too big to fail" doctrine has been applied to institutions whose mistakes were deemed to pose a systemic risk. Moving credit default swaps onto an exchange would likely create the necessity for the government to protect these entities were the market to collapse due to a credit market meltdown. After all, these exchanges would stand at the center of the derivatives market and their failure pose a new threat to financial stability. Bailing out these exchanges might also provide protection for many institutions (i.e., members of the new derivatives exchange) that may not themselves be systemically vital, further extending the government safety net and moral hazard to places they do not belong.

Proponents of listing requirements argue that an exchange-based system will allow regulators and others to better track trading derivatives volumes and exposures and thereby better measure overall systemic risk. While having access to that information would be an improvement over the situation that existed prior to the financial crisis, it is questionable how useful such information will ultimately prove. The credit default swap market was $60 trillion in size at the time of the crisis, although that figure included many offsetting positions and the net exposure of financial institutions to these instruments was lower (again, nobody knew or knows the real figures). As of the end of 2014, this figure reportedly had shrunk to about $20 trillion as parties worked doggedly to reduce their exposures after seeing what happened to AIG, the bond insurers, numerous hedge funds, and others who drank the credit default swap Kool-Aid. But even at $20 trillion, the market is still vast and complex and filled with instruments that few if any of the regulators and senior executives charged with overseeing them understand. It may be helpful for regulators to have some idea of the total number of outstanding credit default swaps as a first step to figuring out how to regulate them. More likely, however, it will prove of limited utility since they still won't understand what they are regulating.

Moreover, heavy lobbying by the financial industry limited the types of contracts that must be listed on exchanges to conventional or standard derivatives contracts. Nonstandard contracts and contracts used to hedge commercial business risks are still not required to be listed. As a result, efforts to move derivatives onto clearing houses have been only partially successful. As of July 17, 2015, for example, the U.S. Commodity Futures Trading Commission (CFTC) reported that of the $257.4 trillion gross notional amount of interest rate swaps that it tracked, only 61.7 percent were traded on exchanges (leaving $98.5 trillion trading elsewhere). Of the $5.4 trillion of total credit default swaps it tracked as of that date, only 29.8 percent were traded on exchanges (leaving 70 percent or $3.8 trillion trading privately). If the idea was to capture all of derivatives in these exchanges, regulators were still far short of meeting their goals.[15]

Proponents for such exclusions argued, among other things, that such information is proprietary. This is another self-serving red herring that should be ignored. Steps can be taken to protect truly confidential information whose disclosure would be harmful to certain businesses.

Counterparty Surveillance

While simply listing derivatives on an exchange misses the mark, the goals of transparency and systemic stability would be much better served by requiring fuller public disclosure by the parties trading these instruments. As some observers, including this author, warned in the period leading up to the financial crisis, one of the most serious flaws in the credit derivatives regime was the inadequacy of counterparty risk monitoring. Not only did regulators and important market participants have no idea of who owed what to whom, but they had no real understanding whether the parties involved in credit default swap transactions were capable of meeting their obligations.

One of the most egregious examples of what can happen when parties fail to perform proper (or any) due diligence on their counterparties involved the Swiss banking giant UBS. UBS purchased $1.31 billion of credit insurance on the oxymoronically termed "super-senior tranche" of a subprime collateralized mortgage obligation (CMO) from a small Connecticut-based hedge fund, Paramax Capital, which had only $200 million of capital under management. Wisely unwilling to put all of its eggs in one basket, Paramax formed a special purpose entity to provide the credit insurance and capitalized it with only $4.6 million of its capital. The special purpose entity was subject to future capital calls if the value of the underlying CMO declined, which it inevitably did (this occurred in 2007), and ultimately Paramax defaulted after posting more than $30 million in collateral. Needless to say, when the hedge fund couldn't make good on its obligation, UBS sued it, and naturally Paramax sued UBS back. If this transaction is typical of UBS's business practices, it is little wonder that UBS announced on December 10, 2007 that it was taking a $10 billion write-down in the fourth quarter of 2007, most of it related to the type of super-senior instrument that it had somehow expected the diminutive Paramax to insure.[16]

Counterparty risk is separate and apart from the risk associated with the underlying debt instrument that is insured under a credit default swap agreement. It is a measure of whether the party selling the credit insurance will be capable of making good on its obligation. In order to properly evaluate counterparty risk, a party entering into a credit default swap contract needs to be able to analyze the financial condition of the other party to the transaction. This requires full disclosure of all of that party's financial obligations, something that is an extremely tall order in today's opaque financial world in which typical counterparties are involved in numerous balance-sheet and off-balance-sheet transactions of various degrees of complexity.

The odds of a typical counterparty being in a position to adequately measure this type of risk are extremely low. The current state of financial disclosure is inadequate to provide the type of information necessary to give counterparties the type of comfort they need to enter into these types of transactions. Reliance on financial institutions' public financial statements or their credit ratings still leaves the system with insufficient information to evaluate counterparty risk on an institution-specific or system-wide basis. For a truly effective system to work, standards of disclosure must be significantly intensified and include provisions to protect confidential and proprietary information. Requiring parties to disclose such information could create a huge disincentive for many of them to engage in such transactions and could be an effective way of limiting speculative trading in these instruments. Increasingly opaque financial markets cannot leave the monitoring of counterparty risk in private hands; government must step in to enforce high standards of disclosure. We have already seen the results of leaving this responsibility in the hands of private sector regulators such as FINRA. Adequate disclosure would include not only counterparties' complete financial condition (including all balance-sheet and off-balance-sheet obligations), and a complete listing of their derivative positions. While Dodd-Frank imposes significant reporting requirements on large hedge funds and other market participants that provide some of this transparency, it remains questionable whether the reams of information being disclosed can be meaningfully analyzed by regulators.

In the wake of the financial crisis, heightened disclosure requirements were greeted with howls of protest by hedge funds and other

investors purporting to claim that their trading positions and strategies constituted trade secrets that need to be protected like matters of
national security. These protests were properly dismissed for at least two
reasons. First, regardless of what hedge fund operators like to claim, there
is little that is proprietary about their positions or strategies. The only
proprietary aspect of their operations is what occurs inside the heads of
the funds' managers, the thought processes that cannot be duplicated
merely by viewing their positions. Moreover, in markets that operate
on the basis of milliseconds, a disclosure regime that operates in arrears
builds in a sufficient time delay to render this concern moot. Second, the
vast majority of these hedge funds' trades are speculative in nature; they
are not increasing the productive capacity of the economy. Accordingly,
the merits of disclosure in terms of enhancing systemic stability should
outweigh any potential limitations on these funds' profitability. Regulation should favor stability and productive investment over instability and
speculation. The real challenge is that regulators are now in possession
of so much information that it is questionable whether they are capable
of analyzing it effectively.

Increasing Collateral Requirements

Higher collateral requirements come closer to the mark but still fall
short of creating the type of economic incentives that would effectively
discourage speculation. It was far too easy for speculators to manipulate
the short-term borrowing rates of firms like Bear Stearns and Lehman
Brothers (and even Goldman Sachs and Morgan Stanley) through the
credit default swap market in the midst of the financial crisis. Large
investment banks or hedge funds could simply add these trades to their
existing credit lines and mount bear raids on other firms in a completely
unregulated environment.

The real question comes back to the type of instrument represented
by a credit default swap. These are insurance contracts that, in the case of
naked swaps, do not require the party purchasing the insurance to own
an insured interest. As a result, their economic interest in the outcome of
the trade remains limited and their incentive to see companies fail remains
high; increasing collateral requirements does little to change either of these
conditions. Limited liability provides enormous incentives for investors

to speculate and is another aspect of the moral hazard problem that haunts the U.S. financial system. Increasing collateral requirements in the absence of requiring an insurable interest in credit default swaps will do little to stem the type of speculation that contributed to the 2008 financial crisis. At best, such a regime will force some weak hands out of the market.

At the end of the day, it is difficult to escape the conclusion that anything less than an outright ban on naked credit default swaps will accomplish the goal of directing more financial and intellectual capital into productive rather than speculative uses while improving systemic transparency and stability. The advent of credit default swaps has done little to improve liquidity in underlying cash markets; in fact, it has produced the opposite effect as trading capital has migrated out of those markets and into the derivatives markets.[17] Moreover, the types of perverse incentives these instruments create to see companies fail rather than succeed suggest that the system could do with fewer of them. Requiring purchasers of credit insurance to have an insurable interest in the underlying debt instrument would be the surest way of addressing the most significant regulatory challenges they pose.

One of the arguments in favor of naked swaps is the same argument in favor of naked short-selling of stocks. Proponents argue that such a strategy imposes an important discipline on companies and provides an incentive for them to maintain strong credit quality. But as George Soros has pointed out, credit default swaps work in a completely different manner than selling stocks short.[18] When an investor is short a stock, an increase in the stock price raises his exposure and renders it increasingly expensive to maintain the position. Moreover, the margin rules require the short-seller to post additional collateral to hold the position (although short positions effected through options and other derivatives can minimize margin requirements). These pressures discourage short-selling.

Credit default swaps do not discourage short-selling because they offer limited risk and unlimited reward. An investor who wants to short a credit can purchase a credit default swap for a fixed amount of money and limit his exposure to that amount of money. As that credit deteriorates, the value of his swap increases and he does not have to post additional collateral (and may, depending on his agreement with his lender, be able to withdraw collateral). This encourages the short-selling of credit. Taking the other side of this trade is much less attractive (that is, selling the credit insurance) because the seller of insurance must continue to post additional collateral as the underlying credit deteriorates. The asymmetry between selling insurance (going long) and buying insurance (going short) can encourage short-selling and introduce a significant short bias into the marketplace. This is far different from imposing an honest discipline on companies to improve their balance sheets and maintain strong credit quality. Instead, credit default swaps introduce a strong incentive to speculate on the short side, which is hardly conducive to directing capital to productive economic uses. The structure of credit default swaps therefore renders them far more destabilizing to markets than other types of hedging instruments and bolsters the case for limiting their usage to situations in which the buyer owns the underlying debt.

***

There is another wonderful scene in *Jurassic Park* when the scientists are touring the laboratory where the dinosaurs are bred. One of the scientists tries to explain to Dr. Malcolm that the park has bred only female velociraptors, a particularly dangerous breed of dinosaurs that come to wreak their own special havoc throughout the film (and its many sequels). Dr. Malcolm responds that it isn't possible to limit the breeding to females, and the scientist condescendingly explains that it's really a rather simple matter of excluding a male hormone from the genetic mix. Dr. Malcolm disagrees and simply says, "Life finds a way." The same is true of Wall Street when it comes to regulation. Wall Street will find a way to manipulate its way around restrictions placed on its ability to create new products and generate profits regardless of the systemic risks its behavior poses.

One of the methods that institutions have employed to avoid restrictions on their derivatives operations since the crisis has been to shift derivatives trades to overseas affiliates, primarily those in London that are no longer guaranteed by their U.S. parent or alternatively to revoke guarantees on specific transactions. In June 2015, the CFTC finally approved a proposal to close this loophole and require the offshore units of U.S. institutions to adhere to CFTC rules even when they are not explicitly on the hook for the trades.

As this book was going to press, the proposed rule was still subject to comments and has to be voted on a second time to go into effect. The constant cat-and-mouse game between regulators and traders is an age-old competition that will continue as long as there are markets. That is why it is incumbent upon every individual and institution that is affected by what occurs in the financial markets to not only understand derivatives but to appreciate why they can't be allowed to run wild like dinosaurs in a china shop.

CHAPTER 8

The Road to Hell

I n 1998, my firm visited with a prominent money manager in New
York City. At the time, we were trying to raise money to invest in
less-than-investment-grade corporate debt. We attended the meeting and, to put it politely, we were given the brush off. That was no big
deal—it happened all the time. But what that money manager said struck
us as very odd. "Why should I give you guys money?" he asked. "You
can't make me one point a month like my friend Bernie." We knew who
Bernie was, and responded, "It's not a 'point-a-month' world."

Several years later, in 2005, we were sitting in front of another group
that said it was interested in raising money for us. The talks proceeded
to the point where we were invited to meet with the company's founder
and his top lieutenants. These gentlemen explained they were looking
for another product to add to the offering of their largest existing manager (whose identity was treated like a national security secret) who was
producing consistent monthly returns in the 80 to 100 basis point range.
They stressed repeatedly that they could not consider a strategy that
experienced losses of as much as 2 percent a month. We told them that

it would be impossible to guarantee that there would not be monthly losses. Needless to say, the talks went nowhere.

The money manager we met in 1998 was Ezra Merkin, whose funds lost a reported $2.4 billion with Bernard Madoff. The money management firm we met in 2005 was Fairfield Greenwich Group, whose clients reportedly lost more than $7 billion in the Madoff fraud. Madoff, of course, was the top secret manager whose identity they refused to disclose. The firm's now disgraced founder Walter Noel attended that meeting but let his minions do most of the talking.

Satan in the Garden

Bernard Madoff Investment Securities offered investors what they think they are supposed to seek in all of their investments: steady returns and minimal risk. This is the mantra of fiduciary thought. Unfortunately, when the curtain was pulled back on that particular wizard, what was discovered was a virtual checklist of the worst imaginable investment practices that knowledgeable investors such as Merkin and Fairfield Greenwich were paid obscene amounts of money to sniff out and avoid. These practices included: a total lack of transparency; financial statements prepared by a hole-in-the-wall accounting firm; and an investment strategy that could not possibly be carried out in any markets on the planet Earth (the so-called "split strike conversion strategy"). Yet fiduciaries such as Merkin and Fairfield Greenwich, as well as a laundry list of other respected investment institutions such as Tremont Group Holdings (owned by MassMutual), Banco Santander of Spain, the Swiss fund-of-funds firm EIM, and many other prominent investors were lured by the promise of month-after-month of consistently positive (but not *too* positive, which was an essential part of the scam) returns. The knowledge that such returns are virtually unattainable and that their purveyor refused to reveal how he produced them was apparently insufficient to dampen investors' hunger for them, suggesting just how rare and valuable such a return profile would be if it were truly achievable in the real world.

Madoff's scheme had a deeply pernicious effect on the investment management business long before it was revealed to be a complete fraud. In addition to casting a cloud of suspicion on other money management firms, particularly independent firms that are not part of large institutions, Madoff's scheme distorted investors' perceptions about the kind of returns they can reasonably expect. This aspect of the Madoff affair has been insufficiently acknowledged and is an essential part of the reason why capital continues to be so poorly managed by the professional investment class.

The essence of Madoff's scheme was the proffer of consistent returns with low risk. To some people, this may seem like a reasonable proposition, but experienced and knowledgeable market participants should know better. This should particularly have been the case with respect to Madoff's track record, which purported to show consecutive years of positive monthly returns with few if any negative months and no correlation to what was occurring in the financial markets. As we told Mr. Merkin in 1998, it is not a "point-a-month" world; it is a world of fat tails and, in the term that Nassim Nicholas Taleb made famous a few years later, Black Swans. Yet Madoff's return pattern captured the imagination of the professional investment class and led it down the road to ruin. It also led to many imitators as institutional investors came to demand that other managers offer the same impossible model. This is one of the ways that the road to investment hell became littered with fiduciary intentions.

Reverse Black Swans

It is hardly a coincidence that the explosion of so-called alternative investments in the hedge fund industry coincided with the growth of investment strategies that offered consistent low-risk returns. By the end of 2006, the cusp of the financial crisis, Hedge Fund Research, Inc., estimated that the global hedge fund industry held $1.43 trillion in assets. These assets were spread among 11,000 different funds of which approximately one-third were funds-of-funds, according to the European Central Bank. This was a huge jump from 1990, when hedge funds held less than $400 billion in assets, and even from 2005, when the $1 trillion mark was passed.

Since the financial crisis, hedge fund assets more than doubled again to $3.118 trillion as of June 2015 according to eVestment.[1] This growth paralleled the growth of private equity assets and related strategies that invest increasing amounts of capital in nonpublic securities that can only be valued by their managers rather than by reference to any objective market standard that is independently verifiable. The two concepts—alternative investments and consistent positive returns—were joined at the hip in a symbiotic relationship that turned into a dance of death during the financial crisis. With some exceptions, the hedge fund model became one in which managers offered investors the prospect of consistent, uncorrelated positive returns in exchange for exorbitant fees.

As we saw with private equity returns, when we pull back the kimono on hedge fund returns from a risk-adjusted basis (that is, adjusted for liquidity, leverage, concentration risks and fees), many of them turn out to be far less attractive than advertised. This is particularly true with respect to credit strategies that invest predominately in nonpublic securities, most of which lost enormous amounts of money in 2008. There were profound structural flaws in the investment strategies of credit hedge funds that were responsible for many of them ending up on the wrong side—and same side—of the market in 2008. These flaws included the following:

- They owned a lot of illiquid assets.
- They used too much leverage.
- Their positions were correlated.
- They took a lot of fat tail risk.
- They financed themselves with unstable capital on both the equity and debt sides of their balance sheets.
- They carried assets at book value (misrepresenting actual values).
- They extrapolated the past into the future and ignored statistically or historically improbable events.

As a result, hedge funds—especially those that reported years of strong performance during the bull market in less liquid asset classes that involved the trading of corporate bonds, loans and credit derivatives—were susceptible to blowing up. They did not disappoint in 2008.

What these funds did was effectively adopt a reverse-Black Swan investment model in which they offered the illusion of steady high returns with low risk. In his book *The Black Swan: The Impact of the Highly Improbable*, best-selling author Nassim Nicholas Taleb described the Black Swan investment strategy, which is characterized by trades that yield small losses over time but can generate extraordinary returns if the market or individual stocks make extreme downward moves. Many hedge funds marketing low volatility strategies inadvertently flipped this strategy on its head and tried to create a series of small but steady returns against the small possibility of large losses due to expectations that market volatility would remain within historical limits. Some funds did this using highly liquid securities and high degrees of leverage, such as credit arbitrage funds, and others invested in non-public debt and equity securities in the credit space, like the many highly leveraged credit-oriented hedge funds that blew up in 2008. These funds collected a lot of illiquid investments and ended up retaining the least valuable ones through a process of adverse selection when forced to sell. Many of these funds either blocked redemptions (i.e., "gated" their funds) or offered to return assets "in-kind" to investors (which from an investor's standpoint is the equivalent of winning the booby prize). Realistically, there is nothing else these funds could do with these investments; they certainly couldn't sell their illiquid assets to anybody at the bottom of the market.

In order to deliver steady streams of positive returns, however, hedge fund managers claimed they were following strategies that were uncorrelated with the financial markets. What does uncorrelated mean? We all know what it is supposed to mean—returns that are not correlated with the movements of other risk assets such as stocks. What uncorrelated really came to mean was something else entirely: Madoff-type returns, which were simply fraudulent, or private-market-type returns, which were based on nonpublic market valuations that could not be confirmed by liquidity events except on a sporadic basis. The latter type of investments included private equity, direct lending to small and midsize companies, structured products, and similar investment strategies. Some of the largest hedge funds in the world managed by firms such as Cerberus Capital Management, LLC, GoldenTree Asset Management, L.P., and Highland Capital Management, L.P. engaged in these strategies and grew to enormous sizes before running aground in 2008. Their losses called into question their reported returns in earlier years to the extent those returns included unrealized gains that were later reversed by losses. But in order to compete to manage the money of institutions that believed in the prospect of low-volatility/high returns, firms that wanted to grow had little choice but to follow these strategies.

This approach worked out just fine as long as the markets were rising, or at least when they weren't experiencing extreme volatility. As long as global liquidity was robust and markets were stable, these strategies looked successful on the surface. Funds could continue to borrow to bid up the prices of financial assets, and managers could continue to convince investors that their investments were worth more each year. But when credit markets seized up, these strategies were swamped by three simultaneous tsunamis. First, the value of their leveraged assets started to decline precipitously. Second, their lenders became nervous and demanded more collateral to support their positions. And third, these firms could no longer convince investors to keep feeding them money and in many cases were faced with requests to return capital. When the markets sold off, many investors wanted their money back. The problem was that these investments were completely illiquid and investor capital could only be returned in kind or not at all. Returning cash to investors was out of the question because capital had died. This was how Madoff's Ponzi scheme came apart: It relied on a continual stream of new money to pay interest on investor capital and to handle the return of capital to investors who requested their money back. But when such requests grew increasingly large (reportedly to $5 or $6 billion by late 2008), there simply wasn't enough new money coming in for Madoff to honor them and the scheme fell apart.

Many legitimate hedge funds (that unlike Madoff's actually engaged in real investing and trading strategies) suffered the same fate and were forced to suspend redemptions, return capital in kind, or close shop. This was not only another example (like the banking industry's SIVs) of a flawed financial strategy that confused long-term solvency with short-term liquidity by borrowing short to lend long, but also emblematic of the fact that institutional investors were seeking an impossible Holy Grail of consistently high positive returns with low risk. One has to wonder how differently things might have turned out had Madoff's fraud been discovered much earlier and the investment community come to an earlier understanding that markets don't serve free lunches.

The real question that should be asked is how so many investors could be led to believe that such strategies were prudent (or even possible). After all, the prudent man rule is the basis on which most fiduciaries base their conduct. How could an entire generation of investors be duped into believing in concepts that are so blatantly false? Like many of the other intellectually corrupting influences discussed in this book, investors were given a mighty helping hand by the political and academic authorities. In particular, the U.S. legal system adopted a doctrine of fiduciary duty that narrowed the focus of those charged with investing other peoples' money to the single goal of economic gain. Other societal interests such as the rights of labor, the environment, and the distinction between productive and speculative investment, were pushed aside.

Moreover, an entire industry of consultants and academics developed the intellectual scaffolding to dress up this mandate in pseudo-scientific language. Concepts like "Sharpe ratio" and "R-squared" and the infamous Greek chorus of "alpha" and "beta" were used to justify investment strategies that could theoretically deliver steady returns with low volatility and low correlation with the stock market. These arcana dressed the consultants in the garb of a secret ministry holding the keys to the kingdom of gold. The only problem is that when one pulls back the curtain, one finds that that there is no wizard and that the magic formula is malarkey. There is a perfectly good reason many of the strategies recommended by the consultant community and other investment advisers don't correlate with financial markets: They are not marked-to-market or even capable of being marked-to-market in any meaningful manner. Accordingly, the entire industry is operating under an illusion from which it would be extremely painful to break free.

It should be noted that there are absolute return strategies that are uncorrelated with the market that can generate consistent high returns without employing high leverage or investing in illiquid assets. I know because I manage one such strategy in The Third Friday Total Return Fund, L.P., which is discussed further in Chapter 11. This strategy was developed over two decades and has been tested successfully through several market cycles. But such strategies are rare.

Birth of the Prudent Man

There are two aspects of modern fiduciary doctrine that are deeply troubling. First, how did the prudent man rule become warped into a blind pursuit of financial profit at the expense of the other, arguably equally important economic and societal values? And second, how did substantive thinking about investing devolve into thinking that the Madoff model of consistent monthly returns is realistic?

The prudent man rule dates back to the 1830 Massachusetts court case *Harvard College v. Amory*, 26 Mass (9 Pick.) 446 (1830). That court held that "all that can be required of a trustee to invest, is, that he shall conduct himself faithfully and exercise a sound discretion. He is to observe how men of prudence, discretion, and intelligence manage their own affairs, not in regard to speculation, but in regard to the permanent disposition of their funds, considering the probable income, as well as the probable safety of the capital to be invested." Most important, the case held that "trustees are not to be made chargeable but for gross neglect and willful mismanagement," standards of conduct that still apply today.

Like many legal standards, this one is extremely broad and leaves many of the details to be filled in by legislators, practitioners, and judges as specific situations arise. There have been a number of landmark advances in the thinking governing this rule over the years. In 1942, the Model Prudent Man Statute was adopted that codified this rule and influenced the passage of many state statutes. In 1972, the Uniform Management of Institutional Funds Act was issued as a model law designed to guide institutional investors to adopt total return strategies for their investment portfolios. This was followed in 1974 by the Employee Retirement Income Security Act (ERISA), a comprehensive federal pension law that codified the prudent man standard of care. ERISA 29 USC § 1104(a) states that

[A] fiduciary shall discharge his duties with respect to a [retirement] plan solely in the interest of the participants and beneficiaries and—

    A. for the exclusive purpose of:
        i. providing benefits to participants and their beneficiaries; and
        ii. defraying reasonable expenses of administering the plan;
    B. with the care, skill, prudence, and diligence under the circumstances then prevailing that a prudent man acting in a like capacity and familiar with such matters would use in the conduct of an enterprise of a like character and with like aims;
    C. by diversifying the investments of the plan so as to minimize the risk of large losses, unless under the circumstances it is clearly prudent not to do so;...

But ERISA did more than simply codify the prudent man rule—it added a duty of diversification. This requirement was an endorsement of the modern portfolio theory developed by Harry Markowitz in one of the most famous papers in modern finance, "Portfolio Selection."

Markowitz's article appeared in the March 1952 issue of the *Journal of Finance* and was written when the author was only 25 years old. Markowitz followed this article with a more detailed discussion in a book entitled *Portfolio Selection: Diversification of Investment,* which was published seven years later in 1959. In the key passage in the article, Markowitz argued, "[i]t is necessary to avoid investing in securities with high covariances among themselves. We should diversify across industries because firms in different industries, especially industries with different economic characteristics, have lower covariances than firms within an industry."[2]

This means that securities in the same industry, for example, will not provide sufficient diversification because they tend to react to the same types of business and economic risk factors in the same way. A portfolio composed of an undue concentration of companies in a single industry would be too vulnerable to the risks facing that industry. "A portfolio with sixty different railway securities," Markowitz wrote, "would not be as well diversified as the same size portfolio with some railroad, some public utility, mining, various sorts of manufacturing, etc. The reason is that it is generally more likely for firms within the same industry to do poorly at the same time than for firms in dissimilar industries."[3] Markowitz's paper was considered revolutionary at the time because it introduced the concept of risk-adjusted returns. Previously, the concept of diversification had not been considered essential to portfolio management. Instead, investors were primarily focused on maximizing their returns without regard to the risks involved. Markowitz introduced the important concept that returns are related to the amount of risk associated with an investment. As noted previously with respect to the discussion of private equity returns, this is an essential insight that is too often overlooked even today.

In constructing portfolios that were sufficiently diversified to protect against risk, Markowitz added the mathematical concept of mean variance optimization, which in layman's terms means "efficiency." In mathematical terms, efficiency means maximizing output for a given input, or minimizing input for a given output. In portfolio terms, this means maximizing the anticipated return for the amount of risk taken, or minimizing risk for the amount of return achieved. In Peter Bernstein's words, an efficient portfolio "offers the highest expected return for any given degree of risk, or that has the lowest degree of risk for any given expected return."[4] This concept still guides much of the money management industry today. Unfortunately, it has done little to help the industry avoid repeating the same mistakes over and over again.

The other theory that has exercised enormous (and undue) influence on fiduciaries is the wholly discredited efficient market theory, which was set forth in a 1965 article by economist Eugene F. Fama. An efficient market is defined as one in which:

> There are large numbers of rational, profit-maximizers actively competing, with each trying to predict future market values of individual securities, and where important current information is almost freely available to all participants. In an efficient market, competition among the many intelligent participants leads to a situation where, at any given moment in time, actual prices of individual securities already reflect the effects of information based both on events that have already occurred and on events which, as of now, the market expects to take place in the future. In other words, in an efficient market at any point in time the actual price of a security will be a good estimate of its intrinsic value.[5]

Although this is clearly a definition that only someone completely lacking in market experience could actually accept as a reflection of reality, it has exercised an undue influence on fiduciary thought.

In fact, the efficient market theory was endorsed in the *Restatement Third of Trusts* (1992), where the Reporter's General Note on Restatement Section 227 reads:

> Economic evidence shows that, from a typical investment perspective, the major capital markets of this country are highly efficient, in the sense that available information is rapidly digested and reflected in the market prices of securities. As a result, fiduciaries and other investors are confronted with potent evidence that the application of expertise, investigation, and diligence in efforts to "beat the market" in these

publicly traded securities ordinarily promises little or no payoff, or even a negative payoff after taking account of research and transaction costs. Empirical research supporting the theory of efficient markets reveals that in such markets skilled professionals have rarely been able to identify underpriced securities (that is, to outguess the market with respect to future return) with any regularity.[6]

The introduction to the *Restatement* and the prefatory note to the Uniform Prudent Investor Act passed two years later stressed the influence of modern portfolio theory, of which Markowitz was one of the founding fathers. In fact, this landmark restatement of the law of trusts was primarily intended to incorporate modern portfolio theory into the rules governing fiduciaries. Among the principles laid out in the *Restatement* was that both passive and active investment strategies would be deemed prudent, but that active strategies would be required to meet a higher standard in justifying that they were adding value (which came to be known as "alpha," one of the Greek gods of current investment argot). The *Restatement* outlined five principles of prudence for fiduciaries to follow: diversification; a reasonable relationship between risk and reward; minimizing unnecessary and unreasonable fees; balancing preservation of capital and production of current income; and giving trustees the duty and authority to delegate investment decisions to others. With the exception of the bald assertion of the necessity of diversification, this is a reasonable list.

It is little wonder that typical fiduciaries at large institutions tend to stumble into one investment trap after another; they invest as though they actually believe that the markets are efficient and that diversification really pays off. They might as well believe that the earth is flat or the moon is made of green cheese, two propositions for which there is just as much empirical proof as there is for the efficient market theory and Harry Markowitz's "Portfolio Selection." This is the type of thinking that leads institutions into the private equity trap, the distressed debt trap, and other illiquid strategies that they are told do not correlate with public equity and debt markets when, in fact, they correlate strongly with such markets with the added handicap of enjoying limited liquidity, employing greater leverage, incurring higher fees, and producing lower risk-adjusted returns. These theories completely overlook market realities. The efficient market theory ignores not only the wisdom of thinkers like Smith, Marx, Keynes, and Minsky that markets are highly inefficient because they are driven primarily by human emotion, but the reams of data that illustrate beyond a shadow of a doubt that market prices are imprecise measures of underlying valuation metrics that are themselves unstable indicia of value. The Portfolio Selection thesis overlooks the fact that the concept of correlation has changed dramatically since the time that Markowitz wrote his paper. Investors treat the concept of correlation like a law of nature rather than a human construct, and therefore engage in profound intellectual error. In fact, it is ironic that when Markowitz wrote the paper in 1955, it was difficult to test his thesis because of limited computer power, while today the advanced computer power that permits every conceivable type of financial instrument to be deconstructed into 1s and 0s renders the very concept of diversification obsolete.

The Fallacy of Diversification

In Chapter 3, we discussed the role that the prudent or reasonable man played in the work of Adam Smith as he tried to design a just society based on commercial exchange. We saw the flaws in that approach as it cedes power to groupthink and the madness of crowds. Add that to an almost religious belief in diversification and efficient markets and one can begin to understand how the evolution of fiduciary law created the conditions for most shepherds of capital to consistently produce suboptimal returns.

Diversification came to be taken for granted as the gravamen of prudent investment management. But the world changed, and diversification in the early twenty-first century no longer means what it did half a century ago before derivatives and Ponzi finance came to dominate the financial landscape. So while the concept of diversification had a great deal to recommend it in the investment world of the 1950s, it has turned out to be a trap for investors in the twenty-first century. Today, asset classes that are not ostensibly covariant (to invoke Markowitz's terminology), such as equities and debt, have been rendered covariant by new financial technology. The ability to deconstruct all types of securities and financial instruments into their constituent parts (1s and 0s) has erased the differences between asset classes, nullifying the boundaries between different types of securities in ways that render the concept of diversification completely outmoded. During the financial crisis, investors discovered, much to their distress, that while they thought their portfolios were invested in different types of risks, they were, in fact, largely exposed to the same risks. The most significant risk was the enormous amount of leverage embedded in all asset classes. Another way of saying this, in the terminology of Hyman Minsky, is that they were at greater risk than they realized that the Ponzi finance structure of the U.S. and global economy would come apart. The economy became populated by so many economic actors—individual homeowners, corporations—that were so highly leveraged that virtually their entire capital structures (equity and debt) effectively consisted of borrowed money. As a result, both the equity and debt components of their capital structures were equally vulnerable not only to changes in individual debtors' financial situations but also to deterioration in the financial markets. What once was uncorrelated suddenly turned out to be highly correlated because all asset classes were vulnerable to the risk of a credit crisis.

Perhaps the grossest abuse of the concept of diversification was committed by the U.S. credit rating agencies, Moody's Investors Service and Standard & Poor's, in their ratings of structured products. The intellectual poverty of the agencies' approach to modeling correlation is writ large in the fact that the agencies subsequently found themselves compelled to reject their earlier ratings and admit that the models on which the entire trillion dollar edifice of structured finance was constructed was deeply flawed. Aided and abetted by large Wall Street underwriters of CDOs, these oligopolists concocted so-called black box models that were intended to measure the correlations among individual mortgages, bonds, or loans. In the case of mortgages, as noted earlier in Chapter 4, they simply ignored the fact that the borrower data (FICO scores) they were using had never been tested in an economic downturn. In the case of corporate bonds and loans, they applied grossly understated corporate default and recovery assumptions (ones that predated the 2001–2002 period in which corporate defaults exceeded 10 percent for two consecutive years) and then categorically restated their assumptions in 2009 after the worst of the crisis had passed with little rationale and without distinguishing among different securities. Their actions effectively forced stable collateralized loan obligations into slow motion liquidations at the nadir of the financial crisis that rendered them incapable of purchasing additional bank loans and further damaged the market. The fact that hundreds of billions of dollars of transactions were premised on default assumptions that were unilaterally altered (at a time, by the way, when the default outlook was improving due to companies enjoying better access to capital that enabled them to refinance their debt) was apparently of no account to these self-appointed doyens of credit that had demonstrated beyond a shadow of a doubt that they know nothing about credit. With banks having exited this market, this unilateral and ill-considered *post hoc* action further shrunk the sources of capital available to fund less-than-investment-grade companies in the United States and Europe.

The only positive sign that the credit agencies were going to be held accountable for their fecklessness was the fact that New York Federal Court Judge Shira Scheindlin rejected their argument that their intellec-tually vacuous credit opinions were protected by the First Amendment. Judge Scheindlin held that First Amendment protection does not apply "where a credit rating agency has disseminated their ratings to a select group of investors rather than to the public at large." I would simply add that when rating agencies are paid large amounts of money for their opinions, the First Amendment veneer of free speech should not protect them from their mistakes.

The high-yield bond area has been a Petri dish for misapplied finan-cial theories and assumptions for years. As noted earlier, high yield bonds are properly understood as hybrid securities that possess the characteristics of both debt and equity. Yet most investors in this asset class focus on the "spread" at which a bond trades. The spread is the number of basis points (1/100s of a percentage point) above a benchmark yield at which a bond trades. In the case of high yield bonds, Treasury bonds are considered the benchmark on the basis that they are riskless securities (an assumption that itself is questionable in view of the United States' increasingly pre-carious fiscal posture). Spread represents the risk premium that investors demand for owning a security that is riskier than a Treasury bond.

There are two problems with this approach. First, conceding for the sake of argument that Treasury securities are riskless in the sense that their repayment in nominal terms by the U.S. government is assured, their interest rates have been kept artificially low since the early 1990s by pro-cyclical Federal Reserve policy. This phenomenon intensified after the Fed lowered the Federal Funds rate to zero during the financial crisis and kept it there for seven years while also engaging in several rounds of quantitative easing, policies that distorted interest rates beyond recognition. These low rates are signs that all is not well in the economy, a condition that adds further risk to high yield bond investments that are generally highly sensitive to economic conditions. In periods when interest rates are extremely low, these low rates are indicative of economic weakness, not strength. Accordingly, high yield bond investors are being grossly underpaid for the risks they are assuming.

Second, spread is a fixed income measurement and high yield bonds are not simple fixed income instruments; they contain a significant component of equity risk (that far too many investors have swallowed firsthand, to their dismay). The market is applying a tool designed to measure fixed income risk to what is in large part an equity security. This is particularly true with respect to lower rated bonds (bonds rated Ba/B or lower by Standard & Poor's and Moody's). Lower rated bonds are extremely risky and are really not fixed income instruments at all; they are best described as "equities in disguise" or "equities with a coupon." In fact, these bonds always end up trading at equity-like yields (which translates into much lower prices and very high yields) when the market recognizes their subordinated, equity-like character.

Combining the wrong benchmark with the wrong tool to measure risk virtually assures investors of a bad outcome. The primary reason spread is used to value high yield bonds is because it appeals to the quantitative side of the investment universe. Unfortunately, it is an extremely poor tool that continues to be used by investors to their detriment.

Another bogus assumption in the high yield bond market that led to billions of dollars of investor losses in the 2001–2002 credit collapse was the set of default expectations underlying a now mercifully extinct product, the collateralized bond obligation (CBO). CBOs were a form of collateralized debt obligation whose collateral was comprised primarily of high yield bonds. CBOs were underwritten by the largest and most respected financial institutions in the world using the basic assumptions that only two percent of the bonds in a diversified portfolio would default each year and that the recovery rate on these bonds would be 40 percent. These assumptions had little basis in reality, as the bond market collapses of 1990–1991, 1998, 2001–2002 and 2007–2008 demonstrated. Yet for some reason, the major credit rating agencies continued to issue investment grade ratings on the various tranches of CBOs based on these erroneous assumptions. Even worse, highly respected investment firms continued to hawk these products based on these same assumptions, and large institutional investors continued to purchase securities while believing them.

Interestingly enough, Harry Markowitz would be very open to suggestions that investment mantras like diversification should be subject to question in view of changing conditions. In 1995, Markowitz wrote a fascinating paper for the *Financial Analysts Journal* entitled "Market Efficiency: A Theoretical Distinction and So What?" in which he subjected William Sharpe's Capital Asset Pricing Model (CAPM) to some revisionary thinking. The CAPM is among the most influential theories in the recent history of investment management despite the fact that it depends on wholly unrealistic assumptions about the way in which markets and investors operate in the real world.[7] Among the assumptions of the CAPM that do not jive with the real world of investment are first, the assumption that taxes, transaction costs, and other friction costs can be ignored, and second, that investors share the same predictions for expected returns, volatilities, and correlations of securities. Both of these assumptions are obviously false. Moreover, the predictive record of this model is notoriously poor. As Eugene F. Fama and Kenneth R. French wrote in 2004: "(t)he empirical record of the model is poor—poor enough to invalidate the way it is used in applications.... The CAPM, like Markowitz's ... portfolio model on which it is built, is nevertheless a theoretical tour de force. We continue to teach the CAPM as an introduction to the fundamentals of portfolio theory and asset pricing.... But we also warn students that, despite its seductive simplicity, the CAPM's empirical problems probably invalidate its use in applications."[8] Despite these flaws—it is based on bogus assumptions and has poor predictive power—the CAPM has exercised an enormous influence on the thinking of investment professionals. There are valuable lessons to be learned from this model. But it is also a lesson that the investment management business—and on a broader basis, human knowledge—is built on error. The trick is learning from those errors and building on them to come to a deeper understanding of the truth—not repeating them.

Peter Bernstein argued powerfully in his final book, *Capital Ideas Evolving*, that "investors have learned from CAPM that they must recognize the fundamental distinction between investing in an asset class and selecting individual securities on which they hope to earn an extra return. The choice of asset classes—for example, stocks, bonds, emerging market equities, real estate, or subdivisions of those markets—is in essence the choice of beta risks, or the volatility of entire markets rather than their individual components."[9] This may be true but does not help solve the conundrum facing investors when all asset classes correlate because they have been reduced to 1s and 0s. Theory has yet to catch up to practice and fiduciaries need to understand the new reality if they are to properly fulfill their obligation to first do no harm before worrying about how to generate attractive risk-adjusted returns for their flocks.

Market dislocations like those that occurred in 1998 and 2008 demonstrated that allegedly non-covariant asset classes like debt and equity can (and likely will) collapse at precisely the same time, and that stocks in different industries are far more interconnected than Markowitz's theory contended. True diversification turns out to require a far more radical approach than that proposed by Markowitz's model and legislated by ERISA and other codifiers of fiduciary standards in the mid-to-late twentieth century, as market events have demonstrated. Fiduciary law, like much of the thinking governing financial markets as they barely escaped the 2008 financial crisis and appeared headed toward another one a decade later, has been left in the dust.

CHAPTER 9

Finance after Armageddon

For many men and women who spent their professional lives on Wall Street, the year 2008 felt like Armageddon. Not only did many of them lose their jobs, but they also lost the wealth and financial security they spent decades accumulating. Regulators and others in the seats of government surely felt as though they were facing the end-of-days when confronted with the death of capital. The global financial system was virtually paralyzed in September and October of 2009, and unimaginable measures were taken to resuscitate it.

The financial crisis was nearly an extinction-level event. Anybody who believed that the system could continue without drastic reform afterward was probably beyond convincing or stood to profit too much personally from maintaining the status quo. Each succeeding financial crisis of the last three decades was more severe than the last because the underlying imbalances that caused it were growing exponentially, distorting the economy more profoundly and becoming less susceptible to correction without inflicting severe hardship on significant parts of society. After each of the previous crises, serious financial reform was sloughed off and the reins on risk-taking were further loosened in the name of free markets. For example, conduct that increased systemic instability, such as the creation of off-balance-sheet entities to conceal debt, continued to receive favorable treatment under bank capital rules even after the abuse of such entities by Enron Corp. caused a crisis of confidence in 2001 that inflicted serious damage on the markets. Increasing tolerance for behavior that escalated systemic risk created a system characterized by extreme moral hazard in which gains are privatized in the hands of a small elite while losses are socialized among the effectively disenfranchised and overburdened American taxpayer. American economics had become little more than socialism for the rich and capitalism for the poor.

For those who still believed that capital can be a force for good in the world if wisely managed and regulated, the financial crisis created an opportunity for serious discussion about what could be changed within the limitations of a corrupt political system and a financial-political complex that exercises power over all aspects of society. The time was long overdue for a serious call-to-arms to reform a system that has the capability of doing great good but has inflicted great harm by being repeatedly diverted into wasting its resources on leverage and speculation.

Despite the profound crisis that capitalism experienced in 2008, serious discussion of reform was quickly sidelined by powerful lobbying interests. After markets hit their nadir in March 2009, a veneer of stability returned to the financial world. But below the surface, serious instabilities continued to boil. Seven years later, as the United States prepares to elect its first new post-crisis president, the enormous mountains of debt that were created to triage the global economy are weighing down sovereign balance sheets and limiting governments' ability to deal with future challenges before they lurch into a new crisis. At the same time, despite the massive shift of debt from the private to the public sector, corporate balance sheets in the U.S. are significantly more leveraged than before the financial crisis. Low interest rates disguise the negative effects of increased leverage, but the global economy is feeling the strain in terms of slower growth. The weakened condition of the global system renders reform more urgent than ever.

Regulatory reform must be approached within the context of the consequences of what economic instability really means and what it can lead to. This requires a much greater focus on the long-term consequences of failing to act rather than concerning ourselves exclusively with reacting to short-term emergencies. The failure of a single institution is, in the long run, a relatively minor event. The system and its constituent parts will find a way to survive. But the long-term consequences of rescuing every poorly managed firm are extremely negative because of the moral hazard they create in a system that has grown accustomed to seeing risk socialized and profit privatized.

In order to develop long-term solutions to the problem of financial stability, one must learn to think in terms of the arc of history. Modern markets and media have shortened our attention spans to the point where historical consciousness has been all but obliterated, and it requires a special effort to focus on anything beyond the immediate moment. Despite the urgent necessity to remember the past and learn from it, people today have forgotten how to think historically. As the social and literary critic Frederic Jameson has written, people need "to think the present historically in an age that has forgotten to think historically in the first place."[1] This is particularly imperative at junctures when it feels like the center cannot hold, periods in which prior assumptions fail us and new answers are needed.

And what better place to start thinking about the consequences of Armageddon than to return to the gates of the place where barbarism last reigned when humanity failed us? After all, in 2015 the forces of barbarism are raging again in the Middle East and Eastern Europe and, due to our lack of vigilance, are spilling blood in the streets of Western cities as well.

In 1969, Theodor Adorno called for an uncompromising standard for education that should be applied more widely to all areas of human endeavor:

> The premier demand upon all education is that Auschwitz not happen again. Its priority before any other requirement is such that I believe I need not and should not justify it. I cannot understand why it has been given so little concern until now. To justify it would be monstrous in the face of the monstrosity that took place. Yet the fact that one is so barely conscious of this demand and the questions that it raises shows that the monstrosity has not penetrated people's minds deeply, itself a symptom of the continuing potential for its recurrence as far as peoples' conscious and unconscious is concerned. Every debate about the ideals of education

is trivial and inconsequential compared to this single ideal: never again Auschwitz. It was the barbarism all education strives against.[2]

Some readers may view it as alarmist to compare the obligation to prevent genocide from reoccurring to the obligation to maintain stable financial markets. But such a connection is absolutely necessary. It is blindness to such comparisons that leads to barbarism, and the conditions that led to the monstrosities that occurred in Germany 70 years ago are no less present in our world today. Just ask the people fleeing ISIS in the streets of Paris or San Bernardino or the barrel bombs of Bashar al-Assad or Vladimir Putin's forces in the Ukraine. This isn't happening by accident; it is a direct result of the failure of America to stand up to tyrants and to enforce high standards of conduct at home and abroad. Because we fail to imagine the worst, we are unprepared to deal with the worst when it descends upon us. The world keeps teaching us that, if only we are willing to pay attention.

Adorno also wrote in the same essay quoted above: "[a]mong the insights of Freud that truly extend even into culture and sociology, one of the most profound seems to be that civilization itself produces anti-civilization and increasingly enforces it." Nearly four decades after Adorno's warning, insufficient attention is paid to the fact that without functioning financial markets that are capable of raising capital for productive uses and creating opportunity for the disenfranchised, the world is far more likely to spin into anarchy. We are already seeing that happen in the Middle East, Eastern Europe, and Africa. The economic grievances that led to Nazism's vicious rise to power in the 1930s are echoed in similar complaints around the world today. Having exported economic disaster to all corners of the world in the 2000s and then laid down in the 2010s while our enemies run roughshod over our interests around the world, the United States and its allies need to reorder their moral and strategic priorities as they heal their economies in order to create a more equitable and stable global order.

As the tools of finance become more sophisticated, the obligation to regulate them prudentially increases exponentially. With great power comes great responsibility. This is the reverse of the Obama doctrine, which believes that with great power comes no responsibility, but it is the only doctrine befitting a still great power like the United States.

In *Modernity and the Holocaust* (1991), the sociologist Zygmunt Bauman argued that two of modernity's signal achievements made the holocaust possible: technology and bureaucracy.[3] In fact, he argues that the genocide of the Jews (and murder of millions of others) was carried out in a manner that was completely consistent with the norms of how business was conducted at the time. In other words, Auschwitz was an example of modernity cannibalizing itself. Why shouldn't the same be said about modern finance and the succession of increasingly destabilizing financial crises that damaged the financial markets over the past two decades? Beginning with portfolio insurance, which contributed to the stock market crash of 1987, and continuing through credit default swaps, which swept away some of the world's largest financial institutions in 2008, financial technology itself was the tool that almost destroyed the very system it was designed to protect from risk. What could be a better example of Adorno's "civilization creating anticivilization?" And if it is indeed the case that our most advanced tools are also the ones most capable of destroying us, mustn't we better educate ourselves to prevent that from happening? As the perpetrators of the crisis try to sneak away from the scene of their crimes unseen, it is incumbent upon the rest of us to ensure that the intellectual and moral lapses that caused so much damage are exposed for what they are. Only after their errors and crimes are exposed can they be disposed of.

Yet Congress fiddles while Rome burns, cheered on by special interests that serve to benefit from the status quo. Proposals for reform were derailed and diluted by Wall Street interests that want us to forget that 2008 even happened. According to the Center for Responsive Economics, the finance, insurance, and real estate industries spent $223 million on lobbying in the first half of 2009, a period in which these very institutions were still in serious financial distress and could have used that money to bolster their weakened balance sheets.[4] Nobody should be fooled. The enemies of reform are not just enemies of reform; they are enemies of a more just and fair society in which the rewards of capital are shared rather than slopped up by a small elite like pigs gorging out at a feeding trough. Reform must start from within and it must begin now.

It is almost impossible to overstate the urgency of financial reform if we are to avoid the social and political consequences of severe economic instability. Maintaining stable and equitable financial markets is not just an economic but a strategic and moral imperative. The status quo, and any system that resembles it, is certain to lead the world into further cycles of boom and bust that will exceed the abilities of both markets and governments to repair. As our readings of Smith, Marx, Keynes, and Minsky suggest, and as our historical experience demonstrates, boom-and-bust cycles are deeply embedded in the nature of capitalism. While some may argue that the authorities effectively prevented a wholesale collapse of global finance in 2008, the need to maintain unprecedented policies long after the crisis passed is *prima facie* evidence that their policies are seriously deficient. The fact that financial markets suffer from imbalances of such extremity that they not only nearly collapsed in 2008 but years later still suffer from sluggish growth and terminal debt problems illustrates that the system requires radical reform. In 2008, the markets were not remotely capable of fixing themselves, and governments managed to return the system to stability by employing temporary fixes.

The unprecedented measures governments were forced to take in 2008 imposed long-term destabilizing effects on the global economy. Those actions were not permanent solutions to the economic imbalances that led to crisis; they were merely temporary bandages applied to triage the patient. They did not create the conditions necessary for sustainable economic growth; all they did was treat a debt problem by creating more debt. The post-crisis period wasn't the first time that underlying imbalances that caused a crisis were left unresolved. In fact, they followed the pattern of the last three decades where one crisis after another caused by flawed monetary and fiscal policy was addressed by short-term fixes that left underlying imbalances unresolved. The imbalances kept growing and distorting the global economy beyond any chance of returning to equilibrium. In 2016, the result is $200 trillion of global debt that is suffocating economic growth and can never be repaid. This is a road to ruin rather than rebirth.

There is a further reason why the financial system desperately needs to be reformed to minimize the chances of future crises. Emergencies give government license to flout the rule of law. The death of capital can lead to the death of liberty and human rights, which is another reason why the moral obliquity of financiers who contribute to serial financial meltdowns is so reprehensible. Their conduct is not only wrong in itself, but because it tempts the government to abuse its power. Each time there is a financial crisis, the SEC and Justice Department throw out the rule of law at the behest of politicians seeking to divert attention from their own mistakes. As each financial crisis grows in severity, this type of *post hoc* criminalization of finance becomes a greater threat to our liberty. While privileged individuals who bleed the system for their own benefit deserve no special pleading, it remains incumbent on the government in a crisis to respect the rule of law. Unfortunately, all too often it does the opposite. Government by show trial should be associated with a gulag, not a republic.

The steps taken to address the 2008 crisis were in many ways a natural extension of the government's conduct after the 9-11 attacks. The passage of the Patriot Act had already seriously weakened civil liberties by giving law enforcement powers to do virtually anything it deemed necessary in order to protect the country from potential terrorist attacks. This came to include such questionable practices as warrantless wiretapping of U.S. citizens, the practice of "extraordinary renditions," the suspension of *habeas corpus*, and the torture of suspected terrorists (and these are only the practices we know about). The financial crisis of 2008 threatened such extreme economic and social chaos that the Obama administration took it upon itself to ignore the rule of law by abrogating the bankruptcy laws in the General Motors and Chrysler bankruptcies. It then used questionable measures to pass ObamaCare, make dubious recess appointments to the National Labor Relations Board (which the Supreme Court later deemed illegal), pass an illegal nuclear arms deal with Iran, and to push through countless executive orders of questionable legality. An administration that demonstrated an early proclivity to exercise raw power in the name of crisis management fell into the regular habit of ignoring the Constitution and other laws in the face of toothless Republican opposition. The most effective way to limit the government's opportunity to rob us of our freedom in the future is to minimize the potential for future crises to occur in the first place.

By the time the economic imbalances being created today come home to roost, it will be too late to introduce the reforms necessary to strengthen institutions to withstand the coming storms and the increasingly draconian measures the government will feel licensed to take to deal with them. Accordingly, meaningful financial reform must be instituted as soon as possible to prepare the system for the instability that is

certain to come when everyone least expects it (for that is what instability is, a disruption that occurs when the system is least prepared to
handle it). A well-fortified and stable system will be the best protection
against government again overstepping the bounds of law to manage
the next crisis.

The consequences of failing to act are not theoretical. On a global
basis, they include a widening gap between rich and poor, high levels
of hunger and poverty not only in disenfranchised areas of the world
but here at home, ecological devastation, and political instability. On
a national level in the United States, the effects include the ruination
of neighborhoods and communities through poverty and violence,
sustained high levels of unemployment (particularly among youths
and minorities), widening wealth inequality, increasing political divisiveness, and a seriously deteriorating fiscal situation. Despite all the
advances that mankind is making in science and technology, there is
much more work to do to fulfill even our most modest obligations to
billions of people around the world. We will not have even the smallest
chance of doing so without a stable financial system. Only a strong and
prudently regulated global financial system whose benefits are shared
equitably will be able to effectively meet the challenges posed by future
threats. We do not have such a system today, and we certainly did not
have one leading into the financial crisis. Instead, the system encouraged speculation at the expense of production, debt at the expense of
equity, and short-term gain at the expense of long-term investment.
True financial reform must be designed to reverse these priorities in
order to prevent capital from dying again.

Obama Goes to Wall Street

In September 2009, on the first anniversary of the day Lehman Brothers
filed for bankruptcy, President Barack Obama flew Marine One up
from Washington, D.C. to make a lunchtime speech at Federal Hall on
Wall Street to discuss financial reform. By this time, much of Wall Street
(or what remained of it after 2008) had already returned to the practices
that contributed to the financial crisis: exorbitant, asymmetric compensation schemes; trafficking in highly complex and highly leveraged

credit derivatives; and the issuance of record levels of debt, including debt associated with leveraged buyouts and other speculative forms of investment. By mid-September 2009, it was obvious to many observers that the battle for meaningful financial reform had already been lost.

The president's speech repeated proposals contained in a white paper authored by Treasury Secretary Timothy Geithner and the director of the National Economic Council Lawrence Summers that was released on June 14, 2009, entitled "Financial Regulatory Reform: A New Foundation." President Obama brought all of his considerable oratory skills to bear on his audience that day, a group that included many of the most influential legislators in the financial arena as well as key representatives from the largest financial institutions and hedge funds. His message was blunt: "We will not go back to the days of reckless behavior and unchecked excess that was at the heart of this crisis, where too many were motivated only by the appetite for quick kills and bloated bonuses," he warned his audience. "Those on Wall Street cannot resume taking risks without regard for consequences and expect that next time, American taxpayers will be there to break their fall." To say that Obama's plea fell flat, however, would be an understatement. His words were largely greeted with silence, according to *The New York Times* reporter Andrew Ross Sorkin,[5] who was in the audience. Most of the financial executives in attendance were trying to position the traumas of 2008 as ancient history and were actively lobbying the government to allow them to go back to their old ways. The model of socializing risk and privatizing gain had worked exceedingly well for the financial elite sitting in Federal Hall that day while impoverishing significant portions of the general population and weakening the economic fabric of the United States. This audience was not interested in changing the status quo. And as it turned out, Mr. Obama lacked the political will and leadership skills to back up his fancy rhetoric.

The sad truth was that the reform train had left the station a long time ago. While just one year earlier the entire financial system was staring into the abyss, trillions of dollars of intervention from the U.S., European, and Chinese governments had created the illusion that all was well with the world economy. Credit markets were functioning again; the stock market had risen approximately 50 percent from its March 2009 lows of 666 on the S&P 500 and 6,547 on the Dow Jones

Industrial Average; and many Wall Street firms had repaid the government money they had taken (or been forced to take) in late 2008 and were now focusing on how to overpay their employees once again. While Wall Street firms were not as leveraged as they were before the crisis, they were again taking outsized risks with their balance sheets. And while there were competing legislative proposals before Congress regarding how to overhaul financial regulation, the old set of laws was still in place with diminishing prospects for meaningful change.

A year after the death of capital, comprehensive regulatory reform of the type needed to truly stabilize the financial system was all but dead. There were some small signs of progress, such as potentially aggressive actions taken by the Federal Reserve and Treasury Department on compensation reform and by the SEC on dark pools. But on more systemically serious matters such as derivatives legislation and monetary policy management, there was little sign that serious change would be effected. This was profoundly disappointing because future financial instability, which is a certainty, rendered radical regulatory reform an urgent necessity.

Principles of Reform

Regulatory reform must be comprehensive in nature in order to maximize financial stability. Earlier in this book, I proposed specific reforms with respect to two areas that have contributed to the overall instability of the economic system—private equity (see Chapter 6) and derivatives (see Chapter 7). On a broader basis, six key areas must be addressed in order to provide a proper foundation for a more stable financial system that would no longer reward speculation at the expense of productive investment or socialize risk and privatize profit:

1. Taxing speculation.
2. Creating a unified regulator.
3. Addressing the "too big to fail" doctrine.
4. Improving the capital adequacy of financial institutions.
5. Reforming monetary policy management.
6. Improving systemic transparency.

Each of these areas is highly complex and requires a comprehensive approach. The complexity of the modern financial system is the major challenge of financial reform, but one that can be overcome by thoughtful and patient legislation. Partial solutions will leave too much room for abuse and the return of instability. A reform program must integrate all of the principles enunciated above in order to be effective.

The current regulatory system is based on the assumption that markets are efficient and investors are rational. Accordingly, regulation was designed to minimize governmental interference with the efficient and rational operation of markets. (Not to put too fine a point on it, but that is a polite way of saying, "garbage in, garbage out.") Those who warn that markets are obviously inefficient and investors far from rational beings are largely marginalized in terms of influencing policy. That is unfortunate, because markets consistently demonstrate their inefficiency, and investors repeatedly exhibit their irrationality. Regulatory reform must start from the premise that markets are inefficient and investors are irrational.[6] Our society should not have to continue to pay such a high price for clinging to beliefs that are consistently shown to be false. Working with any other set of assumptions will lead reform down the wrong path.

The election of Barack Obama offered some promise that things would change, but his choice of Timothy Geithner as treasury secretary, Lawrence Summers as his top economic advisor, and Mary Schapiro as head of the SEC were signs that little would change. These failed stewards of the status quo were the least likely individuals to deliver meaningful reform. Truly comprehensive and meaningful change requires the raw power of new ideas and the political courage to put them into effect rather than reshuffling the same tired old faces through the revolving door.

If financial reform is going to be effective, it must address the two most profound flaws that currently plague Western capitalism. The first is the phenomenon discussed throughout this book—the predominance of speculative over productive investment. This issue has been addressed with far more forthrightness in the United Kingdom than in the United States, where Britain's chief financial regulator, Adair Turner, raised the ire of bankers and other members of the financial services establishment by publicly questioning the purpose of much of the activity in modern finance. In September 2009, Turner told a group of financiers at a dinner held at Mansion House, the grand residence of the Lord Mayor of London, that banks "need to be willing, like the regulator, to recognize that there are some profitable activities so unlikely to have a social benefit, direct or indirect, that they should voluntarily walk away from them."[7] While honest observers welcome such outspokenness, this message was greeted with a fair degree of disdain by the audience. But Turner, who in March 2009 authored "The Turner Review," a fairly scathing report on the financial crisis, is on to something. The global economy simply cannot sustain a regime in which increasing amounts of capital are devoted to churning money out of money rather than adding to the productive stock of the world. Banks in particular, but other financial institutions as well, especially those that operate under the aegis of government licensure that gives them certain rights that non-licensed businesses do not enjoy, possess a public utility function that was thrown to the wayside in recent years by the obsession with free markets. It is time to restore some balance to these institutions to ensure that society is not completely sacrificed at the altar of the profit motive.[8]

The second flaw is the model that socializes risk and privatizes reward. This model is not only economically defective because it places an undue burden on governments and the taxpayers that fund them, but is morally retrograde in absolving individuals of responsibility for their actions, imposing the highest costs on those least responsible for harming society. This regime also widens the gulf between rich and poor and exacerbates social instability.

The basic premise of any regulatory regime must be that it creates the proper incentives that favor productive investment over speculation and more fairly distributes economic gains and losses among the populace. Society must come to understand that the way investors generate profits is just as important as the amount of profits they generate. This is why human beings were vested with moral sentiments—so they could distinguish the quality of human conduct from the quantity of what that conduct produces. And only by appreciating the quality of economic output as well as its quantity will society be able to increase productive investment and improve the quality of life for all of its citizens.

Impose a Tax on Speculation

Toward the end of 2009, proposals were floated in Congress to impose a modest tax on certain types of securities transactions. One proposed piece of legislation, titled "Let Wall Street Pay for the Restoration of Main Street," would have imposed a 0.25 percent tax on the sale and purchase of stocks, options, derivatives, and futures contracts. Wall Street is unalterably opposed to any such tax, but it is a good idea for a number of reasons:

- Tax policy should be used to create the proper types of economic incentives, and to discourage types of behavior that damage the economic system and society at large. One of the indisputable lessons of the 2008 financial crisis is that far too much capital is being devoted to speculation and far too little is being channeled to productive investments. Increasing the cost of speculation is a logical and economically efficient way of discouraging unproductive activities.

- The U.S. government is running unsustainable deficits and is desperately in need of revenues. In addition to ending egregious tax breaks for financial interests such as the "carried interest tax" on private equity profits and permitting hedge fund billionaires to defer their taxes for periods of as long as 10 years (a boondoggle that was finally terminated), the government should be raising revenue from socially unproductive activities. The financial industry can easily afford to pay a tax on its speculative activities. Moreover, a significant amount of securities trading today is not for the purpose of providing growth capital for corporations but is merely done to churn financial profits. By 2015, approximately 75 percent of daily trading activity had nothing to do with fundamental investing but was instead tied to high frequency trading and ETF trading strategies that contribute little to capital formation or the productive capacity of the economy. Accordingly, a tax on these activities would be a perfectly reasonable and economically harmless way to raise revenues.

Transactions such as credit default swaps and leveraged buyouts and recapitalizations have extremely wide profit margins built into them by Wall Street dealers and can easily bear the type of tax proposed here. As someone who has worked in these markets for more than two decades, I can assure readers that Wall Street arguments to the contrary are both self-serving and false. One of the points of such a tax would be to make Wall Street firms and their clients think twice about engaging in speculative activities that contribute nothing positive to society, and force them to give something back economically if they are hell-bent on engaging in such activities.

Rather than a flat 0.25 percent tax on securities trading, I would propose a sliding scale tax rate applied to the face amount of the following types of transactions:

- Naked credit default swaps if they are not banned entirely (1.25 percent tax).
- Debt and preferred stock issued in leveraged buyouts, leveraged recapitalizations, or debt financings used to pay dividends to leveraged buyout sponsors (0.60 percent).
- Quantitative trading strategies (0.35 percent).
- Equity derivatives (options, futures contracts) (0.25 percent).
- Large block trades (0.25 percent).
- All other stock, bond, and bank loan trades (0.15 percent).

Coupled with other measures aimed at reducing systemic risk (i.e., increasing capital adequacy at financial institutions, increasing collateral requirements, and imposing listing requirements for credit default swap trades, and so on), such a tax would impose a cost on activities that add little in the way of productive capacity to the economy and increase systemic instability. Obviously any such tax would have to include provisions to prevent forum shopping so investors and traders could not avoid the tax by moving their activities abroad. Such a tax regime would also contribute to the progressivity of our tax system by asking those who benefit the most from our economy to pay a little more in the way of taxes. The tax should not be imposed on stock, bond, and bank loan investments in retirement accounts under $1 million in size (IRAs, 401ks, etc.).[9]

End Balkanized Regulation

One aspect of the current regulatory regime that must be reformed in order to fortify systemic stability is its balkanized structure. The current regulatory system must be replaced with a unified system. Whatever the historical and political sources of the existing multiple (and often conflicting) agencies that regulate the financial industry (the Securities and Exchange Commission, the Federal Deposit Insurance Corporation, the Commodities Futures Trading Corporation, FINRA, state banking and insurance regulators, and the Federal Reserve), this structure has been rendered archaic by changes in markets and financial technology. In a world where all financial instruments can be deconstructed into 1s and 0s, effectively erasing the barriers among insurance, banking, securities, and real estate firms and rendering any one of them capable of creating systemic risk, the existing regulatory regime is a surefire recipe for disaster. There is no longer a rationale for regulating securities firms, commercial banks, and commodities firms from separate federal agency silos while leaving states to regulate mortgage brokers and insurance companies. Instead, a single regulatory body should assume responsibility for overall regulation of the financial industry and then form separate sub-agencies to regulate each separate type of firm. In a networked global economy, all of these industries are closely linked (for instance, they all trade with each other as counterparties) and must be regulated at the federal level by a unified regulatory body that is guided by the principles of regulation discussed here—encouraging production over speculation, transparency over opacity, and stability over instability.

Moreover, a single, independent regulatory body is needed to monitor and regulate systemic risk. The Federal Reserve has been touted by some observers (and by its own chair) as the most qualified candidate for the role of super-regulator. Such a choice would be unwise for several reasons.

First and foremost, the central bank's track record in managing monetary policy is nothing short of disastrous. Despite the fact that monetary policy is almost impossible to get just right, the Federal Reserve's monetary policy methodology is a case study in pro-cyclicality, is based on deeply flawed intellectual premises, and has placed the U.S. economy on an unsustainable path of speculation and indebtedness. A central bank that sat idly by while obvious bubbles built up and burst hardly seems qualified to prevent the same thing from happening in the future.[10] This track record alone renders the institution a poor choice to serve as the party responsible for monitoring the very systemic risk its own policies consistently exacerbate.

Furthermore, the Federal Reserve's own practices set a poor example of the type of transparency that the system requires to improve stability. It is frankly anachronistic that the central bank refuses to issue real-time releases of the minutes of the Open Market Committee meetings, and instead discloses this information only after significant time delays that leave the markets guessing as to the thinking of the most powerful monetary regulator in the world. In a day and age when information travels around the globe in the blink of an eye, and markets uncover information with astounding speed, the attempt to delay disclosure of the central bank's deliberations borders on absurdity (and antiquity). Moreover, the central bank needs to make a greater effort to make its operations understandable to laymen rather than to economists and market experts. Ben Bernanke and Janet Yellen have been far more constructive in this respect than their predecessor Alan Greenspan, who never met a sentence he couldn't mangle whenever he testified before Congress or otherwise spoke publicly. The decision-making of the Federal Reserve should not be a state secret—it should be a process subject to public scrutiny and debate. That does not mean that the Federal Reserve should lose its independence; one can only imagine the damage that would be done to the economy if monetary policy were subject to more direct influence by Congress, which demonstrates with every passing year its inability to manage complex long-term economic issues with any degree of foresight and responsibility. But the system needs an independent risk monitor that will lead by example, and the Federal Reserve is not that body. Instead, an independent nonpartisan oversight board should be appointed to fill such a role.

Too Big to Fail

In the wake of passage of Dodd-Frank stand a smaller number of "too big to fail" institutions sitting on top of a powder keg of hundreds of trillions of dollars of derivatives contracts. Instead of reducing the threats posed by these institutions, post-crisis reforms concentrated them in fewer hands. While Dodd-Frank established wind-down procedures to deal with the failure of large financial institutions, it failed to effectively address one of the key factors that could cause them to fail in the first place: undue concentrations of derivatives on their balance sheets, a topic addressed elsewhere in this book.

The 2008 financial crisis taught the world a valuable lesson: Institutions that are too big to fail are equivalent to government protectorates. Or put another way, only the government is too big to fail, so any institution that is too big to fail must be taken over by the government. The regime that was in place before the crisis privatized these institutions' profits before they ran into trouble and then, when they hit the skids, socialized their losses. That is unacceptable. Only the government should be considered too big to fail, and, frankly, if the United States continues on its current fiscal and monetary path, that belief will be tested as well. But the concept of permitting private institutions to grow sufficiently large to pose systemic risk in a system that privatizes their profits but socializes their losses must end. As a practical matter, there is little prospect that the government is going to break up JPMorgan Chase, Bank of America, Goldman Sachs, Morgan Stanley, or any other firm whose failure would pose systemic risk. Accordingly, we must accept the reality that there are institutions that are too big to fail but must also impose a regime that requires a bailout of such firms to result in government ownership so that the American taxpayers can share in both the gains and the losses of the enterprise, rather than limiting the gains to insiders and shifting the losses to outsiders.

There are currently several institutions whose failure could pose a serious systemic risk. In one category are institutions that are already owned by the U.S. government like Fannie Mae, Freddie Mac, and others that were owned by the government and returned to private ownership like Citigroup and AIG. Then there are other institutions like JPMorgan Chase, Wells Fargo, Goldman Sachs Group, Inc., Bank of America, Morgan Stanley, and several major insurance companies that are not owned by the government whose demise, while currently unlikely, would cause severe systemic stress. Nonetheless, the collapse of some members of this latter group of firms is not impossible, particularly without meaningful reform of derivatives The combination of lowering balance sheet leverage, reducing the risk embedded in asymmetric compensation schemes, and improving transparency through the elimination of structured investment vehicles (SIVs) have been important steps in minimizing the possibility that a single large firm could destabilize the financial system.

Nonetheless, systemically important firms have a special dual role in the economy and in society. They are not simply profit generators; their size and reach effectively render them public utilities whose continued health is vital to the continued viability of the economy. They have gained that status in part through government licensure, which should be considered a privilege rather than a one-way grant of a right to print private profits. The best approach to the too-big-to-fail doctrine is one that ensures that gains and losses are properly allocated among different societal constituencies. Merely limiting the size of an institution will not ensure that result.

Accordingly, there must first be a regime under which large institutions are regulated to minimize the risk that they will suffer large losses that can place them—and therefore the system—at risk. Such a regime would address issues such as capital adequacy, vulnerability to financial products of mass destruction such as naked credit default swaps and other derivatives, and the imposition of countercyclical approaches to balance sheet management. Secondarily, the system must no longer be designed to address failures, which are inevitable in any capitalist economy, by socializing the losses and privatizing the gains. This would entail reforming compensation practices to better align executive rewards with risk, as well as providing the government with an ownership stake in businesses that have to be bailed out. The fact that the U.S. government profited from its investment in Goldman Sachs, Morgan Stanley, and other companies that received TARP funds was entirely appropriate. It is also why it would be inappropriate to reward shareholders of Fannie Mae, Freddie Mac, or AIG that brought lawsuits claiming that the government unlawfully deprived them of their property when it stepped in to rescue those companies. Had the government not bailed out these three companies, their stockholders would have been wiped out. The only reason stockholders are able to conjure up any claim today is because the government did not want to consolidate those companies' trillions of dollars of debt on its own balance sheet, which is a technical matter that should not lead to unjust enrichment of opportunistic investors. If we want to have an ownership society, gains and losses have to be shared more equitably than they were after the financial crisis.

Improving Capital Adequacy

One of the lessons of the 2008 crisis is that financial institutions rarely have sufficient capital cushions to sustain themselves through true market calamities or even severe economic downturns. Financial institution shareholders demand high returns on equity to boost the value of their stockholdings, particularly where employees own large amounts of stock. Unfortunately, such demands conflict with sound balance sheet practices and lead to excessive leverage and other reckless management behavior. One of the frustrating characteristics of capital is that it is most available when least needed, and least available when most desperately needed. Policy must be changed to ensure that financial institutions are required to maintain stronger balance sheets in prosperous times, even if this reduces their return on equity and lowers their stock prices. In the end, this will reduce the volatility of their stock prices and reduce their odds of failure.

Limiting Banks' Balance Sheet Leverage

Important steps were taken after the crisis to reduce the balance sheet leverage of commercial and investment banks from the dangerously high levels that contributed to the financial crisis. Bear Stearns and Lehman Brothers both sported leverage ratios of more than 30-to-1 when they failed in 2008, a direct result of the loosening of their net capital rules in August 2004. These levels did not include the off-balance-sheet leverage that these firms were concealing from regulators and investors. Such high leverage was the financial equivalent of playing Russian roulette with five of the six chambers of the gun loaded. Once the off-balance-sheet leverage with legal or reputational recourse to the sponsoring institution was added, it was the equivalent of placing a bullet in the sixth chamber. Less than a 3 percent drop in the value of these firms' assets was sufficient to wipe out their equity. Such a thin cushion was insufficient for a traditional bank and was woefully inadequate for investment banks whose business models were based on proprietary trading and trafficking in highly complex financial instruments whose liquidity (and value) could (and did) suddenly evaporate.

Today, most of the large commercial banks and investment banks have reduced their leverage ratios significantly below where they were when the crisis began. Both Dodd-Frank and the second set of banking regulations set forth by the Basel Committee on Banking Supervision (Basel II) imposed much stricter capital requirements on banks designed to prevent a repeat of the financial crisis. Lower leverage will undoubtedly mean that these firms will be less profitable in rising markets. The flip side of that observation is that these firms will be more profitable and less prone to large losses in falling markets and thereby still be able to fulfill their public utility roles when most needed.

Regulation should be geared toward ensuring the stability of financial institutions, not maximizing their profitability. The fact that reducing their balance sheet leverage will reduce their profitability should be completely irrelevant in determining the best manner in which to maintain their capital adequacy. Moreover, if financial institutions were less profitable, they would likely be in a weaker position to lure America's most talented students with lucrative compensation offers to become investment bankers and derivatives and mortgage traders. That would be nothing but a boon for U.S. society, which would greatly benefit if these talented individuals were instead to become scientists, engineers, doctors, and teachers.

Capital requirements also need to be maintained on a countercyclical rather than pro-cyclical basis. For too long, financial institutions were permitted or encouraged to reduce their capital when times were good, leaving them with insufficient capital cushions when economic conditions deteriorated. The old adage about saving money for a rainy day may be quaint, but it has survived for hundreds of years because it makes a great deal of sense. Regulators and stockholders frown upon banks and other financial institutions over-reserving for losses because this results in understating earnings, but a more sophisticated approach to reserves (and measuring bank profitability) is needed. Annual financial results are nothing more than an accounting convention, and many of the financial arrangements into which banks and other institutions enter are far longer in tenor than one year. Accordingly, it would be far more appropriate to tie reserves on longer-dated contracts to their tenor on a fully disclosed basis to permit investors to make a more informed evaluation of an institution's reserve policy. Moreover, regulators are generally ill-equipped to set predetermined reserve requirements for complex financial instruments, and if anything should encourage institutions to err on the side of over-reserving rather than under-reserving in order to ensure that there will be adequate capital cushions when markets inevitably seize up again. A far more flexible regime is needed than a one-size-fits-all capital model. Finally, little attention should be paid to stock market investors on this issue. Reserves are intended to prevent exactly the type of irrational panics to which stock market investors are particularly prone, and they are the least qualified arbiters of capital adequacy in the marketplace.

FDIC insurance should also become subject to a countercyclical regime. In the past, prosperity has given rise to reductions in the amounts of insurance that banks were required to pay into the insurance fund. This proved to be a fateful mistake as the FDIC was rendered seriously insolvent in 2009 by a rash of bank failures. It would be far wiser for insurance rates to be maintained at high levels in strong markets, when banks can afford them, than to create a situation where these fees have to be drastically increased in the middle of a crisis to keep the fund from running out of money. Like many things, management of the FDIC is subject to the human proclivity to believe that current conditions will persist, particularly when such conditions are healthy. Regulators need to exercise imagination and consider that benign conditions are likely to encourage risk-taking and lead to trouble for which a bigger insurance fund will be needed.

Compensation Reform

Any attempt to rein in financial institutions' balance sheet leverage after the crisis needed to include compensation reform. Asymmetric compensation schemes that favored short-term profitability over sustainable long-term financial health greatly exacerbated the balance sheet weaknesses that contributed to the financial crisis. Paying out hundreds of millions of dollars of cash compensation to their executives left firms such as Bear Stearns and Lehman Brothers with diminished capital cushions to absorb losses on their mortgage and loan portfolios when the crisis occurred. Compensation reform was needed to stabilize the capital bases of systemically important institutions.

The good news is that the Obama administration (as well as European governments) took important steps to rein in—at least for the moment—the most egregious pay practices in the financial industry. On October 22, 2009, the Obama administration's Special Master for of Compensation, Kenneth Feinberg, and the Federal Reserve, unveiled a two-front attack on Wall Street's pay practices. Mr. Feinberg, working out of the Treasury Department, set limits on the compensation practices of companies that received financial aid from the government during the crisis and had not yet paid it back: Citigroup, Bank of America, AIG, GMAC, General Motors Corp., Chrysler Corp., and Chrysler Financial Corporation. While these limits reportedly still left several dozen employees at these firms earning in excess of $1 million of long-term compensation, they could fairly be described as draconian (at least in Wall Street terms).[11] On the same day, the Federal Reserve announced that it would incorporate compensation reviews into its routine regulatory supervision of banks, which would affect all institutions regulated by the central bank, including those that received government support during the crisis and were able to pay it back. At the time, Federal Reserve Chairman Ben Bernanke said the purpose of the new rules was to tie pay to long-term performance and to ensure that pay schemes do not create "undue risk for the firm or the financial system."[12] While these steps did not cure the plague of overcompensation in the financial services industry, they were a constructive attempt to remove the asymmetry from previous pay schemes that led executives to make one-way bets with what turned out to be other peoples' (that is, the government's or the American taxpayer's) money.

The payment of huge amounts of cash compensation severely weakens the balance sheets of financial institutions. Accordingly, limits must be placed on the amount of cash compensation that is paid out every year by these firms. A much greater percentage of compensation should be paid in the form of stock that vests over an extended period of time. This will strengthen balance sheets in two ways—first by increasing the firms' cash balances, and second by increasing the amount of equity on their balance sheets. It will also help to align the incentives of the biggest earners with those of the stockholders and other stakeholders who want the firm to survive by taking prudent risks. But even if it doesn't align these interests, it will at least keep more cash where it belongs: inside the firm.

While the senior executives of failed firms owned enormous stock positions (worth hundreds of millions of dollars or more at their peak valuations), these large ownership stakes still failed to instill the necessary ownership mentality and fear of risk. This is likely because these executives were not only granted obscenely large stock option grants annually, but were also paid tens of millions of dollars of cash compensation and retirement benefits each year by the boards of directors and compensation committees that were stacked with their cronies. A study by three Harvard Law School professors showed that executives at Bear Stearns and Lehman Brothers cashed out $1.0 billion and $1.4 billion, respectively, of performance-based compensation from cash bonuses that were not clawed back and from stock sales during the 2000–2008 period.[13] Lehman Brothers' former chairman and chief executive officer Richard Fuld reportedly cashed out more than $500 million of compensation while Bear Stearns' former chairman and chief executive officer James Cayne made off with more than $350 million. Though these men lost hundreds of millions of dollars in stock value when their firms failed, they remained among the wealthiest Americans in the wake of the crisis and the collapse of their firms. This is the epitome of the heads-I-win, tails-I-win-anyway compensation schemes that most executives on Wall Street enjoyed in the years leading up to the 2008 crisis.

Moreover, simply as a matter of common sense and moral decency, Wall Street compensation became grossly disproportionate to any contributions any individual could possibly make to a public company or to society. It is one thing when the owner of a private company earns outsized compensation; that individual is assuming the entire risk of the enterprise. In a public company, all of the expenses of operating the business are paid by others and do not fall on individual executives. Public company executives are sheltered from business risks (for example, the costs of defending litigation) by the financial wealth of the corporation, and there should be some sort of limitation on the upside that accompanies that protection from the downside. Effectively, public company executives have a one-way ticket to earn cash compensation with no return ticket to put any of that cash at risk. This is the real objection to the sky-high bonuses that were paid on Wall Street—they reflected a completely one-sided compensation arrangement in which executives suffer limited pain if their firms experience failure. These types of arrangements must be terminated because they breed a loss of confidence in the fairness of the system, which in turn erodes the moral bonds that encourage the types of constructive conduct that allows markets to function. If the directors of these firms are not prepared to make the necessary changes to these schemes, then the government should step in. The government properly has a role to play in limiting such schemes if losses are going to be socialized when financial firms fail. Firms simply cannot be permitted to perpetuate such asymmetric compensation schemes in an era when the ultimate risk of payment falls on the U.S. taxpayer.

In view of the fact that large amounts of money will continue to be paid to financial executives (even with the Federal Reserve and Treasury Department breathing down their necks), the lion's share of compensation should be paid in the form of stock whose ownership vests over an extended period of years. Stock compensation should be based on several years of performance and include provisions that adjust awards appropriately (known in Wall Street parlance as claw back provisions) in order to avoid the error of rewarding executives for short term performance that later turns out to be illusory. For example, a senior investment banker should not be rewarded with a blank check for working on a transaction that later turns out to fail; his or her ultimate compensation should be related to the success or failure of the deal. This would be an important step to leading investment bankers to work on deals that are likely to succeed and avoid working on deals that are likely to fail (such as a highly leveraged private equity transaction). Regulators should permit firms to maintain reserve accounts and make other arrangements to facilitate these types of compensation structures and require detailed disclosure to keep investors fully informed.

Moreover, such compensation arrangements would ideally focus executives on the overall financial health of their firms and lead them to be more prudent when taking risks. They would also be designed to inculcate a culture focused on shared responsibility and respect for risk-taking, two attributes that are far too rare in the financial services industry. This might also encourage firms to develop cultures in which professionals are required to speak up when they spot reckless behavior or wrongdoing, which would further enhance systemic health. These are ideals, of course; we all know that individuals go to Wall Street primarily to make large sums of money, not to rescue puppies. Nonetheless, it is long past the time when society stopped divorcing doing well from doing good. Generous compensation and respect for the system and the institutions that pay compensation should not be mutually exclusive. In fact, the sooner people realize that these values are mutually reinforcing, the healthier and wealthier the financial system will be.

Compensation is particularly important because the powerful interests in our society repeatedly decide to bail themselves out at the expense of the disenfranchised. After the financial crisis, Former Federal Reserve Chairman Paul Volcker pointed to this flaw in the system and urged bank speculation to be reined in. "I do not think it reasonable that public money—taxpayer money—be indirectly available to support risk-prone capital market activities simply because they are housed within a commercial banking organization. Extensive participation in the impersonal, transaction-oriented capital market does not seem to me an intrinsic part of commercial banking. . . . I want to question any presumption that the federal safety net, and financial support, will be extended beyond the traditional commercial banking community."[14] Volcker was suggesting—correctly—that it would be a profound policy error to continue to permit institutions to speculate in a system that socializes their losses. His influence led to the so-called Volcker Rule that now prevents federally insured institutions from speculating with their own capital.

Reforming Monetary Policy

It is time to acknowledge that the pro-cyclical policies of the Federal Reserve consistently place the United States' economy on an unsustainable path and that a countercyclical policy approach must be adopted. The evidence for this is the pattern of booms and busts that dominated the financial markets over the past 30 years. This pattern proved to be highly disruptive to economic growth as well as damaging to the returns that investors earn on their capital. Furthermore, important trends in the financial markets exacerbated the pro-cyclical bent of monetary policy: the globalization of markets, the digitalization of finance, and the consolidation of the financial industry.[15] With markets increasingly likely to lean in the same direction, it has become imperative that monetary authorities learn to lean in the opposite direction to temper imbalances. The age of allowing imbalances to build until they burst and then cleaning up the mess should have come to an end with the crisis of 2008, but most surely it did not.

Alan Greenspan will probably spend the rest of his life defending his tenure as chairman of the Federal Reserve. Once considered the elder statesman of The Committee to Save the World, his tenure was significantly discredited by the financial crisis that unfolded shortly after he departed the most powerful position in global finance. The "Greenspan put," which morphed into the "Bernanke put" in the hands of his successor and then into the "Yellen put" in the hands of his successor Janet Yellen, created an environment of moral hazard that was repeatedly exploited by the private sector. By constantly resorting to what some economists have termed "preemptive easing" to prevent short-term pain,[16] Greenspan may have won individual battles but managed to lose the war. His policies set the United States on an unsustainable path.

The pattern of policy making since the mid-1980s was clearly pro-cyclical and created an environment that encouraged moral hazard, beginning with the reaction to the stock market crash of 1987. In order to reassure the markets in the aftermath of their 508-point drop on October 19, 1987, Chairman Greenspan promised them that the Federal Reserve stood ready to make available whatever liquidity was necessary to assure their smooth operation. This was a highly appropriate response to an unprecedented one-day drop in the stock market averages. Unfortunately, however, it became the canned response to far less critical threats. Monetary easing in response to real or perceived crises spawned bubble after bubble.

Easing in the late 1980s led to a property bubble that resulted in the savings and loan crisis in the United States in the early 1990s. Low rates in the early 1990s that were invoked to deal with fallout from the savings and loan crisis and resulting recession spurred a decline in the U.S. dollar in the mid-1990s (and dollar-linked Asian currencies in Thailand and Indonesia) and contributed to the Asian bubble that burst in 1997. Low rates also played a large role in the Long Term Capital Management debacle of 1998 (allowing the hedge fund to borrow virtually infinite amounts of cheap money to leverage itself into oblivion) as well as the

Russian default of that year, which led to further emergency easing that contributed to the absurd and unsustainable boom in technology stocks beginning in 1999 and ending in tears in 2001. Greenspan also didn't miss a chance to react to the false alarm that all of the world's computers would supposedly shut down at midnight on December 31, 1999 (we all might be better off if they had) by keeping rates lower than he should have in the middle of what was the most obvious stock market bubble in recent memory (the NASDAQ peaked at a price/earnings ratio of 351 times during that folly). When the Internet bubble burst and dragged down the corporate credit markets that were dominated by billion-dollar debt offerings for telecommunications and technology companies that in many cases didn't even qualify as early stage venture capital start-ups, the Federal Reserve maintained low rates in order to protect the markets from themselves once again. This led to the credit bubble of the mid-2000s that fed mortgages and corporate credit with the able assistance of the shadow banking system of structured credit, SIVs, and derivatives. By the time that bubble burst, the systemic imbalances that were permitted to build up under the aegis of the Federal Reserve were so profound that it was little wonder that capital had to be given its last rites in the fall of 2008.

The Federal Reserve and its misguided chairman didn't accomplish this alone. The nation's inability to bear the least amount of economic pain contaminated every level of the financial and political system. Every time the "R" word (recession) was mentioned, the political classes went into a trance and began quoting Joseph Conrad's Mr. Kurtz— "The horror! The horror!" The United States had fallen far from the days of the Greatest Generation. The American body politic has grown insufferably intolerant of the least degree of hardship. The possibility of a mere recession has become such an anathema to the political classes of this country that it leads policy makers to pull out all the short-term stops to prevent a downturn while completely ignoring the long-term consequences of such a strategy.

This inordinate fear of the slightest economic downturn ignores the fact that recessions are completely normal and absolutely necessary in a capitalist economy. More important, it neglects the basic economic truth that pain deferred is pain increased. Little or no attention was paid each time the potential of an economic slowdown was raised to whether the remedies would sow the seeds of deeper problems later. The Federal Reserve chairman found more-than-willing co-conspirators in the United States Congress, whose inability to rein in spending over the past three decades illustrates beyond a shadow of a doubt that today's U.S. government bears little resemblance to the one envisioned by the Founders. No doubt there was corruption back when the country was formed, and there has been corruption ever since in various forms, but today's corruption is so deeply embedded into the system that it threatens the very future of this country. Drastic measures are needed to reverse course.

The Federal Reserve is justifiably subject to intense criticism by certain members of the political class not only for its actual performance, which has fed one bubble after another, but also for its lack of transparency. Congressman Ron Paul has been in the forefront of this movement. Certainly there should be no reason why the central bank should not set an example for high standards of transparency. In fairness, under Chairman Ben Bernanke and his successor Janet Yellen, the central bank has taken major steps to become more open in its operations. But the bigger issue is one of substance, not form. The Federal Reserve must make an intellectual shift toward a countercyclical policy approach and away from the pro-cyclical policy regime that it has followed since the Greenspan years. Effectively, the Federal Reserve has functioned as a massive momentum machine, feeding liquidity into the market at points when it perceived that it was needed and letting it run too long. You can't day trade a twenty trillion dollar economy, yet that is what the Federal Reserve is trying to do. This has left the U.S. economy with too much debt, too much capacity in too many industries and too few sources of internal growth. In September 2009, capacity utilization in the U.S. and European factory sectors (they are linked in today's global economy) had fallen to a depressed 65 percent and facing a slow recovery. Other sectors of the U.S. economy, such as retailing, hospitality, commercial real estate, and financial services (the latter after shrinking significantly in 2008 and 2009), were also suffering from significant overcapacity. It has taken years for capacity utilization to recover and it is still below optimal levels in 2015. The repercussions of pro-cyclical policy will reverberate through the economy for years to come.

Private sector actors are going to do whatever they can to maximize their profits. After all, as discussed in the previous chapter, it is their fiduciary duty to do so, even if their actions hurt the overall economy. If low-cost leverage is available and can increase profits, economic actors will use it. Accordingly, the maintenance of artificially low interest rates is an invitation for people to borrow and spend.[17] Part of the goal of monetary policy at various times in recent years was clearly to encourage risk-taking and the use of leverage. Until the financial crisis forced Chairman Bernanke and his colleagues to become far more aggressive and creative in employing the tools of the central bank (some might argue in contravention of the law), the primary tool used to manage monetary policy was the Federal Reserve's ability to set the overnight lending rate between banks, known as the Federal Funds rate or the discount rate. The problem is that the overall policy bent has been highly asymmetric—the Federal Reserve has been much quicker to lower rates and ease liquidity at the least sign of economic stress than to raise rates and tighten the flow of money when conditions improved.[18]

But during the Greenspan years, and the first couple of years of Bernanke's term that preceded the crisis, the Federal Reserve also refused to aggressively address growing imbalances in the economy. One reason for this hands-off approach was the oft-stated rationale that monetary policy should only be tightened to battle inflationary threats. This approach was based both on a narrow interpretation of the central bank's mandate and on Alan Greenspan's belief that it is impossible to identify a bubble when it is occurring. While one would have hoped the latter view would have been discredited by the Fed's failures, it is clear by the Fed's refusal to take any action to raise rates until December 2015 that it has not.

Contrary to Greenspan's oft-repeated assertion that it is impossible to identify a bubble, there are clear indicia of when asset prices are rising to unsustainable levels. Moreover, it doesn't require a bubble to justify the imposition of countercyclical policies. Any significant departure from long-term valuation trends should capture the attention and concern of central bankers and trigger a response. But the types of deviations from the norm that occurred in the decade preceding the crisis of 2008 were far more than mere departures from long-term trends; they were obvious bubbles that required no special economic knowledge to identify. Stock prices traded at a multiple of 351 earnings on the NASDAQ Stock Exchange at their peak on March 10, 2000; the average price/earnings multiple at previous market peaks was no higher than 20.[19] The risk premium (known as spread) on Credit Suisse's High Yield Index reached 271 basis points over Treasuries on May 31, 2007, a record level that exceeded the historical average of 570 to 580 basis points by over 50 percent.[20] Asking central bankers to rein in liquidity when markets reach such extreme points of overvaluation is a far cry from asking them to overstep their mandate. Central bankers have the tools at their disposal to counteract such trends, and they should use them more proactively than the Federal Reserve has done. There is a better answer than simply choosing between stepping aside and letting bubbles run their course and creating a command economy with too much government intervention and control.

It was apparent to many observers, including this author,[21] that technology and Internet stocks were experiencing a bubble at the turn of the millennium. The Nasdaq Composite Index was trading at a valuation of more than 20 times higher than its previous peak. The housing market was experiencing a similar unsustainable rise in prices in the mid-2000s when housing prices were well outpacing the growth in personal income. The corporate debt market was trading at unsustainable levels on the eve of the financial crisis when spreads were more than 50 percent tighter than historical norms. The fact that the Federal Reserve either did not recognize these bubbles or simply ignored them is either a severe indictment of its monetary management or a clear sign that formal reform of its mandate is overdue. Today's economy and markets would be unrecognizable to the people responsible for founding the Federal Reserve in 1913, and the central bank's original mandate needs to be revisited. The world cannot afford more pro-cyclical policies that ignore bubbles that are blowing up in central bankers' faces and inflicting damage for which future generations will be left to pay.

Respected authorities such as the Bank for International Settlements have begun to call for countercyclical monetary policy management in recent years. Such a policy is often confused—deliberately perhaps by opponents—as a form of targeting asset prices, but such criticism is misplaced. Asset prices are a symptom of an underlying disease, not the disease itself. Monetary policy is designed to treat diseases, not symptoms, and should be more proactive in addressing burgeoning imbalances in order to help avoid the immense damage that market crises impose on economies and societies. No system can be perfect and eliminate imbalances, but a better system than the one operating today would proactively tighten policy by raising interest rates and tightening liquidity conditions based on movements in certain economic indicators.

Economist William White suggests the following indicators as some of those that might give rise to proactive tightening: "unusually rapid credit and monetary growth rates, unusually low interest rates, unusually high asset prices, unusual spending patterns (say very low household saving or unusually high investment levels)." He also suggests that "unusually high external trade positions" be considered.[22] I would add a series of more specific indicators, including corporate credit spreads, mortgage spreads, differentials between changes in house prices and changes in personal income levels, and the absolute level of existing interest rates. The key question monetary authorities should be asking is whether markets are underpricing risk. The proper pricing of risk (which is an art and not a science) is one of the most effective ways to prevent systemic imbalances from growing out of control and creating threats that turn into crises. Consideration of these factors in the fashioning of monetary policy would be a major improvement over the current narrow focus on inflation, which is itself a far different phenomenon than it was in 1913 when the Federal Reserve's original mandate was implemented.

Enhancing Systemic Transparency

One of the keys to encouraging productive investment and discouraging speculation would be to improve systemic transparency. Obscurity is the enemy of stability. If investors are deprived of the information necessary to evaluate specific securities or markets, they are incapable of accurately determining the level of risk they are assuming or that financial institutions are assuming. If they are not provided with the information regarding the holdings of financial institutions because these holdings are being concealed in off-balance-sheet entities, investors can't possibly evaluate the financial condition of these institutions. Without the ability to make that determination, investors are deprived of the ability to accurately evaluate financial industry or systemic risk. This increases uncertainty, which in turn leads investors to lose trust more easily in their counterparties and the markets themselves. Increasing uncertainty and decreasing trust in market mechanisms leads to less rational behavior as investors act to protect their own interests regardless of the consequences for the system, leading to full-blown market sell-offs like those we saw in 2008. Opponents of transparency need to understand that they are not only harming the system but they are hurting their own interests by ultimately promoting systemic instability.

If there is one common denominator among speculative practices in the financial markets, it is that they tend to be opaque. Earlier chapters in this book examined two of these practices in detail: private equity (and related strategies that invest in nonpublic market securities) and derivatives. Each of these strategies depends in part on the ability to obscure investment holdings (and their valuations) from the prying eyes of investors and regulators. This is done in a number of different ways. For private equity and other nonpublic market strategies, obscurity is obtained through investments in securities that are not traded on a public market and can only be valued through highly subjective procedures that are unverifiable with any degree of certainty by reference to independent pricing sources. For derivatives (and related quantitative strategies), prices are obscured by how the instruments or trades themselves are dressed up in mathematical complexity that most investors and regulators are incapable of understanding.

As a result of these stratagems, these investment programs are effectively operating in regulatory and due diligence vacuums with few checks and balances. At best, it is up to auditors to confirm the validity and the accuracy of prices and investment returns, and auditors only offer *post hoc* reviews of investments and trades and can do little to prevent fraud or other abuses while they are occurring. Moreover, auditors generally have limited knowledge of the substance of what they are reviewing, so any protection they afford is extremely limited. Accordingly, the link between non-productive investment strategies and opacity is deeply embedded and intentional. That link must be identified, and then these strategies must be forced into the light.

Ban Structured Investment Vehicles

There were times during the 2008 crisis when it felt as though the authorities were not going to be able to stop the stampede of panic selling that was threatening to send the markets into a tailspin from which they would never recover. Perhaps the greatest fear motivating panic sellers was fear of the unknown, which was hardly surprising in view of the revelations about hundreds of billions of dollars of highly risky assets that the world's largest financial institutions were concealing in undisclosed SIVs. The assets held in these vehicles were not included in traditional measures of these firms' leverage, which left regulators and investors in the dark with respect to the risks that these institutions were facing. As these entities lost their access to short-term funding in late 2007, legal commitments as well as reputational concerns and governmental and regulatory pressures forced tens of billions of dollars of these assets back onto the balance sheets of their sponsoring institutions, further burdening already overleveraged balance sheets and in some cases threatening outright insolvency. These SIVs were a large part of the shadow banking system that was able to operate outside the purview of regulators and permitted financial institutions to employ even more leverage than the already high levels of leverage they used on their balance sheets. Figure 9.1 shows the growth of these vehicles in the years prior to when the walls came crashing down.

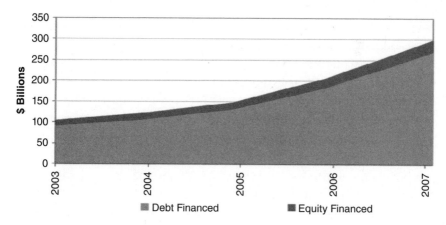

Figure 9.1 Growth of SIVs' Total Assets
SOURCE: Standard & Poor's.

Off-balance-sheet entities produced nothing but trouble in the decade leading to the financial crisis. The regulatory solution to this problem is very simple. All types of off-balance-sheet entities should be banned, plain and simple. They serve no purpose other than to conceal information from regulators and investors. As economist Roger W. Garrison writes, "a market system whose credit markets involve risks that are partially concealed from the lender and partially shifted to others will be biased in the direction of excessive risk-taking. And excessive risks are converted in time into excessive losses."[23] Banks in the United States and U.K. ended up having to take failed SIVs' assets back on their balance sheets and then limp hat in hand to their governments for multibillion dollar bailouts. These losses landed on the doorsteps of taxpayers and their heirs, who are going to be paying the bills for the losses caused by these borrow-short/lend-long schemes for years to come. When it comes to reckless financial ideas (borrowing short-term funds to purchase complex, illiquid long-dated securities), SIVs were at the top of the list. There is no other solution than to remove them from the list permanently.

Virtually without exception, these vehicles were designed to reduce the amount of debt that financial institutions incurred directly on their balance sheets, which in turn artificially preserved their credit ratings and lowered their borrowing costs based on false premises. That was how Enron was able to maintain an investment-grade credit rating while the company teetered on the verge of insolvency; the debt that was so dangerous to its survival was effectively concealed from the prying eyes of investors in undisclosed entities. Other companies, including some of the Big Three automakers and NYNEX Corp. before it became part of Verizon Communications, Inc., used these structures to their advantage to finance large building projects. NYNEX, for example, financed the multibillion dollar construction of its cable and telephone franchises in the United Kingdom through the use of complex off-balance-sheet structures developed by Citigroup in the 1990s. Outside investors (including the author's firm) were brought in and guaranteed a fixed return by NYNEX in exchange for serving as the so-called "equity" in the transactions. There was, of course, no real equity in these transactions because these investors were provided with a corporate guarantee on their investment by NYNEX's parent corporation, but tax attorneys

were willing to provide opinions that granted the necessary equity qual-
ification to the investment to keep the project off NYNEX's books.
NYNEX was able to construct modern telecom and cable systems in
the United Kingdom while preserving its credit rating, something it
could have done at a slightly higher cost on its balance sheet. That project and many others had happy endings. Enron's story did not.

Enron's utilization of off-balance-sheet finance turned into a total
debacle. What was once an innovative industrial and manufacturing
company transformed its balance sheet into a house of cards by shuffling
an increasing percentage of its assets into hidden entities with the active
assistance of Citigroup, JPMorgan Chase, and Merrill Lynch. Enron took
the idea of off-balance-sheet financing to its logical conclusion; by the
time the company collapsed, most of its most valuable assets had been
transferred off of its balance sheet and Enron Corporation was rendered
virtually an empty shell. Due to Enron's obfuscation of its true financial
condition (ably assisted by its attorneys and accountants), the energy
company was able to hang on to its investment-grade credit rating until
shortly before its collapse.[24]

Enron's failure caused a sharp sell-off in the credit markets that
inflicted serious losses on investors in the United States and around the
world. Previously, few if any investment-grade companies had ever collapsed in such a dramatic fashion, plummeting from investment grade to
insolvency in a short period of time. The very validity of an investment
grade rating was thrown into doubt, although the market regained its
confidence soon enough to permit the issuance of hundreds of billions
of dollars of incorrectly rated AAA-rated mortgage securities. Little did
anybody realize that the losses caused by Enron's demise would be nothing compared to what would come to pass when hundreds of billions
of dollars of AAA-ratings turned out to have been issued in error by
Moody's and Standard & Poor's just a few years later.

The Enron story was sad enough on its own in terms of the losses
of jobs and pensions suffered by its many well-intentioned employees.
But there were actually more tragic (Karl Marx would call them farcical)
aspects to what happened at Enron. The company's abuse of off-balance
sheet vehicles and corporate disclosure laws was just a warm-up for the
much larger abuses of off-balance sheet financing that were committed
by the world's largest financial institutions.

One would think that Enron's collapse would have given rise to serious reforms to prevent further abuses of off-balance-sheet vehicles. Yet nothing of the type occurred. After Enron collapsed, members of Congress pulled out their torches and pitchforks and took a brief break from the rubber chicken circuit to swear that off-balance-sheet entities would never again be permitted to damage the U.S. financial system. While they were making these statements for the cameras, the largest financial institutions in the world were busy as beavers sponsoring and underwriting even larger off-balance-sheet entities whose subprime mortgages and other financial instruments were far riskier than the industrial assets held by Enron in its side-pockets.

Moreover, these entities were hiding in plain sight because the debt obligations they issued had to be rated by Moody's and Standard & Poor's. In a report dated March 13, 2002, entitled "Structured Investment Vehicle Criteria," Standard & Poor's wrote that it "rates the senior liabilities of all of the SIVs in the market 'AAA/A-1+,' [Standard & Poor's] highest long- and short-term rating categories. Standard and Poor's also provides counterparty ratings of 'AAA/A-1+' for all such vehicles." The methodology Standard & Poor's used was "to determine whether the senior debt of the vehicle will remain 'AAA/A-1+' rated until the last senior obligation has been honored in the event that the SIV needs to be wound down for whatever reason." In other words, the credit agency's "focus is on the tail end of the transaction." This focus on the end of the transaction is difficult to reconcile with the gross timing mismatch between the entity's assets and liabilities. When Standard & Poor's analyzed the risks that an SIV may face, it clearly acknowledged this mismatch, noting that "their weighted-average liability maturity is usually about four to six months, whereas the assets in the vehicle will have considerably longer average maturities." It is precisely at the end of the transaction that this mismatch will matter.

The report reads like a very reasonable document on its face until one realizes that these entities were almost entirely comprised of the "AAA/A-1+" securities that had very little capital below them (a typical SIV held less than 5 percent equity capital as a cushion against losses). Moreover, the quality of the assets that were being purchased were wholly dependent on credit ratings being granted by no less than the same agencies that were rating the liabilities, the oligopolists

Moody's and Standard & Poor's. The rating agencies' complicity in rating SIVs should have raised serious concerns about the competence and good faith of these agencies and served as a warning that the rating agencies were unsuited for the job to which the regulators had anointed them.

It is inexcusable that none of the leaders of the firms that financed or traded with these SIVs ever spoke out against them or took any action to reduce the systemic risk they posed. Anyone who is presumed to be qualified to manage a bank or investment banking firm should possess the intelligence to understand that borrowing short to lend long is and has always been an idiotic proposition. Using enormous amounts of short term leverage to purchase complex securities that in the most liquid markets only trade by appointment can only lead to one result— disaster. SIVs were not simply an accident waiting to happen—they were actually perfectly designed to create systemic risk and any other outcome would have been a miracle. Each of these men (there were no women in such positions) bears a grim responsibility for allowing the SIV farce to continue for so long and inflict so much damage on the markets. It was also the height of hypocrisy for any member of the Senate Finance Committee or House Finance Committee to pretend that they were surprised that these time bombs existed. Yet no individual was ever held to account for the damage these entities wrought. There is no place for such Ponzi-structures in our financial system, and they should never see the light of day again.

Prohibit Dark Pools and High-Frequency Trading

Apparently hiding hundreds of billions of dollars of assets beyond the purview of regulators and investors did not sate Wall Street's hunger for making money in places where it can be concealed. Even before all of the insolvent SIVs were liquidated, Wall Street was actively building covert trading networks that fed its insatiable desire for secrecy and opacity. Appropriately called "dark pools," a name that could have been torn from the pages of a novel by the paranoid science fiction writer Philip Dick, these private trading exchanges became major profit centers for large financial institutions and hedge funds in the mid-2000s. Dark pools are electronic trading networks that allow institutional investors to buy and sell stocks anonymously. These networks allow investors to conceal their identities as well as the number of shares they are buying or selling. At the time of the first edition of this book, Goldman Sachs operated one such network called SIGMA X; Credit Suisse Group AG operated one called Crossfinder; and there were others called Liquidnet, BATS, and Direct Edge. According to *The Economist*, there were 40 dark pools operating in the United States in mid-2009 that accounted for an estimated 9 percent of traded equities. Other sources estimated the volume to be higher, which highlighted the fact that nobody knew exactly what was going on in these hidden corners of the investment universe because their very *raison d'être* was to conceal information from the eyes of regulators and investors. Having just experienced an unprecedented financial crisis that was caused partly by a lack of transparency on the part of the world's largest financial institutions, dark pools qualified as one of the most dangerous ideas to come to life on Wall Street since SIVs and naked credit default swaps. These secret trading networks pose systemic risks because they suppress the very transparency that builds confidence in markets. The minute these networks came to light, they should have been closed down. Michael Lewis' best-seller *Flash Boys* garnered a great deal of attention to this subject when it was published in 2014.

High-frequency trading is a phenomenon that often takes place on these dark pool exchanges. Actually, the correct term is high-frequency algorithmic trading, because it is a trading strategy based on using algorithmic formulas to analyze market data and then predict and exploit likely market movements. High frequency trading is closely linked to something called "flash trading," a Wall Street invention in which dark pool exchanges allow traders to briefly see and react to certain orders ahead of the rest of the market. Flash trading is nothing more or less than a thinly disguised version of front-running, a blatantly illegal activity. By giving certain traders a preview of order flow, it gives these traders an unfair advantage over other traders who are not privy to such information. The fact that some of the world's largest financial institutions were engaging in this practice right under the noses of regulators is a sad commentary on how deeply inequities are embedded in the financial system.

Wall Street loves these private trading networks, where business is booming and profits are growing. For example, Citadel Investment Group LLC disclosed in litigation that its high-frequency trading business produced more than $1 billion in profits in 2008 (a year in which the firm's hedge funds lost billions of dollars). Needless to say, the type of quantitative trading that occurs on these dark pools is nothing more than mere money-shuffling and adds nothing to the productive capacity of the economy. Moreover, these strategies had a deleterious effect on markets in recent years by increasing volatility and causing securities prices to move without any connection to fundamental changes in the underlying company's financial condition. By 2015, it was estimated that 75 percent of daily trading volume was accounted for by high frequency trading and ETF slicing-and-dicing strategies that have nothing to do with fundamental investing. Proponents of these activities argue that dark pools enhance market liquidity, but liquidity without transparency breeds market volatility and uncertainty. Why can't these trades be done with full disclosure and in the full light of day? How does hiding these trades in the shadows enhance liquidity or market stability?

No less than Paul Wilmott, a highly respected figure in the quantitative investing world (and founder of the quantitative finance journal *Wilmott*), warned of the dangers of high-frequency trading in an opinion piece in *The New York Times:* "Thus the problem with the sudden explosion of high-frequency trading is that it may increasingly destabilize the market. Hedge funds won't necessarily care whether the increased volatility causes stocks to rise or fall, as long as they can get in and out quickly with a profit. But the rest of the economy will care."[25] Moreover, the economy will care because the financial markets do not simply provide an outlet for financial speculation; like banks, they also provide a public utility function whereby they serve as a source of growth capital for companies. Dark pools are private playgrounds that hedge funds and investment houses use to trade in secret; allowing them to operate is singularly bad public policy. As we saw in 2008, when the markets fail and can no longer perform their public utility function because of damage caused by excessive speculation, the economy suffers severe damage. One of the best ways to ensure the healthy operation of markets is to require them to operate transparently, and high-frequency trading on dark pool exchanges is designed to do precisely the opposite.

Dark pools stand in sharp contrast to other recent regulatory efforts to bring greater transparency to trading markets. Several years ago, corporate bond trading was forced into the open through the introduction of the TRACE system, which requires all broker-dealers to report all public bond trades within a few minutes of execution. In view of the consensus in favor of transparency, and the obvious dangers of opacity, it makes absolutely no sense to permit large parts of the equity markets to retreat into the shadows while at the same time forcing corporate bond trading into the light. Such a regime can only contribute to market confusion and instability.

While efforts have been made to rein in dark pools, high frequency trading and similar strategies have grown to dominate stock markets since the financial crisis. With 75 percent of trading driven by machines today, there have been several "flash crashes" in the years since the financial crisis that demonstrate the perils of this type of trading dominating the markets. Regulators have failed to take meaningful steps to address these problems, leaving markets heavily exposed to opaque and speculative trading strategies. When markets are left to the mercy of the machines, there is a high risk of trouble ahead.

**

It is a dead certainty that financial reform cannot prevent another market crisis in the relatively near future. Even if the finance industry wasn't committed to blocking many of the types of financial reform necessary to create genuine financial stability, it is impossible to regulate human nature. But the cynical manner in which Wall Street has worked to block meaningful financial reform is both a tragedy and a farce. It is a tragedy because future crises are not avoidable but could be rendered far less damaging if intelligent reforms were adopted. It is a farce because the world suffers every day from regulatory failures and blind spots. To put it bluntly, we know better and we still refuse to do what is necessary to save ourselves. Accordingly, we will have nobody but ourselves to blame the next time we are staring into the abyss.

CHAPTER 10

Unfinished Business

C hapter 9 was originally written for the first edition of this book. It set forth a series of financial reforms necessary to prevent another financial crisis. While some of those reforms were adopted, many were not. Moreover, some of those that were adopted led to unintended consequences such as negative interest rates and market illiquidity. Clearly, additional reforms are needed to address continuing problems such as pro-cyclical monetary policy, ineffective or non-existent fiscal policy, an unproductive tax code, shrunken military spending in the face of rising geopolitical threats, a broken immigration system, and a variety of other areas.

The United States is at a tipping point as it faces a global economy far more leveraged than on the eve of the financial crisis and a geopolitical landscape far more fractured and unstable than at any time since the end of the Cold War. America has a choice: It can continue to pursue failing policies or adopt new ones that will actually have a chance of solving the challenges staring it in the face.

The single most important economic problem facing the world—and the single greatest obstacle to future prosperity and stability—is the $200 trillion *of debt that is crushing economic growth and sapping the world's financial and intellectual capital. We are spending money we don't have. The world economy cannot continue borrowing from the future without triggering another financial crisis in the near future.*

As noted in Chapter 1, history teaches us that periods of economic stress and volatility lead to social instability. In a globalized and interconnected world, we must acknowledge the threat posed by runaway debt and deal with it before it hands humanity a mortal blow.

If policymakers continue to treat the symptoms of too much debt by creating more debt, which is all they've done since the financial crisis, there is no hope of setting the United States and the world on a more productive and stable course. Nothing less than radical policy changes are required to accomplish this. If it is not self-evident by now, it should be—current fiscal, monetary policies are responsible for drowning us in obligations that we can never hope to meet. We owe it to ourselves and our children to have the courage to change course.

The following are some additional policy changes that are necessary to achieve economic and geopolitical sustainability and recovery in the years ahead.

Monetary Policy

In the previous chapter, I called for countercyclical monetary policy on the part of the Federal Reserve. Such a policy would replace the procyclical policies central bankers have pursued for decades that created the series of booms and busts that plagued the economy in the decades leading to the financial crisis.

It is increasingly apparent, however, that such a change is beyond the intellectual capabilities of our central bankers. The current Federal Reserve Open Market Committee is incapable of making such a change in policy because it is dominated by academic economists with little knowledge of how the real economy functions.

In order to change course, we need to place our monetary policy in the hands of people who understand how the real world works. The Federal Reserve Act should be amended to require that at least 50 percent of the members of the Federal Open Market Committee have worked in the private sector (excluding a university or academic position) for at least 10 years prior to their appointment. Individuals with experience in the real economy are far better qualified to understand how real people respond to economic incentives than academic economists who depend on abstract models. Until we end the tyranny of the professors, we have little hope of benefiting from a monetary policy that accords with reality.

In a 2014 speech to The Cato Institute, the brilliant financial writer and trenchant Federal Reserve critic James Grant warned:

> My generation gave former tenured economics professors discretionary authority to fabricate money and to fix interest rates. We put the cart before the horse of enterprise. We entertained the fantasy that high asset prices made for prosperity, rather than the other way around. We actually worked to foster inflation, which we called "price stability" (this was on the eve of the hyperinflation of 2017). We seem to have miscalculated.[1]

Miscalculated indeed. After maintaining short-term interest rates at zero for seven years while purchasing trillions of dollars of government debt in the years after the financial crisis, the Federal Reserve failed to accomplish virtually any of its policy goals. The economy remained mired in sluggish growth while debt increased to unsustainable levels. Rather than acknowledge failure and change course, however, the denizens of the Eccles Building continued to cling to their broken models and persist in error.

Over the past three decades, the body of academic economists entrusted with guiding the U.S. economy has steered it from one crisis to another. Since the end of the financial crisis, the Yellen-led Fed attempted to calibrate an exit from zero interest rate policy while trying to meet its dual mandate to maintain both low inflation and maximum employment. It did so by trying to day-trade a $20 trillion economy while relying on inflation statistics that have no relationship to real-world prices and confusing structural and cyclical employment trends. The odds of successfully exiting from years of crisis era policies while misinterpreting key data are virtually zero—actually, they are less than zero and guarantee another financial crisis in the near future. Markets began to awaken to that reality in January 2016.

By leaving interest rates at zero for years and repurchasing trillions of dollars of government bonds, the Fed distorted and drained liquidity from the credit markets, destroyed the ability of markets to send accurate pricing signals, and facilitated massive misallocations of capital through-out the economy. While the Fed admittedly operated in a fiscal policy vacuum, its policies only made matters worse.

In addition to misinterpreting structural changes in the workforce as cyclical in nature, the members of the Federal Open Market Committee kept interest rates low based on the belief that low rates would incentivize consumers and businesses to increase their spending and borrowing. Instead, economic actors did the opposite because they interpreted emergency policy measures as a signal to act cautiously. While low interest rates may provide stimulus during a recession or a crisis, there was little chance they would do so in a post-crisis U.S. economy. Behavioral economists understand this; unfortunately, none of them influence monetary policy.

Based on the work of Atif Mian and Amir Sufi in their landmark book *House of Debt: How They (and You) Caused the Great Recession, and How We Can Prevent It from Happening Again,*[2] we know that the huge build-up in household debt in the mid-2000s led to a collapse in house-hold spending during the 2009–2010 recession. Between 2000 and 2007, household debt in the United States doubled to $14 trillion and the household debt-to-income ratio skyrocketed from 1.4x to 2.1x. This was the greatest increase in household debt since the Great Depression.

Both the Great Depression of the 1930s and the Great Recession of 2009–2010 were preceded by collapses in household spending. Mian's and Sufi's work as well as that of other economists[3] demonstrate that large increases in private debt burdens tend to precede severe recessions. Mian and Sufi conclude that, "Economic disasters are almost always pre-ceded by a large increase in household debt. In fact, the correlation is so robust that it as close to an empirical law as it gets in macroeconomics. Further, large increases in household debt and economic disaster seem to be linked by collapses in spending."[4] And sure enough, between the second half of 2008 and early 2013, household debt in the U.S. fell by a cumulative $940 billion as U.S. consumers severely retrenched.

The economy experienced what economist Richard Koo has termed in the context of Japan's economy a "balance sheet recession."[5] In a balance sheet recession, corporations, and individuals focus on repairing their balance sheets by minimizing their debts rather than on spending or borrowing money. In the post-crisis period, this meant they didn't respond to low interest rates by behaving as the Fed's economists expected; instead they spent and borrowed less and focused on saving. The significant drop in U.S. household debt and a slow recovery in lending after the financial crisis should have told the Federal Reserve that consumers and businesses were following the script written by Mr. Koo.

Unfortunately, this behavior didn't fit with the Federal Reserve's preconceived understanding of how the economy works, so it continued to pursue zero interest rate and quantitative easing policies far too long. The credit crunch that hit the U.S. economy in the years after the crisis is typical of what happens in a balance sheet recession. U.S. consumers bolstered their balance sheets; having been burned by the financial crisis, they were reluctant to tempt fate again by increasing their borrowings even with interest rates at record lows.[6]

In contrast to the sharp post-crisis reduction in household debt (which actually began to reverse in the first quarter of 2013), the U.S. corporate sector saw record levels of borrowing since 2009. To a significant extent, the corporate sector has increased its debt load in response to incentives that reward corporate executives based on the performance of their companies' stock prices. This led U.S. corporations to repurchase more than $2 trillion of their own stock since 2009, much of it with cheap borrowed money thanks to the Federal Reserve's zero interest rate policy.

As a result, in 2014, U.S. net corporate debt was actually 40 percent higher than it was in 2007 according to the work of Société Générale economist Andrew Lapthorne.[7] These higher debt levels were disguised by the low cost of borrowing in the post-crisis years. In addition to funding an unprecedented volume of debt buybacks, much of this debt was incurred to refinance higher cost debt that could not be paid off due to insufficient corporate free cash flow. Despite a raging bull market and high corporate cash balances, net corporate debt was higher than ever in 2014, a fact that was totally ignored by investors.

Both consumer and corporate behavior demonstrate that economic actors react to incentives; economic behavior is dynamic, not static. Unfortunately, monetary policy operates on precisely the opposite assumption—that behavior is static rather than dynamic. The Federal

Reserve consistently fails to take into account that consumers and businesses alter their behavior in response to the incentives created by monetary policy and other factors in the economic environment.[8] Low interest rates signal that the economy is struggling; zero interest rates—particularly zero interest rates for a prolonged period—signaled that the economy was in serious trouble. While lowering rates to zero was appropriate at the height of the financial crisis, keeping them at zero for seven more years signaled that the economy was struggling and that economic actors should take less risk, not more risk as central bankers theorized they would.

Among other consequences, low rates robbed savers of hundreds of billions of dollars of interest earnings on their capital and rendered it much more difficult for institutions such as pension funds to meet their future funding obligations. Unfortunately, institutions' future liabilities are still rising at high single digit rates, leaving them increasingly (and terminally) underfunded. Low rates that were theoretically designed to make it easier to borrow money also made it much harder to save money or generate decent investment returns. As a result, they had outlived their usefulness as a tool of monetary policy and should have been put to bed much earlier.

Federal Reserve policy would be more effective if the Federal Reserve's Open Market Committee included more members who understand how the real economy works. Fed apologists will no doubt object to imposing any requirements on the selection of Federal Reserve governors, but it is obvious that the current regime creates consistently sub-optimal policy. The public statements of numerous Fed officials in recent years demonstrate beyond a shadow of a doubt that they lack an adequate understanding of how the economy actually functions. There is more than sufficient evidence to demonstrate that economic actors have not responded to their policy initiatives as their models projected. Rather than persist in error, we should have the courage to admit that the current system is failing and change it.

Fiscal Policy and the Federal Deficit

Fiscal policy has long been a farce as Congress spends money like a bunch of drunken sailors. Both parties share the blame for failing the American people. The Obama years set a new standard for fecklessness when, largely due to the efforts of Senate Majority Leader Harry Reid, the Senate did not pass a working budget during the first six years of the Obama presidency. The stimulus bill passed early in Mr. Obama's first term to deal with the financial crisis failed to fuel economic growth because it was badly designed and failed to direct capital to areas that could increase the productive capacity of the economy.

For the rest of Mr. Obama's presidency, fiscal policy was paralyzed by the inability of both parties to work together to govern effectively, resulting in a failure to take any action to address a burgeoning entitlements crisis or an unproductive tax code while allowing military spending to drop in the face of rising global threats. The low point was the budget sequester, which substituted a spending freeze for the exercise of legislative judgment. This governance mess left the Federal Reserve as the only game in town, and it has not been up to the task intellectually or institutionally.

The situation is so bad that many observers are now celebrating the fact that the federal deficit is only half a trillion dollars a year (*The Wall Street Journal's* editorial page is particularly guilty of this), suggesting a severe loss of perspective. This reprieve will be short-lived as entitlement spending (including ObamaCare) increases and profits from Fannie Mae and Freddie Mac taper off over the rest of the decade. It is time for Congress to start making responsible decisions about how to spend money again. By the end of the Obama presidency, the federal deficit will be nearly $20 trillion and will have increased over Mr. Obama's two terms by a cumulative amount greater than all previous presidents combined. To say that the situation is unsustainable is to give understatements a bad name. The following are the areas that will need to be addressed to bring the deficit under control.

Entitlements

While annual federal budget deficits have dropped significantly from their trillion dollar-plus levels in 2009–2012, they are still running at half-a-trillion dollars a year and will soon increase sharply again unless entitlement spending is reformed (see Figure 10.1). In fiscal 2013, entitlement spending constituted roughly 57 percent of federal spending ($2.0 billion of $3.5 billion of outlays). Entitlements include the major health care programs, Medicare and Medicaid, to which we will start adding the full cost of ObamaCare after its architect Mr. Obama leaves office in early 2017, Social Security, and a variety of income security, government retirement, and veterans benefit programs.[9]

The government projects that the Medicare Trust Fund will run dry in 2030.[10] The Social Security trust fund is scheduled to remain solvent a little longer, through 2034.[11] Social Security's disability insurance program was slated to run out of money in 2016 largely due to a highly suspicious increase in the number of disabled Americans since President Obama took office and lowered eligibility standards. Shortly before publication of this book, however, it was saved by a budget deal that diverts funds from the main Social Security Trust (which holds not money but just IOUs from the government) to keep the disability fund solvent. In the words of the non-partisan Congressional Budget Office: "Throughout the next decade … an aging population, rising health care costs per person, and an increasing number of recipients of exchange subsidies and Medicaid benefits attributable to the Affordable Care Act would push up spending for some of the largest federal programs if current laws governing those programs remain unchanged."[12]

The CBO is currently projecting deficits of between $400 billion and $500 billion for the 2016–2020 period based on a series of assumptions that are likely to prove optimistic. They don't provide, for example, for the possibility of a sharp spike in interest rates; a mere 1 percent increase in interest rates would increase the deficit by $180 billion within a relatively short period of time since the average duration of U.S. debt is relatively short. They also don't provide for any increase in spending due to natural disasters or unanticipated military needs, both of which could easily occur.

There are no easy answers, and certainly no politically painless ways, to deal with entitlements. But that's why strong leadership is required to explain why the choice is between manageable pain today and unmanageable pain tomorrow. There are some obvious steps that should be taken immediately to start limiting entitlement spending before it

	2006	2007	2008	2009	2010	2011	2012	2013	2014
Deficit	-$248	-$161	-$459	-$1,413	-$1,294	-$1,480	-$1,100	-$719	-$514

Figure 10.1 Federal Budget Deficits ($ in billions)
SOURCE: Congressional Budget Office.

consumes the federal budget in future years as Baby Boomers retire and the number of workers supporting these programs declines.

First, all entitlements should be means-tested; the era of sending Social Security checks or paying for routine medical checkups and procedures for people with annual incomes over $200,000 should come to an end immediately.

Second, the eligibility age for all entitlements should be raised to 70 to reflect rising life expectancies for Americans born after 1965.

Third, new workers should be offered alternatives to Social Security so that they can start saving for their own retirements early.

Fourth, standards for eligibility for disability payments should be tightened up. The explosion in disability payments since Mr. Obama took office in January 2009 and lowered eligibility requirements has created a culture of dependency and is unsustainable.[13]

The next step is to repeal the Affordable Care Act and replace it with a market-based system. We must disabuse ourselves of the myth that the Affordable Care Act reduced healthcare costs. Like President Obama's promise that Americans would be able to keep their doctors, the mantra that ObamaCare bends the cost curve is demonstrably false. While the Obama administration claimed that ObamaCare would be revenue neutral or save money, estimates now place the cost at close to $2 trillion (conveniently incurred after Mr. Obama leaves office).

A new entitlement that offers free healthcare to millions of Americans—who have no concern about the cost of services for which they are not paying—is not going to lower costs. It is already apparent from rising healthcare premiums, skyrocketing costs for drugs, and the failure of nine of the 23 insurance co-ops set up under ObamaCare by late 2015 that a new effort is required to deal with reining in medical costs because the ACA failed miserably in this respect.

At this point, the law is providing healthcare to millions of Americans who need it (although as of July 2015 more eligible Americans had turned down coverage under the law than accepted it due to rising premiums and deductibles and more than 30 million Americans remained uninsured) but at the cost of grossly enriching the healthcare and pharmaceutical companies whose support the Obama administration bought off to pass the law. Regardless of the politics, the law is going to have to be fixed or else it will collapse under its own weight.

At some point, the Age of Entitlements is going to come crashing down on the heads of the Americans who voted for them. Americans (especially the young and minorities) are going to have to educate themselves to the fact that voting for politicians that offer them more free entitlements without asking for anything in return is not only a dead end but a profound betrayal of their own interests. This should have already dawned on the people trapped in West Baltimore or South Chicago and countless other failed communities who have been betrayed by 50 years of failed progressive policies. People don't want hand-outs; they want to be empowered and that requires a government that values their contributions to society. The only way to accomplish this is to demand that recipients of government assistance lead responsible lives and contribute something in return (to the extent they are mentally and physically capable of doing so). Instead, the Obama administration demonstrated a deep disrespect for the very people it purported to be empowering by making it easier for them to depend on the government without demanding that they learn to do more for themselves. The result is a more arthritic and divided nation where the people at the bottom of the socio-economic ladder are deprived of the tools to improve their lives by a government that is crippling rather than empowering them.

End Corporate Welfare

The government plays far too intrusive a role in the American economy, distorting incentives and producing sub-optimal outcomes. Steps must be taken to eliminate subsidies that serve small segments of the business establishment while costing American taxpayers billions of dollars without providing them any commensurate benefit in return.

While there are too many corporate subsidies provided by the government to list here, the following should be at the top of the chopping block. First, all farm subsidies including ethanol subsidies should be eliminated. These subsidies distort agricultural markets and in many cases are paid to parties who don't need them. Second, the Export-Import Bank should be closed. In 2013, a Mercatus study found that 76 percent of the Ex-Im Bank's subsidies went to benefit only ten companies, including General Electric, Boeing, Caterpillar, and Bechtel. These companies should not be receiving subsidized financing from the U.S. government. Finally, Medicaid and Medicare should not be prohibited by law from negotiating drug prices with pharmaceutical companies. Outside the United States, other governments that fund healthcare payments for their citizens pay far less for drugs because they are allowed to negotiate for lower prices. The legal prohibition on doing so that applies to Medicare and Medicaid is an obvious political sop to the pharmaceutical industry that costs insurers and patients billions of dollars a year and has no place in a market economy.

Military Spending[14]

On October 22, 2015, President Obama vetoed the $612 billion defense spending bill for the 2016 fiscal year. He objected to the fact that the bill failed to close the U.S. detention facility at Guantanamo Bay, Cuba, and remove the terrorists housed there to federal prisons in the United States mainland. He also criticized the bill for adding $89.2 billion in supplemental war funding in a manner that avoided the automatic budget cuts to military programs known as "sequestration." Under sequestration, $1 trillion of cuts were made to the federal budget and were drawn equally from military and non-military spending despite the fact that military spending represents far less than half of government spending.

Military experts agree that sequestration is wreaking havoc on American security. It contributed to Mr. Obama's abandonment of America's longstanding "two war" strategy that provided for a military force of sufficient size to defeat two enemies in two geographically separate theaters simultaneously. It set the country on a path to have a Navy smaller than at any time since 1915, an Army smaller than it has been since 1940, and an Air Force with the smallest and oldest combat aircraft force in its history. It leaves the United States in a poor position to combat rising cyberattacks and completely unprepared to deal with a potential electromagnetic attack that could cripple its civilian and military infrastructure. It also allowed the country's nuclear capabilities to lag. Finally, military veterans have been treated shamefully by the Department of Veterans Affairs during the Obama years; thousands have died while awaiting medical treatment. The latter scandal was not so much a result of the sequester as a symptom of an administration whose policies and behavior demonstrate that it has little affinity for or genuine respect or appreciation for the military.

Mr. Obama's veto came on the same day that his former Secretary of State, Hillary Clinton, testified before the Congressional Committee investigating the attack on the embassy in Benghazi, Libya that resulted in the death of four Americans, including Ambassador Christopher Stevens. Americans heard irrefutable evidence during Mrs. Clinton's hearing that she and other members of the Obama administration lied to the American people regarding their knowledge of the attack on the embassy. The liberal media naturally praised Mrs. Clinton's "performance" during the hearing while ignoring the fact that the presumptive Democratic candidate for president in 2016 had been caught in another in a seemingly endless series of lies.

A country's military represents its character. When it was discovered that American soldiers were torturing detainees during the Bush administration, Barack Obama and other Democrats were the first to claim that this conduct was a stain on this country's honor and a betrayal of its values. Yet these same individuals have no trouble gutting the military budget or refusing to defend our embassies. They paid lip service to the death of Ambassador Stevens and his three colleagues but were more concerned about the political ramifications of a tragedy that inconveniently occurred a few weeks before the 2012 election. The actions and policies pursued by the administration during Mr. Obama's second term demonstrate beyond a shadow of a doubt that military spending is a low priority for this administration. Unfortunately, the result has rendered America less safe and respected at home and abroad.

Unfortunately, the need for military spending is increasing just as Mr. Obama wants America to retreat from the world. It is now clear that he always intended to reduce military spending regardless of world events. But there is a direct correlation between the rise of global instability and American retreat. The combination of the rise of ISIS, Iran's growing domination of the Middle East, China's aggression in the South China Sea, and Russia's invasion of the Ukraine and direct threat to NATO require more U.S. military spending, not less. So will the Iran nuclear deal, once Mr. Obama or his successor figures out what the rest of the world already knows—that Iran has no intention of complying with its terms or ending its funding of Hezbollah and Hamas and other terrorists around the world.

The sequestration of military spending needs to be terminated immediately. The Gates fiscal 2012 defense budget was the last one prepared using the normal defense planning process. It requested $661 billion for national defense for the 2016 fiscal year. This budget was developed before the rise of ISIS, the collapse of the Iraqi government, the Syrian civil war, the fall of Libya to Islamic militants, the fall of Yemen to Iranian-backed rebels, Russia's invasion of Ukraine, China's stepped up aggression in the South China Sea, and cyberattacks on U.S. government personnel systems. This budget should become the minimum baseline for military spending going forward. At the same time, a non-partisan civilian taskforce should be assigned to eliminate wasteful spending in the budget. In a budget as large and politicized as the U.S. defense budget, there are undoubtedly tens of billions of dollars that can be eliminated. But just as the U.S. cannot borrow and spend itself into prosperity, it cannot cut its military budget into security.

Tax Reform

The tax code is the DNA of any economy. There is widespread agreement that the U.S. tax code requires an overhaul but there are many disagreements regarding the details. Nothing less than a complete tax overhaul will place the U.S. economy on a sufficiently productive path to pay its current and future obligations. Some may view the following proposals as radical, but they are necessary. Whether they are feasible depends on whether we can summon the political and moral courage to enact them.

Lower Individual Tax Rates and Tax Ordinary and Capital Gains Equally

- Ordinary income tax rates should be lowered and all individual deductions (with two exceptions) reduced or eliminated. The only tax deductions that should be kept in place are the charitable deduction, which should be capped at 20 percent of income annually, and retirement plan contribution deductions for taxpayers with income below $500,000 per year. Taxpayers with higher incomes should be permitted to contribute to these plans but their deductions should be capped.

- Businesses should continue to be able to deduct their ordinary and necessary business expenses (salaries, rent, etc. but not interest—see below) from their income to determine taxable income.
- Individual tax rates (including payroll taxes) should be lowered to 10 percent on all incomes below $100,000 per year, 20 percent on all income below $1,000,000 per year, and 25 percent per year for all income above $1,000,000.
- The lower capital gains tax rate should be eliminated; all income whether ordinary or capital in nature should be taxed at the same rate.

People who rely on selling their labor are the most heavily penalized by high tax rates and would most directly benefit from lowering them. Inequality is exacerbated by taxing labor at a higher rather than capital because the wealthy are the only ones who are in a position to sell their capital in the first place. If the tax rate for ordinary income were the same as that for capital gains, it would level the playing field between those who earn their living by selling their labor and those who earn their living by selling their capital. The most effective way we can start to reduce income inequality is to stop taxing labor at a significantly higher rate than we tax capital. Furthermore, if the tax rate on ordinary income were lowered, it would increase incentives for businesses to invest.

Eliminating the capital gains tax would also end the carried interest tax, which taxes labor as capital with no rational policy justification.

These changes would broaden the tax base and promote tax fairness. Liberals like to argue that the way to promote "fairness" is to raise taxes: that type of thinking is the product of minds that understand little of economics and less about human nature. Lower tax rates benefit everyone but particularly those who aspire to the top of the economic pyramid. Higher tax rates discourage economic activity and encourage people to avoid taxes.

The government is an inefficient allocator of capital. Higher tax rates reduce the return on capital, create disincentives for investment, and reduce the amount of capital available for investment in productive activities such as technology, education, building new factories and capital goods, and research and development. They also reduce the capital available to invest in raising labor productivity to enhance economic growth and income gains. Leaving more income in the hands of the private sector is the surest pathway toward economic revival.

Eliminate Deductions for Interest on Debt

- One of the biggest flaws in the tax code is that it creates enormous incentives to borrow money. This makes the U.S. government—which means the U.S. taxpayer—a partner in every debt transaction in the economy. Every time someone borrows money, he or she is subsidized by his fellow citizens. Is it any wonder that debt never stops growing? An essential step that must be taken to fix the tax code and strengthen the economy is ending the interest deduction for all debt—and that includes the hallowed home mortgage deduction. Once we start treating equity and debt equally, the foundation of the American economy will strengthen as equity replaces debt in individual and corporate capital structures. An appropriate period to phase-in this change (i.e., five years) should be provided, but we must bite the bullet and recapitalize our economy with equity.

End the Estate Tax

- The estate tax should be eliminated. First, this wealth has already been subject to income tax and taxing it a second time is fundamentally unfair and confiscatory. Second, the wealthy have numerous ways to avoid the estate tax including leaving their wealth to a foundation that can carry out their philanthropic goals rather than allowing the government to take half their wealth. More of the wealthy, especially technology entrepreneurs, are likely to pursue this path and play an active role in directing their philanthropy rather than let the government take their money. The estate tax collects a relatively modest amount of revenue but causes an enormous amount of resentment among successful people who spend their lives building businesses and legacies for their families. Rather than promoting tax fairness by confiscating the life's work of the most accomplished people in society, the estate tax is a socialist relic that is easily avoided and accomplishes little. It should be given a decent burial and free up financial and intellectual capital for more productive uses.

Eliminate Retirement Plan Abuses

- In November 2014, the U.S. Government Accountability Office published a Report to the Chairman of the Senate Finance Committee entitled "Individual Retirement Accounts: IRS Could Bolster Enforcement of Multimillion Dollar Accounts, but More Direction from Congress Is Needed." Widespread abuse of retirement plans by wealthy taxpayers deprives the government of much-needed revenues and should be eliminated. Such abuses include self-dealing and other prohibited transactions. While IRAs and other retirement plans were designed to give ordinary Americans an opportunity to save for retirement, some wealthy Americans are using them to finance their businesses, invest in hedge funds that they manage, and engage in other activities to shelter their income in ways that are both illegal and contrary to the intended purposes of such accounts. Such abuses, like the carried interest tax, further widen the gulf between rich and poor and corrupt the tax system and should be aggressively audited by the IRS. Serious consideration should also be given to limiting deductions to retirement plans for high income taxpayers, as suggested earlier in this section.

Lower Corporate Tax Rates, Stop Taxing Dividends, and Facilitate Repatriation of Foreign Income

- The U.S. corporate tax rate of 35 percent is among the highest in the world; it should be cut in half to 17.5 percent and applied to net income after all reasonable and necessary business expenses. Special tax breaks should be eliminated except where they relate to scientific or medical research. High U.S. corporate tax rates are placing American corporations at a serious competitive disadvantage because they make the United States an undesirable location for corporate headquarters and investment. Rather than criticize U.S. companies for taking advantage of perfectly legal strategies to reduce their tax burdens, Congress should lower these tax burdens and make it more attractive for U.S. companies to remain domiciled and invested in their own country. Corporations respond to incentives, and the U.S. tax code currently incentivizes them to get out of town.

Corporate dividends should no longer be taxed. When a corporation generates one dollar of income today, it is taxed at a 35 percent rate at the corporate level and a second time at a 23.8 percent rate (for taxpayers in the highest tax bracket) plus additional state income tax charges. This means that the federal government takes roughly half of every dollar of corporate earnings through taxation. Of course, few if any corporations pay the full 35 percent rate, so the actual take in many cases is less, but corporate earnings should not be subject to anywhere near this level of taxation.

Taxing corporate earnings twice reduces the amount of capital available for reinvestment while introducing unnecessary complexity into the tax code. It would be one thing if the government were a wise allocator of capital, but it is precisely the opposite because capital is allocated based on political rather than economic considerations. More capital should be left in the hands of the market and less should be delivered into the grasp of the government to misallocate. One way to do that is to give the government only one bite at the apple of corporate profits. Eliminating the taxation of dividends while eliminating the deductibility of interest as recommended above would also render equity financing significantly more attractive on its own terms and relative to debt financing, an important step in promoting an equity-based economy.

The system that taxes U.S. corporations on their world wide income should be modified to prevent abuses such as the shifting of income to shell corporations in low tax jurisdictions. The incentives for corporations to keep trillions of dollars of cash offshore also need to be eliminated. Funds currently held abroad should be repatriated and taxed at 10 percent (with full credits for any taxes paid to foreign jurisdictions on that income) and corporations should be prevented from avoiding taxes by keeping funds offshore. It makes absolutely no sense for corporations like Apple, Inc. and Microsoft Corp. among others to keep tens of billions of dollars offshore simply in order to avoid paying taxes on them in the United States. It makes even less sense for a company like Apple, which was sitting on over $200 billion of cash as of June 30, 2015, to borrow money to return capital to shareholders for the same reason. Policies that lead to such behavior need to end. Special attention should be also paid to creating incentives for U.S. companies to keep their intellectual property inside the United States rather than shifting it to other countries to lower their tax bills. It is hard to conceive of a tax code more poorly designed to encourage corporations to behave in ways that would benefit the U.S. economy.

Like monetary policy, tax policy suffers from the flawed belief that economic actors do not respond to incentives. Tax policy loses the forest for the trees; it focuses on tax rates rather than overall tax revenues. Each time tax rates were lowered, tax revenues increased because economic growth increased. It is common sense that tax-payers will spend less time avoiding taxes if they are required to pay lower rates and if they believe the system is taxing them fairly. If overall corporate tax rates were lower, more revenue would remain in the U.S. and more taxes would be paid here which, after all, is the point of the tax code in the first place.

Raise Sin Taxes
- Taxes should be raised significantly on cigarettes, alcohol, legal gambling and guns. In addition, if marijuana is legalized as it should be, it should be taxed heavily. All of these activities (with the possible exception of marijuana usage) contribute to higher health-care costs and should be discouraged by the government that ends up paying for much of the damage they cause. The most effective and equitable way to accomplish this is by making those who use these products compensate society directly through higher taxes.

Domestic Policy

There are many areas of domestic policy that have an important bearing on the economy. The following areas are desperately in need of reform in order to promote economic growth in the United States.

Immigration Reform
- We need to enforce our immigration laws and defend our borders. There is something profoundly misguided about an immigration policy that deports highly educated legal immigrants to their home countries after they are allowed to study at an American university but refuses to defend the border to keep

out uneducated and impoverished illegal immigrants. Yet that is precisely what U.S. immigration policy does today: It forces foreigners who come to this country to study for advanced degrees (usually in math and science) to return to their home countries while failing to properly police our borders or enforce our laws against illegal immigrants that burden the system. Millions of illegal immigrants remain in this country with impunity while no path is provided to legal status for themselves or their children. This state of suspended animation must end and a path to legal status provided. People who broke the law to come to this country, should not be rewarded with citizenship; legal status is sufficient to protect them and vindicate the rule of law. Immigration is the lifeblood of our economy, but our immigration policy is draining the life out of our economy. Illegal immigrants are straining our educational, healthcare, and law enforcement resources without any prospect of bringing these individuals into the tax base and providing them with a means of becoming fully productive and participating members of society. It is time to address this issue before it consumes more of our resources without giving us anything in return. Further, the policy of sanctuary cities must end; cities should not be permitted to violate federal immigration law with impunity. The Obama administration's tolerance of sanctuary cities is unacceptable and unlawful.

Antitrust Enforcement

- On July 22, 2015, Dennis K. Berman, *The Wall Street Journal*'s Finance Editor, tweeted the following: "Competition in America, 2015: 4 airlines, 4 banks, 3 health insurers, 2 operating systems, 2 wireless carriers." America has seen an unprecedented boom in mergers and acquisitions since the financial crisis that resulted in industries dominated by a much more limited number of large companies. This is true of virtually every industry but is most noteworthy in finance, transportation (particularly airlines), healthcare, energy, and telecommunications. But the truth is that any industry that wanted to merge did so with impunity under the Obama administration; antitrust enforcement has been virtually non-existent since the financial crisis. And on the rare occasion when deals were blocked, like the Comcast/Time Warner merger, it was based on highly questionable market and economic analysis. The argument supporting the boom in mergers is that American companies need to compete in a global world and require greater size and scale to do so. The problem is that more concentration inevitably leaves consumers facing higher prices and employees facing job losses while these transactions enrich shareholders and corporate executives. One of the major policy initiatives that unleashed an enormous merger wave was ObamaCare, which resulted in a series of mergers among health insurers, hospital chains, and pharmaceutical companies that were unopposed by antitrust regulators. While even paranoids have enemies, only the most naïve among us should ignore the obvious fact that these industries were bought off by the Obama administration in exchange for their support of its most highly cherished domestic policy achievement and were allowed to merge at will (while also raising their prices at will). A more highly concentrated economy will be more rigid and less responsive to a rapidly changing global economy. It will also lead to higher prices for consumers (something that is already apparent in higher airline fares and higher healthcare costs) and fewer choices. The next administration needs to restore genuine antitrust enforcement to its list of priorities.

Term Limits/Lobbying Ban

- Until we have term limits, this country will continue to be governed by an ossified and corrupt political class that serves its own interests rather than those of its constituents. Not that long ago, people entered public service in order to serve the public; today they enter public service to serve themselves and pave the way for lucrative private sector careers that would not be available to them without their public service. The spectacle of former government officials monetizing their government officials is destructive to faith in government. In order to put an end to this sorry regime, it is time for a constitutional amendment to change Congressional terms and impose term limits. The terms for members of the House of Representatives should be extended from two to four years with a two-term limitation (eight years in total) and Senate terms should remain at six years and be limited to two terms

(12 years in total). Former members of Congress and their staff members should be prohibited from lobbying for a period of ten years after leaving office.

Legal System Reform

Our legal system is broken. It takes too much time and money for litigants to assert their rights because the system is abused by too many parties. The following reforms are urgently needed to improve the economy and the quality of life in this country:

- We should adopt tort reform with the "loser pays" rule to reduce frivolous litigation. The failure of ObamaCare to include tort reform neutered much of the law's ability to lower healthcare costs. Medical malpractice claims are rife with abuse by ambulance-chasing lawyers of low character and intellect and clog the courts with frivolous claims that force doctors into practicing defensive medicine that imposes enormous and unnecessary costs on society. Tort reform alone would contribute to a significant reduction in healthcare costs and must be adopted immediately.

- The litigation privilege that allows litigants and their attorneys to lie with impunity in order to try to gain a tactical advantage in litigation should be eliminated. There should be no legal right to defame somebody and the legal system should not provide a shield to people who do. Lawyers who engage in such behavior should be disbarred and made personally liable for damages.

- The standards for filing frivolous lawsuits, which clog courts and harm litigants with legitimate grievances, should be tightened and the penalties for filing such lawsuits should be significantly increased against litigants and their attorneys. State bar associations fail miserably to police bad behavior by their members because they are controlled by other attorneys; they are, in a word, an organized fraud that protects lawyers but not the public. Self-policing of the legal profession should be terminated and taken over by the government. Attorneys who routinely violate the rules, abuse the system and cause enormous economic and systemic damage should be disbarred. There are too many attorneys and the legal system is a blight on this country (and I say that as someone with two law degrees from one of the finest law schools in the country).

Substantive Law Reforms

There are also several laws on the books that need to be changed in order to improve the quality of life and the economic trajectory of this country:

- While law abiding citizens have every right to own guns, gun control laws should be tightened to reduce access to guns by the mentally ill and those with criminal records. Further, the sale of automatic weapons that have no use other than killing multiple human beings quickly should be strictly limited. The Second Amendment does not provide a right to carry weapons of mass murder and the American people need to stand up to the bullying of the NRA on this issue. Finally, the so-called "gun show loophole" in the Brady Bill that allows private parties to sell guns without conducting a background check should be closed.

- We should legalize marijuana nationally (and tax it heavily) and stop prosecuting people for marijuana possession. It is absurd that people are allowed to drink alcohol but prohibited from smoking marijuana. To the extent marijuana usage leads to abuse of more dangerous drugs, the same can be said of alcohol. Several states have already moved in this direction and more will likely follow.

- We should eliminate prison sentences for non-violent drug possession (but not drug distribution offenses) where there is strong evidence that the offender does not pose a risk of committing a violent crime in the future and replace them with financial penalties and community service. American prisons do not rehabilitate anybody; sending the genuinely non-violent to prison for the possession of drugs significantly increases the likelihood that they will emerge with a much higher propensity and tolerance for criminal behavior in the future.

A little common sense would go a long way to improving our economy and quality of life. But in order for common sense to overcome special interests and ideology, men and women of good will must rise up and be heard. The political classes are destroying the world. The question you have to ask yourself is whether you are going to remain silent or stand up and be counted for change.

CHAPTER 11

How to Save Yourself

Your Grace, I feel I've been remiss in my duties. I've given you meat and wine and music, but I haven't shown you the hospitality you deserve. My King has married and I owe my new Queen a wedding gift.
—Lord Walder Frey to the guests at the wedding of Edmure Tully and Roslin Frey in *Game of Thrones*

The guests invited to the wedding of Edmure Tully and Roslin Frey in *Game of Thrones* were lulled into a false sense of security by their host, Lord Walder Frey. They never expected Lord Walder to harm them after he offered them *guest right*, a tradition that provides that after a man invites a guest into his home, neither the guest nor the host can harm each other for the length of the guest's stay. *Guest right* was considered one of the most sacred and inviolable social rules in their world, yet they were about to learn that nothing is sacred in the land of Westeros. The wedding celebration was a set-up all along and a blood-bath known as the Red Wedding ensued.

There is no such thing as *guest right* in the financial markets though investors continue to behave as though they are entitled to safe harbor protection from central bankers. They mistakenly believe that the invitation by central bankers to take greater risks after the financial crisis will protect their investments from losing value, but that is a terrible error of judgment on their part. While The Committee to Destroy the World may not be deliberately plotting to slaughter them like Lord Walder, it is nonetheless creating the conditions for another Red Wedding in the markets.

Investors must take the world as it is, not as they would like it to be. While the previous two chapters set forth a series of policy changes that could set the world on a more productive path, idealism is not an investment strategy. Neither is denial nor relying on the continued generosity (or fecklessness) of central bankers. Just as markets are guided by greed and fear, monetary policy will continue to be guided by people who have no genuine understanding of the real world while fiscal policy will always be made by politicians guided by self-interest and the next election cycle. Policymakers will continue to create havoc—but investors need not succumb to their mistakes. Speaking as a hedge fund manager, I have to make money for my clients all the time. I don't have the luxury of waiting for politicians and central bankers to come to their senses—and neither do you.

The world is currently populated by far too many unqualified people who are managing money and, in many cases, responsible for enormous pools of capital. We live in a world that too easily allows people to fail upward and makes excuses for failure. It remains shocking that investors remain loyal to managers who produce years of underperformance or blow up portfolios due to inadequate risk controls.

In January 2015, numerous macro hedge funds suffered huge and in some cases catastrophic losses when Switzerland decided to break the peg between the Swiss franc and the Euro currency. Exposing investors to this risk was inexcusable; the Swiss National Bank's balance sheet had already swelled to 86 percent of Switzerland's GDP as Swiss authorities tried to defend the peg and the European Central Bank was widely expected to imminently launch a huge quantitative easing program that would place further pressure on the Swiss franc. Yet these macro hedge funds were caught totally flat-footed and lost huge amounts of money (including one well-known $830 million fund, Everest Capital, that literally vaporized 100% of its capital overnight, and another, the Fortress Group's Macro Fund, that closed later in the year after losing more than $100 million on this trade). Even more disturbing was that many macro funds had been underperforming for years, yet investors had stuck with them. Inertia seems to be an unfortunate characteristic of many investors, particularly large institutional ones. It is little wonder that large pension funds remain terminally underfunded.

The biggest challenge facing investors is that nobody knows what the future holds. Despite the pundits parading on television confidently predicting the future, the reality is that they don't have a clue what is going to happen. But saying "I don't know" doesn't get you invited back for future interviews (though providing consistently bad advice apparently does). In a sound-bite world, the only thing worse than being wrong is being uncertain. Unfortunately, hubris can lead straight to the poorhouse. In order to invest profitably over the long run, investors need to maintain humility, recognize the limits of their knowledge, and acknowledge that the only certainty in this world is uncertainty. They must construct a view of the world that is as accurate and comprehensive as possible but also flexible and hedged. Once they complete that task, they must "connect the dots" and pursue investment strategies that are consistent with that world view. In a networked and globalized world, that view must include not only economics but geopolitics, culture, technology, science and the environment. All of these areas work together to influence markets. Everything is connected.

In order to formulate a realistic investment strategy, investors must acknowledge the following characteristics of the post-crisis global economy and markets at the beginning of 2016:

1. There is too much public and private sector debt in the United States, Europe, Asia, and emerging markets that is never going to be repaid in constant dollars.
2. The value of fiat currencies is being actively debauched by the deliberate policies of central banks. Everybody's buying power is being demolished. This means that monetary inflation is raging regardless of what "official" inflation statistics report. Deflation is a fairy tale central bankers tell themselves to justify their inability to raise interest rates because of the damage that would cause an over-indebted world.

3. Central banks have distorted markets by artificially suppressing interest rates to levels that render fixed income investments certificates of confiscation in nominal and real (i.e., inflation-adjusted) terms. The government is slowly stealing savers' money via inflation and currency devaluation.

4. Governments are not pursuing pro-growth fiscal policies capable of generating robust economic growth. This is a political and moral failure rather than an intellectual failure. There are countless policies available to stimulate growth but political leaders don't have the courage or integrity to implement them and their constituents are too focused on their narrow self-interests to demand them. Slow growth will hurt future economic growth and depress future equity returns.

5. Geopolitical instability is rising to dangerous levels in the Middle East, Eastern Europe, and the South China Sea. War is raging around the world while narcissistic Western elites diddle in Davos and engage in false illusions of stability. The world is one wrong step away from a serious military conflict that would seriously disrupt financial markets.

6. All financial assets are grossly inflated in value—not only stocks and bonds but real estate, art, and collectibles. Put another way, the income flows generated by these assets are insufficient to support their valuations seven years after the financial crisis.

After an epic bull market that began in March 2009, investors are likely to experience a much tougher road in the years ahead. They will have to adjust to a prolonged period of below-trend growth as the suffocating weight of debt saps the vitality from the global economy. Interest rates will likely stay low for a prolonged period of time because economic growth is destined to remain low. If economic growth is somehow able to defy the downward gravitational pull of the rising tide of debt, interest rates will rise and exert their own pressures on corporate profits and growth. Either way, the prospects for high returns in most asset classes are poor.

The most likely scenario—persistent sluggish growth—will leave equity prices in the hands of central banks that have come to believe that their job descriptions include boosting equity prices to promote financial stability. Unfortunately, their policies are promoting precisely the opposite—financial fragility. And they have run out of ammunition to employ when the next recession or crisis arrives. With trillions of dollars/euros/yen weighing down their balance sheets and their official interest rates stuck at zero, central banks are left with limited means of stimulating economies or bailing out markets the next time they are called upon. Betting on central banks was a successful strategy since the financial crisis, but it is unlikely to remain one much longer. Printing money only works for so long before it ends in tears. Investors will need to start relying on themselves rather than on unelected former tenured economics professors to secure their economic futures.

In a slow growth world, however, not all investments grow slowly or perform poorly. The key to investment success is properly diagnosing the macroeconomic environment and choosing the proper investments to profit from that environment. One key concept investors need to understand is the difference between "nominal" and "real" returns. Governments thrive on their citizens' failure to understand this difference. "Nominal" returns on capital are measured in constant dollars unadjusted for inflation. "Real" returns on capital are measured in inflation-adjusted dollars. As described in the Introduction, the U.S. government promotes the fiction that the prices of goods and services are increasing when real world prices (other than energy since mid-2014) actually are rising at double-digit rates. For this reason, investors need to earn at least high single digit returns on their capital to keep up with rising prices; lower returns leave them with very low or even negative real or inflation-adjusted returns, meaning their dollars buy less of what they need to live every year. The reason there is so much political discussion about low wage growth is that American workers keep falling behind in terms of what their paychecks buy them in the real world. No less is true with respect to their investment returns although this technical point receives far less media attention.

Ironically, the policymakers who complain about wealth inequality and the impoverishment of ordinary Americans are the very ones responsible for policies that suppress interest rates and investment returns and damage these same constituencies. The Federal Reserve destroyed bonds as an investment class with zero interest rates and quantitative easing. For evidence of this, we need look no further than the performance of the two largest bond funds in the world. For the 3-year period ended May 1, 2015, the PIMCO Total Return Fund and the Vanguard Total Bond Index Fund generated annualized returns of only 2.78 percent and 3.46 percent, respectively. On a nominal basis those returns are unimpressive enough, but on an inflation-adjusted basis they are effectively zero. By May 1, 2015, the PIMCO Total Return Fund had lost more than 65 percent of its assets from its peak of $293 billion in April 2013. While many have attributed these outflows to the departure of Bill Gross as the fund's manager, the real reason is consistently poor performance that started well before Mr. Gross's exit.

While these large bond funds market themselves based on relative performance (i.e., how they perform against their peers), investors should tire of being told that "in the kingdom of the blind, the one-eyed man is king." They can't eat relative real returns of zero. While PIMCO's and Vanguard's returns reveal that these funds have been reduced to little more than glorified money market funds, they are actually much riskier than money market funds because they employ huge amounts of derivatives and leverage to earn these paltry returns. This means that their risk-adjusted returns are even worse than they appear and investors should be looking for alternatives. If these funds were half as adept at investing as they are at marketing, investors would have nothing to worry about. Then again, that could be said of most of the products sold by Wall Street.

In order to deal with the headwinds facing global markets in the next few years and protect their capital, investors need a plan. That plan should involve structuring a portfolio that can generate income and protect capital on both a short-term and a long-term basis. While reasonable men and women can differ on the proper portfolio mix, the following is one model portfolio for a typical individual investor based on the state of the post-crisis world. Investors should discuss their investments with a professional to insure that their portfolio is suited for their specific needs and circumstances.

1. Gold, precious metals, tangible assets—10–20 percent
2. Cash—10–20 percent
3. Absolute return strategies—20–40 percent
4. Dividend paying equities—20 percent
5. Income generating securities—10–20 percent

The first thing readers will notice is that there is an allocation to "income generating securities" but not to bonds per se such as investment grade and municipal bonds and Treasuries. Many absolute return strategies will provide some bond exposure. But beyond that, investors should minimize their bond exposure. Bonds have been rendered certificates of confiscation by post-crisis central bank policies that artificially suppressed interest rates around the world to zero (or less). As discussed above, the largest bond funds in the world have struggled to generate positive returns since 2012.

Some highly regarded investors believe that interest rates will drop sharply over the next few years. Since they are already very low, interest rates would have to drop sharply to generate high returns. For example, it would require the yield on the 10-year Treasury to decline from 2% to 1% over 12 months to generate a total return of 12.8% (and 13.7% for 10-year zero coupon Treasuries). For the 30-year Treasury bond, a decline from 2.9% to 2.0% over a 12-month period would generate a 22.4% return (32.8% on 30-year zero coupon Treasuries). Such sharp declines in interest rates would almost certainly mean that the economy entered a recession (or worse) and that equities and other risk assets suffered severe, if not catastrophic, losses. Alternatively, only small jumps in interest rates would result in big losses for investors.

While I believe there is a reasonable likelihood that rates will move lower as the U.S. and global economy struggles in the years ahead, I believe the risk/reward with respect to high quality bonds (Treasuries, investment grade corporate, and municipal bonds) is poor. The most likely scenario is that bonds will continue to offer poor real (inflation-adjusted) returns for a prolonged period of time in the best of circumstances and pose a serious risk of generating negative returns if central bank policies trigger higher inflation and higher interest rates. If central bankers have demonstrated anything, it is that they will double down on failed policies until they trigger a crisis. That crisis could manifest itself in higher inflation that will seriously hurt bond returns.

The second thing that is not readily apparent from the proposed model portfolio is that investors should hold as many of their assets as possible in U.S. dollars. While the value of all paper currencies will continue to be destroyed by central banks, the U.S. dollar should fare much better than other major currencies like the Euro and the Japanese yen. China will also continue to cheapen its currency in order to remain competitive. To the extent investors hold assets that are denominated in fiat currencies, that fiat currency should be the U.S. dollar.[1]

One of the biggest threats to all paper investments is that the currencies in which they are denominated are being actively devalued every day by the failed monetary policies of the world's central banks and the complete absence of meaningful pro-growth fiscal policies of the sort laid out earlier in this book. The only way to protect yourself is to first, diversify some of your assets out of paper currencies, and second, concentrate your paper currency holdings in the U.S. dollar.

With those two provisos, the following is a discussion of my model portfolio.

Gold

I end every issue of *The Credit Strategist* with words to the effect "Buy gold and save yourself." Gold remains highly controversial among the thinking and non-thinking classes but it is going to be worth a lot more in the future than it is today. Gold spiked to $1,900 an ounce in late 2011 as a result of a number of exogenous factors, including fears about the viability of the European currency union and the flow of money into newly created investment vehicles such as the SPDR Gold Shares ETF (GLD). By mid-2015, it had sold off by roughly 40 percent even as central banks kept pouring trillions of newly created paper money into financial markets and the global economy.

As of late 2015, gold was among the most out-of-favor investments in the world and was vulnerable to trading lower primarily (but not exclusively) because of a rising dollar. But investors were taking a very short-sighted view. Long-term investors who are interested in protecting their wealth should continue to buy gold. Gold should comprise between 10 percent and 20 percent of any portfolio. As James Grant has argued, gold is an investment in global monetary disorder, a condition of which we can be assured for many years. Gold is a hedge against both inflation and deflation and an excellent way to pass wealth down through generations.

The first thing to understand is that gold should be considered a currency, not a metal or commodity, in today's world. But unlike other currencies (with the exception of digital currencies such as bitcoin), it is the anti-fiat currency. In mid-2014, the U.S. dollar began to rise against the Euro, the Japanese yen, and other currencies as U.S. monetary policy began to diverge from those of other major central banks in Europe, Japan, and elsewhere. The Federal Reserve ended quantitative easing in October 2014. In contrast, the Bank of Japan and European Central Bank were about to double down on their versions of this doomed-to-fail policy, which they did in October 2014 and January 2015, respectively.

While the dollar is likely to continue rising against the Euro and the yen long after the publication of this book, the question remains: What will happen to the value of the dollar itself in a world where the Federal Reserve has made no secret of its desire to increase inflation as its official policy? The answer to that question is that it will decline against the value of gold and other tangible assets over the long run. The explosion in financial asset prices since the financial crisis is a manifestation of the destruction of the value of all fiat currencies including the dollar. It is no accident that the wealthiest people in the world are shifting money out of paper currencies into high end real estate, collectibles, art, and other tangible assets. Eventually gold and other precious metals will appreciate sharply along with these beneficiaries of dollar depreciation.

There are several ways to own gold. The preferred way is to own physical gold through the purchase of coins and gold bars. I also recommend the Central Fund of Canada (CEF) and the Sprott Physical Gold Trust ETF (PHYS), which often trade at a discount to the spot price of gold. The SPDR Gold Shares ETF (GLD) is a third way to own gold but tends to attract more speculative fund flows than the other two.

Gold mining shares are another way to gain exposure to gold. In January 2016, the Philadelphia Gold and Silver Index (XAU) was trading at its lowest level since November 2000, when gold was priced at $266 per ounce. While investing in gold mining companies involves exposure to the operating issues involved in investing in any business, it provides another way to invest in gold while also providing exposure to a deeply distressed sector that offers significant upside potential when the price of its primary product recovers. Investors should focus on well-capitalized miners and avoid highly leveraged ones that could suffer from a prolonged period of low gold prices.

Absolute Return Strategies

Investors who continue to rely on a rising stock market courtesy of the kindness (or errors) of central bankers are likely to be very disappointed in the years ahead. The S&P 500 enjoyed an enviable run since hitting its post-crisis low in March 2009, more than tripling in value by mid-2015. This performance was due to two primary factors: (1) a strong recovery in corporate earnings from 2009 recession lows; and (2) massive liquidity flowing into the market courtesy of the trillions of dollars of new money created out of thin air by the Federal Reserve and other global central banks. Unfortunately, those policies failed to create sustainable economic growth and reached the point of diminishing returns not only from an economic but also from a market standpoint by the end of 2015. In fact, it is arguable that the post-crisis bull market ended around the time the Fed terminated its quantitative easing program in October 2014.

Looking forward, traditional investments are unlikely to produce attractive returns over the next decade. The days of investing in an S&P 500 index fund and closing your eyes and hoping for the best are over. Two of the most highly respected strategists in the investment world, Rob Arnott at Performance Analytics and Jeremy Grantham at Grantham Mayo van Otterloo (GMO), are forecasting that stocks are likely to produce negative real (inflation-adjusted) returns over the next 7–10 years (more on this below). Among other things, that means that index investing is going to disappoint a lot of people and active managers are going to have an opportunity to regain the reputations that were tarnished during the great post-crisis bull market.

Since 2008, investors reluctantly but steadily increased their investments in risk assets theoretically capable of providing higher returns like stocks, junk bonds, venture capital, and real estate. This was the result of policies that drove interest rates down to zero, rendering fixed income investments unattractive. But now they face years of low returns on risk assets because the Federal Reserve cannot suppress interest rates forever. Either the economy will begin to grow at better than 2 percent, which would lead interest rates to rise and pressure the value of financial assets, or the economy will continue to struggle and keep interest rates low and depress returns on financial assets. The third scenario, the so-called

"Goldilocks" world in which the economy grows just enough to keep markets and financial assets afloat, is highly unlikely since a significant amount of post-crisis growth and investment gains were based on debt that is becoming harder for companies and governments to service. Goldilocks will end up being devoured by the bears and it won't be a fairy tale.

Stocks have been trading at the upper end of historical valuation ranges since 2013. After they finally experienced their first 10 percent correction in four years in August 2015, they were still trading above historical mean valuations and certain sectors such as social media and biotechnology stocks remained in bubble territory. The high yield credit markets, which were approximately $2.35 billion size at the end of 2014 ($1.5 billion in bonds, $850 billion in bank loans), were heading toward a period of higher defaults and lower returns in the 2016–2019 period as it became clear that the post-crisis credit boom reached its limits in late 2014. In other words, neither stocks nor bonds are likely to offer investors attractive risk-adjusted nominal or real returns over the next few years. Even more significant, commodity prices began to collapse in mid-2014 as a result of two factors: (1) the rise in the U.S. dollar; and (2) a slowing global economy driven by a sharp slowdown in China and other emerging markets. Commodities were sending a signal that the post-crisis recovery in global growth was stalling, causing serious problems for investors.

This has led many investors to invest in what are called "alternative strategies" that take many different forms. What these strategies generally have in common—or are supposed to have in common—is the ability to generate attractive risk-adjusted returns regardless of the performance of the stock or bond markets. These strategies are offered by mutual funds, ETFs, and hedge funds as well as by money managers in managed accounts. Many of these strategies require an investor to commit capital for a long period of time and to sacrifice liquidity. Strategies such as private equity and hedge funds (provided they charge reasonable fees) can be attractive, but only a minority of managers of these strategies generate consistently attractive risk-adjusted returns, as I discussed in Chapter 6 with respect to the returns of the private equity industry. There is a limited number of talented managers who can deliver the types of returns that investors will need to survive in the years ahead; but you have to be able to identify them and perform the proper due diligence on their strategies and businesses.

The institutionalization of the alternative investment space has predictably resulted in the compression of investment returns. Institutions impose limitations on managers in the name of controlling risk that often hamper the ability of truly talented managers to generate high returns. Sadly, the people performing this due diligence often lack the qualifications to do so since they never managed money themselves. The days of being able to "pig out" on great investment ideas, as the legendary investor Stanley Druckenmiller famously advises, are over except in rare circumstances where investors are willing to trust a manager to use his or her judgment to generate true alpha. With 10,000 hedge funds now in existence, only a small number are deserving of such trust. The by-product of an increasingly overcrowded and institutionalized industry is significantly lower returns.

Investors need to be extremely selective in choosing alternative managers and must learn how to properly measure risk-adjusted returns. Risk-adjusted returns adjust nominal returns for factors such as leverage, position concentration, fees, liquidity, and similar factors. As noted in Chapter 6 in the discussion regarding private equity returns, nominal returns are often far less attractive than risk-adjusted returns because managers are taking enormous risks to generate those returns. If a strategy requires high amounts of leverage, for example, it is much riskier than a strategy that does not require leverage. Investors need to understand precisely what risks their managers are taking to generate their returns, particularly in the alternatives and hedge fund spaces where many absolute return strategies are offered.

The key to any absolute return strategy is that it not depend on the stock market moving in a particular direction. A long-only strategy, for example, requires a rising stock market to flourish while a short-selling strategy needs the opposite. While there are many different types of absolute return strategies, all of them generally share the ability to go both "long" and "short" the market. The most popular type are "long-short" equity strategies that are really just stock-picking strategies that are only as good as the manager executing them. During the bull market that began in 2009, most "long-short" managers were forced into becoming "long-only" managers since shorting stocks became extremely unprofitable. And it is no secret that active managers of all sorts employing these strategies failed to keep up with a raging S&P 500 as well as other benchmarks during the post-crisis bull market and began losing serious

The Third Friday Total Return Fund, L.P.

The Third Friday Total Return Fund, L.P. is an absolute return hedge fund available to accredited investors managed by the author.

Third Friday employs a disciplined strategy of selling at-the-money S&P 500 index option straddles on a rolling three-month basis and hedging them with out-of-the-money puts and calls. A straddle is a simultaneous put and call. A put is a bet that the index will drop in value while a call is a bet that the index will rise in value.

Because the fund sells puts and calls simultaneously, it is taking a market neutral position and its returns are not dependent on whether the stock market rises or falls. It extracts returns from the time value embedded in options and from the volatility of the market, characteristics that are always present regardless of market direction. The fund invests its underlying collateral in a diversified portfolio of low-risk income generating assets.

From inception in May 2007 through December 31, 2015, Third Friday generated an annualized return of +7.86 percent compared to +2.75 percent for the HFRI Composite Hedge Fund Index and +6.41 percent for the S&P 500. This includes a +0.12 percent return in 2008 when most funds and the S&P 500 suffered large losses. The fund's Sharpe Ratio, an important risk metric, is 1.18 above. These returns are audited by RSM U.S. LLP through December 31, 2014. Past performance is no guarantee of future performance.

Third Friday generates equity returns with low volatility despite using no leverage. It maintains a cash balance at all times of at least 30 percent of assets. Unlike many absolute return strategies and hedge funds, Third Friday is extremely liquid and offers attractive redemption terms to investors. These characteristics mean that the fund's risk-adjusted returns rank among the best in the industry.

Readers can obtain more information on Third Friday at www.thethirdfriday.com. This description should not be construed as an offering of securities or a solicitation to purchase any security.

money when the bull market ended in 2015. If a fund is "long-only" but charging performance fees (i.e., a management fee plus a performance fee), it is taking unfair advantage of its clients. Only strategies that truly hedge or require a unique skill should be charging performance fees because those are the only strategies that will protect investors from catastrophic losses in a bear market and generate consistent and attractive risk-adjusted returns net of fees over long periods of time.

Investors are well-served by searching out truly unique strategies such as the Third Friday Total Return Fund, L.P. that I manage and is described in the box on page 351. Third Friday's investment strategy was developed over a 20-year period and has successfully weathered several market cycles. At the risk of talking my book, there may be 10,000 hedge funds but there are only a handful with track records and pedigrees comparable to Third Friday's. On a risk-adjusted basis, Third Friday's returns rank among the best in the hedge fund world.

Equities

Investors should have 20 percent of their portfolio invested in stocks. This is lower than the traditional allocation recommended by financial advisors, but the return prospects for equities over the next decade are poor. Furthermore, many absolute return strategies will include additional exposure to equities, so the 20 percent figure is not as low as it appears on its face.

If equity exposure takes the form of index products (such as an S&P 500 mutual fund or ETF), investors should treat it as a "buy and hold" investment and should not attempt to trade it. Over long periods of time, equities should continue to generate high single digit total rates of return (consisting of capital gains plus dividends). As David Rosenberg of Gluskin Sheff & Associates, Inc. teaches, it is time "in" the market rather than "timing" the market that generates solid long-term equity returns. Individuals holding specific stocks need to employ disciplined buy and sell strategies that include stop loss limits to prevent outsized losses in specific stocks and sectors. Investors who failed to employ such strategies with respect to energy stocks and master limited partnerships suffered catastrophic losses between mid-2014 and late 2015 after oil dropped by more than 60 percent. Many of these stocks dropped by as much as 80 percent during that period. There is no reason to buy-and-hold stocks in the face of those types of declines.

As noted above, two of the most highly respected strategists in the investment world, Rob Arnott at Performance Analytics and Jeremy Grantham at Grantham Mayo van Otterloo (GMO), are forecasting that stocks are likely to produce extremely low returns over the next 7–10 years.

As of December 31, 2015, GMO's 7-year real (i.e., inflation-adjusted) return forecasts are the following compared to the 6.5 percent long-term historical return for U.S. equities:[2]

U.S. Large Cap	−1.8%
U.S. Small Cap	0.1%
U.S. High Quality	0.1%
International Large Cap	0.3%
International Small Cap	−1.2%
Emerging Markets	4.0%

Performance Analytics had similar 10-year real return projections as of mid-year 2015:[3]

S&P 500	1.1%
Russell 2000	0.5%
MSCI EAFE (International)	5.3%
MSCI Emerging Markets	7.9%

Both firms forecast that only non-U.S. equities are likely to generate meaningful returns over the next decade, and even those returns are relatively muted.

The post-crisis bull market was only partially the result of a recovery in corporate profits from the 2009 recession; the primary contributors to stock gains were unprecedented central bank liquidity operations and massive financial engineering conducted by Corporate America. Since 2009, U.S. corporations have repurchased more than $2 trillion of their own stock. For the 454 companies listed continuously on the S&P 500 between 2004 and 2013, stock buybacks consumed 51 percent of net income and dividends accounted for an additional 35 percent, leaving only 14 percent for other purposes such as research and development and construction of new plants and facilities and capital expenditures. This was a sharp break with earlier periods; in 1981, buybacks only accounted for

2 percent of the S&P 500's total net income, rising to 25 percent in the 1984–1993 period for the 248 firms continuously listed in the S&P 500 and 37 percent in 1994–2003. Between 2004 and 2013, some of the country's best known corporations such as IBM returned more than 100 percent of their income to shareholders in the form of stock buybacks and dividends, leveraging up their balance sheets with cheap debt in the process.[4]

While defenders of stock buybacks argue that they are done when management deems their shares to be undervalued, companies repeatedly buy more stock as the price rises. The primary reason buybacks are done is because they increase short-term share prices, enrich management, and give short-term oriented investors what they want. They feed the fiduciary culture discussed in Chapter 8 that privileges short-term thinking without taking into account the long-term costs of sacrificing capital that could be spent on productivity-enhancing investments rather than on buying back increasingly overvalued stock. Laurence Fink, chairman of Blackrock, the world's largest investment manager, sent the correct message to the leaders of the Fortune 500 in 2014 when he wrote them that "in the wake of the financial crisis, many companies have shied away from investing in the future growth of their companies" by reducing capital expenditures and research and development in order to return capital to shareholders. This trend has only been exacerbated by the pressure by activist shareholders.

It is unrealistic to expect that central banks and corporations will be able to continue supporting stock prices over the next few years as robustly as they have since the financial crisis. The Federal Reserve terminated quantitative easing in October 2014 (although its history of policy mistakes suggests that it could begin buying bonds again at any time and theoretically could toy with negative interest rates if economic or market conditions deteriorate badly enough). Corporations are also reaching the limits of their ability to borrow money to buy back stock and will need to manage their balance sheets and replenish their capital stocks in order to remain competitive globally.

As noted earlier, Société Générale strategist Andrew Lapthorne has shown that net corporate debt was 40 percent higher in mid-2014 than in 2007 but has been disguised by low interest rates,[5] demonstrating that the ability to keep borrowing unlimited amounts of money to return capital to shareholders is reaching its limits. Based on these factors and elevated late 2015 stock valuations, the 7–10 year outlook for equity returns is unattractive, which is why I am only recommending a 20 percent weighting rather than the much higher weightings that most investment strategists suggest.

As noted above, even after the first stock market correction in four years in August 2015, certain long-term valuation measures suggested that the market was significantly overvalued. After the sell-off, the S&P 500 Market Capitalization/GDP Ratio, about which Warren Buffett has spoken favorably, was 1.14x compared to a historical average of 0.75x. The Shiller Cyclically Adjusted Price Earnings Ratio, which measures the market over a rolling 10-year period, was trading at 24.7x compared to a historical average of 16.6x. Returns in the periods after markets reach such heights tend to be disappointing.

One issue that receives less attention than it should but points to the market being even more overvalued than it looks is that the quality of earnings has deteriorated in recent years as companies employ various accounting tricks to inflate their earnings. This subject receives virtually no attention from Wall Street analysts or the financial media. For example, companies increase their reported earnings by so-called "non-GAAP" adjustments that include non-recurring or non-cash charges that distort cash earnings. In addition, earnings are inflated by the massive stock buybacks described above, by artificially low interest rates, and by favorable stock option accounting. On a cash basis, most corporations are earning far less than their reported earnings. By any reasonable measure, the overall stock market remained extremely expensive in late 2015 after its first correction in four years while certain sectors—social media, Internet, and biotech stocks—were solidly in bubble territory. For that reason, it is prudent to limit portfolios to only 20 percent equity exposure until valuations improve markedly.

There may be opportunities in non-U.S. equity markets, however, such as Europe and Japan, that will benefit from cheaper currencies. But betting on markets that are going to rise because their currencies are being hollowed out by cheaper money is a dangerous game best left to professionals.

Japan, for example, could see its stocks rally due to several factors. First, the government has no choice but to continue to weaken the yen in order to deal with Japan's terminal debt and demographic challenges. A cheaper yen will boost Japan's export businesses. Second, Japan's corporations became very competitive globally as a result of having to operate with an expensive currency for so many years. As a result, they are poised to generate strong profits if they can sell more of their goods under a weak currency regime. Third, corporate governance in Japan is finally starting to improve and recognize the rights of shareholders to a greater extent, rendering the country far more hospitable to foreign investors than ever before. Japan faces significant challenges but its stock markets could provide strong returns over the next decade. Investors should be sure to hedge their yen exposure when they invest in Japanese stocks.

India is another market that offers a great deal of promise due to attractive demographics, a reform-minded prime minister and a progressive central bank president.

These Asian markets are more attractive than Europe, which should benefit from a weaker currency like Japan but faces major debt burdens and continues to struggle to enact meaningful labor and regulatory reforms. Further, the European banking sector remains plagued by capital shortfalls and massive bad debts that could pose systemic risks in the near future. The Euro remains a straitjacket for weaker southern European countries like Spain, Italy, and Portugal that will retard their recovery and likely lead to further debt crises in the years ahead.

Income-Generating Securities

With interest rate sensitive instruments unattractive, investors are forced to look for alternatives to generate income. Other parts of our model portfolio will provide income, including dividend-paying stocks and absolute return strategies. The types of investments that should be made to generate income directly are comprised of the following:

1. Bank loans.
2. Closed-end mutual funds and mortgage REITs trading at a discount to NAV and paying high dividends.
3. Event-driven high yield bonds, bank loans, and convertible bonds.

Bank loans are floating rate, senior in the corporate capital structure and collateralized by a variety of assets. They generate returns in the mid-to-high single digits (and in certain cases higher); unfortunately, they are generally only available to institutional investors. There are mutual funds and ETFs that provide individual investors with access to these loans but investors should choose carefully based on the manager and his or her long-term track record.

Closed-end fixed income mutual funds and mortgage REITs can be attractive if they trade at a discount to the net asset value of the fund. This means that the fund can be purchased at a lower price than the value of the securities owned by the fund and that it is likely paying a high dividend. Such funds can generate high single digit to low double digit returns. Investors can benefit from the high yield and the closing of the gap between the value of the fund and the value of the underlying assets.

Event-driven high yield bonds, loans, and convertible bonds are expected to be refinanced at par or at a call premium prior to maturity. The universe of event-driven bonds and loans shrunk steadily between the end of the financial crisis and early 2015 but was growing again in late 2015. Event-driven bonds and loans are often stressed or distressed and need to be refinanced in order to give a borrower relief from financial pressures such as an imminent debt maturity, covenant violations, or similar issues. In contrast to run-of-the-mill high yield bonds that are generally bought by "buy and hold" investors, event-driven bonds have short (1–2 years) to intermediate (3–4 years) durations (duration measures a bond's sensitivity to changes in interest rates). As the high yield credit markets heads into a likely period of higher defaults in 2016-2019, there will be greater opportunities to invest in event-driven situations. As always, it will require an experienced and skilled manager to navigate these complex investments.

I do not recommend investments in long-dated investment grade bonds or Treasury securities. Not only are the yields on these securities extremely low—offering minimal-to-negative real (inflation-adjusted returns)—but there is a significant chance that rising inflation will cause interest rates to rise over their life and trap investors with large mark-to-market losses. The Federal Reserve has succeeded in destroying the value of fixed income investments for years to come. The income-generating investments I have suggested offer sound alternatives until something better comes along.

Conclusion

The next few years are going to be one of those periods when investors would do well to worry more about the return *of* their money than the return *on* their money. But that doesn't mean they should throw up their hands and give up. Many investors will do extremely well in the difficult environment that is likely to persist in the coming years if they keep their wits about them and resist the advice offered by the financial media and Wall Street. These sources of investment advice consistently lead investors over the cliff and into shark-infested waters. Investors will do fine if they keep their eye on the ball, listen to people who are interested in telling the truth rather than currying favor with the media or the consensus, and focus on what is really going on in the economy and the world. The world is reaching a tipping point in terms of its ability to suffer the fools who have been guiding its monetary and fiscal policies. All you have to do is look around to see the consequences of their mistakes and realize that you can follow them and be a victim or you can think for yourself and save yourself and your family from their incompetence. The choice is yours.

Conclusion: "This Is Later"

On April 16, 2007, the American novelist Cormac McCarthy was awarded the Pulitzer Prize for his novel *The Road*. *The Road* is an unbearably painful tale of a father and son, among the last survivors on the planet, traveling an American landscape that has been rendered a post-apocalyptic charnel house by a nuclear conflagration. Their love is that last fragment of human feeling remaining in a world destroyed by hatred and war. Technologically advanced man has left behind a gray and ruined landscape. When men of good will do not stand up and fight the forces of evil, stupidity, and complacency, it leaves the world looking like this:

> In those first years the roads were peopled with refugees shrouded up in their clothing. Wearing masks and goggles, sitting in their rags by the side of the road like ruined aviators. Their barrows heaped with shoddy. Towing wagons or carts. Their eyes bright in their skulls. Creedless shells of men tottering down the causeways like migrants in a feverland. The frailty of everything revealed at last. Old and troubling issues resolved into nothingness and night. The last instance of a thing takes the class with it. Turns out the light and is gone. Look around you. Ever is a long time. But the boy knew what he knew. That ever is no time at all.[1]

Two and a half years later, in December 2009, the film version of the novel was released. In bringing this bleak and complex novel to film, the producers reportedly had a difficult time identifying shooting locations. In the end, however, they didn't have to travel far from the American heartland. Most of the film was shot near Pittsburgh, Pennsylvania. As one of the film's producers explained to *Rolling Stone* magazine, Pennsylvania was chosen because "it offered such a pleasing array of post-apocalyptic scenery: deserted coalfields, run-down parts of Pittsburgh, windswept dunes."[2] Today, scenes like this can be found throughout the Middle East, the Ukraine, and Africa where war rages out of the sight of affluent and narcissistic Westerners who can't see beyond the selfies on their iPhones.

Half a decade after the worst financial crisis since the Great Depression, markets have recovered on the back of trillions of dollars of debt that were created out of thin air to superficially heal them. As is typical of the recoveries that follow debt crises, economic growth has been disappointing. A small elite flourished while the politically disenfranchised fell further behind. The political and economic elite keeps trying to preserve the system that favors them at the expense of everyone else. But it is increasingly obvious that this system, which is based on debt rather than equity and favors speculation rather than productive investment, is unsustainable. At home, new entitlements were created and the eligibility requirements of old entitlements were lowered to create a culture of dependency, resentment, and division. The only way to pay for this culture is higher taxes on the most productive members of society. Regulatory efforts to strengthen the financial system missed the mark and left a more fragile and concentrated financial system in their wake. Powerful financial interests were able to derail meaningful derivatives reforms and academic economists were able to steer monetary policy into a trap. The economy's DNA, the U.S. tax system, continues to create incentives for U.S. businesses to move their most valuable assets abroad and for individuals and corporations to borrow as much money as possible, creating a debt-financed economy that sooner or later will collapse under its own weight. Policy could not be more misguided if it were plotted by our enemies.

The U.S. economy is far more fragile than it appears on the surface because it is built on a foundation of debt that is sapping intellectual and financial capital away from productive uses. As a result of Dodd-Frank, the financial system is populated by a smaller number of "too big to save" institutions that are nominally less leveraged than they were in 2007 but sit on top of hundreds of trillions of dollars of derivatives contracts that have the potential to blow up the global financial system in the blink of an eye. Only hubris or denial allows the individuals who manage these institutions and the officials who regulate them to deny the risk posed by these instruments of mass financial destruction. As investors smugly cling for dear life to their inflated 401K statements, they should pray that their delusions about the state of the world can persist in the face of the risks that are building under the surface. But when their investments melt away in their hands, so will their delusions.

The situation is particularly unsustainable in a world where America has abandoned its global leadership role and created a vacuum for its enemies to pose existential threats to itself and its allies. The world is a much more dangerous place today than during the financial crisis. Noxious forces that were festering for years in the Middle East, Asia, and Eastern Europe/Russia burst out into the open at the first sign of American weakness. The Obama administration's failed foreign policy allowed these forces to destabilize the world.

In 2008, the world wasn't facing the threat of ISIS, America wasn't dealing with homegrown terrorism, Iran was much farther away from achieving nuclear capability, Syria, Iraq, Libya, and Yemen were stable, Russia hadn't invaded Ukraine, and China wasn't aggressively asserting itself in the South China Sea. Today, all of these problems pose serious threats to global and economic stability and the Obama administration has fumbled its handling of every single one of them. While such threats are complex and were in the process of formation long ago, the weak and incompetent American response to them rendered them a clear and present danger.

The media and political elite play a central role in perpetuating these threats. Rather than speak the truth, these groups promote narratives about the state of the world that are superficial, self-serving, and often simply false. On the day that the Senate was voting on the Iran nuclear deal, the most important foreign policy issue in years, the media was focused on an inconsequential personal remark one presidential candidate made about another, a typical example of how the media trivializes the news. The lack of critical thinking applied by most of the media to the work of the Federal Reserve and the foreign policy of the Obama administration gives journalism a bad name and constitutes a profound betrayal of the public. Perhaps it is too much to expect journalists to be experts in the underlying subject matter they are covering, particularly in the financial area where the subject matter requires a modicum of expertise, but then they shouldn't pretend to know what they are talking about. New media blurs the lines between journalism and analysis to the point where too many uninformed people are offering opinions that are treated as authoritative when they are nothing of the sort. When the media fails to take a critical stance toward authority figures, it allows an institution like the Federal Reserve to retain credibility far longer than it deserves. A more informed and critical media might go a long way to improving policy in this country. At the risk of sounding idealistic, I hope there is a market for an informed media in the years ahead; for the most part, we don't have one now.

It should not seem odd to conclude a book on finance with a discussion of the work of Cormac McCarthy. Careful readers of the preceding pages should not find the appearance of one of our greatest living novelists jarring at all. *The Committee to Destroy the World* maintained from the beginning that finance should draw as much from art as science and is intended to serve a larger purpose in the world than a merely economic one. Capital is the lifeblood of society, making it possible for people to eat and be sheltered and learn and heal. Only after people fill these needs can they begin to appreciate the beauty and love that life offers instead of focusing on its struggle and pain. If there is passion in this book, it is because I believe that the forces responsible for the death of capital, if successful, will extinguish the best hope for mankind to move forward and meet the challenges of the future. Those challenges are growing because our leaders are failing. I, for one, will not allow that to happen without speaking out.

Look around at our culture and society. We must be nearing the end of things, the end of something. We are on an unsustainable path of debt and delusion. Debt is growing much faster than the economy. We celebrate when our federal deficit drops—*drops*—to half a trillion dollars a year! Our inner cities are more violent than ever but the mainstream media is afraid to admit that much of the violence is blacks killing other blacks because that irrefutable fact offends the sensibilities of progressives who have failed for more than 50 years to develop solutions to the underlying causes of black-on-black violence. Mass shootings occur around the country on a weekly basis while our politicians cower in fear of the bullies at the NRA, an organization that twists the meaning the Second Amendment to allow the mentally ill to gain easy access to guns, private parties to sell guns without conducting a background check, and overgrown children to purchase weapons of war. Our education system has been hijacked by teachers unions run by incompetents and the forces of political correctness who are destroying our universities in the name of protecting students' feelings from the very intellectual and moral challenges that are the gravamen of liberal education. Government intrusion and technology are debauching privacy and eradicating individual integrity and autonomy. The stock market may have recovered and the economy climbed out of recession, but life in America and around the world fell apart before our very eyes.

Regardless of the narcissism of technology, which is reinforced by breathless and uncritical media coverage, Facebook and Apple are not going to save us if we don't get a lot smarter, a lot tougher, and a lot more courageous in standing up to the forces of political correctness, narcissism, and short-term thinking. Mr. McCarthy could have been writing the coda for our last days when he wrote in the voice of the father in *The Road*: "No list of things to be done. The day providential to itself. The hour. There is no later. This is later. All things of grace and beauty such that one holds them to one's heart have a common provenance in pain. Their birth in grief and ashes. So he whispered to the boy. I have you."[3] The father perishes in McCarthy's tale, and the son is left to carry on without him. While bereft, the son is fortified by the memory of his father's love and the words that they shared as they struggled on the road together, trying to survive the wreckage that other men wrought.

We too have been abandoned by our leaders. They fail and betray us at every turn. We cannot count on anybody else to save us. We are going to have to save ourselves.

Seven years ago, it was not too late to make the necessary changes to stabilize our financial system against instability, avarice, and stupidity. It is still not too late but time is running out, particularly with respect to the uncontrollable debt burdens that are suffocating economic growth.

In the novelist's words: "There is no later. This is later." At the heart of every discussion about finance lies a simple truth: Without a functioning and stable economy, civilization will ultimately fall into barbarism and chaos. That is the undeniable and redundant lesson of history.

The Jewish-German philosopher Walter Benjamin, who committed suicide at the Spanish border in 1940 rather than surrender to the Nazis, set a very high standard for critical thought when he wrote the following: "In every era the attempt must be made anew to wrest tradition away from a conformism that is about to overpower it....Only that historian will have the gift of fanning the spark of hope in the past who is firmly convinced that *even the dead* will not be safe from the enemy if he wins. And this enemy has not ceased to be victorious."[4] In 2008, we met the enemy—and that enemy was us. We survived that crisis (barely) by printing trillions of dollars of debt, but that just delayed the day of reckoning because we failed to take the steps necessary to set the global economy on a sustainable growth trajectory. And while we were failing to fix our economy and remaining our own worst enemies, new enemies materialized out of the turmoil that was boiling under the surface of the Middle East, Asia, and Eastern Europe. These blood enemies now pose a direct threat to both the dead and the living and wishing them away with phony treaties that aren't worth the paper they are written on leaves the world on the brink of new conflicts that can't be extinguished by the printing presses of central banks or the arrogant delusions of former community organizers.

It is the undeniable lesson of history that the human species requires economic well-being in order to keep from destroying itself. The competition for scarce energy and water resources is intensifying among the great powers but the losers will be those whose economies are most heavily impaired by debt and demographics. The most compelling reason to build a robust financial system—for pragmatists as well as moralists—is to ensure that society continues to move forward in a manner that improves human life on this planet for all people, not just a small elite that continues to fool itself into believing that it will be able to defend itself against the leagues of sufferers when they rush the ramparts.

This book has harsh words for many of the established ideas and institutions that control the world's capital. These words are deeply felt but offered in the spirit of the great Romantic poet William Blake's adage, "Opposition is true friendship." But make no mistake. We must loudly condemn and challenge business and political leaders who put their own interests before those of our country and its citizens. We are appeasing our enemies abroad and creating a culture of debt and dependency at home. We cling to faulty financial theories, invest in unproductive strategies that enrich money managers but impoverish investors, and refuse to adopt the pro-growth monetary and fiscal policies so desperately needed to enhance the quality of human life on our planet. Karl Marx never wrote what comes in history's third act, after tragedy and farce. We still have a chance to write that it ends in triumph if we start taking bold action now. But we are running out of time.

NOTES

Introduction

1. McKinsey Global Institute, "Debt and (Not Much) Deleveraging," February 2015, 9. In view of the opacity of China's economic statistics, the country's debt could well be much higher. No doubt it is higher than the 2014 figure of $28 trillion as this book comes to press.

2. The federal deficit was $10.6 trillion on the day Barack Obama took office in January 2009. By April 12, 2015, it had increased to $18.152 trillion.

3. Office of the Federal Register, "Federal Register Pages Published 1936–2013," https://www.federalregister.gov/uploads/2014/04/OFR-STATISTICS-CHARTS-ALL1-1-1-2013.pdf. These statistics are cited in Mark R. Levin, *Plunder and Deceit: Big Government's Exploitation of Young People and the Future* (New York: Threshold Editions, 2015), 171.

4. Office of the Federal Register, "Federal Register Pages Published 1936–2013," https://www.federalregister.gov/uploads/2014/04/OFR-STATISTICS-CHARTS-ALL1-1-1-2013.pdf.

5. See "The Committee to Destroy the World," *The Credit Strategist*, April 1, 2015.

6. At least English professors study human nature for a living. Human nature, not the soft science of economics, was the decisive factor guiding the economy after the financial crisis. Economic actors saw low interest rates as a sign that the economy was floundering and reacted by limiting their economic activity, behavior that escaped the rigid and outmoded models of the Federal Reserve's economists.

7. One had to shudder listening to Fed apologists like former PIMCO economist Paul McCulley appear on CNBC in August 2015 and proclaim that the Fed should "declare victory" and "take a victory lap" with respect to policies that had failed in virtually every respect. Other than preventing a total meltdown of the financial system in 2008 (which their policies led to), these policies have been abject failures. They distorted markets, destroyed liquidity, increased wealth inequality, failed to produce the type of inflation they desired while grotesquely inflating asset prices, failed to promote genuine employment growth (the labor participation rate in 2015 was at its lowest level since the 1970s), and contributed to the largest misallocation of capital in history through the largest debt buildup in history. Federal Reserve governors routinely make public statements demonstrating their total ignorance of how the real economy works while cowering in fear of the markets. They don't trust markets and neither do their apologists. Rather than declaring victory, they and their cheerleaders should be hanging their heads in shame. The intellectual failures of policymakers and those who pimp for them in the media and on Wall Street have inflicted enormous damage on this country and its economy.

8. Hyman Minsky, *Stabilizing an Unstable Economy* (New Haven, CT: Yale University Press, 1986), 3.

9. Some economists like Paul Krugman have argued that the stimulus plan was not large enough. The size of the stimulus plan was less important than the substance. A larger bill that failed to direct money into productive investments would have been no more successful than the plan that was adopted.

10. In the first opinion, *National Federation of Independent Business v. Sibelius* (2012), Justice Roberts ruled that the word "penalty" really meant "tax" to rescue the law, in the process ignoring the long history of jurisprudence that establishes different definitions of the two words. In the second opinion, *King v. Burwell* (2015), Justice Roberts ruled that the term "Exchange established by the State" really meant "Exchange established by the State or the Federal Government" despite the fact that the words "or the Federal Government" were nowhere written in the law and the legislative history clearly showed that Congress intended the law to require states rather than the federal government to set up the exchanges in question. The language was not a drafting error as intellectually dishonest proponents of the law tried to argue in the press and to the Court. These two opinions usurped the legislative function and constituted nothing other than judicial lawmaking and a clear violation of the separation of powers under the Constitution.

11. While there has been endless debate about the efficacy of quantitative easing, even the Federal Reserve's own economists concluded that it has failed in its stated goals. See, for example, Stephen D. Williamson, "Current Federal Reserve Policy Under the Lens of Economic History: A Review Essay,"

Federal Reserve Bank of St. Louis, Working Paper Series, July 2015, http:// research.stlouisfed.org/wp/2015/2015-015.pdf. Mr. Williamson is a Vice President at the Federal Reserve Bank of St. Louis and concludes in this paper that, "There is no work, to my knowledge, that establishes a link from QE to the ultimate goals of the Fed inflation and real economic activity. Indeed, casual evidence suggests that QE has been ineffective in increasing inflation. For example, despite massive central bank asset purchases in the U.S., the Fed is currently falling short of its 2 percent inflation target. Further, Switzerland and Japan, which have balance sheets that are much larger than that of the U.S., relative to GDP, have been experiencing very low inflation or deflation." Of course, it is difficult to determine who is more confused, the Federal Reserve or Mr. Williamson since inflation in the real world is much higher than official inflation statistics suggest and inflation in financial asset prices has skyrocketed as a result of QE. The bottom line is that as long as we leave our fate in the hands of economists, our gooses are cooked. The real problem is that central bankers don't trust markets; the world would be much better off if they stopped interfering in them and allowed markets to operate freely.

12. Irving Fisher, *The Money Illusion*, (New York: Adelphi Company, 1929).

13. European debt traders recklessly traded ahead of ECB purchases of bonds, pushing interest rates into unsustainable territory and setting themselves up for huge losses just a few weeks later when markets began to come to their senses. Several weeks before Bill Gross made his well-publicized recommendation to short German bunds, I recommended in a *Real Vision TV* interview and in *The Credit Strategist* that investors sell short all of the long-dated European sovereign and corporate debt on which they could get their hands. See *The Credit Strategist*, April 1, 2015. As of the end of 2015, that still remained my recommendation.

14. Christopher Whalen, "Central Banks, Credit Expansion, and the Importance of Being Impatient," Kroll Bond Rating Agency, March 20, 2015.

15. In Europe, there is an even bigger risk in entrusting one's money to banks. As the citizens of Cyprus learned, their savings can be confiscated by the government. This calls into question the integrity of the banking and the financial system and the very tenets on which society is organized and is almost certain to lead to social unrest and violence.

16. Luigi Buttiglioni, Philip R. Lane, Lucrezia Reichlin, and Vincent Reinhart, "Deleveraging? What Deleveraging?" Geneva Reports on the World Economy, Centre for Economic Policy Research, International Center for Monetary and Banking Studies, September 2014, 1–2.

17. Ibid., 2.

18. Ibid.

19. McKinsey, "Debt and (Not Much) Deleveraging," vi.

20. Dr. Philippa Malmgren, *Signals: The Breakdown of the Social Contract and the Rise of Geopolitics* (London: Grosvenor House Publishing Limited, 2015), 325.

21. Bank for International Settlements, *BIS Quarterly Review*, June 2015, p. 4; Bank for International Settlements, Derivatives Statistics, June 8, 2015, Table 19, www.bis.org/statistics/derstats.htm.

22. Ibid., 5.

23. Ibid.

24. David Enrich, Jenny Strasburg and Eyk Henning, "Deutsche Bank Suffers From Litany of Reporting Problems, Regulators Said," *The Wall Street Journal*, July 22, 2014.

25. James Rickards, *Currency Wars: The Making of the Next Global Crisis* (New York: Penguin, 2011), 210.

26. Francis Fukuyama, *Trust: The Social Virtues and the Creation of Prosperity* (New York: The Free Press, 1995), 26.

27. "Transparency" is one of those terms that regulators like to use to impress their political bosses that they know what they are doing. The problem with "transparency" when applied to derivatives is that there are very few regulators with the requisite expertise to understand what they are looking at when the curtain is pulled back on these complex financial instruments. Just because regulators are provided with a mountain of data on derivatives does not mean that they possess the ability to understand the information with which they are being provided. In fact, we can virtually depend on the fact that they do not. This is something that the decision makers who decided to leave derivatives in the hands of regulators after the crisis failed to understand.

28. Source: Bank of International Settlements, *Quarterly Review*, September 2014, Statistical Annex; "Foreign Exchange and Derivatives Market Activity in 2007," Bank for International Settlements Triennial Central Bank Survey, December 2007. In November 2014, it was reported that Deutsche Bank was sharply reducing its trading in "single name" credit default swaps relating to individual sovereign issues and U.S. and European companies. Katy Burne and Eyk Henning, "Deutsche Bank Ends Most CDS Trade," *The Wall Street Journal*, November 17, 2014.

29. The Barclays High Yield Index was approximately $1.3 trillion in par amount outstanding in October 2014 while the S&P/LSTA Leveraged Loan Index was approximately $825 billion in mid-December 2014.

30. Only in late 2015, long after the damage was done, did the Justice Department move to adopt formal guidelines designed to foster indictments of individuals responsible for corporate wrongdoing. The new policy, set forth in a memorandum to federal prosecutors from Deputy Attorney General Sally Quillian Yates dated September 9, 2015, states that settlement agreements will not give

companies credit for cooperating with the government unless they turn over evidence against employees involved in wrongdoing.

31. "Financial Crimes: Unfair Cop," *The Economist,* May 23, 2015, 13.

32. Charles Kindleberger, *Manias, Panics and Crashes: A History of Financial Crises* (New York: Basic Books, 1989), 86.

33. Charles Krauthammer, "Are We Alone in the Universe?," *The Washington Post,* December 29, 2011, reprinted in *Things That Matter: Three Decades of Passions, Pastimes and Politics* (New York: Crown Forum, 2013), 129.

34. The National Military Strategy of the United States, June 2015, 2.

35. Thomas Friedman, "A Good Bad Deal," *The New York Times,* July 1, 2015.

36. The National Military Strategy of the United States of America, 2015, 3.

37. Ibid., 2.

38. Ibid.

39. Krauthammer, "Are We Alone in the Universe?," 129.

40. And it's not as though domestic policy has been successful. For a president focused on his political base, Mr. Obama has been a dismal failure. For example, in July 2015, African American youth unemployment was still 31 percent, more than double that of whites. It's sad that Mr. Obama doesn't understand enough about economics to see that his policies are making conditions worse for precisely those he purports to want to help the most.

41. Colin Dueck, *The Obama Doctrine: American Grand Strategy Today* (New York: Oxford University Press, 2015), 105.

Chapter 1

1. Karl Marx, *The Eighteenth Brumaire of Louis Napoleon* (New York: International Publishers, 1972), 15. Actually, what he wrote was the following: "Hegel remarks somewhere that all facts and personages of great importance in world history occur, as it were, twice. He forgot to add: the first time as tragedy, the second as farce."

2. There is a fourth characteristic that receives less attention in this book than it deserves, the fact that the world's economies and financial markets are connected through vast networks in which information is exchanged at the speed of light 24 hours a day. As a result, what happens in one market often has consequences in other markets that are seemingly unrelated and inexplicable in fundamental economic terms. The proverbial anecdote about a butterfly flapping its wings in Africa causing a hurricane in Miami is a reality in modern markets. Because economies and markets function through networks, they generate

both negative and positive feedback loops that tend to significantly increase volatility and risk. This completely redefines key investment concepts such as correlation and diversification as they have been traditionally understood. Today, short-term price movements in securities are primarily the result of so-called "technical" factors, which means that the mechanisms of interlinked markets move prices in ways that can only be understood in terms of the structural logic of these markets and not in terms of what is happening to the underlying companies whose securities prices are being affected.

3. A.G. Haldane, S. Brennan, and V. Madouros (2010). "What Is the Contribution of the Financial Sector: Miracle or Mirage?" In R. Ledyard (ed.), *The Future of Finance*. London: London School of Economics and Political Science.

4. The growth of finance is amply supported by statistical evidence. Between 1994 and 2000, the profits earned by the financial sector doubled and accounted for 75 percent of the increase in total corporate profits after payment of interest accrued. By 2000, financial profits accounted for 40 percent of total corporate profits. Even during the recession of the early 2000s, these profits came to constitute as much as 50 percent of total corporate profits, according to Morgan Stanley. See Steve Galbraith et al., "Bank of America" and "Fading Fog" in Morgan Stanley's *U.S. and the Americas Investment Research*, June 21, 2001 and September 21, 2003, respectively.

5. Lawrence E. Mitchell, *The Speculation Economy: How Finance Triumphed over Industry* (San Francisco: Berrett-Koehler Publishers, 2007), 3. Mitchell's thesis is that "[t]he giant modern corporation was a phenomenon distinct from the forms and processes of industrialization.... The giant modern corporation was created for a new purpose, to sell stock, stock that would make its promoters and financiers rich" (9).

6. Ibid., 3.

7. Charles Kindleberger, *Manias, Panics and Crashes: A History of Financial Crises*, rev. ed. (New York: Basic Books, 1989), 19.

8. Unfortunately, these mathematical trading models turned out to do little more than dress up a variety of momentum-driven leveraged investment strategies. They tell us little about how real-world markets behave. Benoit Mandelbrot, the mathematician who founded fractal theory, calculated that if the DJIA followed a normal bell curve distribution, it should have moved by more than 3.4 percent on 58 days between 1913 and 2003; instead it moved by that amount on 1,001 days. It should have moved by 4.5 percent on six days but moved that amount on 366 days. And it should have moved by more than 7 percent only once in 300,000 years but in the twentieth century did so 48 times. Source: *The Economist*, "A Special Report on the Future of Finance," January 24, 2009, 14.

9. Robin Blackburn, "The Subprime Crisis," *New Left Review* 50 (March/April 2008): 67.

10. Ok, this differential was narrowed when the tax on corporate dividends was lowered by President George W. Bush.

11. See Thomas I. Palley, "Financialization: What It Is and Why It Matters," The Levy Economics Institute of Bard College, Working Paper No. 525, December 2007, 4.

12. The Obama administration, however, attempted to change the shareholder focus of fiduciary law in 2015 by having its Labor Department issue Interpretive Bulletin 2015-01 telling pension funds to include climate change among the factors to use when choosing investments. This is discussed further in Chapter 8, but suffice it to say here that it is highly inappropriate for the government to be dictating the types of investments that pension funds should be making. Interpretive Bulletin 2015-01 is part of the Obama administration's broad agenda to fight climate change without regard to the economic costs of doing so. Carried to its logical extreme, the bulletin could prevent funds from investing in companies involved in vast swathes of the economy including energy, utilities, industrials, and autos.

13. A third manifestation of this changed world, which would play itself out most publicly and painfully in the slow-motion meltdown of the U.S. automobile industry in the first years of the twenty-first century, was the increasing flexibility of global labor markets. By 2008, labor markets had grown much more flexible than they were two decades earlier, and organized labor had lost much of its power. Labor was subject to temporary contracts, immigration pressures, and off-shoring in ways that emasculated its economic strength. Western manufacturing, particularly in industries like autos and textiles, was decimated as the outsourcing of plants to lower-cost jurisdictions, just-in-time production, and other changes rendered high-cost U.S. and European countries uncompetitive. U.S. labor unions effectively negotiated themselves out of business with their demands for lax work rules and expensive health and pension benefits that helped their members in the short-term but contributed to the bankruptcies of their employers in the long-term. It would not be far off the mark to argue that the approach taken by labor leaders in the United States to try to extract as much as possible for their unions was analogous to the approach adopted by fiduciaries in terms of focusing on maximizing short-term economic gains at the expense of long-term noneconomic interests, with similarly damaging results to the overall economic interests of their constituents. See Chapter 7.

14. Source: Federal Reserve's Flow of Funds data. Of course, these ratios have only grown worse since the financial crisis.

15. The other major economic power that suffers from a comparable debt-to-GDP ratio is Japan, which has been hanging in economic suspended animation for two decades. While the U.S. and Japanese economies are profoundly different, they are also increasingly linked in today's globalized world. The

lesson of Japan should not, therefore, be dismissed. And the trend that country represents is not one the United States wants to follow.

16. Moreover, the currency links between developed countries and developing countries forced both groups to pursue similar expansionary monetary policies in the aftermath of the 2008 financial crisis despite the fact that developed countries were highly indebted, deficit-ridden economies while many developing countries were creditor nations running major surpluses. Post-crisis, this appeared to be creating a series of new bubbles around the world, for instance, in Chinese stock and commodities markets.

17. Consider, for example, the theories that were developed to support the Internet bubble by writers such as George Gilder, Kevin Kelly, Ray Kurzweil, and research analysts such as Mary Meeker and Henry Blodget. See Michael E. Lewitt, "New Math or New Economy? Some Ruminations on the 1999 Stock Market Bubble," *Trusts & Estates* (February 2002).

18. IMF Global Financial Stability Report: Market Developments and Issues, April 2006, 51.

19. Scott Lanman and Steve Matthews, "Greenspan Concedes to 'Flaw' in His Market Ideology," Bloomberg.com (October 23, 2008), www.bloomberg.com/apps/new s?pid=20601087&sid=ah5qh9Up4rIg. See also David Leonhardt, "Greenspan's Mea Culpa," Economix (blog), *The New York Times* (October 23, 2008), http://economix.blogs.nytimes.com/2008/10/23/greenspans-mea-culpa/.

20. Hyman P. Minsky, *Stabilizing an Unstable Economy* (New Haven: Yale University Press, 1986), 250–251.

21. Niall Ferguson, *The War of the Worlds: History's Age of Hatred* (London: Allen Lane, 2006), xli.

22. Ibid., lix. Italics in original.

23. Ibid., lxi–lxii.

24. "The State of Public Finances: Outlook and Medium-Term Policies after the 2008 Crisis," International Monetary Fund (March 6, 2009), www.imf.org/external/np/pp/eng/2009/030609.pdf. I am indebted to Thomas Gallagher of the ISI Group for bringing this chart and its implications to my attention.

25. One of these issues, climate change, became a policy priority during the Obama administration with serious economic consequences that manifested themselves in, among other things, severe damage to the U.S. coal industry and the imposition of strict environmental regulations (often via executive order) limiting carbon emissions that are having a profoundly negative impact on the utilities and the energy industry. It is unfortunate that climate change has been politicized as an issue; the only standard for evaluating such matters should be scientific. Regardless of one's view of the evidence regarding this issue, businesses and governments are already aggressively dealing with it.

Regulators are paying special attention to this issue as well and are requiring extensive disclosures by corporations of the potential impact of climate change on their businesses. Standard & Poor's identifies climate change (along with aging populations) as one of two "global megatrends" that will impact countries' balance sheets over the twenty-first century. The insurance industry is wrestling with the potential impact of higher losses from catastrophic weather events caused by changes in the environment. Investors need to keep climate change on their radar. While they need to focus on the science, they cannot ignore the politics because the latter is already playing in important role in shaping the regulatory responses that are directing impacting business.

Chapter 2

1. The Baltic Dry Index is issued daily by the London-based Baltic Exchange. It "provides an assessment of the price of moving the major raw materials by sea. Taking in 26 shipping routes measured on a time charter and voyage basis, the index covers Handymax, Panamax, and Capesize dry bulk carriers carrying a range of commodities including coal, iron ore, and grain." The Baltic Dry Index is considered to be an accurate barometer of economic activity because dry bulk consists of raw material inputs into the production of intermediate or finished goods such as concrete, electricity, steel, and food. It is also one of the data points to which hedge funds and other influential investors pay a great deal of attention. The Baltic Dry Index collapsed again in late 2015 as global trade slowed sharply, signaling that the post-crisis global economic recovery was in jeopardy.

2. Wealth itself is defined by the *Oxford English Dictionary* as "the condition of being happy and prosperous; well-being" and also "an instance or kind of prosperity; a felicity, blessing," as well as "spiritual well-being" and "prosperity consisting in abundance of possessions; 'worldly goods,' valuable possessions, esp. in great abundance, riches, affluence."

3. This is one reason why my tax reform proposal in Chapter 10 includes the elimination of the capital gains tax break. All capital (including labor) should be taxed at the same tax rate, which means that labor should not be taxed at a higher rate than capital as the tax code currently provides by taxing ordinary income, which is income generated by the sale of labor, at a significantly higher tax rate than capital gains, which is generated by the sale of capital.

4. Capital is not money per se, but money is one form of capital as it is viewed by economic actors exchanging economic values in the economy. Money is itself a highly complex form of capital, but it is only one form of capital. For an extended philosophical discussion of money, see Georg Simmel, *The Philosophy of Money* (1900).

5. See, for example, Craig Karmin, "College Try: Chicago's Stock Sale—How the University's Unloading of $600 Million in Shares Divided Its Managers," *The Wall Street Journal*, August 21, 2009, C1. "The endowment model contained a colossal intellectual error in thinking—that long-term investors don't need short-term liquidity," says Robert Jaegar of BNY Mellon Asset Management.

6. Peter Bernstein, *Capital Ideas: The Improbable Origins of Modern Wall Street* (New York: The Free Press, 1992), 2.

7. Peter Bernstein, *Against the Gods: The Remarkable Story of Risk* (New York: John Wiley & Sons, 1996), 334.

8. See, for example, William A. Fleckenstein with Frederick Sheehan, *Greenspan's Bubbles: The Age of Ignorance at the Federal Reserve* (New York: McGraw Hill, 2008); Peter Hartcher, *Bubble Man: Alan Greenspan and the Missing 7 Trillion Dollars* (New York: W.W. Norton & Company, 2006); Frederick Sheehan, *Panderer to Power: The Untold Story of How Alan Greenspan Enriched Wall Street and Left a Legacy of Recession* (New York: McGraw Hill, 2009). Moreover, despite his now infamous 1996 warning that stock prices had reached levels of "irrational exuberance," often it seemed like Greenspan was looking to the stock market for economic guidance.

9. Peter Bernstein, *Capital Ideas Evolving* (Hoboken, NJ: John Wiley & Sons, 2007), xviii.

10. In its most dangerous form, debt came to be disguised as equity in the form of various types of bonds such as lower rated corporate bonds (junk bonds) and mortgage bonds (subprime and Alt-A mortgage bonds).

Chapter 3

1. Professor Robert Brenner of UCLA has done comprehensive work analyzing corporate profitability (or the lack thereof). See Robert Brenner, *The Boom and the Bubble: The U.S. in the World Economy* (New York: Verso, 2002) and Robert Brenner, *The Economics of Global Turbulence* (New York: Verso, 2006). Professor Brenner's work dispels the myths surrounding U.S. productivity growth and demonstrates that much of the economic expansion of the last two decades has been little more than a mirage.

2. Fernand Braudel, *The Wheels of Commerce: Civilization and Capitalism, 15th–18th Century, Volume II* (New York: Harper & Row, 1982), 28–29. Footnotes omitted.

3. This discussion was heavily influenced by the interpretation of Adam Smith's work found in James Otteson's study, *Adam Smith's Marketplace of Life* (New York: Cambridge University Press, 2002).

4. Adam Smith, *The Wealth of Nations* (New York: Random House, 2000), 15.

5. The famous phrase "invisible hand" appears only once in *The Wealth of Nations* in a discussion of imports: "By preferring the support of domestic to that of foreign industry, he intends only his own security; and by directing that industry in such a manner as its produce may be of the greatest value, he intends only his own gain, and he is in this, as in many other cases, led by an invisible hand to promote an end which was no part of his intention. Nor is it always the worse for the society that it was no part of it. By pursuing his own interest he frequently promotes that of the society more effectually than when he really intends to promote it" (484–485). The phrase also appears in *The Theory of Moral Sentiments* (242) in a section making the dubious argument that the wealthy end up consuming no more than what they need and sharing the rest with the poor: "They [the wealthy] are led by an invisible hand to make nearly the same distribution of the necessaries of life which would have been made had the earth been divided into equal portions among all its inhabitants; and thus, without intending it, without knowing it, advance the interest of the society, and afford means to the multiplication of the species."

6. *The Theory of Moral Sentiments*, 3–4.

7. This statement was included in the second, third, fourth and fifth editions of *The Theory of Moral Sentiments* and excluded from later editions, including some popular modern editions. It can be found on page 152 of the Cambridge Texts in the History of Philosophy edition of Adam Smith, *The Theory of Moral Sentiments*, Knud Haakonssen, editor (New York: Cambridge University Press, 2002).

8. For a thoughtful interpretation of Smith's "impartial spectator," see Otteson, *Adam Smith's Marketplace of Life*, 42–64.

9. Dennis C. Rasmussen, *The Problems and Promise of Commercial Society: Adam Smith's Response to Rousseau* (University Park, PA: The Pennsylvania State University Press, 2008), 114.

10. Ibid., 121.

11. Ibid., 122.

12. Smith, *The Theory of Moral Sentiments*, 206, 207.

13. Ibid., 205.

14. Irving L. Janis, *Groupthink* (Boston: Houghton Mifflin Company, 1982), 10.

15. Smith, *The Theory of Moral Sentiments*, 22.

16. Otteson, *Adam Smith's Marketplace of Life*, 124. Footnotes omitted.

17. Stuart Kauffmann, *At Home in the Universe: The Search for the Laws of Self-Organization and Complexity* (New York: Oxford University Press), 8.

18. Ibid., 15.

19. Ibid.

20. See, for example, Christopher Hitchins, "He's Back: The Current Financial Crisis and the Enduring Relevance of Marx," *The Atlantic* (April 2009): 88–95; Leo Panitch, "Thoroughly Modern Marx," *Foreign Policy* (May/June 2009): 140–45.

21. Francis Wheen, *Marx's Das Kapital: A Biography* (New York: Grove Press, 2006), 4. See also Francis Wheen, *Karl Marx: A Life* (New York: W.W. Norton & Company, 1999), 304–311.

22. See David Harvey, *The Limits to Capital* (New York: Verso, 1999), 20.

23. Karl Marx, *Capital*, Vol. 1 (New York: International Publishers, 1967), 154, 155.

24. Ibid., 154–155.

25. Karl Marx, *Grundrisse* (London: Penguin Books, 1973), 260–261.

26. Marx, *Capital,* Vol. 1, 153.

27. This formulation raises profound questions about the moral values a society places on different kinds of work. For example, why does American society value the work of investment bankers more highly than the work of teachers?

28. Marx, *Capital*, Vol. 1, 72.

29. Ibid.

30. Harvey, *The Limits to Capital*, 17.

31. David Harvey, *The Condition of Postmodernity* (Cambridge, MA: Blackwell Publishers, 1990), 100.

32. Leszek Kolakowski, *Main Currents of Marxism* (New York: W.W. Norton & Company, 2008), 227.

33. Ibid., 227.

34. Marx, *Capital*, Vol. 1, 76.

35. Mark C. Taylor, *Confidence Games Money and Markets in a World without Redemption* (Chicago: University of Chicago Press, 2004), 8.

36. Marx, *Capital*, Vol. 1, 102.

37. Ibid., 196.

38. Ibid., 102.

39. Hyman Minsky, *John Maynard Keynes* (New York: Columbia University Press, 1975), 59.

40. John Maynard Keynes, *The General Theory of Employment, Interest and Money* (New York: Harcourt, Brace & Company, 1964), 158.

41. Ibid.

42. Ibid., 155.

43. Ibid., 156.

44. Ibid., 202.

45. Ibid., 161–62.

46. Ibid., 162–63.

47. Ibid., 37.

48. Ibid., 145.

49. Ibid., 154.

50. Ibid., 155.

51. Minsky, *John Maynard Keynes,* 1.

52. Ibid., 11–12.

53. PIMCO's Paul McCulley deserves credit for being the earliest to bring Minsky's work to a wider audience. During the 1998 Russian debt crisis, McCulley coined the term "Minsky moment" to describe the market meltdown. In December 2004, I wrote in an issue of *The HCM Market Letter* entitled "The Ponzi Museum" that I was "firmly of the view that the credit markets are experiencing a bubble no less overblown than the stock market bubble of 1998–2000." *The HCM Market Letter,* December 21, 2004.

54. Minsky, *Stabilizing an Unstable Economy* (New Haven, CT: Yale University Press, 1986), 206–208.

55. Hyman Minsky, "The Financial-Instability Hypothesis: Capitalist Processes and the Behavior of the Economy," in *Financial Crises Theory, History & Policy,* ed. Charles P. Kindleberger and Jean-Pierre Laffargue (New York: Cambridge University Press, 1982), 25.

56. Minsky in Kindleberger, 37. And in a warning that unfortunately came too late for many investors, Minsky pointed out the risks inherent in many investment structures that involve indefinite entry and exit points: "Incidentally, what in retrospect appears to be a fraudulent operation often has its root in a 'speculative' or 'honest Ponzi' financial arrangement where the 'payoff' is not forthcoming as anticipated. 'Fraud' often is an ex-post result and is not always ex-ante in conception."

57. Ibid., 37.

Chapter 4

1. C.M. Reinhart and K. Rogoff, *This Time is Different: Eight Centuries of Financial Folly* (Princeton, NJ: Princeton University Press, 2009).

2. McKinsey Global Institute, "Debt and (Not Much) Deleveraging," February 2015.

3. Martin Wolf, *Fixing Global Finance* (Baltimore, MD: The Johns Hopkins University Press, 2008), 10–11.

4. Ibid., 12.

5. Diversification is designed to prevent individual securities in a portfolio from acting in a correlated manner. As discussed in Chapter 8, this thesis breaks down in many modern markets due to hidden correlations.

6. Robert J. Shiller, *The Subprime Solution: How Today's Financial Crisis Happened, and What to Do about It* (Princeton, NJ: Princeton University Press, 2008), 22.

7. Peter Bernstein, *Against the Gods: The Remarkable Story of Risk* (New York: John Wiley & Sons, 1996), 334.

8. See Gretchen Morgenson, "If Lenders Say 'The Dog Ate Your Mortgage,'" *The New York Times*, October 25, 2009. Morgenson describes a case that was decided in federal bankruptcy court for the Southern District of New York in which Judge Robert D. Drain ruled that the lender, PHH Mortgage, had failed to prove its claim to a delinquent borrower's home and instead wiped out the $461,263 mortgage on the property.

Chapter 5

1. The limited writings on financialization include Robin Blackburn, "Finance and the Fourth Dimension," *New Left Review* 39 (May/June 2006): 39–70; Gerald A. Epstein, ed., *Financialization and the World Economy* (Northampton, MA: Edward Elgar, 2005); Greta R. Kippner, "The Financialization of the American Economy," *Socio-Economic Review* 3 (2005): 173–208; John Bellamy Foster, "The Financialization of Capitalism," *Monthly Review* 58, no. 11 (April 2007); Thomas I. Palley, "Financialization: What It Is and Why It Matters," The Levy Economics Institute, Working Paper No. 525, December 2007; Randy Martin, *Financialization of Daily Life* (Philadelphia, PA: Temple University Press, 2002). More recently, Adair Turner makes an important contribution to the literature on financialization in *Between Debt and the Devil: Money, Credit and Fixing Global Finance*. Princeton, NJ: Princeton University Press, 2015.

2. Peter Gowan, "Crisis on Wall Street," *New Left Review* (January/February 2009): 22.

3. The foremost writers on the cultural aspects of financialization—although they don't use the term—are Frederic Jameson, particularly in *Postmodernism or The Cultural Logic of Late Capitalism* (Durham, NC: Duke University Press, 1991) and the essays in *The Cultural Turn Selected Writings on the Postmodern, 1983–1998* (New York: Verso, 1998), and Mark C. Taylor in *Confidence Games: Money and Markets in a World Without Redemption* (Chicago: The University of Chicago Press, 2004).

4. Taylor, *Confidence Games*, 7.

5. Ibid., 7.

6. Kevin Phillips, *Boiling Point Democrats, Republicans, and the Decline of Middle-Class Prosperity* (New York: Random House, 1993), 193–194.

7. Ibid., 194. For Braudel's observation that the growth of finance is a sign of late stage economic power, see Fernand Braudel, *The Perspective of the World* (Los Angeles: University of California Press, 1992), 243.

8. Kevin Phillips, *Arrogant Capital: Washington, Wall Street, and the Frustration of American Politics* (New York: Little, Brown & Company, 1994), 81. See also Gerald A. Epstein and Arjun Jayadev, "The Rise of Rentier Incomes in OECD Countries: Financialization, Central Bank Policy and Labor Solidarity," in *Financialization and the World Economy*, ed. Gerald A. Epstein (Northampton, MA: Edward Elgar, 2005), 46–74.

9. Ibid., 82.

10. Robert N. McCauley, Judith S. Ruud, and Frank Iacono, *Dodging Bullets: Changing U.S. Corporate Capital Structures in the 1980s and 1990s* (Boston: MIT Press, 1999), 88.

11. Susan Pulliam, "Banks Try to Stiff-Arm New Rule," *The Wall Street Journal*, June 4, 2009, C1.

12. Giovanni Arrighi, *The Long Twentieth Century: Money, Power and the Origin of Our Times* (New York, Verso, 1994), ix. This definition is also adopted by Greta R. Krippner in an important article on financialization. See "The Financialization of the American Economy," *Socio-Economic Review* 3, 2005, 173–208. Among Krippner's most important observations is that nonfinancial firms have come to earn an increasing percentage of their profits through finance as opposed to their nonfinance activities. Examples of this include General Electric Company and General Electric Credit Corporation and many other companies that have entered the finance business, from the retailer Target Corp. to the airplane manufacturer Textron, Inc.

13. David Harvey, *The Condition of Postmodernity: An Enquiry into the Origins of Cultural Change* (Cambridge, MA: Blackwell, 1989), 147.

14. Ibid., 142.

15. Ibid., 147. For further discussion of the compression of time in society, see Mark C. Taylor, *Speed Limits: Where Time Went and Why We Have So Little Left* (New Haven: Yale University Press, 2014).

16. Ibid., 194.

17. Ibid.

18. Arrighi, *The Long Twentieth Century*, ix.

19. Arrighi, *Adam Smith in Beijing*, 161.

20. Ibid., 8.

21. Ibid., 142.

22. Brenner, *The Economics of Global Turbulence*, 307.

23. Ibid., 307.

24. Arrighi, *The Long Twentieth Century*, 5.

25. I would like to thank David Gerstenhaber of Argonaut Capital Management for helping me formulate my thoughts about consumption. See Argonaut Capital Management, "The U.S. Economy in 2010: Will the Inventory Cycle and a Rebound in the Labor Market Power the Economy Back to Trend Growth?," November 23, 2009.

26. The end of the gold standard (1973) unfettered the dollar from precious metal backing and laid the seeds for unconstrained credit growth. The economic consequences of the movement off the gold standard have been incalculable, but the psychic effects have been profound. Gold is considered by many to be an anachronistic investment, others (including this author) consider it a psychological one, but nobody should forget that gold is one of the few forms of tangible money extant. Gold is a promise kept. Gold is the antiderivative, the anticredit default swap, the anti-LBO. More important, it is the antidollar, the antifiat currency. And a fiat currency is the ultimate example of a promise; increasingly, a promise that can't be kept. Ironically, gold may be considered old fashioned because it lacks promissory elements. Of course, there are gold futures and gold derivatives, and the very popular SPDR Gold Trust (GLD), but good old-fashioned gold is just a piece of metal that you hold in your hand or store in a vault. It is a tangible thing in a world that increasingly values intangible things. It is grounded in a world where few things are grounded. Most important, it is a physical good that is limited in supply. If the end of the world ever comes, it will be your best friend. For more on the benefits of investing in gold, see Chapter 11.

Chapter 6

1. "Get Ready for the Private-Equity Shakeout," The Boston Consulting Group, December 2008, 2.

2. Ludovic Phalippou and Oliver Gottschalg, "The Performance of Private Equity Funds." (August 7, 2005. Last revised March 28, 2008.) Working Paper, University of Amsterdam and HEC School of Management, Paris.

3. Source: Estimates by International Financial Services London; Preqin.

4. Michael C. Jensen, "Eclipse of the Public Corporation," *Harvard Business Review*, September–October 1989, 61–73, at 61. While many of Professor

Jensen's arguments in support of leveraged buyouts in this article have become outdated by subsequent events during the past 20 years, he was very perceptive in understanding the constructive role these transactions played in the private equity industry's early days. His biggest error was believing that private equity firms would solve the agency problem rather than simply create new versions of it and in the process badly abuse the trust of their own limited partners.

5. For example, the employment of short-term strategies such as having portfolio companies raise additional debt to pay dividends to their private equity sponsors gave the lie a long time ago to the argument that private equity firms are long-term investors.

6. Hyman P. Minsky, "Schumpeter and Finance," *Market and Institutions in Market Development: Essays in Honour of Paulo Sylos Labini*, ed. Salvatore Biasco, Alessandro Roncaglia, and Michele Salvati (New York: Palgrave, 1990), 112.

7. Jensen, "Eclipse," 64.

8. The fact that Chrysler Corp. was not liquidated upon filing for bankruptcy in early 2009 but was instead forced into the hands of the Italian carmaker Fiat S.p.A. was a failure of industrial policy. Post-bankruptcy, the company remained uncompetitive and a candidate for liquidation even after its deal with Fiat. The Chrysler bailout was nothing more than a jobs bill designed to minimize short-term job losses at a time when the U.S economy was experiencing steep increases in unemployment. Policymakers chose an expedient short-term solution that only exacerbated the long-term problem of excess capacity in automobile manufacturing. As a result, it took longer than necessary for the U.S. automobile manufacturing industry to return to profitability.

9. Robert W. Parenteau, "The Late 1990s U.S. Bubble: Financialization in the Extreme," in *Financialization and the World Economy*, ed. Gerald A. Epstein (Northampton, MA: Edward Elgar, 2005), 134.

10. Ibid., 134.

11. By December 2009, these types of financing structures were already creeping back into the market, suggesting that a new credit bubble was beginning to build as the Federal Reserve felt it necessary to keep interest rates at an effective zero rate. By late 2015, the high yield credit markets were again melting down as the post-crisis cycle came to an end.

12. Ludovic Phalippou, Christian Rauch, and Marc Umber, "Private Equity Portfolio Company Fees." Working Paper 2015-22, Said Business School, November 2015.

13. Phalippou and Gottschalg, "The Performance of Private Equity Funds," August 7, 2005, last revised March 28, 2008.

14. "Calpers' Private-Equity Fees: $3.4 Billion," *The Wall Street Journal,* November 25, 2015, C3. CalPERS reported that it had paid $3.4 billion of performance on $24.2 billion of earnings on investments in hundreds of private equity funds over the past 17 years. This $3.4 billion figure did not include management fees or the additional fees that private equity firms charge for monitoring their portfolio companies or arranging financing or providing other services for them. Leaving aside for the moment the issue that this was the first time CalPERS had bothered to calculate exactly how much it was paying its private equity managers, the magnitude of these fees explains how there could be an extraordinary seven percentage point gap between "gross" and "net" fees.

15. Andrew Metrick and Ayako Yasuda, "The Economics of Private Equity Funds," August 7, 2005, last revised March 28, 2008, Working Paper, University of Pennsylvania, The Wharton School, August 7, 2005, last revised March 28, 2008.

16. "Calpers Paid $3.4 Billion To Private Equity Firms," *The New York Times,* November 25, 2015, p. B3.

17. Robert N. McCauley, Judith S. Ruud, and Frank Iacono, *Dodging Bullets: Changing U.S. Corporate Capital Structure in the 1980s and 1990s* (Cambridge, MA: MIT Press, 1999), 60.

18. For purposes of this discussion, I am leaving aside issues involved in firms engaging in selective disclosure of returns from certain funds and not others, issues involving valuation of nonpublic securities in these funds, and other complex issues that raise further questions about the validity and reality of their risk-adjusted returns.

19. Steve Kaplan and Antoinette Schoar, "Private Equity Performance: Returns, Persistence and Capital Flows," Working Paper, University of Chicago and MIT, 2005.

20. Phalippou and Gottschalg, "Performance of Private Equity Funds."

21. Alexander P. Groh and Oliver Gottschalg, "The Risk-Adjusted Performance of U.S. Buyouts," Working Paper, University of Amsterdam and HEC Paris, 2006.

22. A fraudulent transfer is a transaction that renders a company insolvent and deprives a creditor of repayment.

23. Among the private equity companies that paid dividends and subsequently defaulted on their debts are Mervyns Department Stores, Simmons Company, Buffets, Inc., Maax Corp., Nellson Nutraceutical, Inc. and several companies owned at least in part by the private equity firm Bain Capital—Dade Behring, Inc., American Pad & Paper LLC and KB Toys, Inc.

24. "Buyout Firms Profited As Company Debt Soared," *The New York Times,* October 5, 2009, A1.

25. In earlier periods, public companies enjoyed a significant advantage in that they could raise debt at significantly lower interest rates than private companies. This advantage disappeared in the early 2000s with the advent of the Sarbanes-Oxley Act of 2002, also known as the Public Company Accounting Reform and Investor Protection Act, which was passed in reaction to a series of accounting scandals at large public corporations such as Enron Corp., WorldCom Inc., Tyco International, Ltd., and Adelphia Communications Corporation. Sarbanes-Oxley significantly increased the cost of being a public company and led many public companies to consider going private to avoid heightened public scrutiny.

26. A recent study by consulting firm Hamilton Lane shows that the 25 largest buyouts between 2005-2007 of companies such as Hertz Global Holdings, Caesars Entertainment, Hilton Worldwide Holdings, and TXU produced a median return of only about 4 percent compared to the 7.3 percent return generated by the S&P 500 between 2006 and 2015. These are the nominal returns on these deals. On a risk-adjusted basis these returns are even worse. See "A Meh Decade for Megadeals," Bloomberg Businessweek, February 1, 2016, 35.

27. It should be noted that the buyouts that were done in 2014 and 2015 are showing signs of excess again. While the number of buyouts dropped from 434 in 2007 to 164 in 2013 and 119 in the first nine months of 2015, the average EBITDA multiple had risen to a record 11.2x in the third quarter of 2015. In 2014, these multiples were 9.7x in 2014 and 10.3x in the first nine months of 2015 compared to 9.7x in 2007. Pro forma leverage also crept up to 5.7x in 2014 compared to 6.1x in 2007. Covenant-lite loans also exploded in volume to $66 billion in 2014. As markets enter the late stages of the epic credit cycle that began when the Federal Reserve lowered interest rates to zero during the financial crisis, private equity firms and those financing them were again exhibiting extremely aggressive behavior. Unlike in the mid-2000s, however, leveraged buyouts were fewer and much smaller in number and less likely to pose a systemic threat than a decade earlier.

28. Gregory Zuckerman, Henny Snyder, and Scott Patterson, "Hedge-Fund Crowd Sees More Green as Fortress Hits Jackpot with IPO," *The Wall Street Journal*, February 10, 2007, A1.

29. "For the Love of God," *The HCM Market Letter*, June 13, 2007. In his book on the financial crisis, Charles Gasparino writes the following with respect to this topic: "[B]oth Paulson and Bernanke still seemed unconvinced that the credit crisis was anything more than a much-needed correction to teach Wall Street a valuable lesson in risk management. It was their belief that the overall economy, even the banking system (with a few bad apples) was still sound. Private equity firm Blackstone had just become a public company, and other private equity firms were considering the same. It was a vote of confidence in the markets and the financial system in general." See Charles Gasparino, *The*

Sellout How Three Decades of Wall Street Greed and Government Mismanagement Destroyed the Global Financial System (New York: Harper Business, 2009), 281. While Gasparino does not specifically attribute this thinking to either Paulson or Bernanke, he appears to suggest that these were their thoughts. If that was in fact what they were thinking, it is a startling example of just how clueless the men in charge were about what was occurring in the financial system that they were charged with preventing from running off the cliffs.

30. Philip Augar, *Chasing Alpha: How Reckless Growth and Unchecked Ambition Ruined the City's Golden Decade* (London: The Bodley Head, 2009), 110.

31. Of course, there is little justification for taxing capital at a lower rate than labor in the first place. For that reason, I propose eliminating the capital gains tax break in Chapter 10.

32. "Private Equity Suffered its Worst Year on Record in 2008," *Financial Times*, Aug. 1, 2009.

33. See "At Calpers, the Great and Not-So," *The Wall Street Journal*, December 9, 2009, C3.

34. "Calpers Has Worst Year, Off 23.4%," *The Wall Street Journal*, July 22, 2009, C3.

35. In fairness, many of these investments recaptured most if not all of their losses in 2009. But investments in fixed income are not supposed to experience such dramatic volatility. Volatility generally suggests that the manager has poor risk controls and is otherwise failing to exercise sound investment judgment. Private equity firms should stick to investing in private equity, where they have enough trouble generating decent risk-adjusted returns.

36. Chris Flood and Chris Newlands, "Calpers' Private Equity Problems Pile Up," *Financial Times*, July 12, 2015; Chris Flood and Chris Newlands, "Calstrs: US Private Equity Woes Deepen," *Financial Times*, July 19, 2015.

Chapter 7

1. David Koepp, *Jurassic Park,* a screenplay based on the novel by Michael Crichton and on an adaptation by Michael Crichton and Malia Scotch Marmo. Final draft December 11, 1992.

2. Gillian Tett tells the story of the creation of credit default swaps in her excellent book *Fool's Gold* (New York: Simon & Schuster, 2009). According to Ms. Tett, the idea for these instruments was developed at a fairly raucous retreat for JPMorgan's swaps department at the Boca Raton Resort that occurred about a year after the film *Jurassic Park* was released.

3. Edward LiPuma and Benjamin Lee, *Financial Derivatives and the Globalization of Risk* (Durham, NC: Duke University Press, 2004), 133–134.

4. The following is based on the analysis of David Harvey in *The Limits to Capital*, 245–246.

5. There are other ways for an investor to hedge the risk of owning a MSFT bond. For example, since the primary risk involved in owning such a bond is interest rate rather than credit risk, the investor could simply short Treasuries of corresponding maturities to hedge the risk of rising rates hurting the value of these bonds.

6. Ramez Mikdashi and Mark Whitehouse, "Derivatives Firms Tackle Backlog," *The Wall Street Journal*, March 14, 2006, C4.

7. It should be noted that almost a decade later, similar problems plagued the bank loan market. Until late 2015, the bank loan market, which was about $850 billion in size in 2014, was plagued by the fact that it took more than three weeks to close the trade of a non-distressed bank loan and even longer to close the trade of a distressed bank loan. This was a serious problem in view of the fact that there were large exchange traded funds (ETFs) that were required to provide instantaneous liquidity to their shareholders that own these instruments. By late 2015, the time to close these trades had reportedly shrunk to an average of roughly seven days, still too long but a significant improvement.

8. Henry T.C. Hu, "'Empty Creditors' and the Crisis," *The Wall Street Journal*, April 10, 2009. In September 2009, Professor Hu was named to head the SEC's new Office of Risk Assessment after the financial crisis, which will regulate complex financial instruments such as credit default swaps.

9. George Soros, "One Way to Stop Bear Raids," *The Wall Street Journal*, March 23, 2009.

10. LiPuma and Lee, *Financial Derivatives*, 86–87.

11. This is why articles like Matt Taibbi's irreverent story on the stock market bear raids on Bear Stearns miss the point. See Matt Taibbi, "Wall Street's Naked Swindle," *Rolling Stone*, October 14, 2009. It was not the stock market that drove Bear Stearns (and later Lehman Brothers) into distress; it was the credit market, and in particular credit default swaps that were subject to manipulation and largely misunderstood and misrepresented by the media.

12. Michael E. Lewitt, *The New York Times*, "Wall Street's Next Big Problem," September 16, 2008.

13. The question of the Federal Reserve's emergency powers is a controversial one. Section 13.3 of the Federal Reserve Act provides as follows: "In unusual and exigent circumstances, the Board of Governors of the Federal Reserve System, by the affirmative vote of not less than five members, may authorize any Federal Reserve bank, during such periods as the said board may determine, at rates established in accordance with the provisions of section 14, subdivision (d), of this Act, to discount for any individual, partnership, or corporation, notes, drafts, and bills of exchange when such notes, drafts, and bills of exchange are indorsed or otherwise secured to the satisfaction of the Federal Reserve bank: *Provided*, That before discounting any such note, draft, or bill of exchange for an individual, partnership, or corporation the Federal reserve bank shall obtain evidence that such individual, partnership, or corporation is unable to secure adequate

credit accommodations from other banking institutions. All such discounts for individuals, partnerships, or corporations shall be subject to such limitations, restrictions, and regulations as the Board of Governors of the Federal Reserve System may prescribe." There has been a great deal of debate about the actions of the Federal Reserve during the 2008 financial crisis, many of which were considered outside the scope of its traditional powers. Section 13.3 appears to be the primary statutory basis for such actions. Whatever one's view regarding whether the Federal Reserve acted properly, there is little doubt that Congress would have done worse. Accordingly, Congress should never be given power over the actions of the central bank. As argued elsewhere in this book, a non-partisan oversight body would be the most appropriate solution to this issue.

14. The bailout of AIG was subsequently challenged in court by Starr International Company, Inc., the company controlled by Maurice Greenberg, the company's founder. Starr owned about 10 percent of AIG's stock. On June 15, 2015, in *Starr International Company, Inc. v. The United States*, Judge Thomas Wheeler of the United States Court of Claims found that the government had acted unlawfully by demanding 79.9 percent of AIG's stock in exchange for its support, although he also ruled that Starr was not entitled to damages since the company would have been forced to file for bankruptcy, wiping out the value of the stock, had the government not stepped in. The government ended up making a profit of $23 billion from its investment in AIG. Appeals of the ruling are pending.

15. U.S. Commodity Futures Trading Commission, Weekly Swaps Report, July 17, 2015, https:/www.cftc.gov/MarketReports/Swaps/Reports/L1GrossExpCS.

16. Gretchen Morgenson, "First Comes the Swap, Then It's the Knives," *The New York Times*, June 1, 2008.

17. The shift of capital away from cash markets was exacerbated by the implementation of the Trade Reporting and Compliance Engine (TRACE) that was launched in 2002 by the NASD (now FINRA) to require all broker-dealers to report all corporate bond trades to a public trading system within 15 minutes of execution. The transparency that TRACE introduced into the previously opaque corporate bond markets (particularly less-than-investment grade or junk bonds) rendered trading in such bonds far less profitable and drove many small dealers from the markets.

18. George Soros, "One Way to Stop Bear Raids," *The Wall Street Journal*, March 23, 2009.

Chapter 8

1. "Q2 Hedge Fund Inflows Surpass Q2 2014 Levels; AUM at USD3.118 Trillion," Hedgeweek, July 30, 2015. www.hedgeweek.com/2015/07/30/227599/q2-hedge-fund-inflows-surpass-q2-2014-levels-aum-usd3118-trillion.

2. Harry Markowitz, "Portfolio Selection: Diversification of Investment," *Journal of Finance,* March 1952.

3. Ibid.

4. Peter Bernstein, *Capital Ideas: The Improbable Origins of Modern Wall Street* (New York: The Free Press, 1992), 53.

5. Eugene F. Fama, "Random Walks in Stock Market Prices," *Financial Analysts Journal* (September/October 1965): 55–59.

6. This is discussed in Tim Hattan, *The New Fiduciary Standard: The 27 Prudent Investment Practices for Financial Advisers, Trustees, and Plan Sponsors* (Princeton, NJ: Bloomberg Press, 2005), 35–38. Hattan concludes that "financial markets are efficient" and "most investors cannot profit even from inefficient financial markets" (38). This is patent nonsense, and it is frankly shocking that Bloomberg could not find somebody with a remotely twenty-first-century understanding of investing to write its primer on fiduciary duty.

7. At some point, one must wonder how in the world markets are expected to function when they are guided by theories that are based on assumptions that are consistently and completely divorced from reality. It is little wonder that finance is still guided by the false mantras of efficient markets and rational investors when one studies the work of the early pioneers and Nobel laureates whose work has so little to do with the real world.

8. Eugene Fama and Kenneth French, "The Capital Asset Pricing Model: Theory and Evidence," *Journal of Economic Perspectives* 18, no. 3 (September 2004): 25, 46. Quoted in Peter Bernstein, *Capital Ideas Evolving* (Hoboken, NJ: John Wiley & Sons, 2007), 165–166.

9. Bernstein, *Capital Ideas Evolving,* 173.

Chapter 9

1. Frederic Jameson, *Postmodernism, or The Cultural Logic of Late Capitalism* (Durham, NC: Duke University Press, 1991), ix.

2. Theodor Adorno, "Education after Auschwitz," in *Education to Maturity* (Frankfurt: Suhrkamp, 1971), 88–104.

3. Zygmunt Bauman, *Modernity and the Holocaust* (Ithaca, NY: Cornell University Press, 2000).

4. Jeff Madrick, "They Didn't Regulate Enough and Still Don't," *The New York Review of Books,* November 5, 2009, 54.

5. Andrew Ross Sorkin, "Obama Faces a Tough Crowd Bringing a Bitter Pill to Wall Street," *The New York Times,* September 16, 2009, C1.

6. For example, economist Robert Shiller has performed extensive research demonstrating that the prices of different types of financial assets can diverge from underlying economic value for extended periods of time. See Robert Shiller, *Irrational Exuberance* (Princeton: Princeton University Press, 2000), chapter 9. While Professor Shiller focused his argument on stock prices in the 2000 edition of this book, he updated his argument for the second edition (published in 2005) to include real estate prices. This research led to the development of The S&P/Case-Shiller Home Price Indices, which have become the most widely respected source of data on housing prices in the United States.

7. "A Regulator of Banks Gives Them a Scolding," *The New York Times*, September 24, 2009, A1. In 2015 shortly before this book went to press, Mr. Turner published *Between Debt and the Devil: Money, Credit and Fixing Global Finance* (Princeton, NJ: Princeton University Press, 2015), in which he elaborated on his ideas and set out a comprehensive set of proposals.

8. The December 2009 proposal by the Chancellor of the Exchequer Alistair Darling to impose a 50 percent tax to be paid by banks on banker's bonuses (in addition to the taxes paid by the bankers themselves) is a step too far, however. Such a tax would return the United Kingdom to the days of confiscatory tax rates and ultimately discourage free enterprise. There are better ways to tax speculative and socially unproductive activities, such as the Tax on Speculation proposed later in this chapter.

9. On January 14, 2010, President Obama introduced a proposal to tax banks for the bailout. The proposal would levy a tax on the nondepository assets of banks with more than $50 billion of such assets. The purpose of this tax was to recover the cost of the bailout for the American taxpayers. This proposal, which never became law, was inadequate from several standpoints. By only taxing the banks, it ignores the complicity of many other speculators who benefited from the reckless financial practices that led to the financial crisis, such as hedge funds and other investors who continue to speculate in naked credit default swaps and other dangerous financial instruments. It is widely known by knowledgeable market professionals that the vast majority of trading in such instruments is done for the purpose of speculation, not for the purpose of hedging underlying positions. Accordingly, this proposal gave a free pass to much of the speculative activity that comprises the most profoundly flawed practices in the system. The Tax on Speculation is more precisely aimed at unproductive activities which, if permitted to fester, will continue to push the U.S. economy down the road to ruin. Mr. Obama's proposal also let the banks off easy. The $120 billion price tag over 10 years would have been a drop in the bucket compared to the trillions of dollars of damage that their reckless practices imposed on the American economy. Recapturing just the cost of the TARP does not go far enough to compensate society for the damage that

modern financial practices have imposed. This proposal did not go nearly far enough in imposing financial responsibility on these public utilities.

10. For example, Federal Reserve Governor Edward M. Gramlich publicly urged an investigation into abusive mortgage practices in the early 2000s but was derailed by Alan Greenspan despite the fact that the Federal Reserve clearly had the authority to conduct such an inquiry. See Edmund L. Andrews, "Fed Shrugged as Subprime Crisis Spread," *The New York Times*, December 18, 2007.

11. Ian Katz, "U.S. Clears 66 Executives for at Least $1 Million in Total Pay," *Bloomberg News*, October 23, 2009.

12. Jon Hilsenrath, "Plan Aims to Curb Dangerous Risks," *The Wall Street Journal*, A4, October 23, 2009.

13. Lucian A. Bebchuk, Alma Cohen, and Holger Spamann, "The Wages of Failure: Executive Compensation at Bear Stearns and Lehman 2000–2008," Working Draft, November 22, 2009.

14. Matthew Benjamin and Christine Harper, "Volcker Urges Dividing Investment, Commercial Banks," Bloomberg.com, March 6, 2009.

15. Compare William R. White, who argues that, "major structural shifts within the financial sector have encouraged pro-cyclicality securitization, globalization, and consolidation." "Should Monetary Policy Be 'Lean or Clean'?" Federal Reserve Bank of Dallas, Globalization and Monetary Policy Institute, Working Paper No. 34, August 2009, 17. The digitalization of finance the ability to deconstruct financial instruments into 1s and 0s—that is the underlying technology of securitization remains a dominant force that contributes to pro-cyclicality by blurring the differences between debt and equity and between traditional asset classes. The conflation of different asset classes tends to make different types of securities—for example, stocks and bonds—correlate to a far greater extent than investors expect. This results in the failure of diversified portfolios to protect investors from declines in one asset class, such as equities, because other parts of their portfolios such as bonds join in the decline.

16. See, for example, White, "Should Monetary Policy Be 'Lean or Clean'?"

17. As an aside, leverage does nothing other than increase the profitability of an already profitable investment. It does not turn a bad investment into a good investment, or render a good investment a better investment. Leverage simply magnifies the non-leveraged return on an investment. In general, a useful investment philosophy is that an investment that is unattractive without leverage will also be unattractive with leverage. Certain investment strategies, such as credit arbitrage, create relationships between debt instruments that yield very small returns that are then leveraged up enormously (10 or 15 times) to produce decent returns. These strategies have generally ended in tears when

financial crises have wiped out years of returns in the blink of an eye (such as Long Term Capital Management).

18. One way to understand this is to think about two different rates of interest—the market rate and the natural rate. The market rate is just what it sounds like—the interest rates that are set in the market. The natural rate would be considered to be the prospective growth rate of the economy. Some economists believe that the market rate fell below the natural rate as long ago as 1997 and that the gap between the two continued to increase right through the financial crisis of 2008. See White, "Should Monetary Policy Be 'Lean or Clean'?"; D. M. Knight, "General Manager's Speech," on the occasion of the BIS Annual General Meeting, June 30, 2008, Basel, Switzerland.

19. Richard Russell, *Dow Theory Letters*, March 22, 2000, 3.

20. Source: Credit Suisse, *2009 Leveraged Finance Outlook and 2008 Annual Review*, January 20, 2009, 33.

21. Michael E. Lewitt, "New Math or New Economy? Some Ruminations on the 1999 Stock Market Bubble," *Trusts & Estates*, February 2001.

22. White, 19.

23. Roger W. Garrison, *Time and Money: The Macroeconomics of Capital Structure* (New York: Routledge, 2001), 120.

24. Whether this obfuscation was deliberate or not remains a complex question and lies at the heart of whether what occurred at Enron Corp. was truly criminal in terms of the laws that govern corporate disclosure. Malcolm Gladwell makes the very interesting argument that Enron in fact disclosed significant amounts of information about its off-balance-sheet entities in its public filings with the SEC. The problem, Gladwell argues, is that these entities were so complex in nature that the disclosure was difficult, if not impossible, for the average investor or regulator to understand. Accordingly, he poses the possibility that it was inappropriate to claim that Enron's executives violated laws regarding corporate disclosure because they did, in fact, disclose this information; the problem was that nobody understood it! See Malcolm Gladwell, "Open Secrets Enron, Intelligence, and the Perils of Too Much Information," in *What the Dog Saw*, Malcolm Gladwell (New York: Little, Brown & Company, 2009), 149–176. This article first appeared in *The New Yorker* on January 8, 2007. There were other problems with the Enron prosecutions, including the legal issue of whether the crime of "theft of services" was properly applied in the case (a question that came before the United States Supreme Court in June 2010 in regard to the conviction of former Enron executive Jeffrey Skilling, where the Court sharply limited the scope of the federal "theft of honest services" fraud statute, 18 U.S.C. § 1346, as unconstitutionally vague). Gladwell's argument raises serious and troubling questions about the nature of corporate disclosure as corporations engage in increasingly complex transactions.

25. Peter Wilmott, "Hurrying Into the Next Panic?" *The New York Times*, July 29, 2009.

Chapter 10

1. James Grant, Opening Keynote Speech to The Cato Institute, November 6, 2014.

2. Atif Mian and Amir Sufi, *House of Debt: How They (and You) Caused the Great Recession, and How We Can Prevent It from Happening Again* (Chicago: The University of Chicago Press, 2014).

3. See also Mervyn King, "Debt Deflation: Theory and Evidence," *European Economic Review* 38 (1994): 419–445.

4. Mian and Sufi, *House of Debt*, 9.

5. Richard Koo, *Balance Sheet Recession: Japan's Struggle with Uncharted Economics and Its Global Implications* (Singapore: John Wiley & Sons (Asia), 2001).

6. The one exception to this may be in the auto sector, which saw an explosion of subprime auto loans that boosted auto sales with low quality borrowers, many of whom may default. The age of the U.S. automobile fleet was extremely extended coming out of the financial crisis, however, leading many consumers into the position where they needed to replace their vehicles. But by mid-2015, retail sales and other indicia of consumer behavior suggested that this all-important sector that represents 70 percent of GDP was pulling in its horns.

7. Andrew Lapthorne, Société Générale Cross Asset Research, Global Quantitative Research, June 12, 2014, "Quant Quickie: As US Corporates Pile on Debt, Leverage Should Now Concern the Market." Mr. Lapthorne's findings were confirmed by Goldman Sachs in November 2015. See Robert D. Boroujerdi, Goldman Sachs Equity Research, "What's Eating Corporate America? Leverage, Goodwill and FX," November 10, 2015.

8. This is particularly unfortunate in view of the fact that Fed Chair Janet Yellen is married to the man considered to be one of the leading behavioral economists in the world, George Akerlof. One would think it would occur to Mr. Akerlof to share his insights with his wife.

9. For a full breakdown of these programs in 2013, see "A Closer Look at Mandatory Spending" prepared by Maureen Constantino and Jonathan Schwabish, Congressional Budget Office, April 2014, http://go.usa.gov/k2TA.

10. 2015 Annual Report of The Boards of Trustees of the Federal Hospital Insurance and Federal Supplementary Medical Insurance Trust Funds, July 22, 2015.

11. Ibid.

12. Congress of the United States, Congressional Budget Office, The 2015 Long-Term Budget Outlook, June 2015, 1.

13. In 2014, average disability benefits for new beneficiaries averaged $1,222 a month, making it more attractive for many less skilled individuals to try to receive disability benefits than to work. Research by the Federal Reserve Bank of San Francisco and the Congressional Budget Office attribute nearly half the increase in disability benefits since 1980 to looser eligibility standards and stagnating wages which rendered these benefits competitive with low-skilled jobs. The significant increase in disability beneficiaries during the Obama years coupled with ObamaCare has clearly increased the culture of dependency in America that is slowly bankrupting the nation.

14. This discussion of military spending is heavily indebted to the ideas found in Dick Cheney and Liz Cheney, *Exceptional: Why the World Needs a Powerful America* (New York: Threshold Editions, 2015), 207–231.

Chapter 11

1. Individual investors who want to profit directly from a strong dollar can buy the PowerShares DB US Dollar Bullish ETF (UUP). This ETF closely tracks the US Dollar Index (DXY), which measures the value of the dollar relative to a basket of foreign currencies. The composition of the index is Euro (57.8 percent), yen (13.6 percent), British pound (11.9 percent), Canadian dollar (9.1 percent), Swedish krona (4.2 percent), and Swiss franc (3.6 percent). Almost 70 percent of UUP is tied to the value of the Euro and the yen, two currencies whose value is likely to continue to drop against the dollar as a result of the deliberate policies of their respective central banks.

2. GMO Quarterly Letter, 4Q 2015.

3. www.researchaffiliates.com\assetallocation.

4. William A. Galston, "Hillary Gets It Right on Short-Termism," *The Wall Street Journal*, July 28, 2015.

5. Société Générale Cross Asset Research, Global Quantitative Research, June 12, 2014, "Quant Quickie: As US Corporates Pile on Debt, Leverage Should Now Concern the Market." See also Boroujerdi, Goldman Sachs Equity Research, "What's Eating Corporate America? Leverage, Goodwill and FX," November 10, 2015.

Conclusion

1. Cormac McCarthy, *The Road* (New York: Alfred A. Knopf, 2006), 24.

2. Charles McGrath, "At World's End, Honing a Father-Son Dynamic," *The New York Times*, May 27, 2008.

3. McCarthy, *The Road,* 46.

4. Walter Benjamin, "Theses on the Philosophy of History," in *Illuminations, ed. Hannah Arendt* (New York: Shocken Books, 1968), 255. Italics in original.

BIBLIOGRAPHY AND OTHER SOURCES

Acharya, Viral V., and Matthew Richardson, eds. *Restoring Financial Stability*. Hoboken, NJ: John Wiley & Sons, 2009.

Adorno, Theodor. "Education after Auschwitz." In *Education to Maturity,* 88–104. Frankfurt: Suhrkamp, 1971.

Anders, George. *Merchants of Debt: KKR and the Mortgaging of America*. New York: Basic Books, 1992.

Anderson, Perry. *The Origins of Postmodernity*. New York: Verso, 1998.

Arrighi, Giovanni. *The Long Twentieth Century: Money, Power and the Origin of our Times*. New York: Verso, 1994.

Arrighi, Giovanni. *Adam Smith in Beijing: Lineages of the Twenty-First Century*. New York: Verso, 2007.

Aubrey, Thomas. *Profiting from Monetary Policy: Investing through the Business Cycle*. London: Palgrave Macmillan, 2012.

Augar, Philip. *Chasing Alpha: How Reckless Growth and Unchecked Ambition Ruined the City's Golden Decade*. London: The Bodley Head, 2009.

Baran, Paul A., and Paul M. Sweezy. *Monopoly Capital: An Essay on the American Economic and Social Order*. New York: Monthly Review Press, 1967.

Barbera, Robert J. *The Cost of Capitalism: Understanding Market Mayhem and Stabilizing Our Economic Future.* New York: McGraw-Hill, 2009.

Bartlett, Sarah. *The Money Machine: How KKR Manufactured Power & Profits.* New York: Warner Books, 1991.

Bauman, Zygmunt. *Modernity and the Holocaust.* Ithaca, NY: Cornell University Press, 2000.

Benjamin, Walter. *Illuminations.* New York: Harcourt Brace & World, 1968.

Berle, Adolf A., and Gardiner C. Means. *The Modern Corporation and Private Property.* New Brunswick, NJ: Transaction Publishers, 2007.

Bernanke, Ben S. *Essays on the Great Depression.* Princeton, NJ: Princeton University Press, 2000.

Bernstein, Peter. *Capital Ideas: The Improbable Origins of Modern Wall Street.* New York: The Free Press, 1992.

Bernstein, Peter. *Against the Gods: The Remarkable Story of Risk.* New York: John Wiley & Sons, 1996.

Bernstein, Peter. *Capital Ideas Evolving.* Hoboken, NJ: John Wiley & Sons, 2007.

Biasco, Salvatore, Alessandro Roncaglia, and Michele Salvati, eds. *Market and Institutions in Economic Development: Essays in Honour of Paolo Sylos Labini.* New York: Palgrave, 1990.

Blackburn, Robin. "Finance and the Fourth Dimension." *New Left Review* 39 (May/June 2006).

Blackburn, Robin. "The Subprime Crisis." *New Left Review* 50 (March/April 2008).

Braudel, Fernand. *Civilization and Capitalism, 15th–18th Century, Volume I, The Structures of Everyday Life.* New York: Harper & Row, 1981.

Braudel, Fernand. *Civilization and Capitalism, 15th–18th Century, Volume II, The Wheels of Commerce.* New York: Harper & Row, 1982.

Braudel, Fernand. *Civilization and Capitalism, 15th–18th Century, Volume III, The Perspective of the World.* New York: Harper & Row, 1984.

Brenner, Robert. *The Boom and the Bubble: The U.S. in the World Economy.* New York: Verso, 2002.

Brenner, Robert. *The Economics of Global Turbulence.* New York: Verso, 2006.

Cassidy, John. *How Markets Fail.* New York: Farrar, Straus and Giroux. 2009.

Cendrowski, Harry, James P. Martin, Louis W. Petro, and Adam A. Wadecki. *Private Equity: History, Governance, and Operations.* Hoboken, NJ: John Wiley & Sons, 2008.

Chancellor, Edward. *Devil Take the Hindmost: A History of Financial Speculation.* New York: Farrar, Straus and Giroux, 1999.

Cheffins, Brian. "The Eclipse of Private Equity." Working Paper No. 339, Centre for Business Research, University of Cambridge, March 2007.

Cheney, Dick, and Liz Cheney. *Exceptional: Why The World Needs A Powerful America*. New York: Threshold Editions, 2015.

Cooper, George. *The Origin of Financial Crises: Central Banks, Credit Bubbles and the Efficient Market Fallacy*. New York: Random House, 2008.

Coxe, Donald. *The New Reality of Wall Street*. New York: McGraw-Hill, 2003.

Dienst, Richard. *The Bonds of Debt*. London: Verso, 2011.

Dueck, Colin. *The Obama Doctrine: American Grand Strategy Today*. New York: Oxford University Press, 2015.

Duncan, Richard. *The Dollar Crisis: Causes, Consequences, Cures*. Singapore: John Wiley & Sons (Asia), 2003.

Epstein, Gerald A., ed. *Financialization and the World Economy*. Northampton, MA: Edward Elgar, 2005.

Faber, David. *And Then the Roof Caved In: How Wall Street's Greed and Stupidity Brought Capitalism to its Knees*. Hoboken, NJ: John Wiley & Sons, 2009.

Faber, Marc. *Tomorrow's Gold: Asia's Age of Discovery*. New York: CLSA Books, 2002.

Fama, Eugene F. "The Behavior of Stock Prices." *Journal of Business* 37, no. 1 (January 1965): 34–150.

Fama, Eugene F. "Random Walks in Stock Prices." *Financial Analysts Journal* (September–October 1965): 55–59.

Fama, Eugene F., and Kenneth French. "The Capital Asset Pricing Model: Theory and Evidence." *Journal of Economic Perspectives* 18, no. 3 (September 2004): 25–46.

Fisher, Irving. *The Money Illusion*. New York: Adelphi Company, 1928.

Ferguson, Niall. *The War of the World: History's Age of Hatred*. London: Allen Lane, 2006.

Fleckenstein, William A., and Frederick Sheehan. *Greenspan's Bubbles: The Age of Ignorance at the Federal Reserve*. New York: McGraw-Hill, 2008.

Foster, John Bellamy. "The Financialization of Capitalism." *Monthly Review* 58, no. 11 (April 2007).

Fox, Justin. *The Myth of the Rational Market: A History of Risk, Reward, and Delusion on Wall Street*. New York: HarperCollins, 2009.

Fraser-Sampson, Guy. *Private Equity as an Asset Class*. Hoboken, NJ: John Wiley & Sons, 2007.

Fukuyama, Francis. *Trust: The Social Virtues and the Creation of Prosperity*. New York: Simon & Schuster, 1995.

Garrison, Roger W. *Time and Money: The Macroeconomics of Capital Structure*. New York: Routledge, 2001.

Gasparino, Charles. *Blood on the Street: The Sensational Inside Story of How Wall Street Analysts Duped a Generation of Investors*. New York: Free Press, 2005.

Gasparino, Charles. *The Sellout: How Three Decades of Wall Street Greed and Government Mismanagement Destroyed the Global Financial System.* New York: HarperBusiness, 2009.

Gladwell, Malcolm. *What the Dog Saw.* New York: Little, Brown & Company, 2009.

Goodman, Laurie S., Shumin Li, Douglas J. Lucas, Thomas A. Zimmerman, and Frank J. Fabozzi. *Subprime Mortgage Credit Derivatives.* Hoboken, NJ: John Wiley & Sons, 2008.

Gowan, Peter. "Crisis on Wall Street." *New Left Review* (January/February 2009).

Grant, James. *Money of the Mind: Borrowing and Lending in America from the Civil War to Michael Milken.* New York: Farrar, Straus and Giroux, 1992.

Grant, James. *The Trouble with Prosperity: The Loss of Fear, the Rise of Speculation & the Risk to American Savings.* New York: Times Books/Random House, 1996.

Groh, Alexander P., and Oliver Gottschalg. "The Risk-Adjusted Performance of US Buyouts." Working Paper, Montpelier Business School, HEC School of Management, Paris, 2006.

Hartcher, Peter. *Bubble Man: Alan Greenspan and the Missing 7 Trillion Dollars.* New York: W.W. Norton & Company, 2006.

Harvey, David. *The Condition of Postmodernity.* Cambridge, MA: Blackwell Publishers, 1990.

Harvey, David. *The Limits to Capital.* New York: Verso, 1999.

Hatton, Tim. *The New Fiduciary Standard: The 27 Prudent Investment Practices for Financial Advisers, Trustees, and Plan Sponsors.* Princeton, NJ: Bloomberg Press, 2005.

Hedges, Chris. *Empire of Illusion: The End of Literacy and the Triumph of Spectacle.* New York: Nation Books, 2009.

Hitchens, Christopher. "The Revenge of Karl Marx." *The Atlantic* (April 2009): 88–95.

International Monetary Fund. "The State of Public Finances: Outlook and Medium-Term Policies after the 2008 Crisis" (March 6, 2009). www.imf.org/external/np/pp/eng/2009/030609.pdf.

Jameson, Fredric. *Postmodernism, or The Cultural Logic of Late Capitalism.* Durham, NC: Duke University Press, 1991.

Jameson, Fredric. *The Cultural Turn: Selected Writings on the Postmodern, 1983–1998.* New York: Verso, 1998.

Janis, Irving L. *Groupthink.* Boston: Houghton Mifflin, 1982.

Jensen, Michael C. "Eclipse of the Public Corporation." *Harvard Business Review* (September–October 1989).

Kaplan, Steve, and Antoinette Schoar. "Private Equity Performance: Returns, Persistence and Capital Flows." Working Paper, University of Chicago and MIT, 2005.

Kass, Doug. *Doug Kass on the Market: A Life on the Street.* Hoboken, NJ: John Wiley & Sons, 2014.

Kauffman, Stuart. *At Home in the Universe: The Search for the Laws of Self-Organization and Complexity.* New York: Oxford University Press, 1995.

Kaufman, Henry. *On Money and Markets.* New York: McGraw-Hill, 2000.

Kaufman, Henry. *The Road to Financial Reformation: Warnings, Consequences, Reforms.* Hoboken, NJ: John Wiley & Sons, 2009.

Keynes, John Maynard. *The General Theory of Employment, Interest and Money.* New York: Harcourt Brace & Company, 1964.

Kindleberger, Charles P. *Manias, Panics, and Crashes: A History of Financial Crises.* Rev. ed. New York: Basic Books, 1989.

Kindleberger, Charles P., and Jean-Pierre Laffargue, eds. *Financial Crises: Theory, History & Policy.* Cambridge, England: Cambridge University Press, 1982.

Koepp, David. *Jurassic Park.* A screenplay based on the novel by Michael Crichton and on an adaptation by Michael Crichton and Malia Scotch Marmo. Final Draft. December 11, 1992.

Kolakowski, Leszek. *Main Currents of Marxism.* New York: W.W. Norton & Company, 2008.

Kosman, Josh. *The Buyout of America: How Private Equity Will Cause the Next Great Credit Crisis.* New York: Penguin Group, 2009.

Krauthammer, Charles. *Things That Matter: Three Decades of Passions, Pastimes, and Politics.* New York: Crown Forum, 2013.

Krippner, Greta R. "The Financialization of the American Economy." *Socio-Economic Review* (2005).

Le Bon, Gustave. *The Crowd: A Study of the Popular Mind.* Marietta, GA: Cherokee Publishing Company, 1982.

Levin, Mark R. *Plunder and Deceit: Big Government's Exploitation of Young People and the Future.* New York: Threshold Editions, 2015.

LiPuma, Edward, and Benjamin Lee. *Financial Derivatives and the Globalization of Risk.* Durham, NC: Duke University Press, 2004.

Littell, Jonathan. *The Kindly Ones.* New York: HarperCollins, 2009.

Lowenstein, Roger. *When Genius Failed: The Rise and Fall of Long-Term Capital Management.* New York: Random House, 2000.

Malmgren, Dr. Philippa. *Signals: The Breakeven of the Social Contract and the Rise of Geopolitics.* London: Grosvenor House Publishing Limited, 2015.

Mandel, Ernest. *Late Capitalism.* New York: Verso, 1978.

Markowitz, Harry. "Portfolio Selection." *Journal of Finance* 7, no. 1 (March 1952): 77–91.

Markowitz, Harry. "Market Efficiency: A Theoretical Distinction and So What?" *Financial Analysts Journal* (2005): 17–30.

Martin, Randy. *Financialization of Daily Life*. Philadelphia: Temple University Press, 2002.

Marx, Karl. *The Eighteenth Brumaire of Louis Napoleon*. New York: International Publishers, 1972.

Marx, Karl. *Capital*, Volume I. New York: International Publishers, 1967.

Marx, Karl. *Capital*, Volume II. New York: Penguin Classics, 1991.

Marx, Karl. *Capital*, Volume III. New York: Penguin Classics, 1991.

Marx, Karl. *Grundrisse*. New York: Penguin Classics, 1973.

McCarthy, Cormac. *The Road*. New York: Alfred A. Knopf, 2006.

McCauley, Robert N., Judith S. Ruud, and Frank Iacono. *Dodging Bullets: Changing U.S. Corporate Capital Structures in the 1980s and 1990s*. Cambridge: MIT Press, 1999.

Metrick, Andrew, and Ayako Yasuda. "The Economics of Private Equity Funds." Working Paper, University of Pennsylvania, The Wharton School., June 27, 2007, last revised September 9, 2008.

Minsky, Hyman. *John Maynard Keynes*. New York: Columbia University Press, 1975.

Minsky, Hyman. *Stabilizing an Unstable Economy*. New Haven: Yale University Press, 1986.

Mitchell, Lawrence E. *The Speculation Economy: How Finance Triumphed over Industry*. San Francisco: Berrett-Koehler Publishers, 2007.

Morris, Charles. *The Trillion-Dollar Meltdown: Easy Money, High Rollers, and the Great Credit Crash*. New York: PublicAffairs, 2008.

Muolo, Matthew, and Matthew Padilla. *Chain of Blame: How Wall Street Caused the Mortgage Crisis*. Hoboken, NJ: John Wiley & Sons, 2008.

Napier, Russell. *Anatomy of the Bear*. Hong Kong: New York: CLSA Books, 2005.

Nesvetailova, Anastasia. *Fragile Finance: Debt, Speculation, and Crisis in the Age of Global Credit*. New York: Palgrave Macmillan, 2007.

Nielsen, Kasper Meisner. "The Return to Pension Funds' Private Equity Investments: New Evidence on the Private Equity Premium Puzzle." Job Market Paper, Copenhagen Business School, 2006.

Otteson, James. *Adam Smith's Marketplace of Life*. Cambridge: Cambridge University Press, 2002.

Palley, Thomas I. "Financialization: What It Is and Why It Matters." The Levy Economics Institute of Bard College, Working Paper No. 525, December 2007.

Panitch, Leo. "Thoroughly Modern Marx." *Foreign Policy* (May/June 2009).

Phalippou, Ludovic, Christian Rauch, and Marc Umber. "Private Equity Portfolio Company Fees." Working Paper 2015–22, Said Business School, November 2015.

Phalippou, Ludovic, and Oliver Gottschalg. "The Performance of Private Equity Funds." Working Paper, University of Amsterdam and HEC School of Management, Paris, August 7, 2005, last revised March 28, 2008.

Phillips, Kevin. *Boiling Point: Democrats, Republicans, and the Decline of Middle-Class Prosperity*. New York: Random House, 1993.

Phillips, Kevin. *Arrogant Capital: Washington, Wall Street, and the Frustration of American Politics*. New York: Little, Brown & Company, 1994.

Polanyi, Karl. *The Great Transformation: The Political and Economic Origins of Our Times*. Boston: Beacon Press, 1944.

Posner, Richard A. *A Failure of Capitalism: The Crisis of '08 and the Descent into Depression*. Cambridge, MA: Harvard University Press, 2009.

Rasmussen, Dennis C. *The Problems and Promise of Commercial Society: Adam Smith's Response to Rousseau*. University Park, PA: The Pennsylvania State University Press, 2008.

Reinhart, Cameron, and Kenneth Rogoff. *This Time is Different: Eight Centuries of Financial Folly*. Princeton, NJ: Princeton University Press, 2009.

Rickards, James. *Currency Wars: The Making of the Next Global Crisis*. New York: Penguin Group (USA), 2011.

Rickards, James. *The Death of Money: The Coming Collapse of the International Monetary System*. New York: Penguin Group (USA), 2014.

Ritholtz, Barry. *Bailout Nation: How Greed and Easy Money Corrupted Wall Street and Shook the World Economy*. Hoboken, NJ: John Wiley & Sons, 2009.

Ross, Ian Simpson. *The Life of Adam Smith*. New York: Oxford University Press, 1995.

Sharpe, William F. "Capital Asset Prices: A Theory of Market Equilibrium Under Conditions of Risk." *The Journal of Finance* XIX, no. 3 (September 1964): 425–442.

Sheehan, Frederick. *Panderer to Power: The Untold Story of How Alan Greenspan Enriched Wall Street and Left a Legacy of Recession*. New York: McGraw-Hill, 2009.

Shiller, Robert J. *Irrational Exuberance*. Princeton: Princeton University Press, 2000.

Shiller, Robert J. *The Subprime Solution: How Today's Financial Crisis Happened, and What to Do about It*. Princeton, NJ: Princeton University Press, 2008.

Simmel, Georg. *The Philosophy of Money*. New York: Routledge, 1978.

Smith, Adam. *The Wealth of Nations*. New York: Random House, Inc., 2000.

Smith, Adam. *The Theory of Moral Sentiments*. New York: Barnes & Noble, 2004.

Sorkin, Andrew Ross. *Too Big to Fail*. New York: Viking, 2009.

Soros, George. *The Alchemy of Finance: Reading the Mind of the Market*. New York: Simon & Schuster, 1987.

Soros, George. *The Crisis of Global Capitalism: Open Society Endangered*. New York: PublicAffairs, 1998.

Soros, George. *The New Paradigm for Financial Markets: The Credit Crisis of 2008 and What It Means*. New York: PublicAffairs, 2008.

Stephens, Bret. *America in Retreat: The New Isolationism and the Coming Global Disorder*. New York: Penguin Group (USA), 2014.

Taleb, Nassim Nicholas. *Fooled by Randomness: The Hidden Role of Chance in Life and Markets*. New York: Random House, 2004.

Taleb, Nassim Nicholas. *The Black Swan: The Impact of the Highly Improbable*. New York: Random House, 2007.

Taleb, Nassim Nicholas. *Antifragile: Things That Gain from Disorder*. New York: Random House, 2012.

Taylor, Mark C. *Confidence Games: Money and Markets in a World without Redemption*. Chicago: The University of Chicago Press, 2004.

Taylor, Mark C. *Speed Limits: Where Time Went and Why We Have So Little Left*. New Haven, CT: Yale University Press, 2014.

Tett, Gillian. *Fool's Gold*. New York: Simon & Schuster, 2009.

Thompson, E.P. *The Making of the English Working Class*. New York: Random House, 1963.

Thompson, E.P. *The Poverty of Theory & Other Essays*. New York: Monthly Review Press, 1978.

Turner, Adair. *Between Debt and the Devil: Money, Credit and Fixing Global Finance*. Princeton: Princeton University Press, 2015.

Warburton, Peter. *Debt & Delusion: Central Bank Follies That Threaten Economic Disaster*. London: Allen Lane, 1999.

Wessel, David. *In Fed We Trust: Ben Bernanke's War on the Great Panic*. New York: Crown Business, 2009.

Wheen, Francis. *Karl Marx*. New York: W.W. Norton & Company, 1999.

Wheen, Francis. *Marx's Das Kapital: A Biography*. New York: Grove Press, 2008.

White, Eugene N., ed. *Crashes and Panics: The Lessons From History*. New York: New York University Press, 1990.

White, William R. "Should Monetary Policy Be 'Lean or Clean'?" Federal Reserve Bank of Dallas, Globalization and Monetary Policy Institute. Working Paper No. 34 (August 2009), 17.

Wolf, Martin. *Fixing Global Finance*. Baltimore, MD: The Johns Hopkins University Press, 2008.

Wood, Christopher. *Boom & Bust: The Rise and Fall of the World's Financial Markets*. New York: Atheneum, 1989.

Zizek, Slavoj. *First as Tragedy, Then as Farce*. New York: Verso, 2009.

ABOUT THE AUTHOR

Michael E. Lewitt is a hedge fund manager and author. He has managed billions of dollars of private equity, credit, and equity funds for some of the largest institutions in the world. He currently manages The Third Friday Total Return Fund, L.P. Since 1990, he has been the editor of *The Credit Strategist*, a monthly financial newsletter that is read worldwide. In September, he launched *Michael Lewitt's Sure Money* with Money Map Press. His writing has appeared in *The New York Times*, *The New Republic*, and the Spanish newspaper *El Mundo*. Mr. Lewitt studied at Brown University, Yale University, and New York University School of Law. He lives in South Florida.

INDEX